A Reference Grammar of Modern Hebrew

A Reference Grammar of Modern Hebrew provides a clearly structured and accessible guide to all aspects of contemporary Hebrew grammar. Systematically organized, it presents the basic structures of the language, looking at grammatical categories, phrases, expressions, and the construction of clauses and sentences. Drawing on their extensive experience of teaching Hebrew to English-speaking students, the authors also provide a wide range of examples to illustrate each point, and introduce in a clear and accessible way the writing and pronunciation of the language, its punctuation rules, and its use in context. Wherever possible, equivalent Hebrew terminology is given to facilitate students' use of Hebrew language textbooks. Specialized linguistic terminology is kept to a minimum, and verb and noun tables are provided as well as a comprehensive index of terms, making this both a useful teaching resource and an easy-to-use reference tool for those wishing to look up specific details of the language.

EDNA AMIR COFFIN is Professor Emerita of Hebrew Language and Literature at the University of Michigan, Ann Arbor, specializing in the areas of Hebrew language and literature and in the methodology of teaching. Her previous books include *Lessons in Modern Hebrew* (Level I 1977; Level II 1978), and *Encounters in Modern Hebrew*, volumes 1–3 (1992–6). She has published articles on a variety of topics in Hebrew language and literature.

SHMUEL BOLOZKY is a Professor of Hebrew at the University of Massachusetts Amherst, specializing in Hebrew linguistics. He coordinates the Hebrew program there and teaches Hebrew at all levels. He is the author of *Measuring Productivity in Word-Formation: The Case of Israeli Hebrew* (1999) and *501 Hebrew Verbs* (1996). He has published a number of chapters in books, mostly on Hebrew and Semitic languages, as well as articles in a broad range of journals.

A Reference Grammar of Modern Hebrew

EDNA AMIR COFFIN

Professor Emerita of Hebrew Language and Literature
Department of Near Eastern Studies
University of Michigan

SHMUEL BOLOZKY

Professor of Hebrew
Department of Judaic and Near Eastern Studies
University of Massachusetts

CAMBRIDGE
UNIVERSITY PRESS

PUBLISHED BY THE PRESS SYNDICATE OF THE UNIVERSITY OF CAMBRIDGE
The Pitt Building, Trumpington Street, Cambridge, United Kingdom

CAMBRIDGE UNIVERSITY PRESS
The Edinburgh Building, Cambridge CB2 2RU, UK
40 West 20th Street, New York, NY 10011-4211, USA
477 Williamstown Road, Port Melbourne, VIC 3207, Australia
Ruiz de Alarcón, 28014 Madrid, Spain
Dock House, The waterfront, Cape Town 8001, South Africa

http://www.cambridge.org

First published 2005

Printed in the United Kingdom at the University Press, Cambridge

Typeset by authors

A catalogue record of this book is available from the British Library

ISBN 0 521 820332 hardback
ISBN 0 521 527333 paperback

For Leah, Jonah, Rachel, Aaron and Harlan
For Michal and Noa

CONTENTS

Preface

The main purpose of this book is to serve as a reference grammar for Modern Hebrew. It is designed to teach about the language and to give readers a reference tool for looking up specific details of the language. The intended audience is a varied one; it includes non-native speakers who are students of Hebrew, native speakers of Hebrew who seek a comprehensive coverage of Hebrew grammar, instructors and teachers of Hebrew, students and scholars of Biblical Hebrew who would like to have a better understanding of contemporary Hebrew, students of linguistics, and the general public interested in Hebrew language and culture. Particular care was taken to make the presentation as simple as possible, and to avoid use of excessive linguistic terminology or complex linguistic analyses, in order to make this volume as accessible as possible to everyone, and to give pedagogical considerations equal weight to those of linguistic explanations and analysis.

The book is based on the study of formal Hebrew and of Hebrew as a spoken language, and it includes some historical notes on pre-modern Hebrew (Biblical and Post-Biblical). We consider the Hebrew language both as a system and as a communicative tool. Whenever possible, equivalent Hebrew terminology is given in order to facilitate use of Hebrew grammar and language textbooks.

A Reference Grammar of Modern Hebrew combines modern and traditional approaches in the description of language structures and uses. The term 'normative' is used to convey the adherence to the formal rules of grammar, while 'common use' alludes to the rules applied by educated speakers in their daily use. While most speakers perceive 'correct' Hebrew to be the language usage as prescribed by the formal rules of Hebrew, in fact their own actual language usage, particularly in informal contexts, often departs somewhat from the normative rules. The language is thus described both in its written and more formal contexts, and in the spoken conversational mode, where there is a relaxation of some of the normative rules, as is common to all languages in use.

The formal presentation of rules and tables associated with language structures uses Hebrew texts with vowels, כתיב חסר *ktiv ḥaser,* while the examples, on the whole, use כתיב מלא *ktiv malé*, without vowels, as in daily use in contemporary Hebrew adult texts.

A Reference Grammar of Modern Hebrew is organized according to universal structural categories. The book describes the basic structures of Modern Hebrew, and provides a generous number of examples, based on the authors' experience of teaching Hebrew to English-speaking students, and research work in the field of Hebrew linguistics.

We wish to acknowledge our colleague Robert Hoberman, Professor of Linguistics at the State University of New York Stony Brook, whose feedback comments were very insightful and helpful from both linguistic and pedagogical aspects. We also wish to acknowledge Liz Brater, who as a student of Hebrew gave us much needed insight into learners' needs, and as a professional editor, helped us with organizing the text. We are particularly thankful to her, since she found time during her busy schedule as a Michigan State Senator, to do careful reading of large parts of the text. In addition, we thank Neta Bolozky and Tris Coffin for their steady support during the writing of the book. We also wish to express our gratitude to Cambridge University Press for the opportunity to write and publish this work.

June 2004

Chapter 1
Preliminary discussion

1.1 Parts of speech

One of the major issues in the presentation of grammar is the definition of language categories. Language categories can be described as parts of speech, i.e. language units in isolation, or in terms of their function in context. For instance, a noun can be described as belonging to the parts-of-speech category 'noun', and also as functioning either as a subject or an object within the clause or sentence structure, as the modifier of another noun, etc. While we recognize that all language items belong to a whole network of interrelationships, we shall limit the present discussion to context-free (i.e., parts-of-speech), and context-dependent (i.e., functional) relationships.

The following are the main traditional categories of parts of speech:

Verbs	פעלים
Nouns	שמות
Pronouns	כינויי גוף
Adjectives	שמות תואר
Adverbs	תוארי הפועל
Prepositions	מילות יחס
Conjunctions	מילות חיבור

In many cases, the distinction between the part-of-speech characterization of some item and its function in context is obvious. Thus, for instance, in the noun phrase חנות ספרים 'bookstore', we have two nouns (part of speech), and although the second one is a modifier

of the first, and thus functions as if it were an adjective, it is still a
noun from the part-of-speech point of view. On the other hand, there
are words that even in isolation cannot be assigned unambiguously to a
single category. Every word functions as at least one part of speech,
but there are words that can serve as two or more parts of speech,
depending on the context. For instance, some present participle forms
can function as verbs in the present tense, as nouns or as adjectives:

Noun	The new <u>worker</u> did not arrive at work today.	הַפּוֹעֵל החדש לא הגיע היום לעבודה.
Verb	The computer does not <u>work</u> properly.	המחשב לא פּוֹעֵל כראוי.
Adjective	The <u>executive (working)</u> committee decided to raise membership fees.	הועד הַפּוֹעֵל החליט להעלות את דמי החבר.

The same word can also function as both an adjective and an adverb:

Adjective	The director is a <u>difficult</u> man.	המנהל הוא איש קָשֶׁה.
Adverb	He makes everyone work <u>hard</u>.	הוא מעביד קָשֶׁה את כולם.

Below are some illustrations of parts of speech and grammatical
functions. A more detailed discussion will follow in the main chapters
of the book.

Verbs   פעלים

Verbs in tense
Dan <u>hurried</u> home.

דן <u>מיהר</u> הביתה.

They <u>will oppose</u> the plan for ideological reasons.

הם <u>יתנגדו</u> לתוכנית מסיבות אידיאולוגיות.

Non-finite verbs
Dan wants <u>to run</u> in the Boston Marathon.

דן רוצה <u>לרוץ</u> במרתון בבוסטון.

Nouns and pronouns   שמות וכינויים

Nouns
I have <u>coffee</u> and <u>cake</u> for you.

יש לי קָפֶה וְעוּגָה בשבילך.

Verbal nouns
Dan is a <u>cooking</u> expert.

דן מומחה לְבִישׁוּל.

She proved a profound <u>understanding</u> of the subject.

היא הוכיחה הֲבָנָה עמוקה בנושא.

Personal pronouns
He likes to cook and she likes to eat.

הוא אוהב לבשל והיא אוהבת
לאכול.

Demonstrative pronouns
This food is Moroccan food.

האוכל הזה הוא אוכל מרוקאי.

Adjectives

שמות תואר

Adjectives in noun phrases
He is an excellent cook.

הוא בשלן מצוין.

Adjectives as predicates
This student is talented.

התלמיד הזה מוכשר.

Adverbs

תוארי הפועל

He cooks a lot but eats little.

הוא מבשל הרבה אבל אוכל מעט.

Particles

מילות/מיליות

Prepositions
Dan goes with friends to shows.

דן הולך עם חברים להצגות.

Conjunctions
Do you want to walk or to go by car?

אתם רוצים ללכת ברגל או לנסוע?

Subordinators
They went to the restaurant that I
recommended.

הם הלכו למסעדה שעליה המלצתי.

Interrogatives
Who is this?

מי זה?

Interjections
Ouch! It hurts!

אוי! זה כואב!

1.2 Grammatical functions

Another way to classify the components of an utterance is by their grammatical function. Here are some of the terms that are used to describe the roles the parts of speech play in sentences:

Subject	נושא
Predicate	נשוא
Attribute	לוואי
Object	מושא
Adjunct	נספח

Subject

נושא

Noun phrases
The new cook is from France.

הטבח החדש הוא מצרפת.

Subordinate clauses
That he studied cooking in France is
of no interest to me.

שהוא למד בישול בצרפת לא מעניין
אותי בכלל.

Predicate

נשוא

Verb predicates
Dan started studying in the summer.

דן התחיל ללמוד בקיץ.

Nominal predicates
He is a student in law school.

הוא תלמיד בפקולטה למשפטים.

Attribute

לוואי

Expansion of phrases with additional information
Dan met friends from work at a pub
on the beach.

דן פגש חברים מהעבודה בפאב על
שפת הים.

Object complement

מושא משלים

Direct object
Dan met his friends.

דן פגש את החברים שלו.

Indirect object
Dan got together with his friends.

דן נפגש עם החברים שלו.

Adjunct

נספח

Temporal
Dan was not at home this morning.

דן לא היה בבית הבוקר.

Spatial
Dan traveled in England for three
months.

דן טייל שלושה חודשים באנגליה.

1.3 Words and patterns

מלים, בניינים ומשקלים

All verbs, many nouns, and a good number of adjectives and adverbs
are based on a combination of roots and patterns. The root שורש
shoresh is a consonantal skeleton. It is a hypothetical sequence of
consonants shared by related words. Roots do not constitute actual
words. Each one is applied to a pattern, from which actual words are
formed. In the verb system the pattern is called בניין *binyan*, and
elsewhere it is called משקל *mishkal*.

Verbs

Gloss	Word	בניין	שורש
wrote	כָּתַב	פעל	כ-ת-ב
dictated	הִכְתִּיב	הפעיל	

Nouns and adjectives

Gloss	Word	משקל	שורש
magician (noun)	קוֹסֵם	פועל	ק-ס-מ
charming (adjective)	מַקְסִים	מפעיל	

There are seven verb pattern groups (*binyanim*) in Hebrew. The third person singular in the past tense is traditionally used to represent each of these groups. To label each of these groups generically, a prototypical root is used. The generic verb פעל is used in combination with the pattern of each *binyan*, giving it its name.

	Binyan's name	Citation Form	Root
pa`al	פָּעַל	זָרַק	ז-ר-ק
nif`al	נִפְעַל	נִשְׁבַּר	ש-ב-ר
pi`el	פִּעֵל (פיעל)	סִפֵּר (סיפר)	ס-פ-ר
pu`al	פֻּעַל (פועל)	סֻלַּק (סולק)	ס-ל-ק
hitpa`el	הִתְפַּעֵל	הִתְרַגֵּשׁ	ר-ג-ש
hif`il	הִפְעִיל	הִקְלִיט	ק-ל-ט
huf`al	הֻפְעַל (הופעל)	הֻנְצַח (הונצח)	נ-צ-ח

The root consonant is labeled פ׳ הפועל (marked in English as C_1). The second root consonant is labeled ע׳ הפועל (C_2) and the third root consonant is ל׳ הפועל (C_3).

Verb form	*Binyan*	Root	ל״ הפועל	ע׳ הפועל	פ׳ הפועל
שָׁתַק	פעל	ש-ת-ק	ק	ת	ש
נִכְנַס	נפעל	כ-נ-ס	ס	נ	כ
שִׁלֵּם (שילם)	פיעל	ש-ל-מ	מ	ל	ש
פֵּטַר (פוטר)	פועל	פ-ט-ר	ר	ט	פ
הִתְכַּתֵּב	התפעל	כ-ת-ב	ב	ת	כ
הִכְתִּיב	הפעיל	כ-ת-ב	ב	ת	כ
הֻקְלַט (הוקלט)	הופעל	ק-ל-ט	ט	ל	ק

A comparative note

The verb pattern groups in Hebrew are somewhat similar to special groups of verbs in English, where the base undergoes predictable internal changes, and the modifications within the stem are regular. Some examples of such groups:

(a) drive-drove-driven, write-wrote-written, ride-rode-ridden
(b) speak-spoke-spoken, freeze-froze-frozen, steal-stole-stolen

Although the root does not exist on its own, many words sharing a common root tend to have a common meaning or related meaning.

Verbs

Gloss	Citation form	*binyan*	Root
tie	קָשַׁר	פעל	ק-ש-ר
be tied	נִקְשַׁר	נפעל	
get in touch; get connected	הִתְקַשֵּׁר	התפעל	

Nouns and adjectives

Gloss			Root
tied, connected (adj.)	קָשׁוּר	תואר	ק-ש-ר
tie, connection (noun)	קֶשֶׁר (ז)	שם	
context (noun)	הֶקְשֵׁר (ז)	שם	

1.3.2 Deriving new words   גזירת מלים חדשות

New words in Hebrew, as in other Semitic languages, are formed in two ways:

1. Linearly, without affecting the base for derivation. For instance, the adjective ציבורי 'public, in the public domain' is derived from the noun ציבור 'the public'.

There are also cases of chains of derivations.

Noun	child	יֶלֶד
Abstract noun derived from יֶלֶד-:	childhood	יַלְדוּת
Adjective derived from יַלְדוּת:	childish	יַלְדוּתִי
Abstract noun derived from יַלְדוּתִי:	childishness	יַלְדוּתִיּוּת

2. New verbs can also be derived from an existing root, by combining it with an existing derivation pattern. For instance, the following recent verbs were formed with existing roots and their new combination with patterns:

Existing verb	write	כָּתַב
New verb in *shif'el* pattern	rewrite	שִכְתֵּב
Existing verb	act, do	פָּעַל
New verb in *tif'el* pattern:	operate, activate	תִּפְעֵל

1.4 Gender and number   מין ומספר

Nouns, adjectives and verbs have gender and number features. The gender is either masculine זָכָר or feminine נְקֵבָה. A distinction is made between two major noun categories: [1] nouns that represent living entities: human beings and other living beings with biological gender features, and [2] nouns that represent other entities, mostly inanimate and abstract nouns (for example, objects, concepts, plants and others). The biological gender of living beings and their inherent masculine or feminine features are reflected in their grammatical gender features. Other nouns have an assigned grammatical gender, which is prescribed and cannot be predicted.

There are regular number features, which indicate whether a noun is a singular noun יחיד/יחידה or whether it is a plural noun רבים/רבות. The feminine singular noun endings (יחידה) are frequently marked by a final הָ- -*a* or a final ת- -*t*. The plural noun endings are represented by the suffixes ים- -*im* and ות- -*ot*. In nouns the plural ending ים- -*im* most frequently but not necessarily reflects the masculine gender of the nouns, while the plural ending ות- -*ot* most frequently but not necessarily reflects the feminine gender of the nouns.
(See pp.130-139 for more information)

Verb forms in Hebrew also have gender and number features. In most past and future tenses they also have subject person features, i.e. personal pronoun features (I, you, he), which are often affixed to the verb forms.
(See pp. 36-38 for more information)

1.5 Open and closed word classes

The parts of speech can be classified as belonging to two large categories: to 'open' classes or to 'closed' classes. The open classes consist of these parts of speech: verb, noun, adjective, and adverb. The various particles (prepositions and conjunctions and others) are closed classes. The closed classes are fixed sets of a limited number of function words, whereas the open classes have a large membership.

1.5.1 Open classes

These are productive classes to which new words are continuously added, responding to the need for new vocabulary to serve the changing times. The new words are added either according to existing rules of morphology for the formation of new words, or by borrowing words from other languages and either leaving them as they are, or adapting them to Hebrew structures and patterns. The closed classes resist the addition of new members.

Formation of verbs
Adaptation from existing words:

Gloss	Derived Verb	Derived Root	Gloss	Base
to market	לְשַׁוֵּק	ש-ו-ק >	market	שׁוּק
to report	לְדַוֵּחַ	ד-ו-ח >	report	דו״ח

ת- t- prefix added to existing roots:

Gloss	Derived Verb	Derived Root	Gloss	Root
to communicate	לְתַקְשֵׁר	ת-ק-ש-ר >	tie	ק-ש-ר
to brief	לְתַדְרֵךְ	ת-ד-ר-כ >	guide	ד-ר-כ

ש- sh- prefix added to existing roots:

Gloss	Derived Verb	Derived Root	Gloss	Root
to subjugate	לְשַׁעְבֵּד	ש-ע-ב-ד >	work	ע-ב-ד
to rewrite	לְשַׁכְתֵּב	ש-כ-ת-ב >	write	כ-ת-ב

Formation of nouns
Derived from verbs

Gloss	Derived Noun	Gloss	Base	Root
frame	מִסְגֶּרֶת	close	סָגַר	ס-ג-ר
guard, watch	מִשְׁמָר	guard	שָׁמַר	ש-מ-ר

Derived from other nouns

Gloss	Derived Noun	Gloss	Base
brotherhood	אַחֲוָה	brother	אָח
privacy	פְּרָטִיּוּת	individual	פְּרָט

Derived from adjectives

Gloss	Derived Noun	Gloss	Base
permissiveness	מַתִּירָנוּת	permissive	מַתִּירָנִי
health	בְּרִיאוּת	healthy	בָּרִיא

Borrowing words from other languages

Direct borrowing of nouns:

high tech	היי-טק
prime time	פריים טיים
boss	בּוֹס

Deriving new verbs from borrowed words:

Gloss	Derived Verb	Extracted Root	Gloss	Base
subsidize	סִבְּסֵד	ס-ב-ס-ד	subsidy	סוּבְּסִידְיָה
sympathize	סִמְפֵּט	ס-מ-פ-ט	sympathy	סִימְפַּתְיָה

Borrowed words with Hebrew suffixes

Plural Suffixes	intellectuals	אינטלקטואלים
Feminine ending	Practice	פרקטיקה
Adjective endings	digital	דיגיטלי/דיגיטלית

Note that the noun system is the most open, and nouns from other languages can be adopted into the language without alterations or with little alteration, such as אטום 'atom', טלפוֹן 'telephone', טלוויזיה 'television', טכנולוגיה 'technology', and many others. However, new borrowed verbs and adjectives require adaptation into the existing system. For instance, the verb סִבְּסֵד *sibsed* 'to subsidize' above requires vowel modification from the borrowed noun סוּבְּסִידְיָה *subsídya* 'subsidy' in order to fit into a Hebrew verb pattern.

1.5.2 Closed classes

The closed classes of words consist of the grammatical function words, such as:

1.	Pronouns	אני, הוא, זה
2.	Prepositions	עם, אצל, ל-, ב
3.	Conjunctions	ו, אבל
4.	Determiners	ה-
5.	Quantifiers	כל, הרבה, או מספרים
6.	Subordinators	ש, אשר

All of the above do not have gender or number features, and as a general rule, do not fill the slot of the head of a phrase. They are called closed because they contain a limited number of items, and their membership is not likely to be expanded. Function words are hardly ever borrowed from other languages.

Prepositions   מילות יחס

Prepositions are usually followed by a noun phrase or by a pronoun suffix. Prepositions function as heads of prepositional phrases. Some verbs must be followed by obligatory prepositions. Some prepositions are followed by a subordinating particle -שֶׁ that introduces a subordinate clause.

Prepositional phrase
After the holiday meal   אחרי הארוחה של החג

Subordinating item: preposition + clause
After they ate the holiday meal.   אחרי שהם אכלו את הארוחה.

Determiners, articles and quantifiers   מילות יידוע

Articles, determiners, and quantifiers precede and modify nouns:

Not everyone agrees with you.   לא כל האנשים מסכימים אתך.
He is a billionaire! He has lots of money.   הוא ביליונר! יש לו המון כסף.
Each person brought something.   כל אחד הביא משהו.

Coordinators   מילות חיבור

Common coordinators are -ו 'and' and כי 'because' and או 'or'. They can be found in several levels of the hierarchy: words, phrases, or clauses.
Phrases
Who is the boss here, you, or your   מי הבוס כאן, אתה או אחיך?
brother?
Are you and your brother going to   אתה ואחיך הולכים למשרד?
the office?

Clauses

There is enough food, <u>and</u> you can all
come and eat.

יש מספיק אוכל, <u>ו</u>כולכם
יכולים לבוא לאכול.

Subordinators   מילות שעבוד

The most frequently used subordinator is the particle -שֶׁ 'that', after
which a subordinate clause follows. When the subordinate clause is an
object (complement) clause, the word כי can be used as a subordinator
but only in higher registers. When the subordinate clause is a relative
clause, אשר may be used in higher registers.

Reporting

We all know <u>that</u> you did not mean to
say this.

At a press conference the American
Secretary of State said <u>that</u> an
important strategic change has taken
place.

כולנו יודעים <u>שֶׁ</u>אתה לא התכוונת
לומר את זה.
במסיבת עיתונאים אמר שר
החוץ האמריקני <u>כי</u> חל שינוי
אסטרטגי חשוב.

Introducing a relative clause

The girl <u>who</u> is walking towards us
is my cousin.

The patient's rights law, <u>which</u>
became valid in 1996, is a pioneer
in its field.

הבחורה <u>שֶׁ</u>באה לקראתנו היא בת-
דודתי.
חוק זכויות החולה, <u>אשר</u> נכנס
לתוקפו בשנת 1996, הינו חלוץ
בתחומו.

Introducing an adverbial clause

He did not arrive on time <u>because</u> his
plane was late.

He came to the office <u>even though</u> he
was sick.

הוא לא הגיע בזמן <u>מכיוון</u>
<u>ש</u>מטוסו איחר.
הוא בא למשרד <u>למרות שֶׁ</u>היה
חולה.

Interrogatives   מילות שאלה

Interrogatives are question words or phrases used to transform
statements to questions. They can be pronoun question words מי?
'who?' or מה? 'what?'. They can also be adverbial question words
about time מתי? 'when?' or about location איפה? 'where?'. They can
pose questions about the reason for doing something למה? 'why?' or
ask to quantify things כמה? 'how much? how many?'.

Questions about the subject or object:

<u>Who</u> called you?   ?מִי טלפן אליך

<u>What</u> did he tell you on the phone?   ?מָה הוא אמר לך בטלפון

Questions about time or location:

<u>When</u> is Dan coming?   ?מָתַי דן חושב לבוא

<u>Where</u> is he going?   ?לְאָן הוא הולך

<u>Where</u> will he be this evening?   ?אֵיפה הוא יהיה הערב

Questions about cause or reason:

<u>Why</u> doesn't Dan want to come?   ?לָמה דן לא רוצה לבוא

<u>Why</u> was he so late?   ?מָדוע הוא אחר כל כך

Questions with prepositions:

The question words מי and מה can be preceded by prepositions, as in על מה? 'about what?', or עם מי? 'with whom?'.

<u>About whom</u> did you talk?   ?עַל מִי דיברתם

<u>With whom</u> did you go to the movies?   ?עַם מִי הלכתם לקולנוע

Interjections   מילות קריאה

Interjections are words or phrases used to exclaim or protest or command. They sometimes stand by themselves, but they are often contained within larger structures. Most interjections are usually used in speech.

<u>Nice</u>! You finished everything on time.   .יָפה! סיימתם הכל בזמן

<u>Wow</u>! I won the lottery!   !מְהַמם! הרווחתי את הלוטו

We won – <u>Hallelujah</u>!   !ניצחנו - הָלְלויה

<u>How awful</u>! Everything is lost.   .אוי ואבוי! הכל הלך לאיבוד

1.6 Phrase constituents

Observe the following sentence:

Small children go to kindergarten.   .ילדים קטנים הולכים לגן

The sentence can be clearly divided into two main constituents:

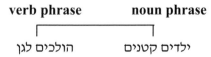

verb phrase	noun phrase
הולכים לגן	ילדים קטנים

Each of these constituents is a phrase and the two of them together form the sentence. The first one is a noun phrase, while the second one is a verb phrase. The central item of the noun phrase is ילדים 'children', while the modifying item is קטנים 'small'. In the verb phrase, the central item is the verb הולכים 'go', and the destination is indicated by the prepositional phrase that completes the verb phrase לגן 'to kindergarten'.

A phrase, as we saw above, consists of an obligatory item, which we call the *head* or *nucleus*, and it is always essential to the phrase. It sets the syntactic category of that phrase. Other elements may be optional. Only words that belong to open classes can be heads of phrases. They combine with other words to form larger units, and within the phrase they constitute the central item around which the other words are organized. Head nouns determine the gender and number of the other components in the phrase, as well as in the sentence.

Types of phrase: noun phrase
Head word - noun: שפה 'language'
In context: [The Hebrew language] changes.   .[השפה העברית] משתנה

Types of phrase: verb phrase
Head word - verb: קנו 'bought'
In context: The children [bought ice cream].   .[הילדים [קנו גלידה

1.7 Rules of agreement
The head of a syntactic unit, such as a phrase, a clause or a sentence determines many of the features of the other nouns, adjectives or verb forms in these units. Beyond the phrase there is agreement between the head noun of a subject and its predicate (verb, noun or adjective), or between any noun and its co-referent pronoun anywhere in the sentence or beyond.
Let's see how the head noun in the following sentence determines the features of some other components in the sentence:

ילדים קטנים הולכים לגן.
- Head noun: ילדים. Gender: masculine. Number: plural.
- Adjective reflects the features of the head noun: קטנים.

- The verb reflects the plural masculine features of the head noun: הולכים.

1.7.1 Gender agreement

1. Noun phrase: head noun + adjective

The new movie sounds interesting.	הסרט החדש נשמע מעניין.
The new exhibit is attracting a lot of visitors. They say that it is very interesting.	התערוכה החדשה מושכת מבקרים רבים. אומרים שהיא מעניינת מאוד.

2. Noun phrase: head noun + demonstrative pronoun

Since demonstrative pronouns can modify nouns in a noun phrase, they agree in gender and number with the head nouns.

This pool is an Olympic pool.	הבריכה הזאת היא בריכה אולימפית.
That game was riveting.	המשחק ההוא היה מרתק.

3. Noun phrase + verb predicate

Nira was accepted to work in the office of an architectural firm. They hired her as soon as she finished her studies.	נירה התקבלה לעבודה במשרד של ארכיטקטים. קיבלו אותה מייד עם תום לימודיה.
Noam works in a bank. Many friends of his work there.	נועם עובד בבנק. חברים רבים שלו עובדים שם.

4. Noun phrase + adjective predicate

Your choice (is) very good.	הבחירה שלך טובה מאוד.
The voting rate (is) low.	שיעור ההצבעה נמוך.

1.7.2 Number agreement

1. Noun phrase: head noun + adjective

The new plays are interesting.	המחזות החדשים מעניינים.
We strolled in the small streets of the town.	טיילנו ברחובות הקטנים של העיר.

2. Sentence: noun phrase + predicate: verb

Moshe and Danny arrived late.	משה ודני הגיעו מאוחר.
Aliza and Dina live in the dorms.	עליזה ודינה גרות במעונות.

3. Sentence: noun phrase + predicate: adjective

These flowers are very pretty.	הפרחים האלה יפים מאוד.
The girls in my class are not particularly friendly.	הבנות בכיתה לא חברותיות במיוחד.

1.7.3 Agreement in person

I will finish the paper tomorrow.	אני אגמור את העבודה מחר.
You didn't hear the bell?	אתם לא שמעתם את הצלצול?

Personal pronouns (subject, object, possessive, etc.) reflect the person that they represent.

The girl said that she was hungry.	הילדה אמרה שהיא רעבה.
Her parents also said that they were hungry.	גם הוריה אמרו שהם רעבים.

1.7.4 Definite/Indefinite status

When the head noun is indefinite, so is the adjective that modifies it. However, when the noun modifier is a prepositional phrase, the head noun does not influence it.

Indefinite head noun

There are small and nice restaurants there.	יש שם מסעדות קטנות ונחמדות.
We bought an old house.	קנינו בית ישן.
Did you visit any art museums?	ביקרתם במוזיאונים לאמנות?

When the head noun is definite, the adjectives that modify it are also definite. A definite concept consists of a noun introduced by a definite article, or one with a possessive suffix, or a proper name. However, when the noun modifier is a prepositional phrase, the head noun does not influence it.

Definite head noun

The blossoming trees are apple trees.	העצים הפורחים הם עצי תפוחים.
His second wife was born in Canada.	אשתו השנייה נולדה בקנדה.
Our Ilana is a gifted musician.	אילנה שלנו היא מוסיקאית מחוננת.

Chapter 2
Writing and pronunciation

2.1 Introduction

In Hebrew, as in other Semitic languages, consonants are regarded as the primary units that compose a word. There are twenty-two letters in the Hebrew alphabet, with eight additional variations. Each consonant is assigned a letter of the alphabet. Four consonants may also represent vowels, but generally, vowel signs are marked by dots and short lines inserted below, above, and inside the consonants.

In contemporary Hebrew texts, sequences of consonants represent words. Vowel signs are not used in most texts, with the exception of poetry, children's literature, textbooks for early grades, and liturgical literature. In writing without vowels, each sequence of consonants can have more than one vowel pattern assigned to it, and thus has several possible pronunciations and consequently several possible meanings, e.g., in a sequence like ספר:

Gloss		With vowels	Without vowels
book; literary work	*séfer*	סֵפֶר	ספר
(1) tell, narrate; talk about	*sipér*	סִפֵּר	סיפר
(2) to cut hair			
be recounted, be narrated	*supár*	סֻפַּר	סופר
count, enumerate	*safár*	סָפַר	ספר
count!	*sfór*	סְפֹר	ספור
barber	*sapár*	סַפָּר	ספר
border, edge, fringe	*sfár*	סְפָר	ספר

The consonantal skeleton of a word carries its basic sense, and the vowel string usually identifies the word grouping to which a particular word belongs. Pattern recognition is aided by affixes (attachments), which facilitate the reconstruction of the associated vowel configuration. The following example demonstrates the combination of a consonantal skeleton with two different word patterns.

Gloss	Patterns		Root	Prefix
number	*mispar*	מִסְפָּר	ס-פ-ר	מִ-
narrator	*mesaper*	מְסַפֵּר	ס-פ-ר	מְ-

2.2 Consonants and sounds   עיצורים וצלילים

In the table below, you will find the Hebrew consonantal alphabet, traditionally arranged. Five consonants have a special form when they come at the end of the word (כ׳ ך׳ ; מ׳ ם׳ ; נ׳ ן׳ ; צ׳ ץ׳ ; פ׳ ף׳). Note that *shin* and *sin* are represented by the same symbol (a dot is used to distinguish between them); and that some consonants were modified with diacritics to also represent non-native sounds (ג׳, ז׳, צ׳). The letters are displayed in both print and script forms. The transcription sign is displayed under the sound column, referring to the sound realization of that letter and the conventional way to transcribe it in English. Short notes about pronunciation are added in a separate column next to each letter.

Note

Single Hebrew letters in isolation are marked with an apostrophe. When the letters are referred to by name in texts, they often have an inverted double comma inserted in between the last two letters, such as in the following examples: אלי״ף, בי״ת, וי״ו, כ״ף, צד״י, תי״ו. The reason for inserting the double inverted comma into the spelling of the names of letters is to avoid confusion with actual words. In the following table neither an apostrophe nor a double-inverted comma are inserted, since there is no confusion as to what they stand for when they appear in a table.

Consonants

Letter		Sound	Notes on pronunciation	Name	
א	**אּ**	Ø	It carries the sound of the following vowel, as in אָבִיב *aviv*. It is never realized at the end of words: קָרָא *kara*, בָּרִיא *bari*.	*'álef*	אָלֶף
		'	In deliberate speech it is realized as a glottal stop with a stressed vowel: קָרְאָה *kar'á*.		
בּ	**בּ**	b	*b*, as in the first sound of <u>b</u>oy, word intially: בֶּן *ben*, or after a closed syllable: הַרְבֵּה *harbe*, or after an open syllable in some patterns: דִּבֵּר *diber*.	*bet*	בֵּית
ב	**ב**	v	*v*, as in the first sound of <u>v</u>ine, after a vowel or at the end of words: סָבְתָא *savta*, כָּתַב *katav*.	*vet*	בֵית
ג	**ג**	g	g as in the first sound in *green*	*gímel*	גִּימֶל
ג׳	**׳ג**	j	as in the first sound in <u>G</u>eorge (ג׳וֹרג׳י)		
ד	**ד**	d	*d* as in the first sound in <u>d</u>oor	*dálet*	דָּלֶת
ה	**ה**	h	Aspirated *h*, as in <u>h</u>ello, before a stressed vowel, e.g., הַר *hár*; or when ה is final, preceded by *a*, preceded by another vowel: גָּבוֹהַּ *gavóah*; or to mark a fem. sing. suffix: לָהּ *lah*.	*hé*	הֵא
		Ø	At the end of a word, following an *a* or *e*: יָפָה *yafá*, יָפֶה *yafé*, or optionally before an unstressed vowel: אֹהֶל *óhel* ~ *óel*		
ו	**ו**	v	*v* as in the first sound of וֶרֶד *véred*, or after a vowel as in קַוֶּה *kiva*, קַו *kav*.	*vav*	וָו
וּ	**ו**	u	The vowel *u* as in קוּם *kum*, קָנוּ *kanu*.		
וֹ	**ו**	o	The vowel *o* as in קוֹף *kof*, בּוֹ *bo*.		
וו	**וו**	v	Alternative for a single ו consonant.		
		w	*w* in foreign words, וושינגטון *Washington*		

ז	**ן**	z	z as in the first sound of <u>z</u>oo.	záyin	זַיִן
'ז	**'ן**	zh	In foreign (borrowed) words, such as the final sound in gara<u>ge</u> (גָּרָאזְ').		
ח	**ת**	ħ	ħ is pronounced as in *Lo<u>ch</u> Ness*. For alternate pronunciation see explanation on page 31.	ħet	חֵית
ט	**6**	t	t as in the first sound of <u>t</u>able	tet	טֵית
י	**ı**	y	y in any position, as in <u>y</u>earn, ka<u>y</u>ak	yod	יוֹד
יִ	**!**	i	The vowel i as in sp<u>ee</u>d, or in s<u>ea</u>l		
יֵ	**ı ⃝**	ey	The diphthong ey as in w<u>ay</u>		
יי	**ıı**	y	Alternative for a single 'י consonant.		
כ	**כ**	k	k as in <u>c</u>an: at the beginning of a word כֵּן *ken*, or after a closed syllable: מַלְכָּה *malka*, or after an open syllable in some patterns: סִכֵּן *siken*.	kaf	כַּף
כ	**כ**	kh	kh is pronounced as in *Lo<u>ch</u> Ness*, after a vowel or at the end of words.	khaf	כַף
ך	**ך**		An orthographic variation at the end of words: רַךְ *rakh*.	khaf sofit	כַף סוֹפִית
ל	**ƒ**	l	l as in the first sound of <u>l</u>ean.	lámed	לָמֶד
מ	**ℵ**	m	m as in the first sound of <u>m</u>other.	mem	מֵם
ם	**מ**		An orthographic variation at the end of words.	mem sofit	מֵם סוֹפִית
נ	**J**	n	n as in the first sound of <u>n</u>ever.	nun	נוּן
ן	**ן**		An orthographic variation of at the end of words.	nun sofit	נוּן סוֹפִית
ס	**ס**	s	s as in the first sound of <u>s</u>un.	sámekh	סָמֶךְ
ע	**ע**	Ø	In standard speech it only carries the sound of the following vowel, just as א does. For alternative pronunciation see explanation on page 31.	'áyin	עַיִן

פ	**כ**	p	p as in the first sound of *pearl*: at the beginning of the word or after a closed syllable: פַּרְפַּר *parpar*, or after an open syllable in some patterns: סִפֵּר *siper*.	*pe*	פֵּא
פ	**כ**	f	f as in the first sound of *fun*: after a vowel: סַפְסָל *safsal* or initially in borrowed words: פֶסְטִיבָל *festivál*.	*fe*	פֵא
ף	**ף**		Orthographic variation of *f* at the end of words: כֶּסֶף *késef*.	*fe sofit*	פֵא סוֹפִית
צ	**3**	ts	ts pronounced as one segment, as in the first segment of צַדִיק *tsadik*.	*tsadi*	צָדִי
ץ	**ף**		Orthographic variation of *ts* at the end of words: קִיבּוּץ *kibbutz*.	*tsadi sofit*	צָדִי סוֹפִית
'צ	**'3**	ch	ch in foreign words, such as *Charlie* (צַ׳רְלִי).		
ץ'	**'ף**				
ק	**ק**	k	k as in the first sound of *kid*.	*kof*	קוֹף
ר	**ר**	r	r as in the first sound of *run*. It is pronounced almost like the r in French or German. Some pronounce it like the rolling r as in Spanish.	*resh*	רֵיש
ש	**e**	sh	sh as in the first sound of *shop*.	*šin*	שִׁין
שׂ	**ė**	s	s as in the first sound of *sun*.	*sin*	שִׂין
ת	**ת**	t	t as in the first sound of *table*.	*tav*	תָו

The following letters, which were historically distinct, have the same sound today. Words with different spelling can have the same sound:

Pronounced		Word 1		Word 2	Letters
kar	cold	קַר	pillow	כָּר	כ, ק
shoté	drink	שׁוֹתֶה	fool	שׁוֹטֶה	ט, ת
alá	went up	עָלָה	club, bat	אַלָה	א, ע
sar	minister	שָׂר	go aside	סָר	ס, שׂ
lakh	to you	לָךְ	humid	לַח	ח, כ
tsav	summons	צַו	turtle	צָב	ב, ו

2.3 Vowels   תנועות

Israeli Hebrew has only five vowel sounds: *i e a o u*. There are many more different vowel signs, reflecting historical differences in vowel quality and length that no longer exist in contemporary use (other than what is determined automatically by the stress pattern and the context).

Pronunciation	Vowel Name		Sign
a (as in *start*)	*kamats*	קָמַץ	סָ
	pataħ	פַּתָּח	סַ
	ħataf-pataħ	חֲטָף-פַּתָּח	חֲ
e (as in *get*)	*segol*	סֶגּוֹל	סֶ
	ħataf-segol	חֲטָף-סֶגּוֹל	חֱ
	shva na`	שְׁוָא נָע	סְ
	tsere	צֵירֶה	סֵ
ey (as in *may*)	*tsere*	צֵירֶה	סֵי
i (as in *dear*)	*ħirik ħaser*	חִירִיק חָסֵר	סִ
	ħirik malé	חִירִיק מָלֵא	סִי
o (as in *stop*)	*ħolam ħaser*	חוֹלָם חָסֵר	סֹ
	ħolam malé	חוֹלָם מָלֵא	סוֹ
	kamats katan	קָמַץ קָטָן	סָ
	ħataf kamats	חֲטָף קָמַץ	חֳ
u (as in *soup*)	*kubuts*	קֻבּוּץ	סֻ
	shuruk	שׁוּרוּק	סוּ
Ø (as in *glue*) short *e* (as in *yeladim*)	*shva naħ* *shva na`*	שְׁוָא נָח שְׁוָא נָע	סְ

In this table the letter 'ס is used as a prototypical consonant, 'ח for a prototypical guttural.

Note 1: Comment on *kamats* vowels

There are two realizations of the קָמַץ *kamats* vowel: The normal realization of the vowel in ָה, for instance, is *a*, but in a few words (as a rule in a closed, unstressed syllable) it is pronounced *o*.

Note 2: Comment on *segol* and related vowels

In Israeli Hebrew, the *segol*, the *ħataf-segol* and the *shva na`* are all realized as *e*, and so are most cases of *tsere* that are not followed by *yod*.

Note 3: Comments on *shva* vowels

The usual realization of *shva* is no vowel, but in some environments where a sequence of consonants is difficult to pronounce (because of the nature of the consonant clusters involved), it is pronounced as a short *e*. Traditionally, the absence of a vowel at the end of a closed syllable, as in מִסְדָּר *mis-dar* or מַשְׁבֵּר *mash-ber*, is called שְׁוָא נָח *shva naħ*. When a *shva* at the beginning of a syllable is realized as *e*, as in לְבָנִים *levanim*, it is called שְׁוָא נָע *shva na`*.

Originally, every word-initial consonant cluster was split by a *shva na`*: גְּ-דוֹ-לִים *ge-do-lim*; however, in Israeli Hebrew, which allows many initial consonant clusters, most initial *shva*'s are realized as zero vowels: גְּ-דוֹ-לִים < גְדוֹ-לִים *ge-do-lim > gdo-lim*. When the consonant clusters are difficult to pronounce, the *shva* will be pronounced as *e*, as in לְ-בָ-נִים *le-va-nim*. This is true when a word begins with a consonant cluster the first member of which is ר׳, נ׳, מ׳, ל׳, י׳, or when the second is א׳, ה׳, or ע׳, which makes the consonant sequence hard to articulate.

levanim	לְבָנִים	*yeladim*	יְלָדִים
neshama	נְשָׁמָה	*mesiba*	מְסִבָּה
zehirut	זְהִירוּת	*reshima*	רְשִׁימָה
she`onim	שְׁעוֹנִים	*te`una*	תְּאוּנָה

The same applies to a *shva* that immediately follows another *shva:*

nivdka > niv-de-ka   נִבְדְּקָה   *tisgru > tis-ge-ru*   תִּסְגְּרוּ

Note 4: Comments on vowels marked with *ħataf*

The four guttural consonants, א׳, ה׳, ח׳, ע׳, are hard to pronounce with no vowel (i.e., a *shva naħ*). There are many word patterns which include a zero vowel in particular positions in the word, so to facilitate the pronunciation of each of the four guttural consonants where a zero vowel was supposed to occur, one of three auxiliary vowels is inserted: shorter versions of the *kamats*, *pataħ* and *segol*. These auxiliary vowels are known as *ħatafim* חֲטָפִים. Today, however, they are no longer short.

Replacement of Ø by auxiliary vowels:

ḥataf-pataḥ	*a*	חֲטָף-פַּתָּח	חֲדָרִים	<	יְלָדִים
ḥataf-segol	*e*	חֲטָף-סֶגוֹל	אֱמוּנָה	<	גְּדוֹלָה
ḥataf-kamats	*o*	חֲטָף-קָמַץ	חֳדָשִׁים	<	צְרָכִים

Note 5: 'furtive' *pataḥ* (*pataḥ gnuva*)

The furtive *pataḥ* is an *a* vowel that is added to a word-final הי, חי, עי
when it is preceded by a vowel other than *a* (as required by the word
formation pattern), because it is easier to pronounce a word-final
guttural, which is a low consonant, when it is preceded by a low vowel,
i.e., by the *pataḥ a*.

Here are some examples:

Pattern:	Final הי	Final עי	Final חי
CaCiC	מַגִּיהַּ	גָּבִיעַ	צָחִיחַ
CaCuC	תְּמוּהַּ	יָדוּעַ	פָּתוּחַ
CaCoC	גָּבוֹהַּ	שָׁמוֹעַ	שָׁכוֹחַ
CoCeC/CaCeC	תָּמֵהַּ	יוֹדֵעַ	פּוֹרֵחַ

However, this rule does not apply when the word-final vowel is *a*.

| CaCaC | גָּבַהּ | שָׁמַע | פָּתַח |

Note on the pronunciation of furtive *pataḥ*

When you see a *pataḥ* under a word-final עי, חי, read it as if a silent אי
with a *pataḥ* has been inserted before it: פּוֹתֵחַ *potéaḥ*, יָדוּעַ *yadúa`*. The
stress is always on the vowel before the furtive *pataḥ*. It never falls on
the furtive *pataḥ* itself.

A historical note

The development of Hebrew orthographic signs for consonants is much
earlier than that of vowels. The first sign of vowels emerges in what are
called אמות הקריאה *matres lectionis,* where some consonants were also
used to represent vowels: וי, יי, final אי and final הי.
1. The letter וי *vav* represents the consonant *v* (historically pronounced
w), as well as two vowels: וֹ stands for *o* (יוֹם, בְּנוֹ), and וּ for *u* (קוּם, קָמוּ).

2. The letter *yod* represents the consonant *y* as well as the vowel *i*
(שִׁיר, בְּנִי), and on some occasions the diphthongs *ay* (עָלַי) or *ey* (בֵּית, פָּנַי)
(diphthongs are vowels combined with the "semi-vowels" *y* or *w*).

3. The use of וֹ and יֹ as vowels applied in medial as well as in final position.

4. In Hebrew orthography as it eventually became stabilized, all final vowels are represented by letters, with ו for *o* and *u*, י for *i, ey* and *ay*, and ה for *a* (בָּנָה) and *e* (יִבְנֶה). Similarly, א is silent at the end of words (קָרָא) or syllables (קָרָאתִי, כָּאן), but is still maintained in the spelling.

Vowel marks and other diacritical signs were added later to the Biblical Hebrew text to aid in the pronunciation of the text.

2.4 With or without vowel signs?

Although native speakers can easily deduce the vowels from the morphological patterns in which words are realized and from the rest of the context, the optional use of *yod* and *vav* to represent the vowels *i* and *o/u*, respectively, has been a long tradition for many generations and has become the norm today. It is taught in schools, documented in all recent dictionaries, and used with complete regularity by publishers. When this is done, we refer to the result as כְּתִיב מָלֵא *ktiv malé*, '*plene* writing', as opposed to כְּתִיב חָסֵר *ktiv ḥasér*, which includes vowels marks (for a summary of *plene* writing rules, see Appendix 5). In a text with *ktiv malé* most *o/u* vowels can be represented with a *vav* throughout, but the use of *yod* for *i* is generally restricted to open syllables, or to alternants of words with open syllables, e.g., דיבר and דיברו, but התלבש, not *היתלבש (see description of open and closed syllables on p. 27).

Although the distinction between כתיב מלא *ktiv malé* and כתיב חסר *ktiv ḥasér* only refers to the presence or absence of optional vowel letters for *i* and for *o/u*, respectively, in practice the former is typically also characterized by the absence of any diacritic vowel marks, which *ktiv ḥasér* usually displays. Note, however, that a 'hybrid' practice is emerging, in which the two representations are merged when users feel the need for it, so as to achieve maximal redundancy, as in דִּיבֵּר alongside דִּבֵּר and דיבר.

It should be emphasized that *ktiv malé* only relates to optional vowels; many vowel signs are obligatory, as in לָקוּם, סְפוּר, לָשִׁיר, מָקוֹם etc. Such vowels have always been obligatory. Also, note that the use of the *matres lectionis* הי and אי to represent *a* and *e* is essentially still limited to the ends of words – although אי is often used in rendering internal *a* in borrowed words and foreign names: סולטאן 'sultan', סונאטה 'sonata', סאדאת 'Sadat'.

Another long-standing tradition associated with *ktiv malé* is to distinguish between consonants and their corresponding vowels by representing the former with a double letter, i.e., וו for *v* from *vav* (חיוור *ḥiver*) and יי for *y* from *yod* (חייל *ḥayal*).

כתיב חסר ומלא

מלא	חסר	מלא	חסר	מלא	חסר
דיבר	דִּבֶּר	יכתוב	יִכְתֹּב	שולחן	שֻׁלְחָן
חיסכון	חִסָּכוֹן	טייסת	טַיֶּסֶת	התכוון	הִתְכַּוֵּן
חוכמה	חָכְמָה	דיבור	דִּבּוּר	עליי	עָלַי

2.5 Other diacritics

Along with the vowel signs that were developed in post-biblical Hebrew, there are other diacritic marks that came to signify either a variant pronunciation of a letter, or its length, or a grammatical function. These diacritic marks are the following: *dagesh kal*, *dagesh ḥazak* and *mapik*. They are marked by insertion of a dot into the middle of a letter. The three have different labels, as they have different values and functions.

2.5.1 *Dagesh kal*　　　　　　　　　　　　　　　　　דגש קל

Historically, six Hebrew consonants were pronounced in two different ways, depending on their position in the word: בי גי די כי פי תי. The *dagesh kal* consists of a dot inserted into these letters to distinguish two variant pronunciations: בי גי די כי פי תי (stops) and בי גי די כי פי תי (continuants), respectively. The latter occurred after vowels, the former elsewhere. Three of the six, בי, כי, פי, have maintained the two variants (*b, k, p* vs. *v, kh, f*, respectively), while the other three, גי, די, תי, have lost that distinction. In texts with vowels, all six letters keep the two distinct variants, indicated by the presence or absence of *dagesh kal*, but only the following are maintained in current pronunciation:

v as in *sevivon*	סְבִיבוֹן	ב	*b* as in *barvaz*	בַּרְוָז	ב
kh as in *mikhtav*	מִכְתָּב	כ	*k* as in *kartis*	כַּרְטִיס	כ
f as in *sifriya*	סִפְרִיָּה	פ	*p* as in *patish*	פַּטִישׁ	פ

2.5.2 *Dagesh ħazak*   דגש חזק

The *dagesh ħazak* uses the same sign as the *dagesh kal*, a dot in the middle of a letter, but has a totally different function. Historically the presence of a *dagesh ħazak* reflected a doubling of the length of the letter. The *dagesh* could be inserted into most of the letters of the alphabet, with the exception of the 'guttural' consonants (א' ה' ח' ע' ר'). In Israeli Hebrew, the *dagesh ħazak* no longer reflects a doubling of the length of a consonant, but it still functions as part of the distinct pattern of some verb and noun groupings. It is also part of the definite article structure: in texts with vowel markings, *dagesh ħazak* is inserted into the first consonant of the noun the definite article -ה is attached to (with the exception of א' ה' ח' ע' ר' – which could not be doubled).

Definite article + consonant with *dagesh*:

| *haséfer* | הַסֵּפֶר | | *habáyit* | הַבַּיִת |

Definite article followed by guttural consonant:

| *ha'árets* | הָאָרֶץ | | *harúaħ* | הָרוּחַ |

Because the length, or doubling, represented by a *dagesh ħazak* no longer exists in Israeli Hebrew, all Hebrew consonants, including the ones with *dagesh ħazak*, are considered and are pronounced "short".

Note

Since the *dagesh* cannot be inserted into the letters א' ה' ח' ע' ר', there were rules for compensating for the absence of the *dagesh* (תַּשְׁלוּם דָּגֵשׁ). This process no longer makes any difference in pronunciation, but in writing, vowels often changed from what used to be short vowels to formerly long vowels. In many cases the following changes occurred:

Short vowel > long vowel   תנועה קצרה > תנועה ארוכה
    pataħ > kamats   סַבָּל > שָׂרָת
    ħirik > tsere   סִפּוּר > תֵּאוּר
    kubuts > holam ħaser   מְסֻפָּר > מְתֹאָר (מתואר)

2.5.3 *Mapik*   מַפִּיק

A dot (*mapik*), though looking the same as a *dagesh*, has a distinct function. It can be inserted into the letter ה' when it is in a final position in the word, to signal an audible *h* sound and to distinguish it from the typical final הי, which is silent. It is used for the small number of items that contain a true *h* as their last root consonant, as in גָּבוֹהַּ, but in most cases it also has a morphological function. It is attached at the end of a noun, or a preposition, to indicate a third person feminine singular pronoun suffix: סִפְרָהּ 'her book', לָהּ 'to her', שֶׁלָּהּ 'her(s)'.

In Israeli Hebrew the final הי is silent. In formal readings, there are those who may pronounce it as an aspirated *h* for stylistic reasons.

Note

The *mapik* is only present in the feminine **singular** third person form of possessive pronouns. When the pronoun is feminine plural, there is no *mapik* in the pronoun suffix.

	without *mapik*			with *mapik*	
her books	*sfaréha*	סְפָרֶיהָ	her book	*sifráh*	סִפְרָהּ

2.6 Syllables   הברות

Words are composed of syllables. There are two types of syllables, הֲבָרוֹת פְּתוּחוֹת 'open syllables' and הֲבָרוֹת סְגוּרוֹת 'closed syllables'. Whereas in English, many syllables start with vowels (e.g., *apple*), most Hebrew syllables start with a consonant. Following the consonant, the syllable has one vowel. The open syllable ends with a vowel, while the closed syllable ends with a consonant (or consonants).

CV =	*sé* = open syllable	*sé-fer*	סֵפֶר
CVC =	*fer* = closed syllable		
CV=	*sha* = open syllable	*sha-*	שָׁמַרְתְּ
CVCC=	*mart* = closed syllable	*márt*	
CCV=	*shmi* = open syllable	*shmi-rá*	שְׁמִירָה
CV=	*ra* = open syllable		

(C stands for consonants and V for vowels).

Note

There are some morphological arguments for assigning consonantal value to the 'guttural' consonants אי, עי, הי in describing the syllabic structure of a word, even when they are not actually realized. One may wish to do so because consonantal slots indicate the morphological pattern to which particular words belong. Insofar as syllable structure proper is concerned, however, it depends on the likelihood of actual

realization. Since under certain circumstances, א׳, ע׳ or ה׳ may be
realized phonetically before a stressed vowel, as in קָרְאָה *kar'á* 'she
read', we may be justified in granting them consonantal value, even
though it is not always pronounced. At the end of a word, the same
letters are even less likely to have consonantal value insofar as the
structure of the syllable is concerned: א׳ is never realized phonetically
(e.g., צָמֵא *tsamé*), nor is ה׳ from original י׳ (e.g., רָזֶה *razé*), and
realization of ע׳ is rare (e.g., רֶגַע *réga'* > *réga*). Such words are thus
regarded as ending with an open syllable. Final ע׳ or ה׳ preceded by *a*,
itself preceded by another vowel, as in יוֹדֵעַ or גָּבוֹהַּ, is just as unlikely to
be realized: *yodéa'* > *yodéa, gavóah* > *gavóa*.

2.7 Stress   הטעמה

Every word has a stressed vowel, which is usually pronounced as a
longer vowel and often more emphatically. Stress is part of the pattern
of the word. Two words can have the same sound sequence (not
necessarily spelled alike), but still have a different stress pattern, and
thus have different meanings. For instance, the sequence *bo-ker* can
have two different stress patterns: The first syllable can be stressed:
בֹּקֶר *bóker*, which means 'morning', or stress can fall on the second
syllable: בּוֹקֵר *bokér*, which means 'cowboy'. (Note that both are
written בוקר when they appear in texts without vowels).

Hebrew stress normally falls on the final vowel of the word, regardless
of the number of syllables. Final vowel stress is called מִלְרַע *milrá'*.

Hebrew	*ivrít*	עִבְרִית
secret	*sód*	סוֹד
thing	*davár*	דָּבָר

There are well-defined word groups, where the stress falls on the vowel
before last (penultimate), called מִלְעֵל *mil'él*, but all other words follow
the general rule. The largest group of *mil'él* words are the *segolate*
nouns known by that name because of the prominence of the *segol*
vowel as part of their pattern:

| *CéCeC* | man | *géver* | גֶּבֶר |
| | way | *dérekh* | דֶּרֶךְ |

A detailed discussion of the *segolate* nouns can be found in Chapter 5,
pp. 153-155. For additional examples, see the noun index.

The feminine singular conjugation of many verbs in the present tense has a similar *segolate* pattern, and thus the same מִלְעֵל stress:

| ...*CéCet* | says | *oméret* | אוֹמֶרֶת |
| | gets excited | *mitragéshet* | מִתְרַגֶּשֶׁת |

Past tense forms in the first and second person (whose suffixes usually start with a consonant) are also stressed מִלְעֵל:

| ...+*ti* | I wrote | *katávti* | כָּתַבְתִּי |
| ...+*nu* | we spoke | *dibárnu* | דִּבַּרְנוּ |

So is the final י *i* or ו *u/o* or *e* of a past or future verb stem (or *a* whose root contains י *i* or ו *u*) that is followed by a suffix vowel:

	they will run	*yarútsu*	יָרוּצוּ
	she explained	*hisbíra*	הִסְבִּירָה
	they got up	*kámu*	קָמוּ
	they will come	*yavóu*	יָבוֹאוּ
	she protected	*hegéna*	הֵגֵנָּה

Another class of items stressed מִלְעֵל is forms with the dual-noun suffix -*áyim*:

| -*áyim* | legs | *ragláyim* | רַגְלַיִם |
| | twice | *pa`amáyim* | פַּעֲמַיִם |

Stress patterns in borrowed words

Generally, borrowed nouns maintain the stress pattern they had in the original language, e.g.,

	artist	*artist*	אַרְטִיסְט
	flashback	*fléshbek*	פְלֶשְׁבֶּק
	maniac	*mányak*	מַנְיָאק

Certain foreign suffixes (especially from Eastern European languages) are associated with non-final stress in the source, and maintain it in Hebrew as well, as in nouns ending with +*ika*:

	politics	*polítika*	פּוֹלִיטִיקָה
	ceramics	*kerámika*	קֵרָמִיקָה
	music	*músika*	מוּסִיקָה

Changes when affixes are added

When an affix is added to a native Hebrew word, stress normally shifts from the stem to that suffix:

Native words:

Stress > last syllable		Suffixed	Stress	Base	
susá	mare	סוּסָה	*sús*	horse	סוּס
shirím	poems	שִׁירִים	*shír*	poem	שִׁיר

In borrowed words and in acronyms, however, stress remains on where it was in the word in isolation:

Borrowed words

Stress unchanged		Suffixed	Stress	Base	
tánkim	tanks	טַנְקִים	*tánk*	tank	טַנְק
jóbim	jobs	גִ'וֹבִּים	*jób*	job	גִ'וֹב

Acronyms

Stress unchanged		Suffixed	Stress	Base	
mankálim	CEO's	מַנְכָּ"לִים	*mankál*	CEO	מַנְכָּ"ל
makámin	radars	מַכָּ"מִים	*makám*	radar	מַכָּ"ם

Stress patterns in casual and rapid speech

Speech is conveyed in a connected stream of words, rather than in singular words, and therefore the stress pattern of words that are strung together may change from the stress pattern of each of these words viewed out of context, as single entities.

What do you mean?	מַה זֹאת אוֹמֶרֶת?
Stress in individual words:	מילים נפרדות :
má zót oméret	מַה + זֹאת + אוֹמֶרֶת?
Rapid speech:	דיבור מהיר :
màstoméret?	מַזְתוֹמֶרֶת?

It is not all right.	זֶה לֹא בְּסֵדֶר.
Stress in individual words:	מילים נפרדות :
ze ló beséder	זֶה + לֹא + בְּסֵדֶר.
Rapid speech:	דיבור מהיר :
zlòpséder	זְלוֹבְּסֵדֶר

Primary and secondary stress

There are two degrees of stress, which are noticeable in such sequences as the ones above: a primary stress, and a secondary stress. In expressions like ?מַה זֹאת אוֹמֶרֶת, the primary stress still falls on the stressed vowel of *oméret*, whereas the secondary stress falls on *mà*. In pronouncing the sequence, the secondary stress is less dominant than the first one, but is still audible. Also, note that in a sequence like הוא אמר לנו שלום *ù amár lànu shalóm* 'he said hello to us', the secondary stress of *lànu* normally moves forward, resulting in *lanù*, to avoid a stress clash with the primary stress of *amár*: *ù amár lanù shalóm*.

2.8 Dialectal variation   שונות דיאלקטית בהגיית עיצורים

In the early days of the revival of Hebrew as a spoken language (late 19th and early 20th centuries), two main dialects were recognized in Modern Hebrew, and in the popular vernacular they were referred to as 'Ashkenazi' and 'Sepharadi'. The Ashkenazi dialect referred to the Hebrew of European Jews or recent immigrants from mostly Eastern European background, while the Sepharadi dialect was used as a general term to refer to the Hebrew of Jews from Arabic-speaking countries, who spoke Arabic as their native tongue, as well as to Jews from the Balkans and parts of the Middle East who spoke Judeo-Spanish (Ladino). However, today Israeli Hebrew is the one standard language. Most variations within Israeli Hebrew involve language registers, but may also reflect communities of speakers by the countries of their origin. (The situation is never stable, since the waves of immigration continue to bring groups of speakers from a variety of countries, for instance, Ethiopia and Russia). There is a formal standard Hebrew, which is used by the media: newspapers, radio and television. An even higher register is used for language of the courtroom and formal speeches and addresses. As in most spoken languages, there are also several informal registers and sub-dialects in Israeli Hebrew, such as street Hebrew, army jargon, pop culture and children's language.

The term *Mizrahí* (Eastern) has now replaced Sepharadi, and it refers to the spoken pronunciation of Israelis from Eastern (mostly Arabic-speaking) backgrounds. The main feature of the *Mizrahí* dialect is the preservation of the original pronunciations of ח and ע. Both are articulated low, in the pharynx, and both are fricative. The difference between them is in voicing; when ע is pronounced, the vocal cords vibrate, while in חׄ they do not. Few older members of Eastern immigrant groups maintain the distinction between כׄ *k* and קׄ *q* that exists in Arabic, pronouncing the latter further back in the mouth (at the uvula). Even more rarely is the historical difference between תׄ and טׄ maintained (this involves the articulation of טׄ like *t*, while simultaneously raising the back of the tongue, creating the impression of emphasis). The historical pronunciation of the letter *tsadi* was *s* with the raising of the back of the tongue, and the articulation of the letter וׄ was *w*. However, in contemporary Hebrew, such features of pronunciation are extinct. There are some who pronounce רׄ not in the back of the mouth as in standard Israeli Hebrew, but as a dental roll, like Spanish or Polish *r*. As a rule, these variations are not characteristic of all of the speakers of Eastern origin and depend a great deal on whether they are immigrant or native Israelis, and in the case of the former, of their age at the time of immigration. Standard Hebrew is gradually replacing other dialects in daily speaking. Some special pronunciation is maintained in the folk tradition, particularly in popular and traditional music, folksongs and story-telling.

Chapter 3
The verb system

3.1 Introduction: verb components

Verbal forms in Hebrew are composed of two main components: verb stems and morphemes of inflection that denote person, gender and number.

Gloss	Suffix	Stem/base	Prefix	Verb form	Root
I closed	תִי-	סָגַר-		סָגַרְתִּי	ס-ג-ר
you will close	י-	סְגְּר-	תִּ-	תִּסְגְּרִי	ס-ג-ר
tells		סַפֵּר-	מְ-	מְסַפֵּר	ס-פ-ר
to guard		שְׁמֹר-	לִ-	לִשְׁמֹר	ש-מ-ר

A traditional constituent of each verb is its root. Roots are not actual words, but rather sequences of consonants, which provide the common base for verbs and nouns. Roots can be common to a number of verb patterns and noun patterns:

Verbs				**Root**
be written	נִכְתַּב	write	כָּתַב	כ-ת-ב
be dictated	הֻכְתַּב	dictate	הִכְתִּיב	
		correspond	הִתְכַּתֵּב	
Nouns				**Root**
handwriting	כְּתָב	spelling	כְּתִיב	כ-ת-ב
correspondence	תִּכְתֹּבֶת	letter	מִכְתָּב	
dictation	הַכְתָּבָה	desk	מִכְתָּבָה	

Verb stems are formations through which roots, which are not actual words but rather sequences of consonants, are organized into a variety of verb forms. The stem sequences are composed of vowel patterns combined with root consonants and in some cases additional consonants. Conjugation markers are added to verb stems in order to indicate person, gender, and tense or mood. For example, the verb form סָגַרְתִּי 'I closed' is made up of the stem -סָגַר and the first person subject suffix -תִּי, which designates first person singular in the past tense. The verb form מְסַפֵּר 'tells' is composed of the stem -סַפֵּר and the -מְ prefix marking the present tense of *pi`el*.

3.2 Citation forms   צורות מילוניות

Verbs are usually entered into the dictionary either by root or by the past tense, third person singular form. Different dictionaries use different principles to organize lexical entries, even when alphabetization is by root. The sub-entries within each root are by the past tense form of the third person masculine singular. A verb form like הִסְבִּירוּ 'they explained', for instance, is never listed as such. One needs to look for the form הִסְבִּיר 'he explained', which would be listed either under the 'root' ס-ב-ר, or as is, in simple alphabetical order, regardless of root. At times the present tense form מַסְבִּיר 'explain, masculine singular' is included as a separate dictionary entry, also irrespective of root. In either case, the form is marked for category (a verb, in this case), and sometimes for verb pattern (here, *hif`il*). This type of dictionary entry is referred to as צורה מילונית, a 'citation form'. An example of a minimal dictionary entry is לָמַד (פ) '(to) study (v)'. More information may be included, such as regarding a preposition that obligatorily follows the verb to link it with an object, as in בָּטַח בְּ- (פָּעַל) 'trust (in)'. The citation form, although it mirrors the third person past tense, refers to the general meaning of the verb, and to all the various possible actual uses, i.e. the entire verb paradigm. For instance, הִסְבִּיר is not only the past tense, meaning 'he explained', but also stands for all the verbal forms associated with that *hif`il* verb.

In English similar representation is achieved by entering verbs under the infinitive 'to explain', or simply 'explain'.

Here is an illustration of the above concepts:

Gloss	בניין	שורש	צורה מילונית
explain	הִפְעִיל	ס-ב-ר	הִסְבִּיר

These are the various forms associated with the dictionary entry הסביר:

Tense/mood	Person	Verb forms	Stems
Past	1st 2nd	הִסְבַּרְתִּי הִסְבַּרְתָּ הִסְבַּרְתְּ	הִסְבַּרְ-
		הִסְבַּרְנוּ הִסְבַּרְתֶּם הִסְבַּרְתֶּן	
	3rd	הוּא הִסְבִּיר, הִיא הִסְבִּירָה, הֵם הִסְבִּירוּ	הִסְבִּיר
Present	all	מַסְבִּיר מַסְבִּירָה מַסְבִּירִים מַסְבִּירוֹת	מַסְבִּיר-
Future	singular	אַסְבִּיר תַּסְבִּיר תַּסְבִּירִי יַסְבִּיר תַּסְבִּיר	-סְבִּיר-
	plural	נַסְבִּיר תַּסְבִּירוּ (תַּסְבֵּרְנָה) יַסְבִּירוּ	
		(תַּסְבֵּרְנָה)	
Imperative	2nd	הַסְבֵּר הַסְבִּירִי הַסְבִּירוּ (הַסְבֵּרְנָה)	הַסְבֵּ(י)ר-
Infinitive		לְהַסְבִּיר	הַסְבִּיר

As can be seen in the above table, each verb stem is present in the actual verb forms listed next to it. Verbs conjugated in tense have a dynamic quality since they express different ongoing processes.

3.3 Verb tenses   זמני הפועל

Verbs can be classified in two different groups: those that are conjugated in tense, and those that are not. Verb tense is the expression of the time frame for the action, state or event that the verb signifies. The verb form itself denotes the time frame. There are three tenses in modern Hebrew: past, present and future. The past tense indicates a completed one-time action, or a process that started at some point in the past and was completed or ceased. Hebrew expresses past perfect by the simple past. The present tense indicates an ongoing action, event or state, or habitual action. The future tense indicates actions or states contemplated, planned or considered for a future time.

3.3.1 The present tense   זמן הווה

The present tense refers to an ongoing state or action repeated with regularity, or a continuous action. The present tense of all verbs has four forms. These forms have gender attributes (masculine or feminine), and number markings (singular or plural). They do not have any person attributes and thus do not include a subject (unlike the past

and future tenses). In the following tables the present tense verb base
(בָּסִיס) and the suffixes that are added to it are represented.

Present tense suffixes

בסיס + ה/ת	אני את היא	בסיס*	אני אתה הוא	יחיד/ה
בסיס + ות	אנחנו אתן הן	בסיס + ים	אנחנו אתם הם	רבים/ות

בסיס, the Hebrew term for 'stem', stands for any present tense stem

Here are some of the nuances conveyed by the use of the present tense:

1. The present moment of the speaker

She cannot come to the phone <u>now</u> because she is working.

היא לא יכולה לדבר <u>עכשיו</u> בטלפון כי היא עובדת.

2. Ongoing progressive activity

She has been sitting and waiting here <u>for hours</u>.

היא יושבת ומחכה כאן <u>כבר שעות</u>.

3. Habitual/repetitive action

<u>Every day</u> they leave home at seven.

<u>כל יום</u> הם יוצאים מהבית בשבע.

4. Completed action resulting in a state

The meal <u>is ready</u>.

הארוחה <u>מוכנה</u>.

The context for the above sentence is a process of meal preparation that took place and was completed, and the result is that now it is ready.

5. Action that started in the past and is ongoing

They have been teaching this course <u>for five years</u>.

הם מלמדים את הקורס הזה <u>כבר חמש שנים</u>.

Grammatical functions of present tense forms

The present tense forms can function as verbs, as adjectives, and as agent nouns. They are referred to as participles צורות בינוני.

1. As verbs:

She <u>closes</u> the door and <u>leaves</u>.

היא <u>סוגרת</u> את הדלת <u>ויוצאת</u>.

We <u>are looking for</u> an apartment.

אנחנו <u>מחפשים</u> דירה.

2. As adjectives:

The dog is a <u>faithful</u> animal.

הכלב הוא חיה <u>נאמנה.</u>

The <u>cooked</u> food is in the refrigerator.

האוכל <u>המבושל</u> נמצא במקרר.

3. As nouns:

There are many <u>distinguished people</u> in the audience.

יש הרבה <u>נכבדים</u> בקהל.

The <u>organizers</u> did a good job.

<u>המארגנים</u> עשו עבודה טובה.

3.3.2 The past tense   זמן עבר

The past tense has nine forms. The subjects of the verbs are suffixed to the verb stems in the first and second persons. Therefore the past tense is sometimes referred to as the suffixed tense. In the third person, both singular and plural, the subject is not included in the verb form and has to be expressed by a noun or pronoun or some other entity.

Past tense suffixes

בסיס + תִּי	(אני)	בסיס* + תִּי	(אני)
בסיס + תְּ	(את)	בסיס + תָ	(אתה)
בסיס + הָ	היא	בסיס	הוא

יחיד/ה

בסיס + נו	(אנחנו)	בסיס + נו	(אנחנו)
בסיס + תֶּן	(אתן)	בסיס + תֶם	(אתם)
בסיס + ו	הן	בסיס + ו	הם

רבים/ות

*בסיס, the Hebrew term for 'stem', stands for any past tense stem

In Hebrew, unlike in English, it is not necessary to have an independent subject pronoun in the first and second persons of the past tense, since these pronouns are already incorporated in the subject suffixes and thus would be redundant.

	Subject	Stem	
I finished	תִּי +	גָמַר =	גָמַרְתִּי (אני)
You finished	תָ +	גָמַר =	גָמַרְתָ (אתה)

However, it is possible to include them as separate pronouns for emphasis, and in common use even without emphasis.

<u>I</u> found the lost item, not he.

<u>אני</u> מצאתי את האבדה, לא הוא.

<u>I</u> finished eating before you.

<u>אני</u> גמרתי לאכול לפניך.

The past tense refers to an aspect of a completed action, an event or a situation that was completed and is no longer taking place.

1. Completed action

I <u>read</u> the book you <u>wrote</u>.	.קראתי את הספר שכתבת

2. Duration of action

The author <u>had been writing</u> the book for ten years.	המחבר כתב את הספר במשך עשר שנים.

3. Past perfect

I <u>had read</u> his last novel, before I <u>started reading</u> his first book.	קראתי את הרומן האחרון שלו, לפני שהתחלתי לקרוא את הספר הראשון שלו.

3.3.3 The future tense   זמן עתיד

The future tense forms combine a prefix subject pronoun with the future stem of the verb. The feminine singular and the plural forms also have suffixes indicating gender and number.

Future tense affixes

א + בסיס	(אני)	א + בסיס	(אני)	יחיד/ה
ת + בסיס + י	(את)	ת + בסיס	(אתה)	
ת + בסיס	היא	י + בסיס	הוא	
נ + בסיס	(אנחנו)	נ + בסיס	(אנחנו)	רבים/ות
ת +בסיס + ו	(אתן)	ת +בסיס+ ו	(אתם)	
(ת + בסיס + נה)				
י +בסיס + ו	הן	י +בסיס+ ו	הם	
(ת + בסיס + נה)				

בסיס, the Hebrew term for 'stem', stands for any future tense stem

Note

As in the past tense, independent personal pronouns are redundant for the first and second persons, since they are already incorporated in the suffixes of these forms. However, they may be added when the pronoun requires emphasizing, as well as in colloquial use. It should be noted that in the first person singular, the independent pronoun אני has become the norm in everyday speech.

There are two variants for the feminine plural meaning of the second person and third person:

1. The first one employs a special form for the feminine second and third person plural: אַתֶּן תִּפְעַלוּ/אַתֶּן תִּפְעַלְנָה ; הן יִפְעֲלוּ/הן תִּפְעַלְנָה. The form תִּפְעַלְנָה, which is found in biblical Hebrew, is rarely in use in contemporary Hebrew. It was considered for many years to be the normative form, but is now restricted to use in formal speech, and sometimes when addressing a female audience.

2. The shared plural form for both masculine and feminine in the second and third persons is the standard form in ordinary speech and is part of the accepted norm: אַתֶּם תִּפְעֲלוּ/אַתֶּן תִּפְעֲלוּ ; הם יִפְעֲלוּ/הן יִפְעֲלוּ.

3.3.4 Planning, anticipation and contemplation

The future tense refers to an action or process that is being planned, anticipated or contemplated.

Plans

Dan will be working on the program during the year.

דן <u>יעבוד</u> על התוכנה במשך השנה.

Anticipation

Everybody hopes that there will not be a strike.

כולם מקווים שלא <u>תהיה</u> שביתה.

Contemplation

They may not (it is likely that they will not) arrive on time, and then we'll be late for the show.

יכול להיות שהם לא <u>יגיעו</u> בזמן, ואז נאחר להצגה.

Conditionals

If there is (<u>will be</u>) a strike, we <u>won't</u> be able to get home, since the trains <u>won't be running</u>.

אם <u>תהיה</u> שביתה לא <u>נוכל</u> להגיע הביתה, כי הרכבות לא <u>יפעלו</u>.

A comparative note

Three tenses in Hebrew cover eight categories of tense in English

1. **Present tense - habitual action**

He goes to work at eight.

הוא הולך לעבודה בשמונה.

2. **Present progressive- action in ongoing present**

He has been driving for eight hours already.

הוא נוהג כבר שמונה שעות.

3. **Past tense - action occurred in the past**

He drove all the way.   .הוא נהג כל הדרך

4. **Past progressive - ongoing action in past**

He was driving along, and did not notice the   הוא נהג ולא שם לב
time.   .לזמן

5. **Past perfect progressive**

He had been working there for eight   הוא עבד שם שמונה שנים ועכשיו
years, and now he called it quits.   .הוא החליט לעזוב את העבודה

6. **Past Perfect**

Before he started working here, he   לפני שהוא התחיל לעבוד כאן, הוא
had been working in another office.   .עבד במשרד אחר

7. **Future**

He will work here if the conditions   הוא יעבוד כאן אם התנאים יהיו
will be satisfactory.   .מספיק טובים

8. **Future Continuous**

He will be working here in the next   הוא יעבוד כאן במשך השבועיים
two weeks.   .הבאים

3.4 Historical notes

1. Many linguists view Biblical Hebrew as having no tenses, only aspects: actions or states are considered as either complete or incomplete, perfect or imperfect, rather than being related to time and tense.

2. In Biblical Hebrew there are two additional verbal forms related to the imperfect: the jussive and the cohortative moods (see below). They are maintained in high registers of Israeli Hebrew, especially in written texts for stylistic reasons.

3. Past tense in Biblical Hebrew is normally indicated by the use of the imperfect form prefixed by the *waw* consecutive. Future tense can be indicated by the use of the perfect form prefixed by a *waw* consecutive. (see discussion below for illustrations).

3.4.1 Jussive and short form of the imperfect   עתיד מקוצר

In classical Hebrew, a brief form of the imperfect (and of some imperatives) exists in some of the "defective" (or non-regular) verb classes and in some regular *hif'il* forms. It is used in the third person, less commonly in the second person, and rarely in the first person:

יִכְרֵת > יַכְרִית, יִבֶן > יִבְנֶה, יֵרָא > יִרְאֶה, יְהִי > יִהְיֶה

The short form of the imperfect can function as a jussive, i.e., a moderated command, as in the following example:

And God said, Let there be light: and there was light. (Genesis, 1:3)

וַיֹּאמֶר אֱלֹהִים: יְהִי אוֹר - וַיְהִי אוֹר. (בראשית א:ג)

When it combines with the special '*waw* consecutive' *wa-* (vs. regular *we-*), it assumes a narrative function, as well as past tense time reference, and is used mostly in narrative style (see discussion below):

וַיַּרְא אֱלֹהִים אֶת הָאוֹר כִּי טוֹב וַיַּבְדֵּל אֱלֹהִים בֵּין הָאוֹר וּבֵין הַחֹשֶׁךְ. (בראשית א:ד)
And God saw the light, that [it was] good: and God divided the light from the darkness. (Genesis, 1:4)

It should be noted, however, that not all imperfect forms used as a jussive are necessarily shortened; many remain intact. A significant number of verb types are unaffected, and even when the singular form is shortened, the comparable plural one may not be.

And he said to his father, let my father sit up and eat of his son's game. (Genesis, 27:31)

וַיֹּאמֶר לְאָבִיו יָקֻם אָבִי וְיֹאכַל מִצֵּיד בְּנוֹ. (בראשית כז:לא)

Abner said to Joab, Let the young men come forward and play before us. (Samuel II, 2:14)

וַיֹּאמֶר אַבְנֵר אֶל-יוֹאָב יָקוּמוּ נָא הַנְּעָרִים וִישַׂחֲקוּ לְפָנֵינוּ. (שמואל ב' ב:יד)

3.4.2 Cohortative　　　　　　　　עתיד מוארך

This is a quasi-imperative mode, used exclusively in the first person (singular and plural), to express a wish, command or request, often in the form of self-encouragement (as one would expect from a "command to oneself"). An -*á* suffix is added to the verb form.

1st person singular	Future	*'eshmor*	אֶשְׁמֹר
	Cohortative	*'eshmerá*	אֶשְׁמְרָה
1st person plural	Future	*nishmor*	נִשְׁמֹר
	Cohortative	*nishmerá*	נִשְׁמְרָה

The meaning attached to this type of future verb is 'let's do something'. In modern Hebrew it is used in the literary register, usually with the

initiating verb of address: הָבָה 'let us', as in the famous tune הָבָה נָגִילָה
וְנִשְׂמְחָה 'Let us rejoice and be happy'.

Here are examples from biblical literature:

| And they said one to another, Go to, let us make brick, and burn them thoroughly. And they had brick for stone, and slime had they for mortar. (Genesis, 11:3) | וַיֹּאמְרוּ אִישׁ אֶל-רֵעֵהוּ, הָבָה נִלְבְּנָה לְבֵנִים וְנִשְׂרְפָה לִשְׂרֵפָה; וַתְּהִי לָהֶם הַלְּבֵנָה לְאָבֶן, וְהַחֵמָר הָיָה לָהֶם לַחֹמֶר. (בראשית יא:ג) |

| Let us go down, and there confound their language, that they may not understand one another's speech. (Genesis, 11:7) | הָבָה נֵרְדָה, וְנָבְלָה שָׁם שְׂפָתָם אֲשֶׁר לֹא יִשְׁמְעוּ אִישׁ שְׂפַת רֵעֵהוּ. (בראשית יא:ז) |

3.4.3 The uses of *waw* consecutive   וו ההיפוך

The '*waw* consecutive' is one of the most frequently used particles in the verb system of Biblical Hebrew. Prefixing this particle to verbal forms turns it into a constituent of a verb sequence (narrative and other), and sets its time reference.

Waw consecutive prefixed to imperfect verb forms

When this particle is prefixed to the imperfect verb form, it places it in a narrative sequence, and sets its time reference to the realm of the past. A shortened form of the imperfect follows this particle in some verb sub-groups, but in many cases the full imperfect form is maintained. The *waw* is always followed by the vowel *a (patah,* with a *dagesh* in the next segment, or a *kamats*, if the next segment is a guttural), which helps distinguish it from the regular conjunction -וְ:

and he said	ו+יאמר = וַיֹּאמֶר	הוא אמר <
and they went	ו + ילכו = וַיֵּלְכוּ	הם הלכו <
I went	ו + אלך = וָאֵלֵךְ	אני הלכתי <

Illustrations:

| And he rose up, and went unto the place of which God had told him. (Genesis, 22:3) | וַיָּקָם וַיֵּלֶךְ אֶל-הַמָּקוֹם אֲשֶׁר-אָמַר-לוֹ הָאֱלֹהִים (בראשית כב:ג) |

| He came to King Solomon, and executed all his work. (Kings I, 7:14) | וַיָּבוֹא אֶל-הַמֶּלֶךְ שְׁלֹמֹה וַיַּעַשׂ אֶת-כָּל-מְלַאכְתּוֹ (מלכים א' ז:יד) |

Waw consecutive prefixed to perfect verb forms

When the *waw* is prefixed to the perfect verb form, it places it in a verb sequence, and sets its time reference to the realm of the future.

and it will come to be	ו + היה = וְהָיָה	הוא יִהְיֶה <
and they will go/turn	ו + פנו = וּפָנוּ	הם יִפְנוּ <
and he will build	ו + בנה = וּבָנָה	הוא יִבְנֶה <
and you (pl.) will guard	ו + שמרתם = וּשְׁמַרְתֶּם	אתם תִּשְׁמְרוּ <

The *waw* is followed by a *shva*, or is realized as וּ before a labial consonant (ב׳, ו׳, מ׳, פ׳) or before a consonant cluster, e.g., *shm* in וּשְׁמַרְתֶּם *ushmartém.*

Illustrations:

| Cursed of the Lord be the man who shall undertake to fortify (lit. who will rise and will build) this city of Jericho. (Joshua, 6:26) | אָרוּר הָאִישׁ לִפְנֵי יְהוָֹה אֲשֶׁר יָקוּם וּבָנָה אֶת-הָעִיר הַזֹּאת אֶת-יְרִיחוֹ. (יהושע ו:כו) |

| For your part, take of everything that is eaten and you shall gather it, and it shall be for food for you and for them. (Genesis, 6:21) | וְאַתָּה קַח-לְךָ מִכָּל-מַאֲכָל אֲשֶׁר יֵאָכֵל וְאָסַפְתָּ אֵלֶיךָ וְהָיָה לְךָ וְלָהֶם לְאָכְלָה. (בראשית ו:כא) |

Since a very large number of verbs in the Bible are either constituents of a verb sequence, and/or are part of a narrative, the forms with '*waw* consecutive' prove to be prevalent. The simple imperfect and perfect without *waw* are generally used only in specific contexts:

1. After certain short words like לֹא 'not', כִּי 'because', מִי 'who', מַה 'what', אָז 'then', אֲשֶׁר 'which/that', e.g., מִי עָשָׂה אֶת-הַדָּבָר הַזֶּה 'who has done this thing?'

2. When the subject precedes the verb, usually for focusing (normally, the verb precedes the subject in Biblical Hebrew), e.g., וְעֵשָׂו אָחִיו בָּא מִצֵּידוֹ 'and his brother Esau came back from his hunting'.

3. When the verb refers to the past-of-the-past (past perfect), i.e., when referring to an earlier "pre-past" occurrence, e.g., וה׳ בֵּרַךְ אֶת-אַבְרָהָם בַּכֹּל 'and God had blessed Abraham with everything'.

4. As the first verb in a verb sequence; the next occurrence(s) would be with a '*waw* consecutive', as in יָקוּם וּבָנָה 'who will rise and will build' above.

3.5 Moods and verbal nouns   דרכים ושמות פועל/פעולה

There are two moods other than the indicative/declarative mood (which refers to the basic regular mode of verbs in tense): imperative, and infinitive. The temporal aspect of the activity or state is not a feature of these moods.

3.5.1 The imperative mood   ציווי

Only five of the *binyanim* have an imperative form. The two passive verb groups, *pu`al* and *hu`fal*, do not have such a form. The imperative mood conveys commands, directions, orders, and instructions. For a negative command, the special negative particle אַל is used, and the future tense forms are added.

Imperative mood: giving commands or directions

| Command | Sit quietly! | שֵׁב בשקט! | ציווי |
| Negative | Don't sit near the door! | אַל תֵּשֵׁב על יד הדלת! | שלילה |

To moderate the force of a command, words like בְּבַקָשָׁה can be added to the imperative.

Come in, please!   היכנסו בבקשה!

In daily speech, the future forms are usually used in lieu of the imperative, but the same may apply in higher registers as well, as an alternative to adding בְּבקשה when issuing a polite request or a directive, rather than a command.

Come in and make yourself at home!   תיכנסו ותרגישו בבית!

3.5.2 The infinitive mood   שם הפועל

The infinitive שם הפועל is the form of a verb that has no inflection to indicate person, number, mood or tense; it only contains information about the base of the verb and reflects the main idea or concept of the verb. It is called "infinitive" because the verb is not made finite, or modified by inflection.

Who wants <u>to speak</u>?   מי רוצה לדבר!   לְדַבֵּר

You have <u>to listen</u> to us!   אתם צריכים להקשיב לנו!   לְהַקְשִׁיב

Hebrew has two infinitives, the infinitive absolute מקור מוחלט and the infinitive construct מקור נטוי. The infinitive construct is used much as an English infinitive, including being preceded by ל- 'to', and with some other prepositions (see below); the infinitive absolute, which is restricted to the higher registers, is used to add emphasis or certainty to the verb, or as a verbal noun, or for emphatic commands (see below).

Like the imperative, only five of the *binyanim* have an infinitive form. The two passive *binyanim*, *pu`al* and *huf`al*, do not have an infinitive form. In literary Hebrew, however, absolute infinitive forms of these two *binyanim* may occur, as in גָּנוֹב גֻּנַּבְתִּי 'I have indeed been kidnapped', or הָזְהֵר הֻזְהַרְתָּ 'you have (unequivocally) been warned!'

3.5.3 Infinitive absolute   מקור מוחלט

The infinitive absolute is used either before a verb in tense, to intensify and increase the force of the statement, or on its own, to serve either as an abstract noun, or as an emphatic command. There is no equivalent to it in English, and therefore it is somewhat difficult to explain. It occurs mostly in Biblical Hebrew. It is not productive in Israeli Hebrew, but individual forms do occur, for example הָלוֹךְ וְחָזוֹר 'back and forth'.

Emphasis	We have indeed eaten	אָכוֹל אָכַלְנוּ	אָכוֹל
	You will say	אָמוֹר תֹּאמְרוּ	אָמוֹר
	He shall indeed die	מוֹת יָמוּת	מוֹת
Emphatic Command	Keep the Sabbath to honor it (Deut. 5:12)	שָׁמוֹר אֶת-יוֹם הַשַּׁבָּת לְקַדְּשׁוֹ (דברים ה:יב)	שָׁמוֹר
Abstract Noun	Eating too much honey is not good (Proverbs 25:27)	אָכֹל דְּבַשׁ הַרְבּוֹת לא-טוֹב (משלי כה:כז)	אָכוֹל

3.5.4 Infinitive construct   שם הפועל (מקור נטוי)

As mentioned earlier, when we refer to the infinitive mood, we are generally referring to its ordinary use, similar to its function in English.

Who wants <u>to speak</u>?   מי רוצה <u>לדבר</u>!   לְדַבֵּר

You have <u>to listen</u>!   אתם חייבים <u>לְהַקְשִׁיב</u>!   לְהַקְשִׁיב

3.5.5 Infinitive as gerund

The infinitive mood is used mostly with the particle ל- 'to', and as such it is more often referred to as שם הפועל and not מקור. However, there are other uses for the infinitive, with one of the four prepositional prefixes ב׳, כ׳, ל׳, מ׳. In such cases it acts as a gerund rather than an infinitive. It is not used often in such a form, except in some written texts. Paraphrasing with a verb in tense is much more common.

gloss	gerund	
while being	בִּהְיוֹת-	ב+ המקור הנטוי/שם הפועל
to the return of	לָשׁוּב-	ל+ המקור הנטוי/שם הפועל
from going	מִלֶּכֶת-	מ+ המקור הנטוי/שם הפועל
as (his) saying	כְּאוֹמְר-	כ+ המקור הנטוי/שם הפועל

Pronoun endings can be added, and they act as the subject of the gerund:

gloss	gerund	
while I was	בִּהְיוֹתִי	ב + שם הפועל+ סיומת גוף
for your return	לָשׁוּבְכֶם	ל + שם הפועל+ סיומת גוף
from her going	מִלֶּכְתָּה	מ + שם הפועל+ סיומת גוף
as he said	כְּאוֹמְרוֹ	כ + שם הפועל+ סיומת גוף

When I was a little girl, I lived abroad.	בִּהְיוֹתִי ילדה קטנה, גרתי בחו״ל.
We waited for his return from abroad.	חכינו לָשׁוּבוֹ מחו״ל.
We avoided going to his home.	נמנענו מִלֶּכֶת לביתו.

The infinitives in the sentences above can be paraphrased by sentences with finite verbs:

<u>ב+ מקור + אני</u>

Infinitive + suffix	while being abroad	בִּהְיוֹתִי בחו״ל
Paraphrase	when I was abroad	כאשר הייתי בחו״ל

<u>ל + מקור + הוא</u>

Infinitive + suffix	We waited for his return from abroad.	חכינו לָשׁוּבוֹ מחו״ל
Paraphrases	We waited till he returned from abroad.	חכינו עד שהוא שב מחו״ל
	We waited for him to return from abroad.	חכינו שהוא ישוב מחו״ל.

3.5.6 Verbal noun שם הפעולה

Verbal nouns are abstract nouns that can be related to verbal roots and are associated with various verbal groups and patterns. Each *binyan* has one or more patterns of nouns that are derived from the roots and/or are associated with that *binyan.*

	שם פעולה	שם פועל	שורש
reading, act of reading	קְרִיאָה (נ)	לִקְרֹא	ק-ר-א
agreement, discussion	הִדָּבְרוּת (נ)	לְהִדָּבֵר	ד-ב-ר
excursion, trip	טִיּוּל (ז)	לְטַיֵּל	ט-י-ל
explaining; propaganda	הַסְבָּרָה (נ)	לְהַסְבִּיר	ס-ב-ר
explanation	הֶסְבֵּר (ז)		
development	הִתְפַּתְּחוּת (נ)	לְהִתְפַּתֵּחַ	פ-ת-ח

3.6 Verb pattern groups בניינים

Traditionally Hebrew grammar classifies verbs into seven basic pattern groups, called *binyanim,* each of which has special inflectional characteristics. In contemporary grammatical descriptions five major pattern groups are recognized, with the two additional ones being "internal passives". The verb conjugations are the various sets of forms of actual verbs. Some of the categories that dictate the form of a conjugated verb are person, gender, and number features.

The third person singular in the past tense is not marked by a suffix, and serves as the citation form for each *binyan.* To capture the citation form, a prototypical root is used, most commonly פעל.

3.6.1 Names of verb pattern groups שמות הבניינים

Each conjugation is named according to its citation form.

Names of verb patterns		Citation forms	
pa`al	פָּעַל	*lamad*	לָמַד
nif`al	נִפְעַל	*nilmad*	נִלְמַד
pi`el	פִּעֵל	*gidel*	גִּדֵּל
pu`al	פֻּעַל	*gudal*	גֻּדַּל
hif`il	הִפְעִיל	*hiklit*	הִקְלִיט
huf`al	הֻפְעַל	*huklat*	הֻקְלַט
hitpa`el	הִתְפַּעֵל	*hitkabel*	הִתְקַבֵּל

3.6.2 Root composition: regular and irregular

There are two major root classifications: regular verbs and irregular verbs. They are also known as "strong" verbs, and "weak" verbs, respectively. In the same manner that each verb belongs to a particular בניין, it also belongs to a particular group of verbs, known as גְּזְרָה (plural גְּזָרוֹת) that classify them by their root composition.

1. The regular verbs belong to a root composition group known as גִּזְרַת הַשְׁלֵמִים ('whole'), as all consonants are present.

2. Verbs that are not fully regular are labeled by the particular root letter, which causes some deviation from a fully regular conjugation. These classifications, the גזרות, provide a frame of reference for addressing irregularities in the verb system. There are two ways of labeling them, either as -נְחֵי, which means that a root consonant, indicated by the label, undergoes some weakening, or as -חַסְרֵי, which means that one of the consonants, indicated by the label, is omitted in part of or in the entire verb conjugation. Root consonants undergo changes in some, but not necessarily all forms in the conjugation concerned.

Root classification groups

C_1=י	י-ש-ן < יָשַׁנְתָּ, תִּישַׁן ; לִישׁוֹן (פעל)	נָחֵי פ״י
	י-ל-ד < נוֹלַד (נפעל) ; הוֹלִיד (הפעיל)	
C_1=י	י-ר-ד < תֵּרֶד, רֵד! ; לָרֶדֶת (פעל)	חַסְרֵי פ״י
C_1=נ	נ-ב-ט < הִבִּיט, מַבִּיט ; לְהַבִּיט (הפעיל)	חסרי פ״נ
C_2= ו/י	ק-ו-מ < קַמְתִּי, קָם ; לָקוּם (פעל)	עי״ו/עי״י
	קוֹמַמְתִּי, קוֹמֵם ; לְקוֹמֵם (פיעל)	
	ש-י-ר < שַׁרְתִּי, שָׁר ; לָשִׁיר (פעל)	
$C_2 = C_3$	ג-נ-נ < הִתְגּוֹנַנְתִּי, מִתְגּוֹנֵן ; לְהִתְגּוֹנֵן (התפעל)	כפולים
C_3= א	ק-ר-א < קוֹרֵא, קוֹרֵאת ; לִקְרֹא (פעל)	נחי ל״א
C_3= י	ר-צ-י < רָצִיתִי, רָצָה ; לִרְצוֹת (פעל)	נחי ל״י (ל״ה*)

*The root classification נחי ל״י is also referred to as נחי ל״ה. The term נחי ל״י assumes that the י which surfaces when suffixes are added is the actual underlying consonant.

3.6.3 Verb roots with four consonants

While most roots in Hebrew consist of three consonants, there are also roots with four consonants (on occasion even five). Traditionally, in order to accommodate such roots, all consonants fit into a three "consonant slot" structure, which is the norm set by the predominant tri-consonantal verb pattern. In the case of שָׁבַר, for instance, the root consonant slots and the *pa`al* stem vowels are divided as follows:

Form	Slot 3	Vowel	Slot 2	Vowel	Slot1	Root
שָׁבַר	ר	a	ב	a	שׁ	שׁ-ב-ר

The four consonant roots are accommodated by the three following *binyanim*: *pi`el*, *pu`al* and *hitpa`el*. They are not found in other *binyanim*.

Pi`el Conjugation

Form	Slot 3	Vowel	Slot 2	Vowel	Slot1	Root
סִפֵּר	ר	*e*	פ	*i*	ס	ס-פ-ר
תִּרְגֵּם	ם	*e*	רג	*i*	ת	ת-ר-ג-מ

Pu`al Conjugation

Form	Slot 3	Vowel	Slot 2	Vowel	Slot1	Root
פֻּטַּר	ר	*a*	ט	*u*	פ	פ-ט-ר
שֻׁכְלַל	ל	*a*	כל	*u*	שׁ	שׁ-כ-ל-ל

Hitpa`el Conjugation

Form	Slot 3	Vowel	Slot 2	Vowel	Slot1	Root
הִתְלַבֵּשׁ	שׁ	*e*	ב	*a*	ל	ל-ב-שׁ
הִתְפַּרְנֵס	ס	*e*	רנ	*a*	פ	פ-ר-נ-ס

Note

The consonantal slots indicate how the extra consonants are accommodated into three slots that form the stem. They do not necessarily represent the syllabic division. For instance, the slot division of ד-רב-נ is not the same as the syllabic division, which divides the word into two closed syllables: דָּרְ-בֵּן.

There are different processes by which four consonantal roots or longer are created:

1. Some roots, which have a base of two consonants, <u>repeat</u> (reduplicate) their consonants.

	Slot 3	Slot 2	Slot1		<u>ב-ל-ב-ל</u>
בִּלְבֵּל	ל	לב	ב		<u>פיעל</u>
בֻּלְבַּל	ל	לב	ב		<u>פועל</u>
הִתְבַּלְבֵּל	ל	לב	ב	הת-	<u>התפעל</u>

The slot division is ב-לב-ל, *while the syllabic division is* בְּלְ-בֵּל.

2. One way of creating new four letter roots is by adding an initial consonant to basic three letter roots, thus forming secondary derived roots having a related meaning. The three consonants used in this process are: א', ש', ת'

Gloss	Derivation	Gloss	Base
diagnose	אָבְחֵן > א + ב-ח-נ	examine	בָּחַן
rewrite	שִׁכְתֵּב > ש + כ-ת-ב	write	כָּתַב
activate	תִּפְעֵל > ת + פ-ע-ל	act	פָּעַל

3. Other four letter roots are derived from native nouns and adjectives

Gloss	Derivation	Gloss	Base
oxidize	חִמְצֵן > ח-מ-צ-נ	oxygen	חַמְצָן
calculate	חִשְׁבֵּן > ח-ש-ב-נ	calculation	חֶשְׁבּוֹן
enumerate	מִסְפֵּר > מ-ס-פ-ר	number	מִסְפָּר

4. A large number are derived from foreign words

Gloss	Derivation	Gloss	Base
phone	טִלְפֵּן > ט-ל-פ-נ	telephone	טֶלֶפוֹן
catalogue	קִטְלֵג > ק-ט-ל-ג	catalogue	קָטָלוֹג

3.6.4 Some shared meanings of roots

Although the root does not exist on its own, most words that share a common root tend to have a common meaning core. These form-and-meaning relationships are only tendencies, and often apply only in part. Some forms never followed the regularity to start with, and most departed from it with time, with varying degrees of deviation. Language is an ever-changing, living entity, and the relationship between form and meaning is not maintained for long. Exceptions consequently abound, and meaning develops independently by extension and by association.

Here is a common root with some shared meanings:

examination, test	בְּחִינָה	examine, test	בָּחַן
examiner	בּוֹחֵן	be examined	נִבְחַן
diagnosis	אִבְחוּן	diagnose	אִבְחֵן
perception, discernment	הַבְחָנָה	notice, discern	הִבְחִין
diagnostician	מְאַבְחֵן	be noticed	הֻבְחַן

3.7 Verb categorization

Verbs in Hebrew can be classified in a number of ways, by their meaning and function, and by structural characteristics. There are transitive and intransitive verbs, active and passive verbs, verbs of action and verbs that describe state. Some verbs describe the process of change from one state to another. Verbs can also be classified in terms of their composition: There are verbs that have to be complemented by objects, and when these objects are not direct, they have obligatory prepositions, which link them with their objects. There are compound verbs, which are constructed of two verbs, usually one conjugated in tense, and another realized in infinitive form. These classifications will be described in the segments below.

3.7.1 Transitive verbs   פעלים יוצאים

A transitive verb is an action verb requiring a direct or indirect object to complement its meaning in the sentence. The action of the verb, performed by the subject, is transferred to the object, the recipient of the action. It is not just a matter of meaning but also of form. The direct object, which directly follows the verb, is either unmarked when the object is indefinite, or is preceded by the particle אֶת when the object is definite. Indirect objects require a preposition. However, it should be remembered that many indirect objects are not complements of transitive verbs.

Transitive verbs with direct objects:
<u>Indefinite direct object</u>

| The parents bought <u>presents</u> for the children. | הַהוֹרִים קנו <u>מתנות</u> לילדים. |

<u>Definite direct object</u>
The parents hid <u>the presents.</u>

ההורים החביאו <u>את המתנות</u>.

Transitive verbs with indirect objects:
Indefinite indirect object
The truck driver hit <u>a streetlight</u> and
<u>a power line post</u>.

נהג המשאית פגע <u>בפנס רחוב</u>
<u>ובעמוד חשמל</u>.

Definite indirect object
I did not mean to hurt <u>Michael</u>.

לא התכוונתי לפגוע <u>במיכאל</u>.

A comparative note
Notice that while there is an indirect object following the verb פגע ב- 'hurt/hit', in English an equivalent verb takes a direct object. In both cases, the fact that the action of the verb is transferred to the object makes the verbs transitive in meaning.

3.7.2 Intransitive verbs   פעלים עומדים

An intransitive verb is one that does not transfer the action to a recipient. The subject is the person or things undergoing or experiencing the action of the verb. Typically, an adverb or prepositional phrase modifies an intransitive verb, or the verb ends the sentence.

Nir and Ilana <u>danced</u>.

ניר ואילנה <u>רקדו</u>.

Afterwards they <u>strolled</u> in the park.

אחר כך הם <u>טיילו</u> בפארק.

Nir's grandfather <u>was born</u> in 1930.

סבא של ניר <u>נולד</u> בשנת 1930.

Some verbs can function as both transitive and intransitive verbs.

Intransitive	Nir and Ilana <u>studied</u>.	ניר ואילנה <u>למדו</u>.
Transitive	They <u>learned</u> new <u>songs</u>.	הם <u>למדו שירים</u> חדשים.

3.8 With and without linking verbs

In the present tense in Hebrew, there are sentences without verbs. They usually have a subject and a noun or noun phrase predicate, or an adjectival one. These sentences are often referred to as nominal sentences:

Dan (is) a bank director.	דן מנהל בנק.
His wife (is) a lawyer.	אשתו עורכת דין.
The twins (are) high school students.	התאומים תלמידים בתיכון.
The car (is) over there.	המכונית שם.

3.8.1 Linking verb 'to be'

Verbless sentences exist in the present tense, however, in the past and future tenses, the verb 'to be' is present and in addition to linking the two parts of the sentence, it marks the tense.

Dan <u>was</u> the director.	דן <u>היה</u> המנהל.
His wife <u>will be</u> a lawyer.	אשתו <u>תהיה</u> עורכת דין.
Their twins <u>will be</u> university students.	התאומים שלהם <u>יהיו</u> סטודנטים באוניברסיטה.

Note

היה may also serve as a full-fledged verb meaning 'exist', rather than as a mere linking verb, as in the beginning of the Book of Job:

There was a man in the land of Uz named Job.	איש היה בארץ עוץ, איוב שמו.

3.8.2 Other related linking verbs

Why do you <u>seem</u> so sad?	למה אתם <u>נראים</u> כל כך עצובים?
They <u>remained</u> our good friends.	הם <u>נשארו</u> החברים הטובים שלנו.
This movie <u>sounds</u> melodramatic.	הסרט הזה <u>נשמע</u> מלודרמטי.

For more information, see Chapter 14, pp. 320-323

3.9 Verbs with obligatory prepositions

There are a number of verbs, which have a preposition as an integral part of their form. The preposition is, by definition, followed by an object, which is a noun, a noun phrase or a pronoun. The meaning cannot be conveyed by the verb alone; it must include the prescribed obligatory preposition that connects it to the following object. The citation form of the verb usually includes that preposition.

Examples of verbs that cannot be used without a preposition and an object following it:

The host hurt our feelings.	פגע ב- המנחה פגע <u>ב</u>רגשות שלנו.

When will you help us get ready for the party?	עזר ל- מתי תעזרו לַנו להכין את המסיבה?

3.10 Action, stative and inchoative verbs

Another way of dividing verbs is by semantic categories like the following: action verbs, stative verbs, and inchoative verbs.

3.10.1 Non-stative verbs

There are many types of dynamic verbs, and most of them describe activities or events, which can have beginning and completion points.

Here are some examples:

<u>Activity</u>	Shira <u>is playing</u> tennis.	שירה מְשחקת טניס.
<u>Process</u>	The food <u>is cooking</u>.	האוכל מתבשל.
<u>Action</u>	He <u>passed</u> the ball.	הוא מסַר את הכדור.

3.10.2 Stative verbs

Stative verbs usually refer to an ongoing state or condition. They can be divided into verbs of perception or cognition (which refer to things in the mind), or verbs of state (which describe an ongoing state).

<u>Describing perception/feeling/attitude:</u>

Ayelet <u>hates</u> science fiction movies.	אילת שונאת סרטי מדע בדיוני.
She <u>loves</u> adventure movies.	היא אוהבת סרטי הרפתקאות.
Ayelet <u>prefers</u> funny movies.	אילת מעדיפה סרטים מצחיקים.

<u>Describing states:</u>

Everybody <u>is asleep.</u>	כולם ישנים.
Nobody <u>is awake</u> at such a time.	אף אחד לא עֵר בשעה כזאת.
He <u>has been sick</u> for a week.	הוא חולה כבר שבוע ימים.

3.10.3 Inchoative verbs

Inchoative verbs are verbs that convey a transformation and change of state, such as 'fall asleep', which indicates the process of changing from being awake to being asleep. The change is usually an internal one, the process of becoming.

Describing changes of state:

Everybody <u>fell asleep</u>.	כולם <u>נרדמו</u>.
Nobody <u>woke up</u> when we knocked.	אף אחד לא <u>התעורר</u> כשדפקנו.
When he <u>gets well</u>, we'll travel to Africa.	כשהוא <u>יבריא</u>, ניסע לאפריקה.
The apples <u>ripened</u> (became ripe).	התפוחים <u>הבשילו</u>.

Chapter 4
Verb pattern groups

In this chapter the seven major *binyanim* (verb pattern groups) will be discussed. They will be presented first in the regular root groups שְׁלֵמִים first, and then in the irregular verb categories.

4.1	*pa`al*	בניין פָּעַל (קל)
4.2	*nif`al*	בניין נִפְעַל
4.3	*pi`el*	בניין פִּעֵל (פיעל)
4.4	*pu`al*	בניין פֻּעַל (פועל)
4.5	*hitpa`el*	בניין הִתְפַּעֵל
4.6	*hif`il*	בניין הִפְעִיל
4.7	*huf`al*	בניין הֻפְעַל (הופעל)

4.1 *Pa`al* conjugation   בנין פָּעַל

The *pa`al* conjugation is traditionally considered the simplest or the most basic of the conjugations. It is an unmarked conjugation, since its verb forms do not contain any special identifying markers other than the root letters, usually tri-consonantal (i.e. composed of three consonants) and the tense/mood/person markers. The *pa`al* conjugation is not identified with any particular semantic trait either and is broad enough to incorporate such categories as:

(1) transitive verbs (e.g. [את התפוח] אָכַל 'eat')
(2) intransitive ones (יָשַׁב 'sit')
(3) stative verbs (יָשֵׁן 'sleep')
(4) inchoative 'change/become' verbs

4.1.1 Regular verbs   שלמים

Regular verbs are verbs in which all the root consonants are present in all the verb forms.

Present tense/participle   זמן הווה/בינוני פּוֹעֵל

In most *pa`al* conjugations, the stem of the present tense consists of the sequence $C_1oC_2eC_3$ (C = consonant) פּוֹעֵל. The vowel *o* חולם מלא, between the first and the second consonant of the root, and the vowel *e* צירה, between the second and third consonants, are the stem vowels for most of the present tense forms. There are four forms of present tense: masculine singular, feminine singular, masculine plural and feminine plural.

to dance לִרְקֹד

יחיד/ה :	(אני, אתה, הוא) רוֹקֵד ; (אני, את, היא) רוֹקֶדֶת ;
רבים/ות :	(אנחנו, אתם, הם) רוֹקְדִים ; (אנחנו, אתן, הן) רוֹקְדוֹת

In the singular forms the stress is on the second vowel of the stem: *rokéd* and *rokédet*. In the plural form the stress shifts to the suffix vowel, which brings about the loss of the last stem vowel *e*: *rokdím* and *rokdót*.

Variation – first stem vowel *a*
In some verbs in the present tense of *pa'al* the first stem vowel is *a* instead of the usual *o*. It characterizes mostly stative verbs.

to sleep לישון

יחיד/ה :	(אני, אתה, הוא) יָשֵׁן ; (אני, את, היא) יְשֵׁנָה ;
רבים/ות :	(אנחנו, אתם, הם) יְשֵׁנִים ; (אנחנו, אתן, הן) יְשֵׁנוֹת

Note
In colloquial Hebrew native speakers tend to use the prevalent *o-e* sequence rather than the normative one for such forms: *יוֹשֵׁן, *יוֹשֶׁנֶת, *יוֹשְׁנִים, *יוֹשְׁנוֹת. It is considered substandard.

Passive participle   בינוני פעול
Many present tense forms in *pa'al* have passive counterparts that describe a state, and generally function as adjectives, as 'broken', 'stolen', etc. do in English.

broken   שָׁבוּר, שְׁבוּרָה, שְׁבוּרִים, שְׁבוּרוֹת

The passive participle stem is פָּעוּל, but when the feminine and plural suffixes are added, the stress moves to the last syllable, and the stem-initial vowel is omitted, resulting in a variation of the stem: -פְּעוּל, to which feminine and plural suffixes are added.

Compare:

I <u>am open</u> to any interesting proposal.   .אני <u>פתוח</u> לכל הצעה מעניינת

The door <u>is open</u>; close it please.   .הדלת <u>פתוחה</u>; סגור אותה בבקשה

When the first consonant is ע׳, ח׳, ה׳, א׳, a *hataf patah* replaces the *shva* in the feminine singular and the plural: אָבוּד, אֲבוּדָה, אֲבוּדִים, אֲבוּדוֹת .

The *pa῾ul* form also provides a base for many adjectives (all of which have four forms):

clear	צָלוּל-צְלוּלָה	important	חָשׁוּב-חֲשׁוּבָה
imperfect	פָּגוּם-פְּגוּמָה	steep	תָּלוּל-תְּלוּלָה

Past tense   זמן עבר

The sequence פָּעַל- provides the stem for the past tense (and the citation form, since פָּעַל is also the third person singular form). A variation of this stem פָּעְל- occurs when a final suffix vowel is added, and the stress shifts to it, again causing deletion of the preceding stem-vowel (*gamrá* גָּמְרָה, *gamrú* גָּמְרוּ). Stress remains on the last stem-vowel only in the first and second person forms (*gamárti* גָּמַרְתִּי, *gamárta* גָּמַרְתָּ, etc.).

to finish   לִגְמֹר

יחיד/ה:	(אני) גָּמַרְתִּי, (אתה) גָּמַרְתָּ, (את) גָּמַרְתְּ,
	הוא גָּמַר, היא גָּמְרָה
רבים/ות:	(אנחנו) גָּמַרְנוּ, (אתם) גְּמַרְתֶּם*, (אתן) גְּמַרְתֶּן*,
	הם גָּמְרוּ, הן גָּמְרוּ

*There are two variants for the plural form of the second person: *gmartém* גְּמַרְתֶּם and *gamártem* גָּמַרְתֶּם. The variant *gmartém* is considered normative, but it is rarely used, except in formal speech. The other variant *gamártem* (considered substandard by some) is commonly used, and is modeled after all other first and second person forms in stem structure and in stress pattern.

Ordinary speech		Normative	
gamártem	(אתם) גָּמַרְתֶּם	*gmartém*	(אתם) גְּמַרְתֶּם
gamárten	(אתן) גָּמַרְתֶּן	*gmartén*	(אתן) גְּמַרְתֶּן

Future tense   זמן עתיד

When regular verbs שְׁלֵמִים are conjugated in the future, they can be divided into two main groups: the major group of verbs that have an *o* stem vowel (such as אֶגְמֹר), and a smaller group of verbs that have an *a* stem vowel (such as in אֶנְהַג).

The personal pronoun prefixes have an *i* vowel, with the exception of the first person prefix, which has an *e* vowel: יִשְׁמֹר, אֶשְׁמֹר.

Verbs with *o* stem vowel

יחיד/ה:	(אני) אֶגְמֹר, (אתה) תִּגְמֹר, (את) תִּגְמְרִי, הוא יִגְמֹר, היא תִּגְמֹר
רבים/ות:	(אנחנו) נִגְמֹר, (אתם) תִּגְמְרוּ, (אתן) תִּגְמְרוּ (תִּגְמֹרְנָה), הם יִגְמְרוּ, הן יִגְמְרוּ (תִּגְמֹרְנָה)

Note

1. The *o* vowel of the future tense is represented by a *holam haser* in normative orthography, but in common use in writing the vowel וֹ (*holam male*) is inserted instead: נגמור, יגמור, תגמור, אגמור

2. There are two variants for the feminine plural form of the second person and third person:

(i) the variant that is commonly used is the same for both the masculine plural and feminine plural. They have become the standard forms in ordinary speech and are considered normative.

(ii) The Biblical Hebrew variant with distinctive feminine plural suffix תִּגְמֹרְנָה is rarely used, except in formal speech, and is now considered somewhat archaic.

Verbs with *a* stem vowel:
to learn, study לִלְמֹד

יחיד/ה:	(אני) אֶלְמַד, (אתה) תִּלְמַד, (את) תִּלְמְדִי, הוא יִלְמַד, היא תִּלְמַד
רבים/ות:	(אנחנו) נִלְמַד, (אתם) תִּלְמְדוּ, (אתן) תִּלְמְדוּ (תִּלְמַדְנָה), הם יִלְמְדוּ, הן יִלְמְדוּ (תִּלְמַדְנָה)

Which verbs have a stem vowel *a*?

1. There are a few verbs that simply have to be memorized as having a stem vowel *a*: the future of לָמַד 'study' = יִלְמַד 'will study', and שָׁכַב 'lie (down)' = יִשְׁכַּב 'will lie down'.

2. When the second or third root letter is ע׳ ,ח׳ ,ה׳ ,א׳:

third root letter guttural	second root letter guttural
תִּקְרָא, תִּגְבַּהּ, תִּשְׁלַח, תִּשְׁמַע	תִּשְׁאַל, תִּנְהַג, תִּרְחַץ, תִּרְעַד

Note

1. The future forms that end in a vowel (the forms of את, אתם/ן, הם/ן) lose the second vowel of the stem when vowel suffixes are added. Consequently, there are two sequential *shva*'s: תִּלְמְדִי, תִּלְמְדוּ. Since such a sequence is difficult to pronounce, the second *shva* is pronounced *e* rather than zero: *tilmedí* , *tilmedú*.

2. The vowel *a* is not reduced when the second or third root letter is a guttural. The vowel חטף-פתח is used:

(את) תִּשְׁאֲלִי, (אתם/ן) תִּשְׁאֲלוּ, הם/ן יִשְׁאֲלוּ

The imperative mood   ציווי

Similar to the forms in the future tense, the imperative forms can be divided into two groups, according to the stem vowel. The division only affects the form of the masculine singular.

Verbs with *o* stem vowel

גְּמֹר (גמור)! גִּמְרִי ! גִּמְרוּ! (גְּמֹרְנָה)*

Verbs with *a* stem vowel

לְמַד! לִמְדִי! לִמְדוּ! (לְמַדְנָה)*

The negative imperative

To form negative imperatives one uses the future tense form with the imperative negative particle אַל 'don't!':

אַל תִּגְמֹר (תגמור)! אַל תִּגְמְרִי! אַל תִּגְמְרוּ!

* Just like in the future, there are two variants for the feminine plural form of the imperative: גִּמְרוּ! and גְּמֹרְנָה!

The variant that is commonly used is the same for both the masculine plural and feminine plural. It is the standard form in ordinary speech and is considered normative.

The infinitive mood שם הפועל

The 'default' stem with *o* in the future tense and in the imperative of the majority of *pa`al* verbs also serves to derive the infinitive לִפְעֹל, including those verbs that belong to the group where the future vowel is *a* (except for isolated forms like לִשְׁכַּב): לִלְמֹד, לִשְׁאֹל, לִשְׁלֹחַ.

The verbal noun שם הפעולה

In addition to the infinitive, there are also verbal nouns (שְׁמוֹת פְּעוּלָה), or nominalizations, that are more 'noun-like', but are still closely related to the verbal *pa`al* form. The form of verbal nouns of regular *pa`al* verbs is generally of the form פְּעִילָה, e.g. סְגִירָה, כְּתִיבָה.

Variants with ב', כ', פ'

1. The letters ב', כ', פ' are realized as *b, k, p*

i. when they occur as the first consonant of the present and past tenses and imperative:

בינוני פועל : בּוֹדֵק, כּוֹתֵב, פּוֹתֵחַ

בינוני פעול : בָּרוּר, כָּתוּב, פָּתוּחַ

עבר : בָּדַק, כָּתַב, פָּתַח

ציווי : בְּדֹק! כְּתֹב! פְּתַח!

ii. when occurring as the second root letter in the future tense, or the infinitive:

עתיד : יִשְׁבֹּר, יִרְכַּב, יִתְפֹּס

שם הפועל : לִשְׁבֹּר, לִרְכֹּב, לִתְפֹּס

2. The letters ב', כ', פ' are realized as *v, kh, f*

i. when they occur as the second root letter in the present, past and imperative:

בינוני : שׁוֹבֵר, רוֹכֵב, תּוֹפֵס

עבר : שָׁבַר, רָכַב, תָּפַס

ציווי : שְׁבֹר! רְכַב! תְּפֹס!

ii. when they occur as the first root letter in the future tense, or the infinitive:

עתיד : יִבְדֹּק, יִכְתֹּב, יִפְגֹּשׁ

שם פועל : לִבְדֹּק, לִכְתֹּב, לִפְגֹּשׁ

iii. when they are in the final position in the word or root.

לִכְתֹּב, דָּרְכוּ, קוֹטְפִים

Variants with guttural root letters

C1 = א׳

When the first root letter is א, the vowel *e* replaces the *shva* vowel in the future, imperative and infinitive. The prefix vowel in these verb forms is also affected:

שם הפועל: לֶאֱסֹף, לֶאֱגֹר, לֶאֱרֹז

עתיד: יֶאֱסֹף, יֶאֱגֹר, יֶאֱרֹז

ציווי: אֱסֹף! אֱגֹר! אֱרֹז!

C1 = ע׳

When the first root letter is ע, the vowel *a* replaces the *shva* vowel in the future, imperative and infinitive. The prefix vowel in these verb forms is also affected:

שם הפועל: לַעֲבֹד, לַעֲבֹר, לַעֲמֹד

עתיד: יַעֲבֹד, יַעֲבֹר, יַעֲמֹד

ציווי: עֲבֹד! עֲבֹר! עֲמֹד!

C1 = ח׳

When the first root letter is ח the vowel *a* replaces the prefix vowel *i*. The first root letter can either be zero *shva*, or the *shva* may be replaced by *a*. Both forms are acceptable, but the pronunciation with the zero *shva* is more common in speech.

שם הפועל: לַחְשֹׁב, לַחְצֹב, לַחְתֹּר (לַחֲשֹׁב, לַחֲצֹב, לַחֲתֹר)

עתיד: יַחְשֹׁב, יַחְצֹב, יַחְתֹּר (יַחֲשֹׁב, יַחֲצֹב, יַחֲתֹר)

C2 = א׳, ה׳, ח׳, ע׳

When the consonant is a guttural a *hataf pataḥ* replaces the *shva*:

שָׁאֲלָה, נוֹהֲגִים, תִּצְחֲקִי, יִבְעֲרוּ

C3 = ה׳, ח׳, ע׳

At the end of the word, if one of these gutturals is preceded by a vowel other than *a*, a 'furtive' *pataḥ* is inserted: שׁוֹלֵחַ, תָּמֵהַּ, לִשְׁמֹעַ

4.1.2 Irregular verbs   גזרות חסרים ונחים

The group of irregular verbs is composed of verbs where one or more of the root consonants are either missing or altered.

Note

1. The classification חסרים stands for verbs where one of the root consonants is absent, while נחים stands for the classification when a root consonant is present in spelling but it is not pronounced.

2. The three root consonant letters by which the irregularities are marked are: consonant 1 = פ׳ , consonant 2 = ע׳ , and consonant 3 = ל׳. When the first consonant is affected, the following label is given to it: פ״י, meaning the first consonant *yod* undergoes a change, and so on. The category of roots classified by irregularity of root consonants is called גזרה 'root classification group'.

The root classification: ע״ו/ע״י

These are roots with a second root consonant ו, such as in ק-ו-מ, or י, such as in ש-י-ר. The verb stems of the past and present tenses are bi-consonantal, i.e. have only two consonants, as the second root consonant is omitted, such as in קָם, שָׁר. In the future, imperative and infinitive, the second root consonants are realized as vowels: the vowel ו *u* for ע״ו verbs, as in קום-, or as the vowel י *i* in ע״י verbs, as in שִׁיר-. Accordingly, this conjugation pattern is called גִּזְרַת ע״י/ע״ו, since it is ע that undergoes changes and thus differs from the regular verb הפועל conjugations.

ע״ו verbs

לָקוּם to get up

Root classification	Verbal Noun	Infinitive	Root
ע״ו	קִימָה	לָקוּם	ק-ו-מ
	הם	היא	הוא
Present	קָמִים	קָמָה	קָם
Past 3rd person	קָמוּ	קָמָה	קָם
Future 3rd person	יָקוּמוּ	תָּקוּם	יָקוּם
	אתם/ן	את	אתה
Imperative	קומוּ!	קומִי	קום

Note

In ע״י/ע״ו verb forms, the stress usually stays on the (only) stem vowel, even when a suffix vowel is added: *káma* קָמָה, *kámu* קָמוּ, *yakúmu* יָקוּמוּ, *kúmi* קומִי, *kúmu* קומוּ. This is always the case in regular speech. In the higher registers, the present tense feminine singular form קָמָה is distinguished from its identical past tense form by the movement of its stress to the suffix (the same as in the plural – *kamím, kamót*):

I/you/she gets up	*kamá*	קָמָה	אני, את, היא	הווה
she got up	*káma*	קָמָה	היא	עבר

As is the case with any verb in the formal register, stress also moves to the suffix in *kamtém/n* קַמְתֶּם, but not so in regular speech (*kámtem/n)*.

Variation of ע"ו verbs:

The stem vowel of the future, imperative and infinitive is *o* when the final root letter is א:

לָבוֹא to come

Root classification	Verbal Noun	Infinitive	Root
ע"ו	בִּיאָה	לָבוֹא	ב-ו-א
	הם	היא	הוא
Future	יָבוֹאוּ	תָּבוֹא	יָבוֹא
	אתם/ן	את	אתה
Imperative	בּוֹאוּ!	בּוֹאִי!	בּוֹא!

ע"י verbs:

The stem vowel is *i* when the medial root letter is י:

לָשִׁיר to sing

Root classification	Verbal noun	Infinitive	Root
ע"י	שִׁירָה	לָשִׁיר	ש-י-ר
	הם	היא	הוא
Future	יָשִׁירוּ	תָּשִׁיר	יָשִׁיר
	אתם/ן	את	אתה
Imperative	שִׁירוּ!	שִׁירִי!	שִׁיר!

The root classification: נָחֵי פ"א

The conjugation is called נחי פ"א because א, its first root consonant, is 'silent' in some verbs. In verbs such as אכל, instead of the expected תֶּאֱכַל* or תֶאֱכֹל* (cf. יֶאֱסֹף above), the form is תֹאכַל *tokhál*, with א silent. The associated vowel becomes *o*. Only the future tense is affected, and the rest of the forms follow the regular verb rules.

לֶאֱכֹל **to eat**

Root classification	Verbal Noun	Infinitive	Root
<u>פ״א</u>	אֲכִילָה	לֶאֱכֹל	א-כ-ל
	<u>הֵם</u>	<u>הִיא</u>	<u>הוּא</u>
Future	יֹאכְלוּ	תֹּאכַל	יֹאכַל
	<u>אתם/ן</u>	<u>אַת</u>	<u>אַתָּה</u>
Imperative	אִכְלוּ!	אִכְלִי!	אֱכֹל!

Another common verb classified as נחי פ״א is the verb לוֹמַר 'to say': אָמַר, תֹּאמַר etc. Note the absence of the א of the root א-מ-ר in אָמַר, אֹכַל and the even more unusual absence of א in לוֹמַר. In all other cases, if the root includes א, the א always appears in writing, even if silent. That the silent א is omitted after an א (אָמַר, אֹכַל) is expected, but לוֹמַר is a real exception, probably the only one. The alternative Biblical Hebrew לֵאמֹר is used with a slightly different meaning, more like 'quote'.

The root classification: חַסְרֵי פ״י

When the first consonant of the root (פ׳ הפועל) is י and that י is absent in the future tense, the imperative, and the infinitive, it is referred to as גִּזְרַת חַסְרֵי פ״י (חָסֵר means 'missing', or 'absent').

לָשֶׁבֶת **to sit**

Root classification	Verbal Noun	Infinitive	Root
<u>חסרי פ״י</u>	יְשִׁיבָה	לָשֶׁבֶת	י-ש-ב
	<u>הֵם</u>	<u>הִיא</u>	<u>הוּא</u>
Future	יֵשְׁבוּ	תֵּשֵׁב	יֵשֵׁב
	<u>אתם/ן</u>	<u>אַת</u>	<u>אַתָּה</u>
Imperative	שְׁבוּ!	שְׁבִי!	שֵׁב!

When חסרי פ״י has a final 'guttural' consonant ח, ע, such as in ידע 'know', the stem vowel *e* changes to *a*. Compare the two:

Imperative	Future	Infinitive	Root
שֵׁב!	יֵשֵׁב	לָשֶׁבֶת	י-ש-ב
דַּע!	יֵדַע	לָדַעַת	י-ד-ע

The root classification: נָחֵי פ״י

When the first consonant of the root is י y, and that י is not deleted, but rather weakened to the corresponding vowel *i* in the future tense and in the infinitive, we refer to the conjugation as גִּזְרַת נָחֵי פ״י.

Unlike חֲסֵרֵי פִּ"י where the י is omitted, notice that the letter י is still included in the verb forms: אִישַׁן but אֵשֵׁב.

לִישֹׁן to sleep

Root classification	Verbal Noun	Infinitive	Root
<u>נֵחֵי פִּ"י</u>	שֵׁנָה	לִישֹׁן	י-שׁ-נ
	<u>הֵם</u>	<u>הִיא</u>	<u>הוּא</u>
Future	יִישְׁנוּ	תִּישַׁן	יִישַׁן
	<u>אַתֶּם/ן</u>	<u>אַתְּ</u>	<u>אַתָּה</u>
Imperative	יִשְׁנוּ!	יִשְׁנִי!	יְשַׁן!

The root classification: פ"נ

This classification includes verbs which have נ *nun* as their first root letter. Such verbs can lose their initial נ in the future and infinitive for a phonological reason: the consonant נ is weakened at the end of syllables, i.e., when no vowel follows. As a result it tends to be totally assimilated into the next consonant (cf. English historical assimilation in *inlegal > illegal*, *inregular > irregular*, etc.). The group of verbs whose נ is assimilated in this manner is known as גִּזְרַת חֲסֵרֵי פִּ"נ.

לִפֹּל to fall

Root classification	Verbal noun	Infinitive	Root
<u>חֲסֵרֵי פִּ"נ</u>	נְפִילָה	לִפֹּל	נ-פ-ל
	<u>הֵם</u>	<u>הִיא</u>	<u>הוּא</u>
Future	יִפְּלוּ	תִּפֹּל	יִפֹּל

In some חֲסֵרֵי פִּ"נ verbs, while the initial נ is lost in the future forms, the נ is kept in the imperative, such as in these verbs: 'fall down!' נְפֹל! נְפְלִי! נְפְלוּ! or 'take' נְטֹל! נְטְלִי! נְטְלוּ!

Other verbs lose the initial נ in both: 'drive' סַע! סְעִי! תִּסַּע, תִּסְעִי, תִּסְעוּ; סְעוּ! or 'give' תֵּן! תְּנִי! תְּנוּ! תִּתֵּן, תִּתְּנִי, תִּתְּנוּ; (see below).

פ"נ verbs that keep their initial נ

1. Verbs that keep the נ in the future, imperative and infinitive are those that have a 'guttural' second root consonant: א׳, ה׳, ח׳, ע׳, as they cannot assimilate any consonants adjacent to them.

Gloss	Infinitive	Imperative	Future	Root
deliver speech	לִנְאֹם	נְאַם	יִנְאַם	נ-א-מ
drive	לִנְהֹג	נְהַג!	יִנְהַג	נ-ה-ג
tack	לִנְעֹץ	נְעַץ!	יִנְעַץ	נ-ע-צ
land (plane)	לִנְחֹת	נְחַת!	יִנְחַת	נ-ח-ת

2. There are other verbs that for no apparent a priori reason keep their initial נ, and that today actually outnumber those in which the נ is assimilated. Among them are:

rebuke	נזף	bark	נבח	germinate	נבט
oppose	נגד	bite	נגס	took steps	נקט

Special verbs:

There are a number of special חסרי פ״נ verbs that combine features of different irregular verb groups.

1. 'to give' לָתֵת : פ"נ/ל"נ

The verb לָתֵת 'to give' is a unique one, since both first and third consonants are נ, either of which assimilates into the next consonant when occurring at the end of the syllable. In addition, the infinitive form not only reflects the loss of the two *n* consonants, but also takes on a special infinitive form partly associated with פ״י verbs.

גזרה	שם פעולה	שם פועל	שורש
חסרי פ״נ	נְתִינָה/מַתָּן	לָתֵת	נ-ת-נ

1. In the present tense the verb נ-ת-נ is conjugated as a regular verb and does not lose any consonants: נוֹתֵן, נוֹתֶנֶת, נוֹתְנִים, נוֹתְנוֹת.

2. In the past tense the third consonant נ is lost, and is assimilated into the subject pronoun suffix: the expected נָתַנְ+תִּי* ends up as נָתַתִּי. This occurs only in the first and second person. A *dagesh ħazak* in the suffix compensates for the loss of the first root consonant.

אתם/אתן	אנחנו	אתה	אני
נתתם	נָתַנּוּ	נָתַתָּ	נָתַתִּי

3. In the third person all consonants are maintained: נָתַן, נָתְנָה, נָתְנוּ.

4. All the future tense forms lose the first נ, which is assimilated into the second consonant (a *dagesh ħazak* in the second consonant

compensates for the loss of the first root consonant): אֶתֵּן instead of
אֶנְתֵּן.

הם/ן	היא	הוא
יִתְּנוּ	תִּתֵּן	יִתֵּן

5. The imperative forms echo the first consonant loss of the future
tense:

	אתם/ן	את	אתה
Imperative	תְּנוּ!	תְּנִי!	תֵּן!

2. 'to touch' לָגַעַת/לִנְגּוֹעַ

The infinitive form has two variants: לָגַעַת loses the first consonant *n*
and takes on a special infinitive form associated with פ״י verbs, while
לִנְגּוֹעַ has a regular verb infinitive and keeps all root consonants.

חסרי פ״נ		מַגָּע/נְגִיעָה	לָגַעַת	נ-ג-ע

All the future tense forms lose the first *n*, which is assimilated into the
second consonant. The stem vowel is *a*, as it is in any such forms that
end with a guttural consonant:

Future   אני אֶגַּע, אתה תִּגַּע, הוא יִגַּע, אנחנו נִגַּע,
                    את תִּגְּעִי, אתם/ן תִּגְּעוּ, הם/ן יִגְּעוּ
Imperative   גַּע, גְּעִי, גְּעוּ

3. 'to travel' לִנְסֹעַ

The infinitive form of this particular פ״נ verb keeps all consonants, but
the future and imperative lose the *n*, like the verbs above:

Future   אני אֶסַּע, אתה תִּסַּע, הוא יִסַּע, אנחנו נִסַּע,
                    את תִּסְּעִי, אתם/ן תִּסְּעוּ, הם/ן יִסְּעוּ
Imperative   סַע, סְעִי, סְעוּ

4. 'to take' לָקַחַת

The root of this verb is ל-ק-ח, and although it does not have a נ׳ or a י׳
consonant, it behaves like a פ״נ verb with a final guttural consonant. It
is conjugated just like the verb נָגַע 'to touch'. The infinitive form loses
the first consonant *l* and takes on a special infinitive form associated
with פ״י verbs. All the future tense forms lose the first ל׳, which is

assimilated into the second consonant. The stem vowel is *a*, as it is in any such forms that end with a guttural consonant ע׳ or ח׳:

<u>Future</u>   אֲנִי אֶקַּח, אתה תִּקַּח, הוא יִקַּח, אנחנו נִקַּח,

                                  את תִּקְחִי, אתם/ן תִּקְחוּ, הם/ן יִקְחוּ

<u>Imperative</u>   קַח, קְחִי, קְחוּ

The root classification: נחי ל"א

In the ל"א conjugation, in which the third root consonant is א׳, the א׳ is kept in spelling, but is not pronounced at the end of the syllable.

to find לִמְצֹא

Root classification		Verbal noun	Infinitive	Root
<u>נחי ל"א</u>		מְצִיאָה	לִמְצֹא	מ-צ-א
	<u>הֵם</u>	<u>הִיא</u>	<u>הוּא</u>	<u>אתה</u>
Present	מוֹצְאִים	מוֹצֵאת	מוֹצֵא	מוֹצֵא
Pa`ul	מְצוּיִּים	מְצוּיָה	מָצוּי	מָצוּי
Past	מָצְאוּ	מָצְאָה	מָצָא	מָצָאתָ
Future	יִמְצְאוּ	תִּמְצָא	יִמְצָא	תִּמְצָא
	<u>אתם/ן</u>		<u>את</u>	<u>אתה</u>
Imperative	מִצְאוּ!		מִצְאִי!	מְצָא!

Note

Notice that in some ל"א verbs, the י׳ substitutes for the א׳ in the בינוני פָּעוּל, following the ל"י pattern, as shown in the table above. However, this is not true for all ל"א verbs, as forms such as שָׂנוּא, כָּלוּא exist as well. At times there is even a 'mixed' case: נָשׂוּי, נְשׂוּאָה 'married'.

The root classification: נחי ל"י

When the third root consonant is י׳ *y*, it is realized as the vowel *e* or *a* in final position, where it is represented in the spelling as ה׳, whereas elsewhere, it is realized as the vowel י׳ *i*, or is elided before another vowel. This conjugation is called נחי ל"י. It is also commonly known as נחי ל"ה because of the final ה׳ of the citation form.

לִקְנוֹת **to buy**

	Root classification	Verbal noun	Infinitive	Root
	<u>לייי</u>	קְנִיָּה	לִקְנוֹת	ק-נ-ה
	<u>הֵם</u>	<u>הִיא</u>	<u>הוּא</u>	<u>אַתָּה</u>
Present	קוֹנִים	קוֹנָה	קוֹנֶה	קוֹנֶה
Pa`ul	קְנוּיִים	קְנוּיָה	קָנוּי	קָנוּי
Past	קָנוּ	קָנְתָה	קָנָה	קָנִיתָ
Future	יִקְנוּ	תִּקְנֶה	יִקְנֶה	תִּקְנֶה
		<u>אַתֶּם/אַתֶּן</u>	<u>אַתְּ</u>	<u>אַתָּה</u>
Imperative		קְנוּ!	קְנִי!	קְנֵה!

Note that in the third person feminine of the past tense, elision of the stem vowel would have merged the form with the masculine counterpart, קָנָה. To prevent that, the historical feminine ת׳ resurfaces, resulting in קָנְתָה.

Marginal root class: ע"ע

In some roots, the second and third root consonants are identical. In *pa`al*, most of them behave like regular verbs in current usage, e.g., חָגַגְתִּי 'I celebrated' from the root ח-ג-ג, but a few maintain a separate form in which the two identical consonants are merged, e.g., חַנּוֹתִי 'I pardoned' from ח-נ-נ.

For full conjugation see Appendix 1.

4.1.3 Associated meanings

As noted above, *pa`al* verbs can be classified into two major groups, verbs of action and stative verbs, but it is hard to go into any further semantic classification, since *pa`al* is the major default verb conjugation, and the meanings of other *binyanim* are often described in relation to the *pa`al* pattern.

4.2 *Nif`al* conjugation   בניין נפעל

The conjugation *nif`al* בניין נפעל is identified by a prefix, *n* (realized as *ni-* to facilitate pronunciation), that is part of its past and present tense stem. Its name reflects the third person singular masculine past tense form, its 'citation form': *ni+CCaC*   נִ+פְעַל. The *ni-* prefix is not maintained throughout the conjugation. Its *n* is totally assimilated into the first consonant of the stem in the future, the imperative, and in the infinitive, and the vowel pattern changes. It is assimilated because it occurs at the end of the syllable in these sub-conjugations (e.g., *ti+n+gamer > tiggamer > tigamer* – cf. *n* assimilation in *pa`al* above). In the imperative and infinitive forms, there emerges an initial הי prefix.

Stem of future		Stem of past and present	
...*i+shamer*	יִשָּׁמֵר	*ni+shmar* נִשְׁמַר/נִשְׁמָר	

Stem of the imperative and infinitive	
hi+shamer	הִשָּׁמֵר

Thus, instead of *niCCaC* נִפְעַל of the past and present, the stem of the future, imperative and infinitive is *(hi)-CaCeC* (הִ)-פָּעֵל. The *dagesh ħazak* in the first root letter was intended to compensate for the loss of the prefix consonant נ *n*. When the text has vowels, the *dagesh ħazak* is visible. When the text has no vowels, the letter י is inserted after the pronoun subject prefix to reflect the vowel *i* (This, of course, excludes the first person singular personal pronoun, as the vowel of that prefix is *e*):

לְהִכָּנֵס	הִכָּנֵס	תִּכָּנֵס
להיכנס	היכנס	תיכנס

The י does not form part of the *nif`al* pattern but is inserted for clarity, sometimes even in vowelled texts, to indicate the *i* vowel.

4.2.1 Regular verbs   שלמים

Regular verbs are verbs in which the root consonants are present in all verb forms.

Present tense   זמן הווה

The present tense forms have a *ni-* prefix, which identifies them as *nif'al* verbs. The stem vowel is קמץ *a* with the exception of the feminine form.

לְהִזָּכֵר ב to recall

יחיד/ה :	(אני, אתה, הוא) נִזְכָּר ; (אני, את, היא) נִזְכֶּרֶת
רבים/ות :	(אנחנו, אתם, הם) נִזְכָּרִים ; (אנחנו, אתן, הן) נִזְכָּרוֹת

In the singular forms the stress of the word is maintained on the second vowel of the verb form: *nizkar,* and *nizkéret*. In the plural form the stress shifts to the last vowel of the word: *nizkarím* and *nizkarót*. The second vowel (or stem vowel) remains *a*, and doesn't change to *e* with the movement of the stress.

Past tense   זמן עבר

The past tense forms also have a *ni-* prefix, which identifies them as *nif'al* verbs. The stem vowel is פתח *a*, with the exception of the forms that end in a vowel.

יחיד/ה :	(אני) נִזְכַּרְתִּי, (אתה) נִזְכַּרְתָּ, (את) נִזְכַּרְתְּ,
	הוא נִזְכַּר, היא נִזְכְּרָה
רבים/ות :	(אנחנו) נִזְכַּרְנוּ, (אתם) נִזְכַּרְתֶּם, (אתן) נִזְכַּרְתֶּן,
	הם נִזְכְּרוּ, הן נִזְכְּרוּ

The stem of the past tense shares the citation form *niCCáC-*. It has a variant *niCCeC-* (the second *shva* is pronounced *e*), resulting from reduction of *a* to *e* when the stress shifts to the last syllable of an added vowel suffix (feminine and plural markers of the third person).

Future tense   זמן עתיד

In the future tense the *ni-* prefix is not present, and instead we find the stem *i(e)* + *CaCeC-*. As noted above, the *n* was there historically, but as in other similar environments was assimilated into the subsequent consonant, resulting in a *dagesh ḥazak* when the letter is not guttural (guttural letters required that the previous vowel be lengthened instead). It has a variant *-iCaCC-* when the stress shifts to the last syllable (feminine and plural markers of the third person), reflecting deletion of the last stem vowel.

יחיד/ה : (אני) אֶזָּכֵר, (אתה) תִּזָּכֵר, (את) תִּזָּכְרִי,

הוא יִזָּכֵר, היא תִּזָּכֵר

רבים/ות : (אנחנו) נִזָּכֵר, (אתם) תִּזָּכְרוּ , (אתן) תִּזָּכְרוּ (תִּזָּכַרְנָה),

הם יִזָּכְרוּ, הן יִזָּכְרוּ (תִּזָּכַרְנָה)

As noted above, the י is usually present, as in תיזכר. Without the י a form like תזכרי can be read as 'you will remember' in *pa`al*, or 'you will recall' in *nif`al*. There is no confusion if the *pa`al* form is written תזכרי and the *nif`al* form is written תיזכרי.

The imperative mood   ציווי
The Imperative shares part of the stem with the future tense, and in addition is preceded by the prefix -הִ *hiCaCeC (hiCaCC-)*

Recall!	הִזָּכֵר! הִזָּכְרִי! הִזָּכְרוּ! (הִזָּכַרְנָה)
Beware! Watch out! Be careful!	הִזָּהֵר! הִזָּהֲרִי! הִזָּהֲרוּ! (הִזָּהַרְנָה)

Often a י is inserted after the prefix: היזכר!

The future forms are used with negative commands, and in daily speech often for positive commands as well.

Come in, immediately!	תיכנסו מייד!
Don't enter the room!	אל תיכנסי לחדר!

Limited use
Directives can occur in *nif`al* only when the verb has an active meaning:

Come in!	היכנס!
Beware!	הִזָּהֲרוּ!

but not when it has a passive meaning:

~~Get broken!~~	~~הישברו!~~
~~Be written!~~	~~היכתבו!~~

The infinitive mood   שם הפועל
The infinitive has the same stem as the future and imperative; in fact, in this case the stem is identical to the imperative stem: לְהִכָּנֵס 'to enter'.

I don't like recalling that story.	.אני לא אוהב להיזכר באותו סיפור
It is impossible to come in; the	.אי אפשר להיכנס, הפתח צר מדיי
opening is too narrow.	
He needs <u>to beware</u> of them.	.הוא צריך <u>להיזהר</u> מהם

The infinitive form can also be translated by the gerund 'doing' (rather than by 'to do'), though not as commonly:

| <u>Entering</u> his house is like entering | <u>להיכנס</u> אליו הביתה זה כמו להיכנס |
| a bank. | .לבנק |

Verbal noun   שם הפעולה

Not all verbs can generate a related verbal noun. Most *nif'al* verbal nouns use the same stem as the infinitive, plus the abstract nominalization suffix -ות. It is always a feminine noun. In these verbal noun forms, the *e* vowel of the stem (of the infinitive, future and imperative) is deleted:

	Verbal noun	Infinitive	Citation form
running into	הִתָּקְלוֹת	לְהִתָּקֵל ב	נִתְקַל ב
state of readiness	הֵעָרְכוֹת	לְהֵעָרֵךְ ל	נֶעֱרַךְ ל

Some forms of the verbal noun are based on the present tense stem:

	Verbal noun		Stem form
determination	נֶחֱרָצוּת	determined	נֶחֱרָץ
willingness, readiness	נְכוֹנוּת	correct	נָכוֹן

Some verbal nouns whose base is *nif'al* are realized in other patterns:

	Verbal noun		Stem form
entrance, entry	כְּנִיסָה	enter, come in	נִכְנַס
caution	זְהִירוּת	watch out	נִזְהַר

Variants with ב', כ', פ'

<u>1. The letters ב', כ', פ' are realized as *b, k, p*</u>

When occurring as the second root consonant in the past and present, or the first root consonant is in the future, imperative and infinitive

| בינוני : נִשְׁבָּר, נִזְכָּר, נִתְפָּר |
| עבר : נִשְׁבַּר, נִזְכַּר, נִתְפַּר |
| עתיד : תִּבָּדֵק, תִּפָּגֵשׁ, תִּכָּנֵס |
| ציווי : הִבָּדֵק, הִפָּגֵשׁ, הִכָּנֵס |
| שם הפועל : לְהִבָּדֵק, לְהִפָּגֵשׁ, לְהִכָּנֵס |

2. The letters 'ב', כ', פ' are realized as *v, kh, f*

i. When it is the first root consonant in the present and past

בינוני : נִבְחָן, נִכְנָס, נִפְתָּח

עבר : נִבְחַן, נִכְנַס, נִפְתַּח

ii. When it is the second or third root consonant in the future, imperative, and infinitive

עתיד : תִּשָּׁבֵר, תִּזָּכֵר, תִּשָּׁפֵט

עתיד : יִגָּנְבוּ, תִּשָּׂרְפִי, יִשָּׁפְכוּ

שם הפועל : לְהִשָּׁבֵר, לְהִזָּכֵר, לְהִשָּׁפֵט

Variations with guttural radicals

1. In the future, imperative and infinitive, the prefix vowel is always *e* and there is no *dagesh ħazak* in the guttural consonants: לְהֵחָשֵׁב.

2. The prefix vowel of *nif'al ni-* in the past and present tenses changes from *ni-* to *ne-* when the first consonant of the verb is ע' ,ח' ,ה' ,א'. An 'echo' vowel replaces the zero vowel of the first consonant, with the exception (in non-formal usage) of first radical ח':

הוא נֶאֱלַץ ; הוא נֶהֱנָה ; הוא נֶעֱדַר ; הוא נֶחְשַׁב

3. When the second letter is 'guttural', the expected zero vowel (*shva*) is replaced by a *ħataf pataħ* in the third person of the past tense (feminine singular, and plural); in the second person singular feminine and in the second and third person plural of the future tense; and in second person singular feminine and plural of the imperative:

נִזְהֲרָה, נִזְהֲרוּ, תִּזָּהֲרִי, תִּזָּהֲרוּ, יִזָּהֲרוּ, הִזָּהֲרִי, הִזָּהֲרוּ

4.2.2 Irregular Verbs   גזרות חסרים ונחים

Irregular verbs are verbs in which one or more of the roots consonants are missing, altered or remain silent.

The root classification: נָחֵי פ"י

When the first consonant of the root is י', it is never deleted; it is replaced by the vowel *o* in the present and in the past tenses, and is converted to the consonant ו' in the rest of the conjugation.

to be born לְהִוָּלֵד

Root classification		Verbal noun	Infinitive	Root
	נחי פ״י	הִוָּלְדוּת	לְהִוָּלֵד	י-ל-ד
	הם	היא	הוא	אתה
Present	נוֹלָדִים	נוֹלֶדֶת	נוֹלָד	נוֹלָד
Past	נוֹלְדוּ	נוֹלְדָה	נוֹלַד	נוֹלַדְתָּ
Future	יִוָּלְדוּ	תִּוָּלֵד	יִוָּלֵד	תִּוָּלֵד

The root classification: נחֵי ל"א

The final consonant א׳ is always silent in forms that end the word or syllable, or precede another consonant that ends the syllable:
1. The past tense first and second stem, and third person masculine singular: נִקְרֵא- (תִי/תָ/ת/נוּ/תֶם/תֶן), נִקְרָא. Note: before a consonant, *a* > *e*.
2. The present tense singular: נִקְרָא, נִקְרֵאת
3. The future, imperative, and infinitive stem (except for forms that end in a suffix vowel): (הִ)קָּרֵא

to be read/named לְהִקָּרֵא

Root classification		Verbal noun	infinitive	root
נחי ל״א		הִקָּרְאוּת	לְהִקָּרֵא	ק-ר-א
	הם	היא	הוא	אתה
Present	נִקְרָאִים	נִקְרֵאת	נִקְרָא	נִקְרָא
Past	נִקְרְאוּ	נִקְרְאָה	נִקְרָא	נִקְרֵאתָ
Future	יִקָּרְאוּ	תִּקָּרֵא	יִקָּרֵא	תִּקָּרֵא
		אתם/ן	את	אתה
Imperative		הִקָּרְאוּ!	הִקָּרְאִי!	הִקָּרֵא!

The root classification: נחֵי ל"י

When the third root consonant is י׳, it is realized as the vowel *e* or *a* in final position, where it is represented in the spelling as ה. Elsewhere, it is realized as the vowel ֵי *ey*, in the past tense: נִרְאֵיתִי, or in the singular feminine present tense היא נִרְאֵית. The final stem vowel is elided before a final vowel when a suffix is added, such as in הם נִקְנוּ, הם יִקָּנוּ, and a ת׳ separates the feminine נִבְנְתָה form from נִבְנָה.

to be built לְהִבָּנוֹת

Root classification		Associated noun	Infinitive	Root
נחי ל"י		הִבָּנוֹת/בְּנִיָּה*	לְהִבָּנוֹת	ב-נ-י
	הם	היא	הוא	אתה
Present	נִבְנִים	נִבְנֵית	נִבְנֶה	נִבְנֶה
Past	נִבְנוּ	נִבְנְתָה	נִבְנָה	נִבְנֵיתָ
Future	יִבָּנוּ	תִּבָּנֶה	יִבָּנֶה	תִּבָּנֶה
		אתם/ן	את	אתה
Imperative		הִבָּנוּ!	הִבָּנִי!	הִבָּנֵה!

*The associated noun is often the verbal noun of the *pa`al* conjugation. The *nif`al* form of the verbal noun is הִבָּנוֹת, but it is rarely used in contemporary Hebrew.

Combined initial guttural and ל"י verb:

The verb לֵהָנוֹת 'to enjoy' combines the features of verbs with initial gutturals with those of נחי ל"י verbs.

to enjoy לְהֵהָנוֹת/ לֵהָנוֹת

Root classification		Associated noun	Infinitive	Root
נחי ל"י		הֲנָאָה*	לֵהָנוֹת	ה-נ-י
	הם	היא	הוא	אתה
Present	נֶהֱנִים	נֶהֱנֵית	נֶהֱנֶה	נֶהֱנֶה
Past	נֶהֱנוּ	נֶהֱנְתָה	נֶהֱנָה	נֶהֱנֵיתָ
Future	יֵהָנוּ	תֵּהָנֶה	יֵהָנֶה	תֵּהָנֶה
		אתם/ן	את	אתה
Imperative		הֵהָנוּ!	הֵהָנִי!	הֵהָנֵה!

*While the verbal noun form הֵהָנוֹת exists, the noun commonly used and associated with this verb is הנאה 'enjoyment'.

Marginal root classes: חסרי פ"נ, ע"ו, ע"ע

In a few verbs, the first נ of the stem is assimilated to the next consonant when it occurs in syllable-final position, and its loss is reflected in a *dagesh ḥazak*, e.g., from נ-צ-ל, נִצַּלְתִּי < נִנְצַלְתִּי 'I survived'.

In the literary register, some ע"ו forms survived, e.g., from ס-ו-ג, נְסוּגוֹתִי 'I retreated', נָסוֹג 'he retreated'. There are also some high register residues of ע״ע verbs, e.g., from ס-ב-ב, נְסַבּוֹתִי 'I turned', נָסַב 'he turned'.

See Appendix 1

4.2.3 Associated meanings

In contemporary Hebrew *nif'al* generally refers to either one of two meanings – passive or inchoative (denoting a change of state). In a few cases, it also carries a reciprocal meaning. The focus of most *nif'al* verbs is on the recipient of the action.

a. Passive meaning

There are several verbs in *nif'al* which are counterparts of transitive verbs, usually in *pa'al*.

Active meaning

Dan <u>sent</u> the letter only yesterday.	דן <u>שלח</u> את המכתב רק אתמול.

Passive meaning

The letter <u>was sent</u> only yesterday.	המכתב <u>נשלח</u> רק אתמול.

When a *nif'al* verb carries a passive meaning, the grammatical subject of the sentence is the recipient of the action, rather than the agent that performs the action.

The minimal components of a sentence with a passive verb are the subject of the verb, which is the recipient of the action, and the *nif'al* passive verb:

נפעל (סביל) נושא: המכתב	פעל (פעיל) נושא: דן
המכתב נשלח. <	דן שלח את המכתב.

The presence or absence of an agent (the one performing the act) is dependent on the context. There are many instances where the agent is as important a focus as the recipient, and thus is included in the passive sentence as well, as an indirect object.

Agent: subject

<u>The police</u> interrogated suspects.	<u>המשטרה</u> חקרה חשודים.

Agent: Indirect object

<u>The suspects</u> were interrogated by the police.	<u>החשודים</u> נֶחקרו על ידי המשטרה.

b. Inchoative (change of state) meaning

Inchoative verbs involve a change of state, e.g. going from wakefulness to a state of sleep, as expressed in a verb like 'fall asleep' נִרְדָּם. A change of state may be 'involuntary'; the process happens without an agent causing it, or without mentioning who caused it.

Dan <u>remembered</u> that he forgot to close the door.

דן <u>נזכר</u> שהוא שכח לסגור את הדלת.

The patient <u>weakened</u> after the difficult treatment.

החולה <u>נחלש</u> אחרי הטיפול הקשה.

Thus, in a sentence like הַזְּגוּגִית נִשְׁבְּרָה 'the window pane broke', the breaking is assumed to have occurred on its own. In Hebrew you cannot make an agent out of an inanimate object. Even if someone may have been involved, their role is not the focus of the statement.

A comparative note

In both Hebrew and English the recipient of the action may actually be the subject of the proposition, but in addition, in English, the verb can be realized as an active verb, whereas in Hebrew it is stated by a *nif'al* form with a passive meaning.

The shops never <u>close</u>.

החנויות אף פעם לא <u>נסגרות</u>.

The result of the action is stated in Hebrew not in *nif'al,* but rather in the passive participle of *pa'al*:

The shops <u>are closed</u> every Tuesday afternoon.

החנויות <u>סגורות</u> כל יום שלישי אחר הצוהריים.

The *nif'al* form describes the process, whereas the *pa'al* passive participle בינוני פָּעוּל describes the state resulting from that process. The person who is causing the action may be at the same time the one undergoing it, in which case the verb is referred to as 'reflexive' (cf. the meanings of *hitpa'el* below). In the illustrations below, Dan can be said to register himself for school, and Joseph to lean himself on the wall.

Dan <u>is registering for</u> school today.

דן <u>נרשם</u> ללימודים היום.

Joseph <u>leaned on</u> the wall.

יוסף <u>נשען על</u> הקיר.

c. Reciprocal meaning

The *nif'al binyan* shares another meaning with *hitpa'el*, that of reciprocity. There are a few reciprocal verbs in *nif'al*, where the causer of the action and the recipient of it are not the same, but may shift roles (usually conveyed in English by 'each other'). Reciprocal meaning can only occur when the verbs are in plural form, since the meaning 'each other' involves more than one entity.

Dan and Rina <u>met</u> at work.	דן ורינה <u>נפגשו</u> בעבודה.
Moshe and Hanna <u>separated</u> after many years.	משה וחנה <u>נפרדו</u> אחרי שנים רבות.

The sentences above can have reciprocal pronouns as their object. This use of these pronouns is optional since they are redundant.

Dan and Rina met <u>each other</u> at work.	דן ורינה נפגשו <u>זה עם זו</u> בעבודה.
Moshe and Hanna separated <u>from each other</u> after many years.	משה וחנה נפרדו <u>זה מזו</u> אחרי שנים רבות.

When the subject is singular these verbs must take an object, usually introduced by an obligatory preposition:

Dan <u>gets together with</u> Rina every evening.	דן <u>נפגש עם</u> רינה כל ערב.
Moshe <u>separated from</u> Hanna after many years.	משה <u>נפרד מרינה</u> אחרי שנים רבות.

The feature of reciprocity is not a unique feature of *nif'al*.

d. Other meanings

Verbs in *nif'al* are not necessarily passive, inchoative, or reciprocal. Many involve none of the above semantic features and can be considered to have an active meaning.

We opened the door and entered the room.	פתחנו את הדלת ונכנסנו לַחדר.
We hurried to help them.	נֶחלצנו לַעזרתם.
Britain fought the Nazi regime.	בריטניה נלחמה בַמשטר הנאצי.
He wrestled with his conscience.	הוא נֶאֱבק עם מצפונו.

4.3 *Pi`el* conjugation   בניין פיעל

The פִּעֵל *CiCeC* sequence characterizes the stem of the third person masculine singular form in the past tense and gives it its name. The vowel sequence *i-e* (with its variants) provides the stem for the past tense. This includes a *dagesh ḥazak* in the second consonant, e.g. הוא דִּבֵּר. In other tenses and moods the vowel sequence is *a-e*: דַּבֵּר-. The *dagesh ḥazak*, which is part of the pattern, exists in all forms of the various tenses and moods, with the exception of the 'guttural' consonants (א׳, ה׳, ח׳, ע׳, ר׳), where a *dagesh* can never be present.

A historical note

The presence of the *dagesh ḥazak* is a historical residue of the doubled (geminated) second radical, which originally marked the doubling of the length of a consonant. Today this feature is no longer in effect phonetically, but the *dagesh ḥazak* is still part of the pattern of the verb, which also means that when the consonant concerned is ב׳, כ׳, פ׳, it is always realized as a stop, *b, p, k*.

4.3.1 Regular verbs   שלמים

The group of regular verbs is composed of verbs in which all the root consonants are present in all the verb forms.

Present tense   זמן הווה

The present tense of this conjugation pattern has a -מְ *me-* prefix, which marks it for present tense.

יחיד/ה:	(אני, אתה, הוא) מְדַבֵּר ; (אני, את, היא) מְדַבֶּרֶת
רבים/ות:	(אנחנו, אתם, הם) מְדַבְּרִים ; (אנחנו, אתן, הן) מְדַבְּרוֹת

Note

The prefix -מ is typical to all verb pattern groups, except for *pa`al* and *nif`al*.

The present tense forms of *pi`el* not only act as verbs, but generate many adjectives and nouns.

Here are some adjectives that have *pi`el* present tense forms:

	Adjective		Citation form		Root
fascinating	מְרַתֵּק	fascinate	רִתֵּק		ר-ת-ק
reinforcing	מְחַזֵּק	reinforce	חִזֵּק		ח-ז-ק
fantastic	מְשַׁגֵּעַ	drive mad	שִׁגֵּעַ		ש-ג-ע

Speakers add new adjectives constantly, e.g.:

	Adjective		Citation form		Root
astonishing	מְהַמֵּם	shock	הִמֵּם		ה-מ-מ

Here are some nouns that have *pi'el* present tense forms:

	Noun		Citation form		Root
immigrant	מְהַגֵּר	immigrate	הִגֵּר		ה-ג-ר
trainer/coach	מְאַמֵּן	train	אִמֵּן		א-מ-נ
narrator	מְסַפֵּר	tell, narrate	סִפֵּר		ס-פ-ר
gambler	מְהַמֵּר	gamble	הִמֵּר		ה-מ-ר

Past tense   זמן עבר

The past tense of *pi'el* has three stem variants:

Masculine singular 3rd person:	*diber*	דִּבֵּר

Masculine singular 3rd person: *diber*   דִּבֵּר

1st and 2nd person forms: *dibar-*   ־דִּבַּרְ

3rd person feminine singular and plural (stem vowel   *dibr-*   ־דִּבְּר
deleted when stress moves to suffix):

---

to speak; to talk לְדַבֵּר

> יחיד/ה : (אני) דִּבַּרְתִּי, (אתה) דִּבַּרְתָּ, (את) דִּבַּרְתְּ,
> הוא דִּבֵּר, היא דִּבְּרָה
> רבים/ות : (אנחנו) דִּבַּרְנוּ, (אתם) דִּבַּרְתֶּם, (אתן) דִּבַּרְתֶּן,
> הם דִּבְּרוּ, הן דִּבְּרוּ

The vowel stem *i* is indicated by the frequent addition of י following the first consonant: דיבר. It is added not only to indicate the stem vowel, but also to further clarify the difference between *pi'el* verbs and *pa'al* verbs, such as between סיפר 'recounted/told' and ספר 'counted'. The י is often inserted even in texts with vowels.

Future tense

זמן עתיד

The future tense of *pi`el* has two stem variants:

1. In all first and second person singulars and first person plurals	*-daber*	־דַּבֵּר
2. In the second person feminine singular and second and third person plural (stem vowel deleted when stress moves to suffix)	*-dabr-*	־דַּבְּר־

(אֲנִי) אֲדַבֵּר, (אַתָּה) תְּדַבֵּר, (אַתְּ) תְּדַבְּרִי, הוּא יְדַבֵּר, הִיא תְּדַבֵּר	יחיד/ה :
(אֲנַחְנוּ) נְדַבֵּר, (אַתֶּם) תְּדַבְּרוּ, (אַתֶּן) תְּדַבְּרוּ (תְּדַבֵּרְנָה), הֵם יְדַבְּרוּ, הֵן יְדַבְּרוּ (תְּדַבֵּרְנָה)	רבים/ות :

The imperative mood

ציווי

The imperative shares the same stem with the future tense.

דַּבֵּר! דַּבְּרִי! דַּבְּרוּ! (דַּבֵּרְנָה)

Future forms used for negative and positive ones in speech:

תְּדַבֵּר!	אַל תְּדַבֵּר!
תְּדַבְּרִי!	אַל תְּדַבְּרִי!
תְּדַבְּרוּ!	אַל תְּדַבְּרוּ!

The infinitive mood

שם הפועל

The *pi`el* infinitive uses the same stem as the present, future, and imperative: לְדַבֵּר, לְתָאֵר, לְשַׂמֵּחַ.

I want to talk to him about what happened yesterday.	אֲנִי רוֹצֶה לְדַבֵּר אִיתוֹ עַל מַה שֶׁקָּרָה אֶתְמוֹל.
Talking to him is like talking to the wall.	לְדַבֵּר אִיתוֹ זֶה כְּמוֹ לְדַבֵּר אֶל הַקִּיר.

Verbal noun

שם הפעולה

The *pi`el* verbal noun uses a form similar to the 'citation form', but the second vowel is *u* rather than *e*:

Gerund	Stem	Gerund	Stem
שִׁדּוּר	שִׁדֵּר	סִדּוּר	סִדֵּר
שידור	שידר	סידור	סידר

Variants with ב', כ', פ'

<u>1. The letters ב', כ', פ' are realized as *b, k, p*</u>

i. When it is the first root letter in the past and imperative:

עבר : בִּקֵּר, פִּזֵּר, כִּנֵּס

ציווי : בַּקֵּר! פַּזֵּר! כַּנֵּס!

ii. When it is the second root letter in all tenses and moods:

עבר : דִּבֵּר, סִכֵּם, סִפֵּר

הווה : מְדַבֵּר, מְסַכֵּם, מְסַפֵּר

עתיד : יְדַבֵּר, יְסַכֵּם, יְסַפֵּר

ציווי : דַּבֵּר! סַכֵּם! סַפֵּר!

שם הפועל : לְדַבֵּר, לְסַכֵּם, לְסַפֵּר

<u>2. The letters ב', כ', פ' are realized as *v, kh, f*</u>

i. When it is the first root letter, preceded by a prefix: in the present, future, and infinitive.

הווה : מְכַנֵּס, מְפַזֵּר, מְבַקֵּר

עתיד : אֲבַקֵּר, אֲכַנֵּס, אֲפַזֵּר

שם הפועל : לְבַקֵּר, לְכַנֵּס, לְפַזֵּר

ii. Whenever it is the last letter in the word or root:

מְבָרֵךְ, מְגָרְפִים, סֵרְבָה

Variations with 'guttural' consonants   א', ע', ח', ה', ר'

1. When the second root letter is א' or ר', the first vowel *i* is replaced by *e* in the past tense and in the verbal noun: בֵּרֵר, תֵּאֵר ; בֵּרוּר, תֵּאוּר

2. When the second root letter is a guttural, the expected zero vowel (*shva*) is replaced by a *ḥataf pataḥ*: נִיהֲלָה, מְנַהֲלִים, יְנַהֲלוּ when the verb form ends in a stressed suffix vowel.

3. When the second root letter is א' or ר', the *pataḥ* under the first one is replaced by a *kamats*, but the pronunciation remains the same: מְתָאֵר, מְגָרֵשׁ, מְבָרֵךְ

4. When the third root letter is ח', ע' and no suffix is appended, the normative form has the stem vowel *a*: שִׁגַּע, יְפַתַּח; however in common speech the second stem vowel changes to *e* and a 'furtive' *pataḥ* is inserted, as in שִׁגֵּעַ, יְפַתֵּחַ. The form with a furtive *pataḥ* is the only option in the present tense: מְשַׁגֵּעַ, מְפַתֵּחַ (note: fem. מְנַצַּחַת, מְשַׁגַּעַת).

4.3.2 Irregular Verbs   גזרות חסרים ונחים

The root classification: ע"ע

Verbs that belong to this group have identical second and third root consonants. They are conjugated as regular verbs.

Some of the ע"ע roots are derived from bi-consonantal adjectives:

Gloss	Infinitive	Future	Present	Past	ע"ע	שם תואר
sharpen	לְחַדֵּד	יְחַדֵּד	מְחַדֵּד	חִדֵּד	ח-ד-ד	חד >
warm up	לְחַמֵּם	יְחַמֵּם	מְחַמֵּם	חִמֵּם	ח-מ-מ	חם >
cool down	לְקָרֵר	יְקָרֵר	מְקָרֵר	קֵרֵר	ק-ר-ר	קר >
embitter	לְמָרֵר	יְמָרֵר	מְמָרֵר	מֵרֵר	מ-ר-ר	מר >

The root classification: merger of ע"ו/ע"י with ע"ע

In *pi'el*, *pu'al* and *hitpa'el* ע"ו/ע"י verbs behave as if they were ע"ע ones, and undergo some additional changes. For both original ע"ע verbs and merged ע"ו/ע"י ones, the final root consonant is duplicated, and the medial consonant ו or י is replaced by the vowel *o*.

Gloss	Infinitive	Future	Present	Past	ע"ע	ע"ו
spin around	לְסוֹבֵב	יְסוֹבֵב	מְסוֹבֵב	סוֹבֵב	ס-ב-ב	(ס-ו-ב)
incite	לְקוֹמֵם	יְקוֹמֵם	מְקוֹמֵם	קוֹמֵם	(ק-מ-מ)	ק-ו-מ

Note

Some ע"ו/ע"י roots have two forms of *pi'el*: one is conjugated as a regular verb in *pi'el*, and the medial semi-vowel ו or י is realized as a consonant. The other follows the merged ע"ע/ע"ו/ע"י pattern above.

Examples

Gloss	Infinitive	Citation form	Pi'el root	Source
fulfill, realize	לְקַיֵּם	קִיֵּם	ק-י-מ	ק-ו-מ
incite, arouse	לְקוֹמֵם	קוֹמֵם	ק-מ-מ	ק-ו-מ

Gloss	Infinitive	Citation form	Pi'el root	Source
aim, direct	לְכַוֵּן	כִּוֵּן	כ-ו-נ	כ-ו-נ
found, establish	לְכוֹנֵן	כּוֹנֵן	כ-נ-נ	כ-ו-נ

The root classification: נָחֵי ל"א

When the third root consonant is א, it is not pronounced at the end of the syllable, although it is maintained in the spelling.

to fill up לְמַלֵּא

Root classification		Verbal noun	Infinitive	Root
נחי ל"א		מִלּוּי/מְלוּאִים	לְמַלֵּא	מ-ל-א
	הם	היא	הוא	אתה
Present	מְמַלְּאִים	מְמַלֵּאת	מְמַלֵּא	מְמַלֵּא
Past	מִלְּאוּ	מִלְּאָה	מִלֵּא	מִלֵּאתָ
Future	יְמַלְּאוּ	תְּמַלֵּא	יְמַלֵּא	תְּמַלֵּא
		אתמ/ן	את	אתה
Imperative		מַלְּאוּ!	מַלְּאִי!	מַלֵּא!

The root classification: נחי ל"י

When the third root consonant is י, it is realized as the vowel *e* or *a* in final position, where it is represented in the spelling as ה, whereas elsewhere, it is realized as the vowel י *i*, or is elided before another vowel.

to discover/reveal לְגַלּוֹת

Root classification		Verbal noun	Infinitive	Root
נחי ל"י		גִלּוּי	לְגַלּוֹת	ג-ל-י
	הם	היא	הוא	אתה
Present	מְגַלִּים	מְגַלָּה	מְגַלֶּה	מְגַלֶּה
Past	גִלּוּ	גִלְּתָה	גִלָּה	גִלִּיתָ
Future	יְגַלּוּ	תְּגַלֶּה	יְגַלֶּה	תְּגַלֶּה
		אתמ/ן	את	אתה
Imperative		גַלּוּ!	גַלִּי!	גַלֵּה!

4.3.3 Derived and newly created verbs

New verbal roots can be created for *pi`el*, which is a very productive *binyan*. There are various ways of creating such new roots, most of which are listed below.

Three-consonantal verbs derived from nouns:

Several agentive verbs (where the subject of the verb is the one carrying out the action) with tri-consonantal roots were and are continuing to be derived from existing nouns, as in:

	Citation form		Noun Stem
place	מִקֵּם (מיקם)	place	מָקוֹם (ז)
report	דִּוַּח (דיווח)	report	דוּחַ (ז)
mechanize	מִכֵּן (מיכן)	machine	מְכוֹנָה (נ)
file	תִּיֵּק (תייק)	file	תִּיק (ז)

Derived four-consonantal verbs

Most Hebrew verbs can be traced to three-consonant roots, but even at earlier stages of the language, some four-letter roots can be attested, all in *pi`el*:

provide livelihood	פִּרְנֵס	gnaw	כִּרְסֵם

However, most four-consonant verbs were derived from pre-existing words or roots. The oldest historical method was to reduplicate the first stem syllable, as in גִּלְגֵּל 'roll (tr.)', בִּלְבֵּל 'confuse'.

a. First stem syllable reduplication:

לְגַלְגֵּל to roll

Root classification		Verbal noun	Infinitive	Root
מרובעים (משוכפלים)		גִּלְגּוּל	לְגַלְגֵּל	ג-ל-ג-ל
	הֵם	הִיא	הוּא	אַתָּה
Present	מְגַלְגְּלִים	מְגַלְגֶּלֶת	מְגַלְגֵּל	מְגַלְגֵּל
Past	גִּלְגְּלוּ	גִּלְגְּלָה	גִּלְגֵּל	גִּלְגַּלְתָּ
Future	יְגַלְגְּלוּ	תְּגַלְגֵּל	יְגַלְגֵּל	תְּגַלְגֵּל
	אַתֶּם/ן	אַתְּ		אַתָּה
Imperative	גַּלְגְּלוּ!	גַּלְגְּלִי!		גַּלְגֵּל!

b. Four-consonantal verbs derived from existing nouns

Another way is to derive such verbs from existing nouns with (at least) four consonants:

Verb meaning	Citation form	Root		Base Noun
interest	עִנְיֵן	ע-נ-י-נ	matter	עִנְיָן
calculate	חִשְׁבֵּן	ח-שׁ-ב-נ	calculation	חֶשְׁבּוֹן
ensure, obtain	שִׁרְיֵן	שׁ-ר-י-נ	armor	שִׁרְיוֹן

c. Verbs derived from foreign words:

The consonants of the foreign words are adapted into root consonants that are realized in the *pi`el* four or five consonantal pattern:

	Citation form		New root	
telephone	טִלְפֵּן/ טִלְפֶּן	←	ט-ל-פ-נ	טֶלֶפוֹן
hypnotize	הִפְנֵט	←	ה-פ-נ-ט	הִיפְּנוֹזָה
fantasize	פִנְטֵז	←	פ-נ-ט-ז	פַנְטַזְיָה
flirt	פְלִרְטֵט	←	פ-ל-ר-ט-ט	פְלִירְט

Note

Most recently many new technology terms have been adapted from English. While technical terms are created by the Hebrew Language Academy based on Hebrew roots, these new terms come from the field, and are created by necessity. They often have a short life as the Academy creates the necessary new roots or new technology replaces the existent one, requiring new terms.

refresh	רִפְרֵשׁ	←	ר-פ-ר-שׁ
compile	קִמְפֵּל	←	ק-מ-פ-ל

Four-consonant roots expanded from three-consonant roots

Some new roots are derived from existing tri-consonantal verbal roots, to which an initial שׁ-, ת-, א-, or מ- are added as the first consonant, to create a new, but related meaning.

a. Four-consonantal verbs: with שׁ as first consonant

Adding an initial שׁ- as the first consonant, creating a new, but related meaning can create new roots.

Verb meaning	Citation form	Root	Gloss		Base
convince	שִׁכְנֵעַ	שׁ-כ-נ-ע	surrender	נִכְנַע	כ-נ-ע
rewrite	שִׁכְתֵּב	שׁ-כ-ת-ב	write	כָּתַב	כ-ת-ב
duplicate, photocopy	שִׁכְפֵּל	שׁ-כ-פ-ל	multiply	הִכְפִּיל	כ-פ-ל

b. Four-consonantal verbs: with initial letters ת, א, מ

The prefixes מ-, א-, ת- characterize some new roots, which are either derived directly from existing nouns, or from existing tri-consonantal verbal roots. New verbs are created, and they have a meaning related to their source words.

Verb meaning	Citation form	Root		Noun
drill, exercise	תִּרְגֵּל	ת-ר-ג-ל	exercise	תַּרְגִּיל
function	תִּפְקֵד	ת-פ-ק-ד	function	תַּפְקִיד
diagnose	אִבְחֵן	א-ב-ח-נ	check, test	בָּחַן
refer	אִזְכֵּר	א-ז-כ-ר	mention	הִזְכִּיר
enumerate	מִסְפֵּר	מ-ס-פ-ר	number	מִסְפָּר
mortgage	מִשְׁכֵּן	מ-שׁ-כ-נ	mortgage	מַשְׁכַּנְתָּה

4.3.4 Associated meanings

Pi`el may be either transitive, e.g. סִדֵּר 'arrange', or intransitive, e.g. דִּבֵּר 'speak'. It is difficult to place all the verbs under one semantic rubric; the closest is 'agentive', i.e. the verb designates a voluntary activity, which is initiated and controlled by the 'actor/doer', who is the subject of the sentence.

The director is a friend of ours and he got us good tickets for the show.	הבמאי חבר שלנו והוא סידר לנו כרטיסים טובים להצגה.

The following subgroups have additional specific features that characterize them.

a. Causative: 'cause to be', or 'cause to become'

The volunteer physicians <u>cure</u> patients in many distant villages.	הרופאים המתנדבים <u>מרפאים</u> חולים בכפרים רחוקים.
The danger <u>unified</u> the family.	הסכנה <u>איחדה</u> את המשפחה.

b. Repeated/intensive action

Some *pi`el* verbs that share roots with *pa`al* add the feature of repeated action to the meaning of the verb. Thus, if קָפַץ *kafats* is 'jump', קִפֵּץ *kipets* is 'jump again and again, or jump back and forth'. Sometimes the activity may be characterized as intensive, so while שָׁבַר *shavar* is 'break' שִׁבֵּר *shiber* is 'smash, shatter'. The intensive activity can also be accounted for by repetition, as 'smash' means 'break again and again'.

The clerks <u>sorted</u> all the files.	הפקידים <u>מיינו</u> את כל התיקים.
We didn't read the book - we only <u>leafed through it</u>.	לא קראנו את הספר, רק <u>דפדפנו בו</u>.
One <u>preserves</u> fruit in this manner.	<u>מְשַׁמְּרִים</u> פירות בשיטה זו.

c. Removal

A small group of verbs in *pi`el* refer to removal (often related to a base noun).

One should <u>uproot</u> violence from the schools.	צריך <u>לְשָׁרֵשׁ</u> את האלימות מבתי הספר.
We'll <u>remove</u> all the thugs.	<u>נְסַלֵּק</u> את כל הבריונים.

4.4   *Pu`al* conjugation   בניין פועל

Pi`el* and *pu`al are related conjugations. All or almost all verbs in *pu`al* are passive counterparts of existing *pi`el* verbs, which in itself suggests that *pu`al* is always *pi`el*-based. However, not every *pi`el* verb has a passive counterpart in *pu`al*. The *pu`al* stem is characterized by the discontinuous *u-a* vowel sequence that internally marks it as being passive. The *u-a* vowel pattern simply replaces the parallel *i-e* one in the corresponding *pi`el* form. As in *pi`el*, the second root consonant is always marked with a *dagesh ḥazak*, which is not audible in current Hebrew, but which at least means that when that consonant is one of the letters בי, כי, פי, it is always realized as *b, k, p* – never *v, kh, f.*

Pattern	Form	Root	Form	Root
CiCeC	תִּקֵּן (תיקון)	ת-ק-נ	סִפֵּר (סיפור)	ס-פ-ר
CuCaC	תֻּקַּן (תוקן)		סֻפַּר (סופר)	

The *dagesh ḥazak* in the second root consonant of the verb is an integral part of the *pu`al* pattern, just as it is an essential component of *pi`el*. The only exceptions are the 'guttural' consonants (אי, הי, חי, עי, רי), which can never have a *dagesh*. As noted above, the presence of the *dagesh* is an historical residue of the doubling in length of the second root consonant. An important feature of the *pu`al* conjugation is that it is limited to the tenses only: present, past and future. This verb conjugation does not have the imperative or infinitive moods and does not have a verbal noun. The *pi`el* infinitive and verbal nouns serve the *pu`al* conjugation. Due to the passive nature of *pu`al*, most forms used in the past, present and future tenses are in the third person only. There are only a few verbs that occur in the first and second person also.

4.4.1 Regular verbs   שלמים

The group of regular verbs includes verbs in which all the root consonants are present in all the verb forms.

Present tense   זמן הווה

All present tense forms are marked by a מְ- *me-* prefix.

to be arranged/neat   לִהְיוֹת מְסֻדָּר

(אני, אתה, הוא) מְסֻדָּר ; (אני, את, היא) מְסֻדֶּרֶת	יחיד/ה :
(אנחנו, אתם, הם) מְסֻדָּרִים ; (אנחנו, אתן, הן) מְסֻדָּרוֹת	רבים/ות :

When the text is without vowels, the ו vowel replaces the *kubuts* [ֻ] *u* vowel mark. In ordinary writing, even when the texts have vowels, the ו is inserted to make deciphering this form easier:

מסודר, מסודרת, מסודרים, מסודרות

Many present tense forms of *pu'al* function as adjectives. This pattern is particularly productive in generating new adjectives.

	Adjective		Citation form	Root
obliged	מְחֻיָּב (מחויב)	be obliged	חֻיַּב	ח-י-ב
riveted	מְרֻתָּק (מרותק)	be riveted	רֻתַּק	ר-ת-ק
connected	מְחֻבָּר (מחובר)	be connected	חֻבַּר	ח-ב-ר
signified/marked	מְסֻמָּן (מסומן)	be marked	סֻמַּן	ס-מ-נ

Past tense   זמן עבר

The past tense of *pu'al* has two variants of the past tense stem:

In the first and second person:	*putar-*	־פֻּטַּר
In the third person feminine singular and plural:	*putr-*	־פֻּטְּר

לִהְיוֹת מְפֻטָּר to be fired

> יחיד/ה : (אני) פֻּטַּרְתִּי, (אתה) פֻּטַּרְתָּ, (את) פֻּטַּרְתְּ,
> הוא פֻּטַּר, היא פֻּטְּרָה
> רבים/ות : (אנחנו) פֻּטַּרְנוּ, (אתם) פֻּטַּרְתֶּם, (אתן) פֻּטַּרְתֶּן,
> הם פֻּטְּרוּ, הן פֻּטְּרוּ

In text without vowels: פוטרתי, פוטרת, פוטר, פוטרנו, פוטרתם, פוטרו

Future tense   זמן עתיד

The future tense uses the following stem: *-CuCaC*. The second stem vowel *a* is lost when the stress shifts to the last syllable.

> יחיד/ה : (אני) אֲפֻטַּר, (אתה) תְּפֻטַּר, (את) תְּפֻטְּרִי,
> הוא יְפֻטַּר, היא תְּפֻטַּר
> רבים/ות : (אנחנו) נְפֻטַּר, (אתם) תְּפֻטְּרוּ, (אתן) תְּפֻטְּרוּ (תְּפֻטַּרְנָה),
> הם יְפֻטְּרוּ, הן יְפֻטְּרוּ (תְּפֻטַּרְנָה)

In text without vowels: אפוטר, תפוטר, תפוטרי, נפוטר, תפוטרו

Variants with ב', כ', פ'

<u>1. The letters ב', כ', פ' are realized as *b, k, p*</u>

i. When it is the first root letter in the past tense

עבר: פֶּטַר,כֶּנֵס

ii. When it is the second root letter in all tenses and moods:

עבר : סֻבַּךְ, סֻכַּם, סֻפַּר

הווה : מְסֻבָּךְ, מְסֻכָּם, מְסֻפָּר

עתיד : יְסֻבַּךְ, יְסֻכַּם, יְסֻפַּר

<u>2. The letters ב', כ', פ' are realized as *v, kh, f*</u>

i. When it is the first root letter in the present and future tenses

הווה: מְבֻקָּשׁ, מְכֻנָּס, מְפֻטָּר

עתיד : יְבֻקַּשׁ, יְכֻנַּס, יְפֻטַּר

ii. When it is the third letter of the root

עֹרַב, בֹּרְכוּ, שֻׁתְּפָה

Variations with root letters א', ה', ח', ע', ר'

In roots where the second consonant is a guttural one (except for ח'),
the *u* is replaced by *o*, in all tenses:

מְבֹהָל, מְפֹאָר, מְקֹרָב, מְשֹׁעָר

With the same consonant (except for ח'), a *ḥataf pataḥ* replaces the
expected *shva*: תֹּאֲרוּ, יְתֹאֲרוּ, יְנֹהֲלוּ, יְשֹׁעֲרוּ.

4.4.2 Irregular Verbs   גזרות חסרים ונחים

The group of irregular verbs parallels that of the *pi`el* conjugation and
undergoes the same processes.

The root classification: merger of ע"ו/ע"י with ע"ע

In *pu`al*, as in *pi`el* and *hitpa`el*, ע"י/ע"י verbs behave as if they were
ע"ע ones: the final root consonant is duplicated. Their first vowel is *o*.

Gloss	Future	Present	Past	<u>ע"ע</u>	<u>ע"ו</u>
be spun around	יְסוֹבַב	מְסוֹבָב	סוֹבַב	ס-ב-ב	(ס-ו-ב)
be incited	יְקוֹמַם	מְקוֹמָם	קוֹמַם	(ק-מ-מ)	ק-ו-מ

The נחי ל"א root classification

When the third root consonant is א', it is not pronounced at the end of
the syllable, although it is maintained in the spelling. In the first and

second person of the past tense, the *a* vowel before the suffix is replaced by *e*.

In the third person singular the *pataḥ* is replaced by *kamats,* which does not affect its pronunciation.

to be filled לִהְיוֹת מְמֻלָּא

נחי ל"א				שורש : מ-ל-א
	הֵם	הִיא	הוּא	אַתָּה
Present	מְמֻלָּאִים	מְמֻלֵּאת	מְמֻלָּא	מְמֻלָּא
Past	מֻלְּאוּ	מֻלְּאָה	מֻלָּא	מֻלֵּאתָ
Future	יְמֻלְּאוּ	תְּמֻלָּא	יְמֻלָּא	תְּמֻלָּא

The נחי ל"י root classification

As in other *binyanim,* when the third root consonant is י, it is realized as the vowel *e* or *a* in final position, where it is represented in the spelling as הי: מְפֻנֶּה, מְפֻנָּה. Elsewhere, it is realized as the vowel ֵי *ey* as in פֻּנֵּיתִי, or is elided before another vowel, as in פֻּנּוּ.

to be experienced לִהְיוֹת מְנֻסֶּה

נחי ל"י				שורש : נ-ס-י
	הֵם	הִיא	הוּא	אַתָּה
Present	מְנֻסִּים	מְנֻסָּה	מְנֻסֶּה	מְנֻסֶּה
Past	נֻסּוּ	נֻסְּתָה	נֻסָּה	נֻסֵּיתָ
Future	יְנֻסּוּ	תְּנֻסֶּה	יְנֻסֶּה	תְּנֻסֶּה

4.4.3 Derived and newly created verbs

New verb forms can be created for *puʿal,* mostly by virtue of its being the almost-automatic counterpart of the very productive *piʿel.* Generally, all new verb formation patterns allowed in *piʿel* can be found in *puʿal* as well. Thus, for instance, when a three-consonant new root can be formed in *piʿel,* it will have generally a *puʿal* counterpart as well:

Gloss	פועל	Gloss	פיעל	Gloss	Base
place	מֻקַּם (מוקם)	place	מִקֵּם	place	מָקוֹם
report	דֻוַּח (דווח)	report	דִוֵּחַ	report	דוּחַ
file	תֻּיַּק (תויק)	file	תִּיֵּק	file	תִּיק

Reduplicated roots

The same *pi`el-pu`al* relationship applies when the first syllable is reduplicated, to form new four-consonant verbs. Alongside בִּלְבֵּל 'confuse' (tr.) in *pi`el*, we find בֻּלְבַּל 'being confused' in *pu`al*.

to be confused לִהְיוֹת מְבֻלְבָּל

Root classification				Root
מְרֻבָּעִים (מֻשׁכְפָלִים)				ב-ל-ב-ל
	הֵם	הִיא	הוּא	
Present	מְבֻלְבָּלִים	מְבֻלְבֶּלֶת	מְבֻלְבָּל	
Past	בֻּלְבְּלוּ	בֻּלְבְּלָה	בֻּלְבַּל	
Future	יְבֻלְבְּלוּ	תְּבֻלְבַּל	יְבֻלְבַּל	

Expansion to four-letter roots

The *pu`al* stem can be expanded to four letters:

to be famous; be advertised לִהְיוֹת מְפֻרְסָם

Root classification				Root
מְרֻבָּעִים				פ-ר-ס-מ
	הֵם	הִיא	הוּא	
Present	מְפֻרְסָמִים	מְפֻרְסֶמֶת	מְפֻרְסָם	
Past 3rd person	פֻּרְסְמוּ	פֻּרְסְמָה	פֻּרְסַם	
Future 3rd person	יְפֻרְסְמוּ	תְּפֻרְסַם	יְפֻרְסַם	

Derived four-consonant verbs

a. Derived from foreign words

The consonants of the foreign words are adapted into root consonants in the same manner as in the *pi`el* conjugation. What distinguishes the two *binyanim* is the vowel sequence.

	pu`al form	*pi`el*		New root	Noun
be hypnotized	הֻפְּנַט	הִפְּנֵט	←	ה-פ-נ-ט	הִיפְּנוֹזָה
be neutralized	נֻטְרַל	נִטְרֵל	←	נ-ט-ר-ל	נִטְרוּל

b. Four-consonantal verbs derived from existing native nouns

	pu`al form	*pi`el*	Root		Base noun
be ensured	שֻׁרְיַן	שִׁרְיֵן	ש-ר-י-נ	armor	שִׁרְיוֹן

c. Four-consonantal verbs: with ‎-ש, ‎-ת, ‎א or ‎-מ as first consonant

The new roots are derived either directly from existing nouns, or from existing tri-consonantal verbal roots.

Verb meaning	*pu`al*	*pi`el*	Root		Source
be rewritten	שֻׁכְתַּב	שִׁכְתֵּב	ש-כ-ת-ב	write	כתב+ש
be drilled	תֻּרְגַּל	תִּרְגֵּל	ת-ר-ג-ל	exercise	תַּרְגִּיל
be reinforced	תֻּגְבַּר	תִּגְבֵּר	ת-ג-ב-ר	overcome	גָּבַר
be diagnosed	אֻבְחַן	אִבְחֵן	א-ב-ח-נ	check, test	בָּחַן
be referred	אֻזְכַּר	אִזְכֵּר	א-ז-כ-ר	mention	הִזְכִּיר
be enumerated	מֻסְפַּר	מִסְפֵּר	מ-ס-פ-ר	number	מִסְפָּר

4.4.4 Associated meanings

Pu`al* verbs are used most commonly in the third person, which can refer to objects as well as to persons. There are few *pu`al verbs that can be conjugated in the first and second person as well. The restrictions are semantic and depend on the specific meaning of the verb:

Pu`al in all persons:

We <u>were hugged</u> and (were) <u>kissed</u>.   חובקנו ונושקנו.

Pu`al in plural:

The workers <u>were</u> <u>organized</u> for the   הפועלים <u>אורגנו</u> לקראת השביתה.
strike.

The singular is not applicable:

~~I was organized for the strike.~~   ~~אורגנתי לקראת השביתה.~~

There are many *pu`al* verbs that cannot be used with a human grammatical subject. Their meaning excludes a person being the recipient of an action.

The show <u>was</u> <u>cancelled</u>.   ההצגה <u>בוטלה</u>.

~~I was cancelled.~~   ~~בוטלתי.~~

Active *pi`el* and passive *pu`al*

Because of the passive nature of the conjugation, the grammatical subject of the sentence with a *pu`al* verb is the recipient of the action rather than the initiator of the action. The subject of the active sentence, the agent, may surface in the passive counterpart as an indirect (or oblique) object, signaled by the preposition 'by' עַל יְדֵי. The recipient is often an object or an entity, which is not a person. A few verbs apply to human recipients of actions.

pi`el

The manager <u>changed</u> the daily schedule.   .המנהל <u>שינה</u> את סדר היום

pu`al

The daily <u>schedule was changed</u> by   .סדר היום <u>שונה</u> על ידי המנהל
the manager.

We also find some *pu`al* verbs used in passive sentences even when the corresponding *pi`el* verb is not transitive, e.g., דִּבֵּר 'talk, speak' and דֻּבַּר 'be talked about':

It <u>was</u> <u>not</u> <u>talked</u> about in the last   <u>לא דובר</u> על כך בישיבת הממשלה
meeting of the government.   .האחרונה

A comparative note

Active verbs in English have passive counterparts. This is not necessarily the case in Hebrew.

Dan <u>did not pay</u> Ron the money	דן לא <u>שילם</u> לרון את הכסף
Ron was not paid the money.	~~רון לא שולם את הכסף.~~
The money <u>was</u> <u>not</u> <u>paid</u> (by Ron).	הכסף <u>לא שולם</u> (על ידי רון).

פִּיעֵל
פֻּעַל
פֻּעַל

Other verbs act in a similar way in Hebrew and English:

The doctors <u>immunized</u> the   הרופאים <u>חיסנו</u> את הילדים   פִּיעֵל
children against measles.   .נגד אדמת

The children <u>were immunized</u>   .הילדים <u>חוסנו</u> נגד אדמת   פֻּעַל
against measles.

Common use

The use of *pu`al* is most often restricted to a high register, which is used in news broadcasts, in formal documents or speeches and in literature. In practice, the use of sentences with third person subjects and the verb in *pi`el* is more characteristic of everyday speech to express the passive sense.

<u>More formal</u>	This bill was paid.	.החשבון הזה שולם פֻּעַל
<u>Everyday Use</u>		.כבר שילמו את החשבון הזה פִּיעֵל

Pu`al participles as adjectives or nouns

There are many participles (present tense forms) of the same verbs that function as adjectives, nouns, or adverbs.

Adjective	The hour is already <u>late</u>.	.השעה כבר <u>מאוחרת</u>
Adverb	I arrived <u>late</u> to the meeting.	.הגעתי לפגישה <u>מאוחר</u>
Noun	All the <u>dignitaries</u> have arrived.	.כל <u>המכובדים</u> הגיעו
Adjective	Professor Schwartz is a <u>highly regarded</u> scholar.	פרופסור שוורץ הוא חוקר <u>מכובד</u>.

4.5 *Hitpa`el* conjugation   בניין התפעל

The stem of *hitpa`el* has two components: *-it* + *pa`el*. The prefix *-it* is the unique marker of *hitpa`el*, and it is always preceded by another marker:

1. It can be initiated by the present tense marker *m*: מִתְפַּעֵל.
2. It can be initiated by *h* in the past tense, imperative and infinitive: הִתְפַּעֵל.
3. In the future tense, the subject person prefixes combine with it, such as in the following forms: אֶתְפַּעֵל, יִתְפַּעֵל .

As in *pi`el* and in *pu`al*, the second root consonant is always marked with a *dagesh ħazak*. Although the *dagesh* is irrelevant in Israeli Hebrew, one consequence is that when that consonant is one of the letters ב', כ', פ', it is always realized as *b, k, p*, respectively.

4.5.1 Regular verbs   שלמים

Regular verbs are composed of verbs in which all the root consonants are present in all the verb forms.

Present tense   זמן הווה

All present tense forms have a *mit-* מִתְ prefix: the *m* indicates present tense, and the following *t* indicates that it is a *hitpa`el* verb.

to get dressed לְהִתְלַבֵּשׁ

(אני, את, היא) מִתְלַבֶּשֶׁת ; (אני, אתה, הוא) מִתְלַבֵּשׁ	: יחיד/ה
(אנחנו, אתן, הן) מִתְלַבְּשׁוֹת ; (אנחנו, אתם, הם) מִתְלַבְּשִׁים	: רבים/ות

Past tense   זמן עבר

The stem of the past tense of *hitpa`el* has three variants:

1. Masculine, singular third person   *hitlabesh*   הִתְלַבֵּשׁ
2. First and second person forms   *hitlabash-*   -הִתְלַבַּשׁ
3. Third person feminine singular and plural   *hitlabsh-*   -הִתְלַבְּשׁ
(deletion resulting from stress shift to the suffix)

יחיד/ה :	(אֲנִי) הִתְלַבַּשְׁתִּי, (אַתָּה) הִתְלַבַּשְׁתָּ, (אַתְּ) הִתְלַבַּשְׁתְּ,
	הוּא הִתְלַבֵּשׁ, הִיא הִתְלַבְּשָׁה
רבים/ות :	(אֲנַחְנוּ) הִתְלַבַּשְׁנוּ, (אַתֶּם) הִתְלַבַּשְׁתֶּם, (אַתֶּן) הִתְלַבַּשְׁתֶּן,
	הֵם הִתְלַבְּשׁוּ, הֵן הִתְלַבְּשׁוּ

A historical note

In Mishnaic Hebrew a variant of *hitpa`el* emerged in the perfect: *nitpa`el*, with *n* replacing *h* in the *hit-* prefix:

take place, exist   נִתְקַיֵּם   be discovered   נִתְגַּלָּה

This variant became the preferred realization in Mishnaic Hebrew. Few verbs maintained the *hit-* prefix in that period. It is very likely that the *h > n* shift resulted from analogy with the *n* of *nif`al*. In modern Hebrew, *hit-* is dominant in everyday use; *nit-* is more typical of higher registers.

Future tense   זמן עתיד

The stem of the future tense of *hitpa`el* has two variants:

1. In all first and second singular and first person plural:	*-tlabesh*	־תְלַבֵּשׁ
2. In the second person feminine singular and second and third person plural (deletion resulting from stress shift):	*-tlabsh-*	־תְלַבְּשִׁ־

יחיד/ה :	(אֲנִי) אֶתְלַבֵּשׁ, (אַתָּה) תִּתְלַבֵּשׁ, (אַתְּ) תִּתְלַבְּשִׁי,
	הוּא יִתְלַבֵּשׁ, הִיא תִּתְלַבֵּשׁ
רבים/ות :	(אֲנַחְנוּ) נִתְלַבֵּשׁ, (אַתֶּם) תִּתְלַבְּשׁוּ, (אַתֶּן) תִּתְלַבְּשׁוּ (תִּתְלַבֵּשְׁנָה),
	הֵם יִתְלַבְּשׁוּ, הֵן יִתְלַבְּשׁוּ (תִּתְלַבֵּשְׁנָה)

The imperative mood   ציווי

The imperative, like the past and the infinitive, includes the prefix *hi-* of the *hitpa`el* pattern in its forms.

הִתְלַבֵּשׁ! הִתְלַבְּשִׁי! הִתְלַבְּשׁוּ! (הִתְלַבֵּשְׁנָה)

Like in the rest of the conjugation, the stem vowel is reduced from *e* to a zero vowel before a stressed suffix ~~hitlabesh+ú~~ * > *hitlabshú*.

The negative imperative

The negative imperative also uses the future tense form with the negative particle אַל 'don't!'

אַל תִּתְלַבֵּשׁ! אַל תִּתְלַבְּשִׁי! אַל תִּתְלַבְּשׁוּ!

The infinitive mood שם הפועל

The *hitpa'el* infinitive mood is formed with the same stem as the imperative: הִתְלַבֵּשׁ, הִתְקַבֵּל, הִתְפַּלֵּל, with the addition of the prefixed letter -לְ 'to': לְהִתְלַבֵּשׁ, לְהִתְקַבֵּל, לְהִתְפַּלֵּל.

I need to get dressed before I leave home.	אני צריכה להתלבש לפני שאני יוצאת מהבית.
He hopes to be admitted to the University.	הוא מקווה להתקבל לאוניברסיטה.

As in other *binyanim* the infinitive form can also be translated as the English gerund equivalent of 'doing' (rather than by 'to do').

Exercising every day is very important.	חשוב להתעמל כל יום.

The verbal noun שם הפעולה

The *hitpa'el* verbal noun appends the suffix ־וּת to its citation form stem. The stem used is the variant *hitlabsh-*, because it is followed by a stressed vowel. Nouns with the suffix ־וּת are always feminine nouns.

Gerund	Stem	Gerund	Stem
הִתְרַגְּשׁוּת	הִתְרַגֵּשׁ	הִתְנַגְּדוּת	הִתְנַגֵּד (ל-)

A verbal noun of a transitive verb is linked to an object by the same preposition as the finite verb:

I have no objection to the decisions.	אין לי כל התנגדות להחלטות.
Familiarity with this domain is very important for the work in the lab.	ההתמצאות בתחום הזה חשובה מאוד לעבודה במעבדה.

Alternate stems with initial: ס, שׂ, שׁ, צ, ז

There are certain alterations that occur in the stem of *hitpa'el* verbs when the first consonant is a sibilant: ס/שׂ *s*, שׁ *sh*, צ *ts*, ז *z*. (In Hebrew the sibilants are known as אותיות שורקות or 'whistling letters' because of their articulation). The changes involve a different placement of the ת of the prefix of *hitpa'el*, which trades places with the first root consonant. It may involve other changes as well. The changes facilitate the articulation of the prefix together with the sibilants and prevent them from merging with the ת, so that they are all heard distinctly.

First root consonant: ס/שׂ *s*, שׁ *sh*

If the first consonant of the root is either ס/שׂ or שׁ, then that consonant and the ת at the end of the prefix change places: *ts* > *st.*

	Actual Form			Expected Form	
histader	הִסְתַּדֵּר	←	*hit+sader*	הִתְ-סַדֵּר*
hishtalem	הִשְׁתַּלֵם	←	*hit+shalem*	הִתְ-שַׁלֵם*

First root consonant: ז *zayin*

When the first consonant of the root is *zayin* ז *z*, the ת of the *hit-* prefix becomes ד, as well as changing places with the first root letter: *tz* > *zd.* The reason for the change from the prefix consonant ת to ד is its proximity to the first root consonant ז, which is a voiced consonant. Instead of the expected voiceless ת, the prefix consonant becomes voiced ד.

	Actual Form			Expected Form	
hizdamen	הִזְדַּמֵּן	←	*hit+zamen*	הִתְ-זַמֵּן*
hizdaken	הִזְדַּקֵּן	←	*hit+zaken*	הִתְ-זַקֵּן*

First root consonant: צ *tsadi*

If the first consonant of the root is *tsadi* צ *ts*, then that consonant and the prefix consonant change places. In addition the prefix consonant ת changes to ט: תצ > צט.

	Actual Form			Expected Form	
hitsta`er	הִצְטַעֵר	←	*hit+tsa`er*	הִתְ-צַעֵר*
hitstalem	הִצְטַלֵם	←	*hit+tsalem*	הִתְ-צַלֵם*

A historical note

The consonant צ *tsadi* was historically an emphatic consonant, pronounced differently than today's pronunciation of *ts* (i.e. it was an *s* with the back of the tongue simultaneously raised towards the velum). Therefore the ת of the *hitpa`el* prefix which preceded it was turned into what was once an emphatic ט *tet* to fit with צ. These qualities were lost in modern pronunciation, but the spelling still reflects the historical process.

Variants with ב', כ', פ'

1. The letters ב', כ', פ' are realized as *b, k, p*

i. When it is the first root letter in all the tenses and moods:

הווה : מִתְפַּלֵּא ; עבר : הִתְפַּלֵּא ; עתיד : יִתְפַּלֵּא

ציווי : הִתְפַּלֵּא! שם הפועל : לְהִתְפַּלֵּא

ii. When it is the second root letter in all tenses and moods:

הווה : מִתְלַבֵּשׁ ; עבר : הִתְלַבֵּשׁ ; עתיד : יִתְלַבֵּשׁ

ציווי : הִתְלַבֵּשׁ!

שם הפועל : לְהִתְלַבֵּשׁ

2. The letters ב', כ', פ' are realized as *v, kh, f*

When it is the last letter of the word or root:

מִתְקָרֵב, מִתְהַפֵּךְ, מִתְעַלְּפִים

Variations with radicals א', ע', ח', ה', ר'

1. When the second root letter is ע' or ר', the first one has a *kamats* rather than a *pataḥ* under it, but the pronunciation remains the same in all tenses and moods: מִתְפָּאֵר, יִתְפָּרֵק

2. When the third root letter is ח' or ע' and no suffix is appended, the usual normative form is: הִשְׁתַּגֵּעַ, יִתְפַּתַּח; however in common speech the second stem vowel changes to *e* and a 'furtive' *pataḥ* is inserted, as in יִתְפַּתֵּחַ, הִשְׁתַּגֵּעַ. The form with a furtive *pataḥ* is the only option in the present tense: מִתְפַּתֵּחַ, מִשְׁתַּגֵּעַ

3. If the second consonant is a guttural that is expected to be followed by a zero *shva*, we have a *ḥataf pataḥ* instead:

הִתְפָּאֲרָה, מִתְנַהֲלִים, יִתְנַחֲלוּ, תִּצְטַעֲרִי

4.5.2 Irregular Verbs   גזרות חסרים ונחים

The root classification: ע"ע

Verbs that belong to this group have identical second and third root consonants. They are conjugated as regular verbs.

Some of the ע"ע roots are derived from bi-consonantal adjectives:

Gloss	Infinitive	Future	Present	Past	ע"ע	שם תואר
get warm	לְהִתְחַמֵּם	יִתְחַמֵּם	מִתְחַמֵּם	הִתְחַמֵּם	ח-מ-מ	חם <
get cooled	לְהִתְקָרֵר	יִתְקָרֵר	מִתְקָרֵר	הִתְקָרֵר	ק-ר-ר	קר <

The root classification: merger of ע"ו/ע"י with ע"ע

As in *pi`el* and *pu`al*, there is also a group of ע"ו/ע"יי verbs in *hitpa`el* which behave as if they were ע"ע verbs. Again the second consonant is duplicated, and the first stem vowel is *o*, for both ע"ע and ע"ו/ע"יי:

Gloss	Infinitive	Future	Present	Past	ע"ע	ע"ו
spin around	לְהִסְתּוֹבֵב	יִסְתּוֹבֵב	מִסְתּוֹבֵב	הִסְתּוֹבֵב	ס-ב-ב	(ס-ו-ב)
wake up	לְהִתְעוֹרֵר	יִתְעוֹרֵר	מִתְעוֹרֵר	הִתְעוֹרֵר	(ע-ר-ר)	ע-ו-ר

Note

Some ע"ו/ע"יי roots have two forms of *hitpa`el*: one is conjugated as a regular verb in *pi`el*, and the medial semi-vowel ו or י is realized as a consonant. The other follows the merged ע"ע/ע"יי/ע"ו pattern above:

Gloss	Infinitive	Citation form	*hitpa`el* root	Source
take place, exit	לְהִתְקַיֵּם	הִתְקַיֵּם	ק-י-מ	ק-ו-מ
rise up	לְהִתְקוֹמֵם	הִתְקוֹמֵם	ק-מ-מ	ק-ו-מ

Gloss	Infinitive	Citation form	*hitpa`el* root	Source
intend, mean	לְהִתְכַּוֵּן	הִתְכַּוֵּן	כ-ו-נ	כ-ו-נ
get ready, plan	לְהִתְכּוֹנֵן	הִתְכּוֹנֵן	כ-נ-נ	כ-ו-נ

The root classification: נחי ל"א

As in other *binyanim*, when the third root consonant is א, that א is not pronounced at the end of the syllable:

to be familiar with/oriented לְהִתְמַצֵּא ב

Root classification		Verbal noun	Infinitive	Root
נחי ל"א		הִתְמַצְּאוּת	לְהִתְמַצֵּא	מ-צ-א
	הֵם	הִיא	הוּא	אתה
Present	מִתְמַצְּאִים	מִתְמַצֵּאת	מִתְמַצֵּא	מִתְמַצֵּא
Past	הִתְמַצְּאוּ	הִתְמַצְּאָה	הִתְמַצֵּא	הִתְמַצֵּאתָ
Future	יִתְמַצְּאוּ	תִּתְמַצֵּא	יִתְמַצֵּא	תִּתְמַצֵּא
		אתם/ן	את	אתה
Imperative		הִתְמַצְּאוּ!	הִתְמַצְּאִי!	הִתְמַצֵּא!

The root classification: נחי ל"י

When the third root consonant is י *y*, it is realized as the vowel *e* or *a* in final position, where it is represented in the spelling as ה, whereas elsewhere, it is realized as the diphthong יְ *ey*, or is elided before another vowel.

to experience, be put to the test לְהִתְנַסּוֹת

Root classification		Verbal noun	Infinitive	Root
<u>נחי ל״י</u>		הִתְנַסּוּת	לְהִתְנַסּוֹת	נ-ס-י
	<u>הֵם</u>	<u>הִיא</u>	<u>הוּא</u>	<u>אַתָּה</u>
Present	מִתְנַסִּים	מִתְנַסָּה	מִתְנַסֶּה	מִתְנַסֶּה
Past	הִתְנַסּוּ	הִתְנַסְּתָה	הִתְנַסָּה	הִתְנַסֵּיתָ
Future	יִתְנַסּוּ	תִּתְנַסֶּה	יִתְנַסֶּה	תִּתְנַסֶּה
		<u>אַתֶּם/ן</u>	<u>אַתְּ</u>	<u>אַתָּה</u>
Imperative		הִתְנַסּוּ!	הִתְנַסִּי!	הִתְנַסֵּה!

4.5.3 Deriving new *hitpa`el* verbs

The focus in *hitpa`el* forms is not on the initiator of the action, but on its recipient, or on the entity undergoing a process, and generally it is intransitive. In many cases *hitpa`el* verbs are verbs of becoming, turning into, or changing from one state to another. Many other verbs in *hitpa`el* are either reflexive (action goes back to self) or reciprocal (mutual action: each other). As such, it is quite open to derivation from existing nouns as well as from verbs. To start with, many new *pi'el* verbs have *hitpa`el* counterparts, similar to what happens in *pu`al*:

Gloss	התפעל	פועל	פיעל	Gloss	Base
settle (intr.)	הִתְמַקֵּם	מֻקַּם	מִקֵּם	place	מָקוֹם
focus (intr.)	הִתְמַקֵּד	מֻקַּד	מִקֵּד	focus	מוֹקֵד
realize (intr.)	הִתְמַמֵּשׁ	מֻמַּשׁ	מִמֵּשׁ	real(ly)	מַמָּשׁ
become subjugated	הִשְׁתַּעְבֵּד	שֻׁעְבַּד	שִׁעְבֵּד		שׁ+עבד
become perfect	הִשְׁתַּכְלֵל	שֻׁכְלַל	שִׁכְלֵל		שׁ+כלל

And parallel to reduplicated forms in *pi'el* like בִּלְבֵּל 'confuse', there exists the parallel *hitpa`el* counterpart הִתְבַּלְבֵּל 'get confused':

to get confused לְהִתְבַּלְבֵּל

Root classification		Verbal noun	Infinitive	Root
מרובעים (משוכפלים)		הִתְבַּלְבְּלוּת	הִתְבַּלְבֵּל	ב-ל-ב-ל
	הֵם / הִיא		הוּא	אתה
Present	מִתְבַּלְבְּלִים / מִתְבַּלְבֶּלֶת		מִתְבַּלְבֵּל	מִתְבַּלְבֵּל
Past	הִתְבַּלְבְּלוּ / הִתְבַּלְבְּלָה		הִתְבַּלְבֵּל	הִתְבַּלְבַּלְתָּ
Future	יִתְבַּלְבְּלוּ / תִּתְבַּלְבֵּל		יִתְבַּלְבֵּל	תִּתְבַּלְבֵּל
	אתם/אתן		את	אתה
Imperative	הִתְבַּלְבְּלוּ!		הִתְבַּלְבְּלִי!	הִתְבַּלְבֵּל!

Often, a *hitpa`el* verb is related to a noun, an adjective, a *pi`el* verb stem, or a *pa`al* verb stem. It is based on the same root consonants and has a related meaning, as in:

1. Derived from adjectives

	Citation Form			Source
become strong	הִתְחַזֵּק	←	strong	חָזָק
become hot	הִתְחַמֵּם	←	hot	חַם
become clear	הִתְבַּהֵר	←	clear	בָּהִיר
get closer	הִתְקָרֵב	←	close	קָרוֹב
distance oneself	הִתְרַחֵק	←	far, distant	רָחוֹק
straighten up	הִתְיַשֵּׁר	←	straight	יָשָׁר

2. Derived from nouns

	Citation Form			Source
calcify	הִתְאַבֵּן	←	stone	אֶבֶן
become focused	הִתְמַקֵּד	←	focus	מוֹקֵד
become a citizen	הִתְאַזְרֵחַ	←	citizen	אֶזְרָח
take a shower	הִתְקַלֵּחַ	←	shower	מִקְלַחַת
acclimatize oneself	הִתְאַקְלֵם	←	climate	אַקְלִים
take some air	הִתְאַוְרֵר	←	air	אֲוִיר

3. Many verbs are derived from transitive *pi`el* verbs

	Citation Form			Source
improve (intr.)	הִשְׁתַּפֵּר	←	improve (tr.)	שִׁפֵּר
make a living	הִתְפַּרְנֵס	←	provide for	פִּרְנֵס
get cold	הִצְטַנֵּן	←	cool (tr.)	צִנֵּן

get spoiled	הִתְקַלְקֵל	←	spoil (tr.)	קִלְקֵל
take a risk	הִסְתַּכֵּן	←	risk (tr.)	סִכֵּן
advance oneself	הִתְקַדֵּם	←	advance (tr.)	קִדֵּם
get trained	הִתְאַמֵּן	←	train (tr.)	אִמֵּן

4. Derived from transitive verbs in *pa`al*

	Citation Form			Source
get washed	הִתְרַחֵץ	←	wash	רָחַץ
get dressed	הִתְלַבֵּשׁ	←	clothe (tr.)	לָבַשׁ
get undressed	הִתְפַּשֵׁט	←	take off clothes	פָּשַׁט

5. A few verbs are derived from intransitive *pa`al* verbs

	Citation Form			Source
become enraged	הִתְרַתֵּחַ	←	boil	רָתַח
get angry	הִתְרַגֵּז	←	be angry	רָגַז
become silent	הִשְׁתַּתֵּק	←	be silent	שָׁתַק

6. Derived from other *binyanim*

	Citation Form			Source
get ready	הִתְכּוֹנֵן	←	prepare	הֵכִין
hide oneself	הִסְתַּתֵּר	←	hide	הִסְתִּיר
trade places	הִתְחַלֵּף	←	replace	הֶחֱלִיף

4.5.4   Associated meanings

Hitpa`el is primarily associated with reflexive and reciprocal meanings. However, it sometimes has other meanings, including passive, repeated action, and feigning doing something.

a. Reflexive meaning

Reflexive verbs are ones for which the instigator of the action ('the agent'), and its recipient ('the patient'), refer to the same entity.

Every morning I wake up at seven.   כל בוקר אני מתעורר בשבע.

Many reflexive verbs in *hitpa`el* can also have related verbs expressed by a different *binyan*, where they refer to an action affecting someone or something other than the subject.

Reflexive - התפעל

In the morning David washes, shaves,
gets dressed and combs his hair.
~~*He washes himself, shaves himself,~~
~~dresses himself and combs his hair.~~

כל בוקר דוד מתרחץ, מתגלח,
מתלבש ומסתרק.
~~הוא רוחץ את עצמו, מגלח את~~
~~עצמו, מלביש את עצמו, ומסרק~~
~~את עצמו.~~

Transitive – with separate recipient - פעל ופיעל

He washed the car.

הוא רחץ את המכונית.

He wore festive clothes.

הוא לבש בגדי חג.

He combs his hair.

הוא מסרק את השיער.

A comparative note

In English there are verbs which have the same form regardless of
whether they are used as reflexive or as transitive verbs. It thus
becomes a source of confusion for learners of Hebrew. It is important
to keep in mind the distinction between the verbs where the recipient of
the action is identical to the instigator of the action, and similar verbs
which require a separate object.

Reflexive

He trained (intr.) for the Olympic
games.

הוא התאמן למשחקים
האולימפיים.

Transitive

He trained many athletes.

הוא אימן הרבה ספורטאים.

The verb הִתְאַמֵּן 'trained' implies that the person was the trainer as well
as the one being trained. The use of the word *self* is part of the meaning
of *hitpa'el*. The English verb *train* can also be a transitive verb, which
requires an object, such as 'trained many athletes'. In Hebrew, the *pi'el*
verb is a transitive verb, as in הוא אימן את הספורטאים, while the
hitpa'el verb is reflexive and can have no separate direct object.

The reflexive meaning is not obvious at all times. In some intransitive
verbs, the action may not be transferred directly to the subject/patient,
but it still indicates a process that affects it. For instance, הִתְקַדֵּם
'advance' includes the meaning of 'advance oneself', הִתְקָרֵב 'get
closer' is equivalent to 'bring oneself close', and הִתְאַמֵּץ 'make an
effort' is an extension of 'exert oneself'.

b. Reciprocal

Reciprocal verbs are ones for which the participants' roles are either equivalent, or shift back and forth between them. When the subject is plural and includes more than one entity, it is not necessary to add the reciprocal expression 'each other', since it is implied. The built-in feature of 'reciprocity' requires a plural subject. For instance, in הם הִתְוַכְּחוּ 'they argued', the reciprocal pronouns 'with each other' are implied. However, in order to shift the focus to one of the participants, the distinction is made between the initiator of the action, and its recipient. The singular verb form accompanies the subject, and the verb is then perceived as transitive. It will thus be followed by an object, which is usually linked by a preposition:

Dan and Dana got married.	דן ודנה התחתנו.

Transitive meaning – focus on the initiator of action

Dan married Dana.	דן התחתן עם דנה.
Dana married Dan.	דנה התחתנה עם דן.

c. Passive

There are several verbs in *hitpa`el* which are counterparts of transitive verbs, usually in *pi`el*.

Active meaning

Dan requested that I meet with him.	דן ביקש ממני להיפגש אתו.

Passive meaning

I was asked to meet with Dan.	התבקשתי להיפגש עם דן.

Active meaning

The president appointed his spokesperson.	הנשיא מינה את דוברו.

Passive meaning

The spokesperson was appointed.	הדובר התמנה.

d. Additional meanings

1. Occasionally *hitpa`el* verbs have a feature of a repeated action:

run around	הִתְרוֹצֵץ	←	run	רָץ
stroll	הִתְהַלֵּךְ	←	walk	הָלַךְ

2. A few verbs carry the meaning feature of 'pretend to, make believe':

feign naivety	הִתַּמֵּם	←	naïve	תָּמִים
pretend to be sick	הִתְחַלָה	←	sick	חוֹלֶה

4.6 *Hif'il* conjugation   בניין הפעיל

The name of the verb pattern *hif'il* reflects the third person singular masculine, its citation form.

1. The stem vowel י *i* of הפעיל is part of its pattern. It is present in most of the forms of this conjugation, with the exception of the first and second person of the past tense, and the singular masculine form of the imperative. It is not affected by any vowel reduction process.

2. The initial vowel of the past tense that follows the prefix *h* is *i*. However, in other tenses that vowel changes to *a*:

	Infinitive	Future	Present	Past	Root
to explain	לְהַסְבִּיר	יַסְבִּיר	מַסְבִּיר	הִסְבִּיר	ס-ב-ר

4.6.1 Regular Verbs   שלמים

The group of regular verbs are composed of verbs in which all the root consonants are present in all the verb forms.

Present tense   זמן הווה

The present tense of this conjugation pattern has a *ma-* prefix that marks it for the present tense: מַפְעִיל. Unlike other *binyanim*, in which the typical feminine singular ending is unstressed *-et*, the feminine singular suffix in *hif'il* is a stressed *-á* הָ-.

לְהַסְבִּיר **to explain**

יחיד/ה :	(אני, אתה, הוא) מַסְבִּיר ; (אני, את, היא) מַסְבִּירָה
רבים/ות :	(אנחנו, אתם, הם) מַסְבִּירִים ; (אנחנו, אתן, הן) מַסְבִּירוֹת

In addition to functioning as present tense verbs, many of the present tense forms are used as adjectives or as nouns:

	Adjectives		Citation form	Root
brilliant	מַבְרִיק	shine	הִבְרִיק	ב-ר-ק
worrisome	מַדְאִיג	worry	הִדְאִיג	ד-א-ג
infectious	מַדְבִּיק	infect; glue	הִדְבִּיק	ד-ב-ק

	Nouns		Citation form	Root
smuggler	מַבְרִיחַ	smuggle	הִבְרִיחַ	ב-ר-ח
believer	מַאֲמִין	believe	הֶאֱמִין	א-מ-נ
listener	מַאֲזִין	listen	הֶאֱזִין	א-ז-נ

Past tense   זמן עבר

The past tense of *hif'il* has only two stem variants:

1. In the first and second person: -הִפְעַלְ
2. In the third person: הִפְעִיל

יחיד/ה :	(אני) הִסְבַּרְתִּי, (אתה) הִסְבַּרְתָּ, (את) הִסְבַּרְתְּ,
	הוא הִסְבִּיר, היא הִסְבִּירָה
רבים/ות :	(אנחנו) הִסְבַּרְנוּ, (אתם) הִסְבַּרְתֶּם, (אתן) הִסְבַּרְתֶּן,
	הם/הן הִסְבִּירוּ

The stress of the past tense is always on the last vowel of the *hif'il* stem, and not on the suffixes. Even though the second person plural form is realized as *hisbartém* and *hisbartén* in formal Hebrew, it follows the stress pattern of the other first and second persons in daily spoken Hebrew: *hisbártem* and *hisbárten*.

Future tense   זמן עתיד

The stem of future tense verbs is -פְעִיל. The prefix vowel is always *a*. The stress is always on the *i* of the stem.

יחיד/ה :	(אני) אַסְבִּיר, (אתה) תַּסְבִּיר, (את) תַּסְבִּירִי,
	הוא יַסְבִּיר, היא תַּסְבִּיר
רבים/ות :	(אנחנו) נַסְבִּיר, (אתם) תַּסְבִּירוּ, (אתן) תַּסְבִּירוּ (תַּסְבֵּרְנָה)
	הם יַסְבִּירוּ, הן יַסְבִּירוּ (תַּסְבֵּרְנָה)

The imperative mood   ציווי

The imperative forms have an *h-* prefix (like the past tense). Its stem is -*CCiC* in the feminine singular and plural forms, and the stem vowel changes to *e* in the singular masculine form.

הַסְבֵּר! הַסְבִּירִי! הַסְבִּירוּ! (הַסְבֵּרְנָה)

The negative imperatives use the future tense form with the negative אַל 'don't!' :

אַל תַּסְבִּיר! אַל תַּסְבִּירִי! אַל תַּסְבִּירוּ!

The infinitive mood · שם הפועל

The *hif'il* infinitive uses the stem *haCCiC*: לְהַסְבִּיר, לְהַרְגִּיעַ, לְהַעֲבִיר

I'll try <u>to explain</u> what I meant.	אֲנַסֶּה לְהַסְבִּיר למה התכוונתי.
It is hard for him <u>to decide</u> whether to stay single.	קָשֶׁה לו לְהַחְלִיט אם להישאר רווק.

Verbal noun · שם הפעולה

There are two main forms of verbal nouns in *hif'il*. Most frequently they have separate meanings, which are sometimes related meanings, as they come from the same verb root and form.

The הַפְעָלָה form:

Gloss	Verbal noun 1	Stem
invitation	הַזְמָנָה	הִזְמִין
decision	הַחְלָטָה	הֶחְלִיט

The הֶפְעֵל form:

Gloss	Verbal noun 2	Stem
difference	הֶבְדֵּל	הִבְדִּיל
quarantine	הֶסְגֵּר	הִסְגִּיר

Some roots can be realized in both forms of the gerund, and they thus form two different nouns with related but somewhat different meanings:

Verbal noun 2		Verbal noun 1			Stem
explanation	הֶסְבֵּר	information	הַסְבָּרָה	explain	הִסְבִּיר
accord	הֶסְכֵּם	agreement	הַסְכָּמָה	agree	הִסְכִּים

Variants with ב', כ', פ'

1. The letters ב', כ', פ' are realized as *b, k, p*

When it is the second root letter of all the tenses and moods (except when it follows first root letter א', ע', ה', ח'):

עבר : הִסְבִּיר, הווה : מַסְבִּיר, עתיד : יַסְבִּיר

ציווי : הַסְבֵּר! שם הפועל : לְהַסְבִּיר

2. The letters ב', כ', פ' are realized as *v, kh, f*

i. When it is the first root letter in all the tenses and moods:

עבר : הִבְדִּיל, הווה : מַבְדִּיל, עתיד : יַבְדִּיל

ציווי : הַבְדֵּל! שם הפועל : לְהַבְדִּיל

ii. When it is the final root letter in all the tenses and moods:

עבר : הִקְרִיב, הווה : מַקְרִיבִים, עתיד : יַקְרִיב

ציווי : הַקְרֵב! שם הפועל : לְהַקְרִיב

iii. When the second root letter follows א׳, ע׳, ה׳, ח׳:

מַאֲפִיל, מַעֲכִיר, מַעֲבִיר

Variations with ע׳, ח׳, ה׳, א׳

1. When the first letter of the root is א׳, ח׳, ע׳, the prefix vowel of the past tense changes from *i* to *e*. In addition an 'echo' vowel *e* replaces the *shva* vowel of the first root letter. In the case of ח׳ as the first root letter, the 'echo' vowel is optional.

Informal	Formal		
הֶחֱלִיט	הֶחֱלִיט	הֶאֱמִין	הֶעֱבִיר

2. In all other tenses and moods, the *a* vowel of the prefix is maintained, and an 'echo' vowel *a* replaces the *shva* of the first root letter:

Informal	Formal		
מַחְלִיט	מַחֲלִיט	מַאֲמִין	מַעֲבִיר

3. When the third root letter is ה׳, ח׳, ע׳ and no suffix is appended, an *a* vowel is inserted (since the previous vowel is not *a*, a 'furtive' *pataḥ* is inserted) : הִשְׁפִּיעַ, הִבְטִיחַ, הִגְבִּיהַּ.

4.6.2 Irregular Verbs   גזרות חסרים ונחים

The ע״ו/ע״י root classification

The *hifʿil* form of ע״י/ע״ו roots is characterized by the absence of the second root consonant. The vowel *e* is the prefix vowel in the present and past tense and the vowel *a* is the prefix vowel in the future tense, imperative and infinitive:

to raise, set up לְהָקִים

Root classification		Verbal noun	Infinitive	Root
עַ״ו/עַ״י		הֲקָמָה	לְהָקִים	ק-ו-מ
	הֵם	הִיא	הוּא	אַתָּה
Present	מְקִימִים	מְקִימָה	מֵקִים	מֵקִים
Past	הֵקִימוּ	הֵקִימָה	הֵקִים	הֵקַמְתָּ
Future	יָקִימוּ	תָּקִים	יָקִים	תָּקִים
		אַתֶּם/ן	אַתְּ	אַתָּה
Imperative		הָקִימוּ!	הָקִימִי!	הָקֵם!

There are alternative forms for the first and second person in the past tense. They are used in the higher register: הֲקִימוֹתִי, הֲקִימוֹתָ, הֲקִימוֹת

The חסרי פ״נ root classification

For verbs belonging to this group, the first root consonant נ of פִי הפועל is missing from the whole conjugation, since it always precedes a consonant, and as shown elsewhere, a נ is often assimilated into the following consonant:

Past	*hinpálti* > *hipálti*	הִנְפַּלְתִּי < הִפַּלְתִּי	עבר
Future	*tanpil* > *tapil*	תִּנְפִּיל < תַּפִּיל	עתיד
Present	*manpil* > *mapil*	מַנְפִּיל < מַפִּיל	הווה
Infinitive	*lehanpil* > *lehapil*	לְהַנְפִּיל < לְהַפִּיל	שם הפועל

to drop, cause to fall לְהַפִּיל

Root classification		Verbal noun	Infinitive	Root
חסרי פ״נ		הַפָּלָה	לְהַפִּיל	נ-פ-ל
	הֵם	הִיא	הוּא	אַתָּה
Present	מַפִּילִים	מַפִּילָה	מַפִּיל	מַפִּיל
Past	הִפִּילוּ	הִפִּילָה	הִפִּיל	הִפַּלְתָּ
Future	יַפִּילוּ	תַּפִּיל	יַפִּיל	תַּפִּיל
		אַתֶּם/ן	אַתְּ	אַתָּה
Imperative		הַפִּילוּ!	הַפִּילִי!	הַפֵּל!

Note

Because the פ״נ *hif'il* pattern ends up being a bi-consonantal stem in practice – since the first root letter *n* is omitted – there is a tendency among speakers to use the present tense forms of עַ״ו verbs for פ״נ ones. A פ״נ verb such as מַכִּיר, whose root is נ-כ-ר, is often pronounced *mekir* rather than *makir*.

Exceptions

There are exceptions to the rule of having the first root consonant נ assimilated into the second root consonant:

1. As in previous פ״נ cases we have looked at, if a guttural follows, there is no נ assimilation, since gutturals cannot be geminated as required by the assimilation rule: הִנְחִיל, הִנְעִים

2. In forms where there are two verbs with separate meanings derived from the same root, or from a different but homonymous one, one verb will omit the נ according to the rules above, while the other one will keep it, as in regular verb forms, to maintain the distinction between them:

Gloss	Citation form	Infinitive	Root
look at, store	הִבִּיט	לְהַבִּיט	נ-ב-ט
germinate	הִנְבִּיט	לְהַנְבִּיט	נ-ב-ט
tell	הִגִּיד	לְהַגִּיד	נ-ג-ד
contrast	הִנְגִּיד	לְהַנְגִּיד	נ-ג-ד

I wanted to let you know that I am fine.	רציתי להגיד לכם שאני בסדר.
He contrasted the two assumptions.	הוא הנגיד בין שתי ההנחות.

Note:

The following verbs with נ as a first root letter can be conjugated either as פ״נ or following the ע״ו pattern:

Gloss	Citation form	Infinitive	Root	Form of
assume	הִנִּיחַ	לְהַנִּיחַ	נ-ו-ח	פ״נ
put down	הֵנִיחַ	לְהָנִיחַ	נ-ו-ח	ע״ו

It can be assumed that everything is alright.	יש להניח שהכל בסדר.
Don't put the book down on the table.	אל תניח את הספר על השולחן.

The נחי פ״י root classification

When the first root consonant is י, it is realized as the vowel *o* throughout the derivation, and the prefix vowel is elided.

to lower, bring down לְהוֹרִיד

Root classification		Verbal noun	Infinitive	Root
נחי פ״יי		הוֹרָדָה	לְהוֹרִיד	י-ר-ד
	הם	היא	הוא	אתה
Present	מוֹרִידִים	מוֹרִידָה	מוֹרִיד	מוֹרִיד
Past	הוֹרִידוּ	הוֹרִידָה	הוֹרִיד	הוֹרַדְתָּ
Future	יוֹרִידוּ	תּוֹרִיד	יוֹרִיד	תּוֹרִיד
	אתם/ן	את		אתה
Imperative	הוֹרִידוּ!	הוֹרִידִי!		הוֹרֵד!

The נחי ל״א root classification

As in other *binyanim*, when the third root consonant is א׳, that א׳ is not pronounced at the end of the syllable.

to invent לְהַמְצִיא

Root classification		Associated noun	Infinitive	Root
נחי ל״א		הַמְצָאָה	לְהַמְצִיא	מ-צ-א
	הם	היא	הוא	אתה
Present	מַמְצִיאִים	מַמְצִיאָה	מַמְצִיא	מַמְצִיא
Past	הִמְצִיאוּ	הִמְצִיאָה	הִמְצִיא	הִמְצֵאתָ
Future	יַמְצִיאוּ	תַּמְצִיא	יַמְצִיא	תַּמְצִיא
	אתם/ן	את		אתה
Imperative	הַמְצִיאוּ!	הַמְצִיאִי!		הַמְצֵא!

In the first and second person of the past tense, the stem vowel *i* is changed into *tsere e*: הִמְצֵאתִי הִמְצֵאת הִמְצֵאתֶם הִמְצֵאתֶן

The נחי ל״י root classification

When the third root consonant is י׳, it is realized as the vowel *e* or *a* in final position, where it is represented in the spelling as ה׳, and elsewhere, it is realized as the diphthong יִ *ey*, or is elided before another vowel.

לְהַרְשׁוֹת to permit, let

Root classification	Associated noun	Infinitive	Root
נְחִי לַ"י	הַרְשָׁאָה*	לְהַרְשׁוֹת	ר-שׁ-י
הם	**היא**	**הוא**	**אתה**
Present מַרְשִׁים	מַרְשָׁה	מַרְשֶׁה	מַרְשֶׁה
Past הִרְשׁוּ	הִרְשְׁתָה	הִרְשָׁה	הִרְשֵׁיתָ
Future יַרְשׁוּ	תַּרְשֶׁה	יַרְשֶׁה	תַּרְשֶׁה
אתם/ן	**את**		**אתה**
Imperative הַרְשׁוּ!	הַרְשִׁי!		הַרְשֵׁה!

* The noun associated with this particular verb is רְשׁוּת 'permission'. The *hif'il* form is הַרְשָׁאָה or הַרְשָׁיָה, both of which are rarely used.

The כפולים root classification

1. When the two last consonants of the root are identical, they merge in *hif'il*: the expected לְהַקְלִיל is realized as לְהָקֵל (*lehaklil > lehakel*).
2. The present and past tense vowel of the prefix changes from *a* to *e*: הֵקֵל, מֵקֵל.
3. The *i* vowel of the *hif'il* stem changes to a *tsere e* and loses the י .
4. When a suffix beginning with a vowel is appended, a *dagesh ħazak* is added to the last consonant; when in addition to that, the stress is moved to the suffix, the vowel preceding the consonant with the *dagesh* is changed from *e* to *i*: מְקִלָּה, מְקִלִּים vs. הֵקֵלָּה, יָקֵלּוּ.

לְהָקֵל to ease, make easier

Root classification	Verbal noun	Infinitive	Root
ע"ע	הֲקָלָה/ הֲקַלָּה	לְהָקֵל	ק-ל-ל
הם	**היא**	**הוא**	**אתה**
Present מְקִלִּים	מְקִלָּה	מֵקֵל	מֵקֵל
Past הֵקֵלּוּ	הֵקֵלָּה	הֵקֵל	הֵקַלְתָּ
Future יָקֵלּוּ	תָּקֵל	יָקֵל	תָּקֵל
	אתם/ן	**את**	**אתה**
Imperative	הָקֵלּוּ	הָקֵלִּי	הָקֵל

4.6.3 Meanings associated with *hif`il*

The commonest meaning associated with *hif`il* is causative, including 'cause to be(come)' and 'cause to do (something)'.

a. Cause to do something

The term causative is used in the sense of causing somebody or something to do something. The actor by his action triggers another action. A good example is כָּתַב 'write' > הִכְתִּיב 'dictate', i.e. 'cause to write', such as in 'The director dictated a letter to the staff' המנהל הִכְתִּיב מכתב לצוות, i.e. the director caused someone else to write the letter to the staff by dictating it.

When realization in *hif`il* makes a basic verb causative, that basic verb may be a true action verb, as in:

The bear danced.	הדוב רקד.	פעל
The gypsy made the bear dance.	הצועני הרקיד את הדוב.	הפעיל

The child ate the soup.	הילד אכל את המרק.	פעל
The mother fed the soup to the child.	האם האכילה את הילד את המרק.	הפעיל

The verb may also be stative, as in:

We saw a beautiful winter coat.	ראינו מעיל חורף יפה.	פעל
The salesman showed us the coat.	המוכר הֶרְאָה לנו את המעיל.	הפעיל

b. Cause to become/cause to happen (on its own)

Although one tends to think of causatives in the sense of causing to do something, the number of verbs referring to causing to happen, or causing to become, is much greater.

1. Verbs associated with *pa`al* > causative *hif`il* verbs

Some verbs share roots with *pa`al*; when they are conjugated in *hif`il*, it adds the feature of causative onto the basic meaning of the verb.

The light is on.	האור דולק.	פעל
He turned on the light.	הוא הדליק את האור.	הפעיל

We forgot everything.	שכחנו את הכל.	פעל
Time made us forget (obliterated) all of the details.	הזמן השכיח את כל הפרטים.	הפעיל

2. Verbs associated with *nif`al* > causative *hif`il* verbs

The children got scared.	הילדים נבהלו.	<u>נפעל</u>
He scared the children.	הוא הבהיל את הילדים.	<u>הפעיל</u>
He failed the exams.	הוא נכשל בבחינות.	<u>נפעל</u>
The teacher failed everybody.	המורה הכשיל את כולם.	<u>הפעיל</u>

3. nouns > causative *hif`il* verbs

Some *hif`il* verbs are derived from nouns.

There is a limit/border to everything.	יש גבול לכל דבר.	<u>שם</u>
He limited us in everything.	הוא הגביל אותנו בכל.	<u>הפעיל</u>

The king ruled for many years.	המלך משל שנים רבות.	<u>שם</u>
Who crowned you (made you a king)?	מי המליך אותך?	<u>הפעיל</u>

4. adjectives > causative *hif`il* verbs

Some *hif`il* verbs are derived from adjectives.

The tea is not sweet enough.	התה לא מספיק מתוק.	<u>תואר</u>
We should sweeten the tea.	צריך להמתיק את התה.	<u>הפעיל</u>

The skies are clear.	השמיים בהירים.	<u>תואר</u>
He clarified a number of things that we did not understand.	הוא הבהיר לנו כמה דברים שלא הבנו.	<u>הפעיל</u>

c. Cause to become/acquire a new characteristic

There is a significant number of instances in which *hif`il* verbs refer to 'becoming' in the sense of 'acquiring quality of colors or some physical/bodily characteristics'. The verbs signify a change of state, of bringing an animate or inanimate object to a new state, described by an adjective, as in אָפוֹר 'gray' > הֶאֱפִיר 'turn gray/become gray':

He is very pale.	הוא חיוור מאוד.	<u>תואר</u>
He became pale when he heard the news.	הוא הֶחֱוִיר כאשר שמע את החדשות.	<u>הפעיל</u>

| The copper vessels are rusty. | כלי הנחושת חלודים. | תואר |
| They became rusty because we left them out all winter. | הם הֶחלידו כי השארנו אותם בחוץ כל החורף. | הפעיל |

| The fruits are not yet ripe. | הפירות עדיין לא בשֵלים. | תואר |
| The fruits have not yet ripened. | הפירות עוד לא הבשילו. | הפעיל |

Some *hif'il* verbs of the same root can be both transitive and intransitive. The intransitive verbs can be paraphrased as נהיה 'become + (quality)', whereas the transitive verbs can be paraphrased as גרם להיות 'causing something to become'.

Intransitive
get dark = החשיכו = נהיו חשוכים
With the setting of the sun, the skies darkened. = עם רדת השמש החשיכו השמיים.
Transitive
cause it to become dark = הֶחשיך = גרם לכך שיהיה חושך
They darkened the room and the show began. = הם החשיכו את האולם וההצגה התחילה.

Intransitive
become/get fat = השמין = נהיה שמן
The more one gets fat, the more one's quality of life goes down. = ככל שמשמינים כך יורדת איכות החיים.
Transitive
cause someone to get fat = השמין= גרם לכך שמישהו יהיה שמן
It is not the jeans that make her fat, but rather the chocolate cake. = זה לא הג'ינס שמשמין אותה אלא עוגת השוקולד.

Intransitive
Became shiny = הבריקו = נהיו מבריקות
His eyes shone in the dark. = עיניו הבריקו בחשכה.
Transitive
caused them to shine = הבריקה = גרמה להם להבריק
She shone/polished the silver. = היא הבריקה את כלי הכסף.

Relationship between verbs in *pa`al, pi`el* and *hif`il*

Sometimes a *pa`al* verb can have two separate, though related, meanings, each of which is realized as a different causative verb. Consider the verb גָּדַל. The first meaning, which denotes 'growing up', has a causative counterpart in the *pi`el* conjugation 'raising (causing to grow up)'.

pa`al: grow up (intransitive)

They grew up on a farm. הם גָּדלו בחווה.

pi`el: grow, raise (transitive)

There they raised turkeys. שם הם גידלו תרנגולי הודו.

The second meaning, which denotes 'getting larger', has a causative counterpart in the *hif`il* conjugation, 'enlarging, increasing (causing to get bigger)'.

pa`al: grow in size/numbers (intransitive)

The business grew. העסק גדל.

Hif`il: to enlarge, increase size or number (transitive)

He increased the size of the business. הוא הגדיל את העסק.
He enlarged the picture. הוא הגדיל את הצילום.

4.7 *Huf`al* conjugation   בניין הופעל

The name of this pattern verb group *huf`al* reflects the third person singular masculine in the past tense, its citation form.

The *hif`il-huf`al* relationship is similar to the *pi`el-pu`al* one: *huf`al* is essentially the internal passive of *hif`il*, and there are virtually no *huf`al* verbs that do not have *hif`il* counterparts. The discontinuous vowel sequence *u-a* appears in all the tenses. Like *pu`al*, the *huf`al* conjugation is limited to the tenses only: present, past and future. Similarly, it does not have an imperative or an infinitive mood, and does not have a verbal noun. The *h-* of the prefix characteristic of the past tense is replaced by *m-* in the present tense, and by the personal pronoun prefixes of the future tense.

The *u* stem vowel is represented by the vowel קֻבּוּץ, such as in הֻבהַר, but in the contemporary spelling, especially in texts without vowels, the ו represents the vowel *u*, such as in הובהַר.

Note

The *huf'al* conjugation is also referred to as the *hof'al* conjugation. Both *u* or *o* vowel are acceptable as the prefix vowels of this *binyan*.

4.7.1 Regular Verbs   שלמים

Present tense   זמן הווה

The present tense of this conjugation pattern has a *mu-* prefix tense marker. The feminine singular stem changes to -*CCéCet*. As is the case in all *huf'al* tenses, the vowel sequence *u-a* is part of the pattern that characterizes it as passive. Present tense forms function as verbs, as nouns and as adjectives. No vowel reduction takes place in the stem when stress moves to the suffix in the present tense.

to be neglected לִהְיוֹת מֻזְנָח

יחיד/ה :	‏(אני, אתה, הוא) מֻזְנָח ; (אני, את, היא) מֻזְנַחַת*
רבים/ות :	‏(אנחנו, אתם, הם) מֻזְנָחִים ; (אנחנו, אתן, הן) מֻזְנָחוֹת

*The usual vowel pattern for the feminine singular is מֻפְעֶלֶת, but the final ח׳, which is a guttural letter, causes the change of vowel from *e* to *a*, as in מֻזְנַחַת.

In texts without vowels :   מוזנח, מוזנחת, מוזנחים, מוזנחות

Passive participles in *huf'al* that function as adjectives:

abstract	מופשט	defined	מוגדר
limited	מוגבל	recommended	מומלץ
absolute	מוחלט	complex	מורכב

Passive participles in *huf'al* that function as nouns:

juror	מושבע	candidate	מועמד
unemployed	מובטל	authorized person	מוסמך

Past tense   זמן עבר

The past tense of *huf'al* has two stem variants:

In the first and second persons: ‎-הֻפְעַל   *huCCaC-*

In the third person feminine singular and plural: ‎-הֻפְעְל   *huCCeC-*

The reduction from *a* to *e* occurs when stress is moved to the suffix.

יחיד/ה: (אני) הֻזְנַחְתִּי, (אתה) הֻזְנַחְתָּ, (את) הֻזְנַחְתְּ,
הוא הֻזְנַח, היא הֻזְנְחָה
רבים/ות: (אנחנו) הֻזְנַחְנוּ, (אתם) הֻזְנַחְתֶּם, (אתן) הֻזְנַחְתֶּן,
הם/הן הֻזְנְחוּ

Future tense   זמן עתיד

The stem of future tense verbs is *-uCCaC-*, becoming *-uCCeC-* when stress moves to the suffix. There are very few verbs in *huf'al* that are conjugated in all persons in the future tense. The forms that are most in use are the third person forms.

יחיד/ה: (אני) אֻזְנַח, (אתה) תֻּזְנַח, (את) תֻּזְנְחִי,
הוא יֻזְנַח, היא תֻּזְנַח
רבים/ות: (אנחנו) נֻזְנַח, (אתם) תֻּזְנְחוּ, (אתן) תֻּזְנְחוּ (תֻּזְנַחְנָה),
הם יֻזְנְחוּ, הן יֻזְנְחוּ (תֻּזְנַחְנָה)

Variants with ב', כ', פ'

1. The letters ב', כ', פ' are realized as *b, k, p*

When it is the second root letter of all the tenses and moods (except when it follows a first root letter א', ה', ח', ע')

עבר: הֻסְכַּם, הווה: מֻסְכָּם, עתיד: יֻסְכַּם

2. The letters ב', כ', פ' are realized as *v, kh, f*

i. When it is the first root letter in all the tenses and moods

עבר: הֻכְשַׁר, הווה: מֻכְשָׁר, עתיד: יֻכְשַׁר

ii. When it is the final root letter in all the tenses and moods

עבר: הֻקְרַב, הווה: מֻקְרָב, עתיד: יֻקְרַב

iii. When the second root letter follows א', ע', ה', ח':

מֻאֲפָל, מֻעֲכָר

Variations with radicals ע', א'

When the first letter of the root is א', ע', the initial vowel *u* becomes a
kamats katan, which is realized as *o*. The חטף קמץ in the first root letter
echoes that initial vowel and is also pronounced *o*:

mo'omad   מָעֳמָד   *mo'ofal*   מָאֳפָל

Whenever a zero *shva* is expected, we find a *hataf patah* instead: הָפְעֲלוּ,
תְּשָׁאֲלִי.

4.7.2 Irregular verbs   גזרות חסרים ונחים

The ע"ו/ע"י root classification

The *huf'al* form of ע"ו/ע"י roots is characterized by the absence of the
second root consonant.

לִהְיוֹת מוּכָן to be prepared

ע"ו/ע"י				כ-ו-נ
		הֵם	הִיא	הוּא
Present		מוּכָנִים	מוּכָנָה	מוּכָן
Past		הוּכְנוּ	הוּכְנָה	הוּכַן
Future		יוּכְנוּ	תּוּכַן	יוּכַן

The חסרי פ"נ root classification

The חסרי פ"נ is the group of *huf'al* verbs in which the first root
consonant נ is missing in the entire conjugation (since it is always
followed by a consonant).

לִהְיוֹת מֻגָּשׁ to be presented

חסרי פ"נ				נ-ג-ש
		הֵם	הִיא	הוּא
Present		מֻגָּשִׁים	מֻגֶּשֶׁת	מֻגָּשׁ
Past		הֻגְּשׁוּ	הֻגְּשָׁה	הֻגַּשׁ
Future		יֻגְּשׁוּ	תֻּגַּשׁ	יֻגַּשׁ

As in other *binyanim*, there is no assimilation if a guttural follows, e.g.,
in הֻנְחַל, and as in *hif'il*, there are a few verbs with separate meanings
derived from the same root, where one verb will assimilate the נ,
according to the rules, while the other one will keep it, as in regular
verb forms, so as to maintain the distinction between them:

Gloss	Citation form	Root
be told	הֻגַּד	נ-ג-ד
be compared to	הֻנְגַּד (ל)	נ-ג-ד

The נחי פ"י root classification

When the first root consonant is י, it is realized as the prefix vowel *u* throughout the derivation. The י and the prefix vowel are conflated into the *u* vowel.

לִהְיוֹת מוּרָד to be taken down

חסרי פ"יי																			י-ר-ד
	הם	היא	הוא
Present	מוּרָדִים	מוּרֶדֶת	מוּרָד
Past	הוּרְדוּ	הוּרְדָה	הוּרַד
Future	יוּרְדוּ	תּוּרַד	יוּרַד

The נחי ל"י root classification

When the third root consonant is י *y*, it is realized as the vowel *ey*, and the י is present in the first and second persons of the past tense. In final position where it is represented in the spelling as ה׳, it is realized as *a* or *e*.

לִהְיוֹת מֻפְנֶה ל to be referred to

נחי ל"י																			פ-נ-ה
	הם	היא	הוא	אתה
Present	מֻפְנִים	מֻפְנֵית	מֻפְנֶה	מֻפְנֶה
Past	הֻפְנוּ	הֻפְנְתָה	הֻפְנָה	הֻפְנֵיתָ
Future	יֻפְנוּ	תֻּפְנֶה	יֻפְנֶה	תֻּפְנֶה

4.7.3 Meaning associated with *huf`al*

Because of the passive nature of the *huf`al* conjugation, the grammatical subject of the sentence is the recipient of the action rather than its initiator. Typically, the agent (the one performing the action) in the active sentence is not retained in the passive version.

Dan <u>deposited</u> the check in the bank.	דן <u>הפקיד</u> את ההמחאה בבנק.
The check <u>was deposited</u> in the bank.	ההמחאה <u>הופקדה</u> בבנק.

The subject of the active sentence, the agent, may surface in the passive counterpart as an indirect (or oblique) object, signaled by the preposition עַל יְדֵי 'by'. In this example, there is an emphasis on the agent, on Dan, as being the one who deposited the check.

The check was deposited in the   ההמחאה הופקדה בבנק <u>על ידי דן</u>
bank <u>by Dan himself</u>.   <u>בעצמו</u>.

The recipient is often an object or an entity (המחאה) and not a person. A few verbs apply to human recipients of actions, as in the following example:

The new immigrants <u>were discriminated</u>   המהגרים <u>הופלו לרעה</u> על
<u>against</u> by the local residents.   ידי התושבים המקומיים.

While *huf'al* is the passive counterpart of *hif'il*, it is important to remember that not all *hif'il* verbs have *huf'al* counterparts. However, the reverse is true: all *huf'al* verbs have an active counterpart in *binyan hif'il*.

Hif'il verbs that are intransitive do not have *huf'al* counterparts.
<u>Intransitive</u>
They did not come early.   הם לא הקדימו לבוא.
                                                  לֹא הֻקְדְּמוּ.

Hif'il verbs that are transitive are likely to have *huf'al* counterparts.
<u>Transitive: active > passive</u>
The engineers activated all the   המהנדסים הפעילו את כל המחשבים.
computers.
All the computers were activated.   כל המחשבים הֻפְעֲלוּ.

Chapter 5
The noun system

5.1 Introduction to the noun system

A noun is a major part-of-speech category that includes words that refer to people, places, things, ideas, or concepts. Nouns may act as any of the following: subject of the verb, object of the verb, indirect object of the verb, or object of a preposition (or postposition). All Hebrew nouns have a grammatical gender.

5.1.1 Noun categories
1. Common nouns   שמות עצם כלליים

Common nouns are nouns, such as סֵפֶר 'book' or כֶּלֶב 'dog', that can be preceded by a definite article or other modifiers:

the book	הַסֵּפֶר
any book	כָּל סֵפֶר
some books	מִסְפָּר סְפָרִים

Common nouns represent one or all of the members of a class. For example, *singer* represents all singers, as distinct from representing a particular singer, such as אריק איינשטיין 'Arik Einshtein', or מָקוֹם 'place', which represents any place, as distinct from a proper noun, such as ירושלים 'Jerusalem', which signifies a particular place.Common nouns can be animate or inanimate. An inanimate noun refers to things that are not alive. An animate noun refers to living things such as people and animals (but not to plants). They can be countable nouns or non-countable nouns:

1. Countable nouns

Countable nouns are ones that have distinct units that can be counted
and have a singular and a plural form:

Gloss	רבים	יחיד
bottle(s)	בַּקְבּוּקִים	בַּקְבּוּק
dog(s)	כְּלָבִים	כֶּלֶב

2. Non-countable nouns

Non-countable nouns are usually mass nouns that cannot be counted.
Most are singular, such as חוֹל 'sand' or סוּכָּר 'sugar'. A few mass
nouns are plural, such as מַיִם 'water', חַיִּים 'life'.

Gloss	רבים	יחיד
flour		קֶמַח
air		אֲוִיר
water (waters)	מַיִם	
sky (skies)	שָׁמַיִם	

Note

Non-countable mass nouns, such as יַיִן, קֶמַח, חוֹל can be made into
countable nouns by adding units of measure, such as:

Gloss	Countable units	Singular
a glass of water	כּוֹס מַיִם	מַיִם
a bottle of olive oil	בַּקְבּוּק שֶׁמֶן זַיִת	שֶׁמֶן זַיִת
a teaspoon of sugar	כַּפִּית סֻכָּר	סֻכָּר

Collective nouns: countable and non-countable

Collective nouns refer to a group of people, animals or objects as a
group: עַם 'nation', מִשְׁפָּחָה 'family', etc. As such, these nouns have a
singular as well as a plural form:

Gloss	Plural	Singular
political party(ies)	מִפְלָגוֹת	מִפְלָגָה
troupe(s), band	לַהֲקוֹת	לַהֲקָה
family	מִשְׁפָּחוֹת	מִשְׁפָּחָה
nation(s)	עַמִּים	עַם

However, the singular form shares a feature of the non-countable nouns
as well, since in order to specify single units of nouns, such as the ones
above, unit nouns have to be used to count them:

Gloss	Countable units	Singular
party member(s)	חֲבֵר מִפְלָגָה – חַבְרֵי מִפְלָגָה	מִפְלָגָה
band member(s)	חֲבֵר לַהֲקָה – חַבְרֵי לַהֲקָה	לַהֲקָה
family member(s)	בֶּן מִשְׁפָּחָה – בְּנֵי מִשְׁפָּחָה	מִשְׁפָּחָה
national(s)	בֶּן עַם – בְּנֵי עַם	עַם

2. Proper nouns   שמות פרטיים

A proper noun is a noun that is the name of a specific individual, place, or object.

Person's name	Daniel	דָּנִיאֵל
	Dina	דִּינָה
Place name	Jerusalem	יְרוּשָׁלַיִם
	Israel	יִשְׂרָאֵל
Object's name	The Knesset	הַכְּנֶסֶת

Titles added to names

When titles are added to names (usually last names) the phrase can be definite or indefinite.

Mrs./Ms. Yisraeli	הגברת ישראלי	גברת ישראלי
Doctor/Dr. Levi	הד"ר לוי	ד"ר לוי
Captain Barzilay	הסרן ברזילאי	סרן ברזילאי

3. Concrete and abstract nouns

A division of nouns can also be made according to the distinction between concrete and abstract nouns. Concrete nouns refer to objects and substances that exist physically, while abstract nouns refer to states, events, concepts, feelings, qualities, etc., that have no physical existence, e.g. חופש 'freedom', אושר 'happiness', רעיון 'idea', מוסיקה 'music'.

Abstract nouns can be countable or non-countable. Most concrete nouns are countable. Some are non-countable.

Abstract nouns – countable

Feminine	נקבה	Masculine	זכר
culture/s	תַּרְבּוּת, תַּרְבּוּיוֹת	symbol/s	סֵמֶל, סְמָלִים
art/s	אֳמָנוּת, אֳמָנוּיוֹת	holiday/s	חַג, חַגִּים

Abstract nouns: non-countable

Feminine	נקבה	Masculine	זכר
joy	שִׂמְחָה	happiness	אֹשֶׁר
physics	פִּיזִיקָה	wealth	עֹשֶׁר

Note

The noun שִׂמְחָה is also used as a countable noun and as such it refers to 'a joyful occasion' and then it can have a plural form שְׂמָחוֹת 'joyful occasions')

4. Adjectives   שמות תואר

Adjectives may be used in noun phrases to modify common nouns and can also serve as predicates. Adjectives are discussed separately in Chapter 8. Adjectival forms sometimes function as nouns, such as in the use of עשיר, עשירים, which stand for 'rich, wealthy', or for 'a wealthy person/the rich' as the head of the phrase or sentence.

5. Pronouns   שמות גוף

Pronouns are used to replace nouns with independent or affixed features of person, gender and number. Pronouns are discussed separately in Chapter 6.

6. Numerals   שמות מספר

Numerals are used in noun phrases that have countable nouns as head nouns. They signify a specific quantity of objects. Numerals are discussed separately in Chapter 7.

5.1.2 Grammatical characteristics of nouns

As a grammatical class, nouns have the following features:

1. All nouns have a gender assigned to them, either זָכָר 'masculine' or נְקֵבָה 'feminine'. There is no neuter gender.

house	בַּיִת (ז), בָּתִּים	apartment	דִּירָה (נ), דִּירוֹת

2. A noun with no article is always indefinite:

a house	בַּיִת	an apartment	דִּירָה

3. One of the markers of a definite noun is the definite article -ה that is prefixed to the noun:

the house	הַבַּיִת	the apartment	הַדִּירָה

4. Another marker of a definite noun is a pronoun suffix of possession:

our house   בֵּיתֵנוּ/הַבַּיִת שֶׁלָּנוּ   my apartment   דִּירָתִי/הַדִּירָה שֶׁלִּי

5. By definition, all proper nouns (names of people and any other entity) are definite, which in itself already suggests that the presence of the definite article ה- is not a necessary condition for determining that a noun is definite.

6. A noun can have an independent form, שֵׁם נִפְרָד, or it can have a dependent form, שֵׁם נִסְמָךְ, when it is the first component of a two-noun phrase or is a noun that has a suffix attached to it.

Independent noun			שֵׁם נפרד
house	בַּיִת	garden	גִּנָּה

Dependent noun   שֵׁם נסמך

a. The first component of a two-noun phrase:

a coffeehouse   בֵּית קפה   a flower garden   גִּנַּת פרחים

b. Has a suffix attached to it:

my house   בֵּיתִי   my garden   גִּנָּתִי

A noun's dependent form may undergo some internal vowel changes, and predictable changes at the end of the word:

‎-ָה < ת-   דירה < דירת-   ‎-ִים < ‎-ֵי   אנשים < אַנְשֵׁי-

Remember

Most learners tend to memorize a singular word, rather than the forms and features that are important for its use in a variety of contexts. To use the noun appropriately in context, the following features of the noun have to be memorized:

1. the form of the independent singular noun,
2. the form of the plural,
3. the form of the dependent singular noun,
4. the form of the dependent plural noun, and
5. its gender.

Illustration of the features of a masculine noun and a feminine noun:

Masculine	זכר	Feminine	נקבה
Singular	יחיד		יחידה
a house	בַּיִת (בֵּית-)	an apartment	דִּירָה (דִּירַת-)
Plural	רבים		רבות
houses	בָּתִּים (בָּתֵּי-)	apartments	דִּירוֹת (דִּירוֹת-)

Dual endings

Dual endings יִם- *-áyim* can signal either 'two of' or 'a pair of'.

1. Some nouns (mostly time units) have three forms: a singular form, a plural form, and a dual form. When the dual form is used it means 'two of'.

	Dual		Plural		Singular
two weeks	שְׁבוּעַיִם	weeks	שָׁבוּעוֹת	week	שָׁבוּעַ
two months	חֳדָשַׁיִם	months	חֳדָשִׁים	month	חֹדֶשׁ

2. The concept of duality can designate 'a pair of', and the dual form points to that feature of the noun, and is considered also its plural form.

	Dual/plural		Singular
a pair of socks/socks	גַּרְבַּיִם	stocking, sock	גֶּרֶב ז.
a pair of hands/hands	יָדַיִם	hand	יָד נ.

The actual counting with such nouns is done by adding the noun זוג 'a pair of' before the singular noun, and using זוגות 'pairs of' if more than one unit is being counted.

I have two pairs of glasses:	:יש לי שני זוגות מִשְׁקָפַיִם
a pair of sunglasses and a pair of vision glasses.	.זוג משקפֵי שמש וזוג משקפי ראייה

In the singular זוג מִשְׁקָפַיִם 'a pair of glasses' the inclusion of the noun זוג 'a pair of' is optional. The only way to form the plural is to add the plural of זוג, זוגות.

Note

When the singular form of the noun ends in ה- in the dual form, the ה- becomes ת- (as it is a dependent form), and the dual ending is added:

Feminine	two years	שְׁנָתַיִם	a year	שָׁנָה (נ) שָׁנִים
	two hours	שְׁעָתַיִם	an hour	שָׁעָה (נ) שָׁעוֹת

5.2 Indefinite and definite noun forms

In Hebrew there is no indefinite article, either in the singular or in the plural:

A young woman entered the store.   אישה צעירה נכנסה לחנות.

Hats and sunglasses are an important   כובעים ומשקפי שמש הם אביזר
accessory in the summer season.   חשוב בעונת הקיץ.

A definite noun usually occurs when the noun is made specific in the context of the discourse, or is understood from the shared context of the speaker and listener outside the text, and it is formally marked in the following ways:

1. The definite article comes in the form of a prefix to the noun:

The house we plan to buy is outside   הבית שאנחנו מתכוננים לקנות
town.   הוא מחוץ לעיר.
We bought books. The books are   קנינו ספרים. הספרים הם ספרי
textbooks.   לימוד.

2. In a construct phrase – that is, a phrase that has two, or at times more nouns in a morphological relationship expressing possession, origin, affiliation, etc. – the definite article is prefixed to the last noun:

the bookstore	חנות הספרים	a bookstore	חנות ספרים
the problems of	בעיות תלמידי	problems of	בעיות תלמידי
school pupils	בית הספר	school pupils	בית ספר

3. Possessive noun phrases are considered definite. When the possessive pronoun is attached to the noun, no definite article precedes it. When possession is expressed by two separate words – a noun followed by שֶׁל 'of' + pronoun – the noun is prefixed by a definite article:

my books	סְפָרַי= הספרים שֶׁלִי	my book	סְפְרִי= הספר שֶׁלִי

For internal changes of the vowel patterns in the forms to which pronoun suffixes are attached, see Appendix 2, Noun Tables.

4. The definite article is also used for abstract nouns, which embody a general concept, rather than an incident or occurrence (in English these nouns are usually capitalized and appear with no article):

All that matters is <u>Truth</u> and <u>Honor</u>.   .כל מה שחשוב זה <u>האמת והכבוד</u>
<u>Time</u> heals all.   .<u>הזמן</u> מרפא את הכל

5.3 Gender features

As noted above, all nouns in Hebrew have a gender feature, either masculine זָכָר or feminine נְקֵבָה. Some noun endings are associated with either the singular form of feminine nouns or with the plural form of both genders. Gender is indicated in most dictionaries. The gender notation is (ז) for masculine and (נ) for feminine.

Except for inherent biological gender features, there does not seem to be a particular reason why certain nouns are masculine, while others are feminine. Even in a class where nouns share a common meaning, nouns do not necessarily share gender features with one another, as shown in the illustrations below.

Example 1: hotels

Gender: masculine	hotel	מָלוֹן/בֵּית-מָלוֹן	מין : זכר
	residence/home	מָעוֹן	
	inn	פּוּנְדָק	
Gender: feminine	inn/hostel	אַכְסַנְיָה	מין : נקבה

Example 2: stores

Gender: masculine	supermarket	מַרְכֹּל/סוּפֶּרְמַרְקֶט	מין : זכר
	minimarket	מִינִימַרְקֶט	
	hypermarket	הִיפֶּרְמַרְקֶט	
	boutique	בּוּטִיק	
Gender: feminine	store	חֲנוּת	מין : נקבה
	bookstore	חֲנוּת סְפָרִים	
	grocery store	מַכֹּלֶת/צְרָכָנִיָה	

5.3.1 Gender: form and meaning

The gender assigned to nouns is language-specific, and does not necessarily share the same noun-specific gender with other languages that also have grammatically assigned gender (such as French, German, Arabic and others).

Concrete nouns

Feminine	נקבה	Masculine	זכר
pool/s	בְּרֵכָה (נ) בְּרֵכוֹת	room/s	חֶדֶר (ז) חֲדָרִים
city/ies	עִיר (נ) עָרִים	record/s	תַּקְלִיט (ז) תַּקְלִיטִים

Abstract nouns

Feminine	נקבה	Masculine	זכר
culture	תַּרְבּוּת (נ) תַּרְבּוּיוֹת	symbol	סֵמֶל
art	אֳמָנוּת	regime	מִמְשָׁל

Event nouns

stage show	הַצָּגָה (נ) הַצָּגוֹת	stage play	מַחֲזֶה (ז) מַחֲזוֹת

Anatomical gender is reflected in the assignment of gender to most animate nouns.

Examples - human beings

Feminine	נקבה	Masculine	זכר
woman/women	אִשָּׁה (נ) נָשִׁים	man/men	גֶּבֶר (ז) גְּבָרִים
actress/es	שַׂחְקָנִית (נ) שַׂחְקָנִיּוֹת	actor/actors	שַׂחְקָן (ז) שַׂחְקָנִים
girl/girls	יַלְדָּה (נ) יְלָדוֹת	boy/boys	יֶלֶד (ז) יְלָדִים

Examples – other living beings

Feminine	נקבה	Masculine	זכר
mare(s)	סוּסָה (נ) סוּסוֹת	horse(s)	סוּס (ז) סוּסִים
female dog(s)	כַּלְבָּה (נ) כְּלָבוֹת/כַּלְבּוֹת	dog(s)	כֶּלֶב (ז) כְּלָבִים
she-donkey(s)	אָתוֹן (נ) אֲתוֹנוֹת	donkey/(s)	חֲמוֹר (ז) חֲמוֹרִים

Some of the nouns that have biological gender features are often assigned a grammatical gender that does not reflect true gender distinctions. For instance, the gender of the noun נָחָשׁ 'snake' is masculine, regardless of whether the snake is male or female. The generic noun צִפּוֹר 'bird', which stands for any bird, is feminine in contemporary Hebrew. Specific categories of birds are assigned either feminine or masculine gender. For instance, while סְנוּנִית 'swallow' and חֲסִידָה 'stork' are feminine, זַרְזִיר 'starling' and טַוָּס 'peacock' are masculine. Plants are also living things and in the natural world have gender features, but in their representation in Hebrew have an assigned gender and are treated in this respect as objects. While the general noun for the category פֶּרַח 'flower' is masculine, specific flowers within this category such as כַּלָּנִית 'anemone' or רַקֶּפֶת 'cyclamen' are feminine, while others like נַרְקִיס 'daffodil' and צִבְעוֹנִי 'tulip' are masculine nouns.

5.3.2 Gender markings

Many nouns that end in -ָה- *-a* or in ת- *-t* are feminine, but it does not apply to all of them. It is a safe assumption for a learner to consider that these nouns are feminine, unless otherwise indicated.

1. The general identification of the -ָה- suffix is the safest, because of the small number of exceptions involved: only a few isolated items, like (penultimately stressed) לַיְלָה 'night', שׁוּלְיָה 'apprentice', are masculine, as is evident from phrases like לַיְלָה טוֹב 'good night'.

2. Many nouns that end in ת- are feminine, as long as that ת- is part of a suffix.

ית- *-it*	mercury	כַּסְפִּית	plan	תָּכְנִית
וּת- *-ut*	openness	פְּתִיחוּת	culture	תַּרְבּוּת
ֶת- *-et*	pipe	מִקְטֶרֶת	rabies	כַּלֶּבֶת
ַת- *-at*	delegation	מִשְׁלַחַת	flu	שַׁפַּעַת

When that ת is a root letter, the gender is unpredictable. It is often masculine:

death	מָוֶת	olive	זַיִת
radio play	תַּסְכִּית	service	שֵׁרוּת

but may be feminine as well:

religion	דָּת	pliers	צְבָת

Similarly sounding ט' is not part of a gender determination, since ט' is never part of the feminine suffix; it is always a root consonant, and words ending with it can be – unpredictably – either masculine or feminine (although in reality, feminine nouns ending with ט' are rare).

record	(ז) תַּקְלִיט	selection	(ז) לֶקֶט
needle	(נ) מַחַט	item	(ז) פְּרִיט

3. When the final vowel is -ֶה- *e*, a noun is likely to be masculine, as in the following example: מַחֲזֶה 'stage play'. The ending -ֶה- *e* is a regular feature in nouns derived from participles.

intern	מִתְמַחֶה	lecturer	מַרְצֶה
drink	מַשְׁקֶה	field	שָׂדֶה

4. Historically, a few nouns were documented in either gender, sometimes masculine, sometimes feminine, such as:

wedge	יָתֵד	way	דֶּרֶךְ	fire	אֵשׁ
bone	עֶצֶם	knife	סַכִּין	coin	מַטְבֵּעַ
sun	שֶׁמֶשׁ	skeleton	שֶׁלֶד	wind	רוּחַ

However, in current Hebrew everyday usage, speakers use only one gender for these. Usually it is conceived of as strictly feminine, except for שֶׁלֶד 'skeleton' that is always masculine today. Only יָתֵד 'wedge' can be heard being used as either masculine or feminine. Similar usage can be observed in the plural word for 'face', פָּנִים, which to this day maintains a masculine-feminine duality.

5. The dual ending םִיַ- can also serve to some extent as a gender cue. Most human (and animal) limbs that end with this suffix, even when not dual in the real world (e.g., שִׁנַּיִם 'teeth'), are feminine:

hand/arm	יָד	knee	בֶּרֶךְ	ear	אֹזֶן
thigh	שׁוֹק	foot/leg	רֶגֶל	eye	עַיִן

On the other hand, םִיַ- forms that are not part of nature tend to be masculine:

pants	מִכְנָסַיִם	מִכְנָס	socks	גַּרְבַּיִם	גֶּרֶב
spectacles	מִשְׁקָפַיִם		scissors	מִסְפָּרַיִם	

But there are exceptions among these too: נַעֲלַיִם 'shoes' is feminine. Because there are significant occurrences in each group, many speakers are often unsure whether the 'non-human-limb' forms are masculine or feminine, and their individual choices in everyday speech are not consistent.

5.3.3 Deriving feminine and plural forms

Nouns that refer to human beings often have four related forms reflecting number and gender features and sharing the same stem. The masculine form is considered to be the 'base' form that provides the basic stem from which the other forms are derived, with special gender or number suffixes added to them.

	רבות	רבים	יחידה	בסיס/יחיד
young person	בַּחוּרוֹת	בַּחוּרִים	בַּחוּרָה	בָּחוּר
dancer	רַקְדָּנִיּוֹת	רַקְדָּנִים	רַקְדָּנִית	רַקְדָּן

Many nouns and all adjectives that are feminine singular are marked by
the gender suffix ‎ָה‎ (the final consonant ה is silent), ‎ִית‎ or ‎ַת‎, which
is added to the unmarked form of the masculine. The stem of the base
form may undergo some changes in vowel composition in the derived
forms, including that of the feminine form (either because the stress
moves to the last syllable, or because the feminine singular has a
slightly different vowel sequence).

	<u>רבות</u>	<u>רבים</u>	<u>יחידה</u>	<u>בסיס/יחיד</u>
painter	צַיָּרוֹת	צַיָּרִים	צַיֶּרֶת	צַיָּר

Participle forms as nouns
Participle verb forms which serve as nouns or adjectives typically have
a ‎ַת‎ -*é-et* or a ‎ָה‎ -*a* suffix for the feminine form.

	<u>רבות</u>	<u>רבים</u>	<u>יחידה</u>	<u>בסיס/יחיד</u>
agent	סוֹכְנוֹת	סוֹכְנִים	סוֹכֶנֶת	סוֹכֵן
volunteer	מִתְנַדְּבוֹת	מִתְנַדְּבִים	מִתְנַדֶּבֶת	מִתְנַדֵּב
secretary	מַזְכִּירוֹת	מַזְכִּירִים	מַזְכִּירָה	מַזְכִּיר

5.3.4 Nouns with different masculine and feminine stems

There is a group of nouns that have totally different words for
masculine and feminine forms.

<u>Humans</u>	father	אָב	mother	אֵם
	husband	בַּעַל	wife	אִשָּׁה
	bridegroom	חָתָן	bride	כַּלָּה
<u>Animals</u>	donkey	חֲמוֹר	she-donkey	אָתוֹן
	goat	תַּיִשׁ	she-goat	עֵז
	bull	שׁוֹר	cow	פָּרָה

5.3.5 Feminine nouns with shared meanings

Other nouns that are assigned feminine gender and have no distinct
feminine endings can be grouped according to shared and common
meanings.

Nouns: cities

	city, town	עִיר	small town	עֲיָירָה

Names of cities

	Jerusalem	יְרוּשָׁלַיִם	Tel Aviv	תֵּל אָבִיב
	London	לוֹנְדוֹן	New York	נְיוּ יוֹרְק

Nouns: countries

| country | אֶרֶץ | state | מְדִינָה | homeland | מוֹלֶדֶת |

Names of countries

Israel	יִשְׂרָאֵל	USA	אַרְצוֹת הַבְּרִית
Spain	סְפָרַד	Mexico	מֶכְּסִיקוֹ
China	סִין	Japan	יַפָּן

Nouns for parts of the body

(ones that come in pairs and other body- related nouns with dual suffix)

ear	אֹזֶן-אָזְנַיִם	leg	רֶגֶל-רַגְלַיִם
hand	יָד-יָדַיִם	eye	עַיִן-עֵינַיִם
knee	בֶּרֶךְ-בִּרְכַּיִם	shoulder	כָּתֵף-כְּתֵפַיִם
thigh	יָרֵךְ-יְרֵכַיִם	cheek	לֶחִי-לְחָיַיִם
nail	צִפֹּרֶן-צִפָּרְנַיִם	tooth	שֵׁן-שִׁנַּיִם

5.4 Number features

The plural endings of nouns are not a clear indication of the gender of the noun. While in adjectival and present tense forms they indicate gender features, in the noun systems they merely indicate that the noun is a plural noun.

Masculine plural

A great number of masculine nouns share the plural suffix: ים-

	רַבִּים	יָחִיד
house(s)	בָּתִּים	בַּיִת
room(s)	חֲדָרִים	חֶדֶר

There are a number of masculine nouns related to verbal roots (mostly with a middle ו) or that begin with the prefix מ-, and often denote a place or institution. These nouns are masculine, but their plural forms end with ות-.

	רַבִּים	יָחִיד
place(s)	מְקוֹמוֹת	מָקוֹם
dormitory(ies)	מְעוֹנוֹת	מָעוֹן

A smaller number of masculine nouns with the same singular shape and composition have the expected ים- ending in the plural form.

	רבים	יחיד
airplane(s)	מְטוֹסִים	מָטוֹס
institute(s)	מְכוֹנִים	מָכוֹן

A number of masculine nouns without the prefix מ- also share the characteristic of having their plural end with -וֹת in the plural form, as in מְקוֹמוֹת above.

	רבים	יחיד
window(s)	חַלּוֹנוֹת	חַלּוֹן
table	שֻׁלְחָנוֹת	שֻׁלְחָן
cupboard, closet	אֲרוֹנוֹת	אָרוֹן
street(s)	רְחוֹבוֹת	רְחוֹב

Note

1. Notice that many nouns that end in -וֹן or in -ן, such as מעון, חלון, שולחן, פתרון, are masculine nouns, and usually have a -וֹת plural ending, while, of course, their gender remains masculine.

2. Plural forms do not necessarily have the same stem as the singular forms. There can be internal changes:

	רבים	יחיד
market(s)	שְׁוָקִים	שׁוּק
rabbi(s)	רַבָּנִים	רַב
tax(es)	מִסִּים	מַס

Feminine plural

By the same token, a great number of feminine nouns, but not all, share the plural suffix: -וֹת.

Feminine nouns with plural suffix: -וֹת

	רבות	יחידה
apartment(s)	דִּירוֹת	דִּירָה
exhibit(s)	תַּעֲרוּכוֹת	תַּעֲרוּכָה

Feminine nouns with plural suffix: -ים

There are a number of feminine nouns that have a feminine ending in the singular form, and yet the plural form suffix is -ים.

The first group includes some living beings:

	רבות	יחידה
woman/women	נָשִׁים	אִשָׁה
ant(s)	נְמָלִים	נְמָלָה

The second group includes many plants:

	רבות	יחידה
pea(s)	אֲפוּנִים	אֲפוּנָה
rose(s)	שׁוֹשַׁנִּים	שׁוֹשַׁנָּה

Others consist of a variety of feminine nouns:

	רבות	יחידה
year(s)	שָׁנִים	שָׁנָה
word(s)	מִלִּים	מִלָּה

Note
The plural נָשִׁים has two possible dependent forms נְשֵׁי- and -נְשׁוֹת.
These dependent forms are also the bases for adding pronoun suffixes:
נְשֵׁיהֶם or נְשׁוֹתֵיהֶם.

The players and <u>their wives</u> were invited to the party. The directors' <u>wives</u> will be included in the list of invited guests.	השחקנים ונשותיהם הוזמנו למסיבה. גם נשי (נשות) המנהלים ייכללו ברשימת המוזמנים.

The plural noun שָׁנִים has a dependent form -שְׁנוֹת, and it is the form to which pronoun suffixes are added.

The (years of the) nineties were years of economic growth.	שנות התשעים היו שנים של צמיחה כלכלית.

5.5 Noun patterns
Many Hebrew nouns and adjectives are formed from specific consonantal roots plus skeletons of fixed vowels and variable consonantal slots with a possible prefix or suffix. We refer to these skeletal patterns as משקלים *mishkalim*. The term *mishkal* means 'canonical pattern'. Included are some illustrations as to how nouns are formed by combining particular roots with *mishkalim*. Notice that a root can provide the basis for several nouns, each distinguished by a specific pattern.

Here are four roots, which combine with patterns to produce nouns:

Gloss	*מַפְעֵל*	Gloss	*פְּעִילָה*	Root
comb	מַסְרֵק	scanning	סְרִיקָה	ס-ר-ק
juicer	מַסְחֵט	squeezing	סְחִיטָה	ס-ח-ט
syringe	מַזְרֵק	shot; injection	זְרִיקָה	ז-ר-ק
propeller	מַדְחֵף	push	דְחִיפָה	ד-ח-פ

Although the root does not exist on its own, most words sharing a common root tend to have a common meaning core, as one can see from horizontal scanning of the examples above. Thus, for instance, most items incorporating the root ס-ר-ק revolve around the notion of combing or scanning; entries with the root ס-ח-ט contain a squeezing core; ז-ר-ק forms have something to do with throwing, including the more restricted sense of injecting, which is a type of throwing of liquid, hence 'shot' can have two meanings reflecting both senses, of 'a throw' (as in basketball) or 'injection by syringe'; and the core of ד-ח-פ 'push' is extended to 'propelling'.

Vertical reading of the tables reveals something else. The non-linear morphological pattern, of a fixed vowel configuration with a possible affix, **also** tends to demonstrate some regularity. For instance, words sharing the discontinuous pattern *מַפְעֵל* often designate instruments, as in מַזְרֵק 'syringe', מַסְרֵק 'a comb', מַדְחֵף 'propeller', מַסְחֵט 'juicer'.

These form-and-meaning relationships do not occur across the board, and at times may not hold at all, or apply only in part. Some forms never followed the regularity to start with, and most departed from it with time, with varying degrees of deviation. Language is an evolving entity, and the relationship between form and meaning is not maintained for long.

5.5.1 Discontinuous and linear derivations of nouns
There are two main mechanical strategies for creating nouns: discontinuous formation of nouns, and linear derivation of nouns.

Discontinuous derivation of nouns
Discontinuous derivation of nouns is the combination of the root with a pattern to yield nouns. It is called discontinuous since the sequence of

the root consonants is intermittent and is 'interrupted' by the vowels of the pattern. The vowels combine with the root consonants and at times with prefixes and suffixes to form the actual words.

Some common patterns are presented in the table below:
(*C* is used to designate any root consonant and the fixed vowels and prefix consonants are presented specifically as required by the particular *mishkal*).

CéCeC פֶּעֶל		*CaCáC* פַּעָל		*CiCCúC* פִּעוּל	
dog	כֶּלֶב	carpenter	נַגָּר	story	סִפּוּר
king	מֶלֶךְ	cook	טַבָּח	speech	דִּבּוּר
slave	עֶבֶד	barber	סַפָּר	visit	בִּקּוּר

CCiCá פְּעִילָה		*miCCáC* מִפְעָל		*maCCéC* מַפְעֵל	
writing	כְּתִיבָה	letter	מִכְתָּב	computer	מַחְשֵׁב
opening	פְּתִיחָה	shelter	מִקְלָט	receiver	מַקְלֵט
examination	בְּדִיקָה	test	מִבְחָן	battery	מַצְבֵּר

maCCeCá מַפְעֵלָה		*CiCaCón* פִּעָלוֹן		*tiCCóCet* תִּפְעֹ לֶת	
test tube	מַבְחֵנָה	memory	זִכָּרוֹן	outfit	תִּלְבֹּשֶׁת
plough	מַחְרֵשָׁה	madness	שִׁגָּעוֹן	hairdo	תִּסְרֹקֶת
camera	מַצְלֵמָה	experience	נִסָּיוֹן	syndrome	תִּסְמֹנֶת

In indicating the *mishkalim*, the *C* represents any root consonant, and the unchanging prefixes, suffixes and vowels (including the stressed vowel) are indicated in lower case.

Linear derivation of nouns

Linearly derived patterns are those in which a suffix is added to a base without affecting the stem or base of the noun. Some vowel changes may occur, such as the loss of the vowel *a* in סַנְדָּל > סַנְדְּלָר *sandál* > *sandlár*, and a change in spelling in *halilán* חֲלִילָן 'flutist', derived from *halíl* חָלִיל 'flute', where a *hataf patah* replaces the *kamats* vowel. These vowel changes are due to the shift in stress, not to any *mishkal*.

Compounding: recent linear derivations

Suffixes	Gloss	Noun		Gloss	Source
-ut	essence	מַהוּת	<	what	מָה
-an	flutist	חֲלִילָן	<	flute	חָלִיל
-iya	carpenter's shop	נַגָּרִיָּה	<	carpenter	נַגָּר
-on	small horse	סוּסוֹן	<	horse	סוּס
-ay	journalist	עִיתּוֹנַאי	<	newspaper	עִיתּוֹן
-it	truck	מַשָּׂאִית	<	load	מַשָּׂא
-ar	shoemaker	סַנְדְּלָר	<	sandal	סַנְדָּל

1. Word prefix compounding

The prefix words used in prefix compounding are largely borrowed from Aramaic and Greek, and modeled on Greco-Latin forms. They generate some nouns but more commonly adjectives:

one-				חַד-
one-way	חַד-סְטְרִי	single parent		חַד-הוֹרִי
two-				דּוּ-
two-way	דּוּ-סְטְרִי	bilingual		דּוּ-לְשׁוֹנִי
				חֲסַר-
inexperienced	חֲסַר נִסָּיוֹן	experienced		בַּעַל נִסָּיוֹן
pre-				קְדַם-
pre-military	קְדַם-צְבָאִי	pre-historic		קְדַם-הִיסְטוֹרִי
inter-				בֵּין-
international	בֵּינְלְאוּמִי	interstellar		בֵּין-כּוֹכָבִי
intra-				תּוֹךְ-
intra-group	תּוֹךְ-קְבוּצָתִי	intracellular		תּוֹךְ-תָּאִי
post-				בָּתַר-
post-Biblical	בָּתַר-מִקְרָאִי	post-congress		בָּתַר-קוֹנְגְרֶס
multi-				רַב-
centipede	רַב-רֶגֶל	multi-faceted		רַב-פָּנִים
sub-				תַּת-
substandard	תַּת-תִּקְנִי	sub-human		תַּת-אֱנוֹשִׁי
super-				עַל-
supersonic	עַל-קוֹלִי	supernatural		עַל-טִבְעִי
non-				אַל-
no-rust	אַל-מַתַּכְתִּי	immortality		אַל-מָוֶת

2. Foreign suffixes

Foreign suffixes can be appended to native stems (mostly in colloquial Hebrew), as in:

Noun		Suffix		Source
army commander	אַגְדוֹנֶר	< ־(וֹ)נֶר	army (e.g. 3ʳᵈ)	אֲגֻדָּה
one who disgraces	בִּזְיוֹנֶר		disgrace	בִּזָּיוֹן
kibbutz member	קִבּוּצְנִיק	< ־נִיק	kibbutz	קִבּוּץ
Likkud party member	לִכּוּדְנִיק		Likkud party	לִכּוּד
nice young man	בָּחוּרְצֶ׳יק	< ־צֶ׳יק	young man	בָּחוּר
very small	קָטַנְצֶ׳יק		small	קָטָן

3. Compounds: blends

Blends involve merging of two independent lexical items into a new word. Some such blends have been part of the lexicon for quite a while, as in:

Blend		Stem 2		Stem 1	
movie theater	קוֹלְנוֹעַ <	movement	נוֹעַ	sound	קוֹל
traffic light	רַמְזוֹר <	light	אוֹר	hint; signal	רֶמֶז
lighthouse	מִגְדָּלוֹר <	light	אוֹר	tower	מִגְדָּל

4. Compounds: clipped blends

Other blends are more recent. In some of them, part of one of the bases is lost in the process of compounding, which makes them less transparent, and speakers may lose the connection to the base after a while.

Some illustrations:

Blend		Stem 2		Stem 1	
pedestrian mall	מִדְרְחוֹב <	street	רְחוֹב	sidewalk	מִדְרָכָה
cable car	רַכֶּבֶל <	cable	כֶּבֶל	train	רַכֶּבֶת
cellular phone	פֶּלֶאפוֹן <	telephone	טֶלֶפוֹן	wonder	פֶּלֶא

5.6 Nouns derived from verbs

Some very large classes of nouns are derived from verbs. In some cases, the verb form itself, in its passive or active participle form, may also function as a noun; so do certain forms of the infinitive. In other cases, certain specific patterns designating abstract nouns are directly related to verbs, and the relationship between a particular *binyan* and its related abstract nominalization is fairly regular.

5.6.1 Active participles functioning as agent nouns

One of the most common sources for nouns is the active participle, which yields agent nouns (initiators of action) or instruments performing the action denoted by the verb.

בניין פָּעַל - בינוני

Gloss	Noun		Citation form		Verb type
governor	מוֹשֵׁל		govern	מָשַׁל	שלמים
worker	פּוֹעֵל		act	פָּעַל	שלמים
baker	אוֹפֶה		bake	אָפָה	ל״יי
courier	רָץ		run	רָץ	ע״וו

בניין פיעל - בינוני

Gloss	Noun		Citation form		Verb type
immigrant	מְהַגֵּר		immigrate	הִגֵּר	שלמים
designer	מְעַצֵּב		design	עִצֵּב	שלמים
conductor	מְנַצֵּחַ		conduct	נִצֵּחַ	ל׳ גרונית
translator	מְתַרְגֵּם		translate	תִּרְגֵּם	מרובעים

בניין הפעיל – בינוני

Gloss	Noun		Citation form		Verb type
guide	מַדְרִיךְ		guide	הִדְרִיךְ	שלמים
voter	מַצְבִּיעַ		vote	הִצְבִּיעַ	ל׳ גרונית
life guard	מַצִּיל		save	הִצִּיל	פ״נ
leader	מוֹבִיל		lead	הוֹבִיל	פ״יי

בניין התפעל – בינוני

Gloss	Noun		Citation form		Verb type
trainee	מִתְאַמֵּן		train	הִתְאַמֵּן	שלמים
adolescent	מִתְבַּגֵּר		mature	הִתְבַּגֵּר	שלמים
assimilator	מִתְבּוֹלֵל		assimilate	הִתְבּוֹלֵל	כפולים
boxer	מִתְאַגְרֵף		box	הִתְאַגְרֵף	מרובעים

5.6.2 Passive participles functioning as nouns

Passive participial forms occasionally function as nouns.

בניין פָּעַל/פִּעֵל – בינוני פָּעוּל

Gloss	Noun	Citation form		Verb type
fiancé	אָרוּס	get engaged	אֵרַס	פיעל שלמים
divorcé	גָּרוּשׁ	drive away	גֵּרֵשׁ	פיעל שלמים
prisoner	שָׁבוּי	capture	שָׁבָה	פעל ל"י

בניין נפעל – בינוני

Gloss	Noun	Citation form		Verb type
elected person	נִבְחָר	be elected	נִבְחַר	שלמים
absentee	נִפְקָד	be counted	נִפְקַד	שלמים
missing person	נֶעְדָּר	be missing	נֶעְדַּר	פ' גרונית

בניין פֻּעַל – בינוני

Gloss	Noun	Citation form		Verb type
notable	מְכֻבָּד	be respected	כֻּבַּד	שלמים
learned	מְלֻמָּד	be taught	לֻמַּד	שלמים
fossil	מְאֻבָּן	be fossilized	אֻבַּן	פ' גרונית
close associate	מְקֹרָב	be brought closer	קֹרַב	פ' גרונית

Gloss	Noun	Citation form		Verb type
jury member	מֻשְׁבָּע	be sworn	הֻשְׁבַּע	שלמים
unemployed	מֻבְטָל	be laid off (work)	הֻבְטַל	שלמים
axiom	מֻשְׂכָּל	acquire knowledge	הֻשְׂכַּל	שלמים
concept	מוּבָן	be understood	הוּבַן	ע"ו

5.6.3 Infinitive forms functioning as abstract nouns

Each *binyan* is associated with particular forms of abstract nouns. These verbal nouns can have the shape of an infinitive absolute מָקוֹר מֻחְלָט or be nouns with assigned form and gender, which combine the root and some pattern related to a specific *binyan*. In the higher registers, the infinitive form of the verb (without ל- 'to') occasionally serves as an abstract noun (sometimes referred to as a gerund). It is commonly prefixed by -בְּ 'with, upon', but follows other particles as well.

	In context	VN	Citation form	
with the coming of night	עם בּוֹא הלילה	בּוֹא	come	בָּא
upon his coming to Israel	עם בּוֹאוֹ לישראל			
upon his return from the front	בְּשׁוּבוֹ מִן הַחזית	שׁוּב	return	שָׁב

5.6.4 Abstract verbal nouns associated with verbs
1. Derived from participles

As already shown, participial forms, either active or passive, may function as adjectives or as nouns. In some *binyanim,* abstract nouns may be derived from these participles by the addition of the common abstract nominalization suffix ‑וּת (which is always assigned a feminine gender).

	Abstract noun			Base	
agency	סוֹכְנוּת		agent	סוֹכֵן	פעל
ignorance	נִבְעָרוּת		ignorant	נִבְעָר	נפעל
obstetrics	מְיַלְדוּת		obstetrician	מְיַלֵּד	פִּעֵל
loyalty	נֶאֱמָנוּת		loyal	נֶאֱמָן	פ׳ גרונית
obligation	מְחֻיָּבוּת		obliged	מְחֻיָּב	פֻּעַל
skill	מְיֻמָּנוּת		skilled	מְיֻמָּן	
secretariat	מַזְכִּירוּת		secretary	מַזְכִּיר	הפעיל
being limited	מֻגְבָּלוּת		limited	מֻגְבָּל	הופעל

2. 'Default' verbal nouns associated with *binyanim*

Each *binyan* has at least one default abstract nominalization associated with it, unrelated to its participial form(s). The relationship is fairly automatic, although in some cases the verbal noun may have acquired a meaning that is an 'offshoot' of the automatic basic one. If there is more than one nominalization associated with a *binyan,* it is usually much less frequent.

The commonest associations between specific *binyanim* and patterns of abstract noun formation are:

	דוּגמה	שׁורש	שׁם פעולה	בּנין
trip	נְסִיעָה	נ-ס-ע	פְּעִילָה	פעל
survival	הִשָּׂרְדוּת	שׂ-ר-ד	הִפָּעֲלוּת (הִיפַּעֲלוּת)	נפעל
improvement	שִׁפּוּר	שׁ-פ-ר	פִּעוּל (פִּיעוּל)	פיעל
behavior	הִתְנַהֲגוּת	נ-ה-ג	הִתְפַּעֲלוּת	התפעל
beginning	הַתְחָלָה	ת-ח-ל	הַפְעָלָה	הפעיל

5.7 Noun patterns associated with semantic features

It is possible to associate meaning categories with formal features of some of the nouns. They may be associated with a particular ending that provides some association of meaning, such as the ‑וּת ending that characterizes many abstract nouns, or the מ‑ prefix which characterizes many nouns of location or instrument. Some of the most common pattern groups will be presented with a short discussion of their meaning and form associations.

5.7.1 Abstract nouns

The commonest abstract noun suffix is ‑וּת. Such abstract nouns may be derived linearly from the base or constitute part of a discontinuous noun pattern. As mentioned earlier, this noun suffix signals that the noun is feminine. These derivations may involve bases consisting of one syllable, or ones consisting of two or more syllables.

Monosyllabic stems

Derived abstract noun			Base
essence	מַהוּת	what	מָה
being easy, light	קַלּוּת	easy, light	קַל
being thin; finesse	דַּקּוּת	thin	דַּק
entity, being	יֵשׁוּת	there is	יֵשׁ

Polysyllabic stems

citizenship	אֶזְרָחוּת	citizen	אֶזְרָח
foolishness	אֱוִילוּת	fool	אֱוִיל
humanity	אֱנוֹשׁוּת	human being	אֱנוֹשׁ
carpentry	נַגָּרוּת	carpenter	נַגָּר

Many of such abstract nouns are derived from adjectives, which end in *i*. For instance, the adjective דָתִי 'religious' provides the base for דָתִיּוּת 'religiosity', and חִילוֹנִי 'secular' provides the base for חִילוֹנִיּוּת 'secularism'.

Note

In texts with vowels, a *dagesh ḥazak* is inserted into the יּ of the ending of abstract nouns derived from ‑י adjectives (it does not affect the pronunciation of the word).

Derived noun			Base
pragmatism	מַעֲשִׂיּוּת	pragmatic	מַעֲשִׂי
festiveness	חֲגִיגִיּוּת	festive	חֲגִיגִי

Abstract nouns derived from present participles were already discussed above. Note that they may have an alternate form of the stem when the -*ut* ending is present, as the stress shifts from the last syllable of the stem to the vowel ו that characterizes the abstract noun ending.

When the first vowel of the stem is *a*, it is reduced to Ø when the -*ut* ending is added and the stress shifts to -*ut*:

	Derived noun			Base
wholeness	*shlemút*	שְׁלֵמוּת	*shalém*	שָׁלֵם
devotion	*dvekút*	דְּבֵקוּת	*davék*	דָּבֵק

The same happens to an *e* vowel at the **end** of the stem:

foolishness	*tipshút*	טִפְּשׁוּת	*tipésh*	טִפֵּשׁ

Form: פְּעִילוּת > פָּעִיל/פָּעוּל

There are many realizations of abstract nouns that have the form of פְּעִילוּת. They are usually derived from several base forms which have an *a* initial vowel:

	Derived noun			Base
mission	*shlihút*	שְׁלִיחוּת	*shalíah*	שָׁלִיחַ
agility	*zrizút*	זְרִיזוּת	*zaríz*	זָרִיז
openness	*ptihút*	פְּתִיחוּת	*patúah*	פָּתוּחַ
duality	*kfilút*	כְּפִילוּת	*kafúl*	כָּפוּל

Pattern: פַּעֲלוּת

There are many underlying bases for the פַּעֲלוּת pattern. Several base forms, including alternates of *segolate* nouns and some common adjectival forms, provide the source from which these abstract nouns are derived:

	Derived noun			Base
childhood	*yaldút*	יַלְדוּת	*yéled*	יֶלֶד
fitness in accordance with Jewish law	*kashrút*	כַּשְׁרוּת	*kashér*	כָּשֵׁר
greatness	*gadlút*	גַּדְלוּת	*gadól*	גָּדוֹל
simplicity	*pashtút*	פַּשְׁטוּת	*pashút*	פָּשׁוּט

5.7.2 Patterns referring to agents

Agents are performers of an action over which they exercise some control. The dominant patterns are the following: פַּעָל, פַּעְלָן, בסיס+ן, בסיס+אי. Some agent nouns with transparent relationship to the base:

Gloss	Agent	Pattern	Gloss	Base
soldier	חַיָּל	פַּעָל	army	חַיִל
painter	צַבָּע		color, paint	צֶבַע
collector	אַסְפָן	פַּעְלָן	collection	אֹסֶף
comedian	בַּדְחָן		joke	בְּדִיחָה
wireless operator	אַלְחוּטָן	בסיס+ן	wireless	אַלְחוּט
professional	מִקְצוֹעָן		profession	מִקְצוֹעַ
journalist	עִתּוֹנָאי	בסיס+אי	newspaper	עִתּוֹן
electrician	חַשְׁמְלַאי		electricity	חַשְׁמָל

5.7.3 Patterns referring to instruments

An instrument is an implement by means of which an action is carried out. Instruments tend to be realized as מִפְעָל, מַפְעֵל, מַפְעֵלָה and פַּעְלָן.

Gloss	Instrument	Pattern	Gloss	Base
receiver	מַקְלֵט	מַפְעֵל	absorb	קָלַט
key	מַפְתֵּחַ		open	פָּתַח
camera	מַצְלֵמָה	מַפְעֵלָה	photograph	צִלֵּם
lathe	מַחְרֵטָה		engrave	חָרַט
air conditioner	מַזְגָּן	פַּעְלָן	moderate	מִזֵּג
dialer	חַיְּגָן		dial	חִיֵּג
softener	מְרַכֵּךְ	מְפַעֵל	soften	רִכֵּךְ
dryer	מְיַבֵּשׁ		dry	יִבֵּשׁ

In common use the pattern of *meCaCeC* often replaces the normative *maCCeC*, such as *megahets* 'iron' for *maghets* מַגְהֵץ < מְגַהֵץ, or *mehashev* 'computer' for *mahshev* מַחְשֵׁב < מְחַשֵּׁב. Both are acceptable and widely used in speech.

5.7.4 Patterns referring to locations

The prevalent location patterns are מִפְעָל, מִפְעָלָה and בסיס+יָה.

Gloss	Location	Pattern	Gloss	Base
army post	מִשְׁלָט	מִפְעָל	control, rule	שָׁלַט
shelter	מִקְלָט		absorb	קָלַט
headquarters	מִפְקָדָה	מִפְעָלָה	command	פָּקַד
restaurant	מִסְעָדָה		dine	סָעַד
deli	מַעֲדָנִיָה	בסיס+יָה	delicacy	מַעֲדָן
shoemaker's shop	סַנְדְלָרִיָה		shoemaker	סַנְדְלָר

Characterizing a pattern as denoting locations is not always easy, particularly since the location concept may partly overlap with other semantic features. A noun like מַדְרֵגָה 'step', for instance, may be regarded as either a location (where one's foot steps on), or an instrument (a means of getting oneself higher).

Note

Several nouns denoting location in the מפעלה pattern have two possible patterns. Pattern A מִפְעָלָה is considered by some to be the correct form, while Pattern B מַפְעֵלָה is considered incorrect. However, in common use the two patterns exist side-by-side and are equally valid.

Gloss	Pattern B	Pattern A
laundromat	מַכְבֵּסָה	מִכְבָּסָה
plant nursery	מַשְׁתֵּלָה	מִשְׁתָּלָה

5.7.5 Patterns referring to collection/group/system

Some nominal derivation patterns may also denote a group, a collection, or a system; characteristic patterns are linear יָה-, מִפְעָל, פַּעֶלֶת and בסיס+וֹן.

Gloss	Noun	Pattern	Source	
library	סִפְרִיָה	יָה-	book	סֵפֶר
song fest	זִמְרִיָה		song	זֶמֶר
array, variety	מִגְוָן	מִפְעָל	color, hue	גָוֶן
encampment	מַאֲהָל		tent	אֹהֶל
questionnaire	שְׁאֵלוֹן	בסיס + וֹן	ask	שָׁאַל
price list	מְחִירוֹן		price	מְחִיר
air squadron	טַיֶסֶת	פַּעֶלֶת	fly	טָס
card file	כַּרְטֶסֶת		card	כַּרְטִיס

5.7.6 Patterns denoting diminution (reduction)

Diminution usually denotes a smaller noun than its base form, or an adjective with the denoted quality reduced. It is often associated with affection, such as in כְּלַבְלָב 'puppy' or in יַלְדוֹן 'little child'. However, it can also have a negative association, when the diminution is used to reduce the value of someone or something, for instance, as in פְּקִידוֹן 'a small, insignificant clerk', which is derived from פָּקִיד 'clerk', probably because the base itself has some inherent negative feature to start with. There are a number of ways of forming diminutives.

Gloss	Noun	Pattern	Gloss	Source
kitchenette	מִטְבָּחוֹן	בסיס + וֹן	kitchen	מִטְבָּח
small roof	גַּגּוֹן		roof	גַּג
little restaurant	מִסְעָדֹנֶת	בסיס + נֶת	restaurant	מִסְעָדָה
little girl	יַלְדֹנֶת		girl	יַלְדָּה

Gloss	Noun	Pattern	Gloss	Source
doggie	כְּלַבְלָב	פְּעַלְעַל	dog	כֶּלֶב
goatee	זְקַנְקַו		beard	זָקָן
bluish	כְּחַלְחַל		blue	כָּחֹל
kitty	חֲתַלְתּוּל	Reduplic. of	cat	חָתוּל
piggy	חֲזַרְזִיר	stem vowel	pig	חֲזִיר

Gloss	Noun	Pattern	Gloss	Source
teaspoon	כַּפִּית	בסיס+-ִית	tablespoon	כַּף
wine glass	כּוֹסִית		glass	כּוֹס

Gloss	Noun	Pattern	Gloss	Source
hot dog	נַקְנִיקִיָה	בסיס + -ִיָה	sausage	נַקְנִיק
cookie	עוּגִיָה		cake	עוּגָה

In contemporary Hebrew the most productive diminutive pattern is *-on* and its feminine counterpart *-ónet*. Essentially, every noun can be made diminutive by an *-on* suffix. This is a process that can even produce other diminutive nouns from diminutive bases, to render them even more diminutive, as in חָתוּל 'cat' > חֲתַלְתּוּל 'kitty' > חֲתַלְתּוּלוֹן 'little kitty'.

5.7.7 Other noun formation patterns

Some other small groups that belong to derivation patterns in the noun system can be characterized in a semantically coherent fashion.

1. The noun pattern פַּעֶלֶת tends to designate sicknesses and other phenomena with negative associations.

Gloss	Noun	Gloss	Base
jaundice	צַהֶבֶת	yellow	צָהֹב
whooping cough	שַׁעֶלֶת	cough	שִׁעוּל
rabies	כַּלֶּבֶת	dog	כֶּלֶב
inflammation	דַּלֶּקֶת	burn (int.)	דָּלַק

Note

There are other nouns in that pattern, such as רַכֶּבֶת 'train', טַיֶּלֶת 'promenade', קַלֶּטֶת 'cassette', כַּסֶּפֶת 'safe', that do not have any negative connotation .

2. Other nouns with negative connotation are formed in the pattern פִּעָלוֹן:

Gloss	Noun	Gloss	Base
madness	שִׁגָּעוֹן	mad	מְשֻׁגָּע
drunkenness	שִׁכָּרוֹן	drunk	שִׁכּוֹר
failure	כִּשָּׁלוֹן	fail	כָּשַׁל
depression	דִּכָּאוֹן	depress	דִּכֵּא

Note

There are other nouns in that pattern, such as זִכָּרוֹן 'memory', נִקָּיוֹן 'cleanliness', נִסָּיוֹן 'experience', עִקָּרוֹן 'principle' that have a positive connotation.

A fairly common pattern, mostly in more recent Israeli Hebrew, is תַּפְעִיל. It often refers to a product of the action denoted by the base verb (often in *hif'il*), as in:

Gloss	Noun	Gloss	Base
budget	תַּקְצִיב	allot	הִקְצִיב
summary	תַּקְצִיר	shorten	קִצֵּר
incentive	תַּמְרִיץ	encourage	הִמְרִיץ
relief	תַּבְלִיט	make prominent	הִבְלִיט

Another is תִּפְעֶלֶת, which refers to a system, or a set of conditions, as in:

Gloss	Noun	Gloss	Base
memorandum	תִּזְכֹּרֶת	remind	הִזְכִּיר
correspondence	תִּכְתֹּבֶת	correspond	הִתְכַּתֵּב
orchestra	תִּזְמֹרֶת	sing	זִמֵּר
hairdo	תִּסְרֹקֶת	comb	סֵרֵק

5.8 Significant patterns (with no semantic association)

There are many common nouns that have a pattern that is not associated with any particular meaning.

5.8.1 The pattern *pa`ál*

One of the more prominent patterns not associated with any particular meaning is פָּעָל:

river	נָהָר	snake	נָחָשׁ
thing; act of speech	דָּבָר	dust	אָבָק

5.8.2 *Segolate* nouns

One large class of nouns has traditionally been referred to as *segolate* nouns, because their two final consonants are split by a *segol e*, and in the largest sub-group, the preceding vowel is also *e*. That preceding vowel carries the word stress:

rain	*géshem*	גֶּשֶׁם	snow	*shéleg*	שֶׁלֶג

Since the *segolate* stress always falls on the syllable before last (penultimate), it obviously follows that the final vowel is always unstressed. The *segolate* base vowel is generally a stressed *é* vowel, as in *géshem*, but can also be a stressed *ó* or *á*, such as in the following:

summer	*káyits*	קַיִץ	winter	*ħóref*	חֹרֶף
morning	*bóker*	בֹּקֶר	gate	*shá`ar*	שַׁעַר

A historical note

Historically, the *segol* was inserted to split what used to be an impermissible consonant cluster at the end of the word.

1. A noun such as מַלְכּ *málk* 'king' became מֶלֶךְ *mélekh*. The feminine form מַלְכָּה *malká* 'queen' and the abstract noun מַלְכוּת *malkhút* 'kingdom', where a suffix is added, preserve the original stem vowel *a* of the מַלְכּ base, and stress falls on the suffix, as it normally does.

2. A noun such as סִפְר *sifr* 'book' became סֵפֶר *séfer*. The dependent form with possessive pronoun preserved the original stem vowel *i* when suffixes were added, e.g., סִפְרִי *sifrí* 'my book', סִפְרוּת *sifrút* 'literature'.

The plural of *segolate* nouns is a *mishkal* in itself, usually פְּעָלִים *(CCaCim)*; stress falls on the plural suffix:

Gloss	Dependent form			Plural		Singular	
children (of)	*yaldey-*	-יַלְדֵי	*yeladím*	יְלָדִים	*yéled*	יֶלֶד	
bridges (of)	*gishrey-*	-גִּשְׁרֵי	*gsharím*	גְּשָׁרִים	*gésher*	גֶּשֶׁר	

The *mishkal* of the plural of *segolate* nouns can also be פְּעָלוֹת.

Gloss	Dependent form			Plural		Singular	
horns (of)	*karnot-*	-קַרְנוֹת	*kranót*	קְרָנוֹת	*kéren*	קֶרֶן	
doors (of)	*daltot-*	-דַּלְתוֹת	*dlatót*	דְּלָתוֹת	*délet*	דֶּלֶת	

When the first stem vowel is *o*, that *o* remains. Sometimes the vowel *o* is maintained in the plural as well, particularly when the first segment is a guttural.

Gloss	Dependent form			Plural		Sing.	
mornings (of)	*bokrey-*	-בָּקְרֵי	*bkarím*	בְּקָרִים	בֹּקֶר	
months (of)	*ḥodshey-*	-חָדְשֵׁי	*ḥodashím*	חֳדָשִׁים	חֹדֶשׁ	
penalties (of)	*'onshey-*	-עָנְשֵׁי	*'onashím*	עֳנָשִׁים	עֹנֶשׁ	
roots (of)	*shorshey-*	-שָׁרְשֵׁי	*shorashím*	שָׁרָשִׁים	שֹׁרֶשׁ	

When the middle consonant of a *segolate* noun is י, the stem sequence *ayi* is reduced to *ey* in the dependent form: *báyit > beyt*:

Gloss	Dependent form	Plural	Singular	
synagogue	בֵּית כְּנֶסֶת, בָּתֵּי כְּנֶסֶת	בָּתִּים	*báyit*	בַּיִת

When the middle consonant of a *segolate* noun is ו, the stem sequence is reduced from *ave* to *o*, in the dependent form, thus *gaven > gon*:

the hue of the sky	גּוֹן הַשָּׁמַיִם	גְּוָנִים	*gáven*	גָּוֶן
hues of the rainbow	גּוֹנֵי הַקֶּשֶׁת			

The last two syllables of some feminine nouns display a *segolate* pattern, with the characteristic final *e* and penultimate stress. In the plural form the stress shifts to the last vowel; the plural pattern often contains the *a* stem vowel characteristic of the *segolate* plural, but a basic *o* is maintained, and is not reduced in the dependent form.

Gloss		Plural			Base
pipe	*miktarót*	מִקְטָרוֹת		*miktéret*	מִקְטֶרֶת
pipes of	*mikterot-*	מִקְטְרוֹת-			
skull	*karkafót*	קַרְקָפוֹת		*karkéfet*	קַרְקֶפֶת
skulls of	*karkefot-*	קַרְקְפוֹת-			
orchestra	*tizmorót(-)*	תִּזְמוֹרוֹת(-)		*tizmóret*	תִּזְמֹרֶת

The dependent form of nouns of the מִפְעָלָה pattern, מִפְעֶלֶת-, displays the segolate pattern:

Gloss		Plural			Base
restaurant	*mis`édet*	מִסְעֶדֶת-		*mis`ada*	מִסְעָדָה
police	*mishtéret*	מִשְׁטֶרֶת-		*mishtara*	מִשְׁטָרָה

5.9 Acronyms

Hebrew uses at least three types of acronyms:

1. Orthographic acronyms, such as WWII in English, that are never pronounced as such, i.e., are read always in full, as in:

		Source	Form
afternoon		אַחֲרֵי הַצָּהֳרַיִם	אחה״צ
God willing!		אִם יִרְצֶה הַשֵּׁם	איי״ה
God forbid!		חַס וְחָלִילָה	חו״ח
negotiations		מַשָּׂא וּמַתָּן	מו״מ

2. Letter acronyms, such as MP in English, in which the full name of each letter is pronounced (essentially restricted to two-letter acronyms), as in:

		Source	Form
military police		מִשְׁטָרָה צְבָאִית	מ״צ
gate guard (lit. battalion policeman)		שׁוֹטֵר גְּדוּדִי	ש״ג
under command (of)		תַּחַת פִּקוּד	ת״פ
company commander		מְפַקֵּד פְּלוּגָה	מ״פ

3. Pronounceable acronyms, like NATO, RADAR in English. Of those some deliberately seek to form sequences that correspond to existing catchy or relevant words (cf. English SALT), as in:

		Source		Form
women's corps		חֵיל נָשִׁים	*ħén*	חי״ן
per diem		אֲכִילָה שְׁתִיָּה לִינָה	*'éshel*	אשי״ל
kibbutz army units		נוֹעַר חֲלוּצֵי לוֹחֵם	*náħal*	נחי״ל

These particular catchy acronyms have an association with the following words:

Gloss	Associated word		Acronym
grace, beauty	חֵן	*ħén*	ח״ן
tamarisk	אֶשֶׁל	*'éshel*	אש״ל
river, stream	נַחַל	*náħal*	נח״ל

Other pronounceable acronyms involve vocalic components, such as:

Gloss	Source		Acronym
United Nations	אֻמּוֹת מְאוּחָדוֹת	*'úm*	או״ם
silverware	סַכִּין כַּף וּמַזְלֵג	*sakúm*	סכו״ם
missile boat	סְפִינַת טִילִים	*satíl*	סטי״ל

However, the major, most productive, acronym-forming device is what some refer to as root acronyms, where word-initial consonants or consonant sequences are treated as root consonants (or slots), and realized as pronounceable acronyms in *mishkalim*, or in a *mishkal*-like pattern based solely on 'plugging in' of the vowel *a* (see below). Of the preferred existing *mishkalim*, there are the *segolate* patterns *CéCeC* or *CáCaC* (when a guttural is involved), as in:

Gloss	Source		Acronym
Israel Defense Forces (IDF)	צְבָא הֲגַנָּה לְיִשְׂרָאֵל	*tsáhal*	צה״ל
training camp	בְּסִיס הַדְרָכָה	*báhad*	בה״ד
Israel's water authority	תִּכְנוּן הַמַּיִם לְיִשְׂרָאֵל	*táhal*	תה״ל
PX	שֵׁרוּת קַנְטִינוֹת מְזוֹנוֹנִים	*shékem*	שק״ם

Most root acronyms, however, are realized in strings that contain the vowel *a* only – the vowel which is the commonest and most prominent in Israeli Hebrew (note that sometimes, more than one segment is pulled from each base word):

Gloss	Source		Acronym
radar (lit. finder of direction and location)	מְגַלֶּה כִּיווּן מָקוֹם	*makam*	מכ״ם
general staff	מנהל כללי	*mankal*	מנכ״ל
chief of staff	ראש מטה כללי	*ramatkal*	רמטכ״ל

Note that acronyms are different from typical Hebrew words in one important respect: like borrowed words, they keep their stress pattern when inflectional suffixes (like the feminine or plural suffixes) are added to them, whereas in native stems, the stress usually shifts to the inflectional suffix:

| friends | *ħaverím* | חברים | friend | *ħavér* | חבר |
| radars | *makámim* | מכ״מים | radar | *makám* | מכ״ם |

Chapter 6
Pronouns

Pronouns are a subclass of nouns. They are used to refer to nouns or noun phrases, whose identity is known or has already been established, either by the context of a conversation or by presence elsewhere in a text, or is implied by the situation:

Noun phrase	We have <u>friends</u> in Haifa.	יש לנו <u>חברים</u> בחיפה.
Pronoun	<u>They</u> work in a hotel.	<u>הם</u> עובדים במלון.

Pronouns can occur in different positions in the sentence and have different syntactical functions.

Subject	Omer is our friend. <u>He</u> works in a bank.	עומר חבר שלנו. <u>הוא</u> עובד בבנק.
Direct Object	We saw <u>him</u> when he entered the bank.	ראינו <u>אותו</u> כשנכסנו לבנק.
Indirect Object	We don't have confidence <u>in him</u>.	אנחנו לא בוטחים <u>בו</u>.

6.1 Forms of personal pronouns

In Hebrew personal pronouns can have the shape of 'stand alone' independent words that function as subjects of clauses and sentences, or they can be dependent elements prefixed to words or suffixed to words. They can have different functions in the sentence: they can be a subject or a direct or indirect object.

Independent Pronoun

<u>I</u> am a student at the university.

אֲנִי סטודנט באוניברסיטה.

Pronoun suffixed to a preposition

<u>My</u> Dad works in a bank.

אבא שֶׁלִי עובד בבנק.

Pronoun suffixed to a noun

<u>My</u> Dad works in a bank.

אבִי עובד בבנק.

Pronoun suffixed to a verb

<u>I worked</u> with my Dad.

עבדתִי עם אבא שלי.

Pronoun prefixed to a verb

In the summer <u>I'll work</u> in the bank.

בקיץ אני אֲעבוד בבנק.

Reference to personal pronouns

Personal pronouns do not necessarily refer to persons. In the third person they can refer to objects, events, abstract notions and any other noun or noun phrase that is not human. In English these pronouns are expressed by the word *it* for the singular. However, in Hebrew there is no neuter pronoun, such as *it*, and since all nouns have a gender assigned to them, they are referred to as 'he' or 'she' or 'they', depending on the gender of the noun.

<u>Person</u>	<u>David</u> works at the bank in town. <u>He</u> is a branch manager.	<u>דוד</u> עובד בבנק בעיר. <u>הוא</u> מנהל סניף.
<u>Animal</u>	<u>These dogs</u> are old. <u>They</u> lie on the rug all day long.	<u>הכלבים האלה</u> כבר זקנים. <u>הם</u> שוכבים כל היום על השטיח.
<u>Object</u>	<u>My television</u> doesn't work. <u>It</u> is being fixed.	<u>הטלוויזיה</u> שלי לא עובדת. <u>היא</u> בתיקון.
<u>Concept</u>	This is a great <u>idea</u>! <u>It</u> can save us a lot of money.	זה <u>רעיון</u> מצוין! <u>הוא</u> יכול לחסוך לנו הרבה כסף.
<u>Event</u>	It is too bad you did not come to <u>the party</u>. <u>It</u> was very successful.	חבל שלא באתם <u>למסיבה</u>. <u>היא</u> הייתה מוצלחת מאוד.

6.2 Independent subject pronouns

Subject pronouns, as implied by their name, occupy the position of subjects in clauses or sentences. Subject pronouns can be independent words, as they are in English, or they can be attached in some way to other words.

Independent subject pronouns

<u>Singular</u>	*Masc./fem.*	I	אֲנִי	*זכר ונקבה*	<u>יחיד/ה</u>
	Masc.	you	אַתָּה	*זכר*	
	Fem.	you	אַתְּ	*נקבה*	
	Masc.	he	הוּא	*זכר*	
	Fem	she	הִיא	*נקבה*	
<u>Plural</u>	*Masc./fem*	we	אֲנַחְנוּ	*זכר ונקבה*	<u>רבים/רבות</u>
	Masc.	you	אַתֶּם	*זכר*	
	Fem.	you	אַתֶּן	*נקבה*	
	Masc.	they	הֵם	*זכר*	
	Fem.	they	הֵן	*נקבה*	

6.2.1 Common bases for pronoun forms

The common basis for the first person pronoun is (א)נ- in אני, אנחנו.

The common basis for the second person is the beginning of the word אַתּ-, while the plural endings signify both plurality and gender: the final -ם is a masculine plural marker and the final ן- is the feminine plural marker.

All third person forms הוא, היא, הם, הן begin with ה-. Unlike in English, where the third person plural *they* refers to both feminine and masculine, in Hebrew the masculine plural pronoun ends with ם- *-m* and the feminine plural pronoun ends with ן- *-n*.

Comparative notes

There are ten independent pronouns in Hebrew. In English, however, there are seven (six of them refer to human nouns, and one refers to other objects or abstract nouns). The gender features of the Hebrew pronouns are present in both the second and third person forms, but not in the first person forms. אני represents 'I' for both masculine and feminine, and אנחנו represents both masculine and feminine 'we'. In English, gender features, i.e. masculine and feminine distinctions, are only present in 'he' and 'she', but not in other pronouns.

Hebrew, like English, has personal pronouns that refer to persons. However, unlike English, there is no personal pronoun *it* that refers to non-human animate or inanimate objects, as well as abstract concepts. The third person pronouns ('he', 'she', 'they' = הוא, היא, הם, הן) are used to refer to non-human nouns as well. Since all nouns have gender and number features, the choice of the appropriate pronoun for non-living objects is clear.

Note

The final הָ- ending, which is usually associated with feminine singular nouns, marks the masculine singular form אַתָּה, while the form אַתְּ without the ending הָ- is used for the feminine singular.

6.2.2 First and second persons

In a conversation mode, the speaker and addressee (person being spoken to) use the first and second pronouns to refer to each other.

<u>Singular</u>	יחיד
David, do <u>you</u> call home every day?	דוד, <u>אתה</u> מתקשר הביתה כל יום?
No. <u>I</u> phone once a week.	לא. <u>אני</u> מטלפן פעם בשבוע.

<u>Plural</u>	רבים
What are <u>you</u> doing? Don't <u>you</u> see that <u>you</u> are stepping on my flowers? <u>We</u> are sorry. <u>We</u> did not pay any attention.	מה <u>אתם</u> עושים? <u>אתם</u> לא רואים שאתם דורכים על הפרחים שלי? <u>אנחנו</u> מצטערים. לא שמנו לב.

A historical note

אני = אנוכי

There are variant forms to some pronouns. In biblical literature, the first person אֲנִי also has the form of אָנֹכִי. This alternate form may appear in Modern Hebrew in formal speech or in literature. This is true particularly in poetry where it is used to create an artistic effect.

Example from biblical literature

"I am a stranger and live amongst you".
(Genesis 23, 4)

גר ותושב אָנֹכִי עמכם.
(בראשית כ"ג: ד')

"Who am I to go to Pharaoh?"
(Numbers 3, 11)

מי אָנֹכִי כי אלך אל פרעה.
(שמות ג: י"א)

Example from poetry

"That's how I am: quiet like the water in the lake".
(Rachel, "I")

כזאת אָנֹכִי: שקטה כמימי אגם.
(רחל "אני").

אנחנו = אָנוּ

The first person plural pronoun אֲנַחְנוּ has a variant form of אָנוּ. While this variation does not appear in biblical texts, its use can be traced back to early Mishnaic Hebrew and it has continued to be used until today. This alternate form appears in formal speech, and in literary texts, particularly in poetry.

Example from Mishnaic literature

...that on all nights we eat leavened bread and *matsa* ...

...שבכל הלילות אָנוּ אוכלין חמץ ומצה...

Example from a literary text

We live in a different world and forget where we came from and where we are going.

אָנוּ חיים בעולם אחר. שוכחים מאין באנו ולאן אָנוּ הולכים.

Example from a popular song

We came to this land to build and be built.

אָנוּ באנו ארצה לבנות ולהיבנות בה.

As mentioned earlier, the third person is not used solely to refer to people, but also to refer to objects, concepts, and events that are included in sentences or larger discourse units (such as a paragraph, or an entire text). There is no neutral third person pronoun *it*, and the masculine and feminine pronouns are used to refer to non-human nouns, depending on the grammatical gender of the noun.

Objects	The <u>library</u> opens at eight. <u>It (she)</u> closes at ten at night.	<u>הַסִּפְרִיָּיה</u> נפתחת בשמונה. <u>הִיא</u> נסגרת בעשר בלילה.
Events	These are interesting <u>events</u>! <u>They</u> can change the results of the elections.	אלה <u>אירועים</u> מעניינים! <u>הם</u> יכולים לשנות את תוצאות הבחירות.
Animals	The <u>lion</u> is the king of the beasts. <u>It</u> lives in Africa.	<u>הָאַרְיֵה</u> הוא מלך החיות. <u>הוא</u> חי באפריקה.

6.2.3 Word order - independent pronouns
Pronoun follows the noun to which it refers
In most cases the noun phrase precedes the pronoun; the pronoun repeats it by a different word. The reference can be not just to a noun or a noun phrase, but also to a sentence or a content expressed by several sentences in a larger discourse unit. (This phenomenon is called anaphoric reference). The examples brought here are from within the sentence domain.

Out of milk? No problem! It's always possible to go to <u>our grocery store</u>, since <u>it</u> is open all night.

נגמר החלב? אין בעיה. אפשר תמיד לקפוץ <u>למכּולת שלנו</u>, כי <u>היא</u> פתוחה כל הלילה.

<u>The students</u> were not here in the summer, but <u>they</u>'ll return at the beginning of the school year.

<u>הסטודנטים</u> לא היו כאן בקיץ, אבל <u>הם</u> יחזרו בתחילת שנת הלימודים.

Pronoun precedes the noun to which it refers
In some cases, the sequential order of the noun phrase and pronoun is reversed. The pronoun precedes the noun phrase that it refers to. We find out only later in the discourse to what the pronoun refers. (This phenomenon is called cataphoric referencing).

Even though <u>he</u> said <u>he</u> would come early, <u>David</u> did not show up till midnight.

אם כי <u>הוא</u> אמר שהוא יבוא מוקדם, <u>דוד</u> לא הופיע עד חצות.

While <u>she</u> conversed with friends, <u>Dina's mother</u> did not pay attention to the fact that Dina disappeared.

בזמן <u>שהיא</u> שוחחה עם חברות, <u>אמא של דינה</u> לא שמה לב לכך שדינה נעלמה.

Ellipsis of subject pronouns

In conversations, or written passages, it is quite common that once the third person subject has been mentioned, the pronoun is omitted in subsequent sentences. Its presence is implied rather than being openly expressed.

<u>Example from a conversation</u>

So what was <u>David</u> doing there?	אז מה <u>דוד</u> עשה שם?
(He) was just standing and waiting for her to come out.	סתם עמד וחיכה לה עד שתצא.

<u>Example from a written passage</u>

<u>Yitzhak Eliyahu</u> put on his professional look anticipating the woman...twenty minutes later (he) stood by the apartment door...only then did (he) turn to ask her to come in.	<u>יצחק אליהו</u> לבש מאור פנים מקצועי לקראת האישה... עשרים דקות לאחר מזה עמד מול דלת הדירה...רק אז פנה להזמין אותה להיכנס.

6.3 Pronoun suffixes and prefixes in verbs and in existential expressions

When verbs appear in the past tense or in the future tense in the first and second persons, the subject pronouns are included in the verb form. For example, in Hebrew the past tense verb form עָבַדְתִּי 'I worked', combines both the subject and the verb stem in the past tense. In English the same notion is expressed by two separate words: one for the subject pronoun and one for the verb.

6.3.1 Past tense suffixes

In the past tense the subject pronouns of the first and second person are suffixed to the past verb stem. Since the verb form itself is marked for number, gender, and person, the independent pronoun becomes redundant, and thus optional.

Here are the first and second person future tense forms with subject pronoun suffixes. The pronoun is the last component of the verb form.

<u>First and second person singular</u>

I, you met	(את) פגשתְּ	(אתה) פגשתָ	(אני) פגש<u>תי</u>

<u>First and second person plural</u>

we, you met	(אתן) פגשתֶן	(אתם) פגשתֶם	(אנחנו) פגש<u>נו</u>

In the third person, however, the independent pronouns are obligatory. The verb form of the third person does not include person features. It includes the features of number (singular/plural) and gender (masculine/feminine) but not person.

Third person singular
he, she met   היא פגשה   הוא פגש
Third person plural
they (masc. and fem.) met   הן פגשו   הם פגשו

There are cases, however, when second person independent pronouns are used with the past tense verb:
1. In informal spoken Hebrew the independent first person subject pronoun is often included: אני כתבתי.
2. Independent subject pronouns are used to emphasize the subject, so as to indicate a contrast between a particular subject and another:

I wrote this letter – not Dan.   אֲנִי כתבתֵי את המכתב ולא דן.

6.3.2 Future tense prefixes
In the future tense the first and second person subject pronouns come at the beginning of each verb form as prefixes to the future verb stem. Look at the following sentence:
We shall meet Dan in a café.   נָפגוש את דן בבית קפה.

Notice that the verbal expression נפגוש 'we shall meet' is rendered by three words in English, but it is one word in Hebrew.

Here are the first and second person future tense forms of the verb with subject pronoun prefixes. The pronoun is the first component of the verb form. As in the past tense, the independent subject pronouns are redundant, and thus optional, but in daily speech the first person singular pronoun is often included, even though it is incorporated in the verb prefix.

First and second person singular
I, you will meet   (את) תפגשי   (אתה) תפגוש   אני אפגוש
First and second person plural
we, you will meet   (אתן) תפגשו   (אתם) תפגשו   (אנחנו) נפגוש

In the third person, as in the past tense, the independent pronouns are obligatory. The verb form of the third person does not include person features. It includes the features of number (singular/plural) and gender (masculine/feminine) but not person.

<u>Third person singular</u>

he, she will meet	היא תפגוש	הוא יפגוש

<u>Third person plural</u>

they (masc. and fem.) will meet	הן יפגשו	הם יפגשו

The affixes for את, אתם, אתן, הם, הן include a prefix and a suffix: the prefix indicates the person while the suffix indicates gender and number.

(את) ת+פגש+י, (אתם/ן) ת+פגש+ו, הם הן י+פגש+ו

6.3.3 Subject pronouns added to existential expressions

In some registers of Hebrew, from biblical Hebrew to present day formal language, there is a restricted use of personal pronoun subjects that are added to some expressions. The subject suffix is most commonly added to the existential expressions יֵשׁ/אֵין. It is also used in some fixed expressions, especially in legal or technical language.

Pronoun suffixes for the negative particle אין

The most common use of this suffixed pronoun is in the negation expression אֵין, which is only used with present tense participles.

אֵינְךָ שומע אותי? אתה חֵרֵשׁ?   Don't <u>you</u> hear me? Are you deaf?

The suffixed pronoun is also used to negate an existential state.

פעם היה כאן תיאטרון, אבל היום   Once there used to be a theater here,

הוא כבר אֵינֶנּוּ.   but today it <u>is gone</u>.

Personal pronoun suffixes for אין

Paraphrase				Paraphrase	
				אני לא	אֵינֶנִּי /אֵינִי
הוא לא	הוא אֵינֶנּוּ/אֵינוֹ			*אתה לא*	אֵינְךָ
היא לא	היא אֵינֶנָּה/אֵינָהּ			*את לא*	אֵינֵךְ
				אנחנו לא	אֵינֶנּוּ
הם לא	הם אֵינָם			*אתם לא*	אֵינְכֶם
הן לא	הן אֵינָן			*אתן לא*	אֵינְכֶן

| Formal | I do not know if he intends to come. | אֵינֶנִּי יודע אם הוא מתכוון לבוא. |
| Daily speech | I don't know if he is planning to come. | אני לא יודע אם הוא מתכוון לבוא. |

The third person forms are also used in the negation of nominal sentences in the present tense. The suffixes reflect the subject gender and number features.

The house is not new.	הבית אֵינֶנּוּ חדש.
The university is not big.	האוניברסיטה אֵינֶנָּה גדולה.
The children are not at home.	הילדים אֵינָם בבית.
The girls are not in the room.	הבנות אֵינָן בחדר.

Pronoun suffixes for the existential expression יש

The positive existential expression יש 'there is/there are' can carry third person subject pronoun suffixes. A noun may follow it, or it may be preceded by a subject pronoun. It often serves as the link between subject and predicate, much as the verb 'to be' serves that function in English.

3rd person suffixes to the positive particle יש

Gloss	Paraphrase	
he is	הוא נמצא/קיים	הוא יֶשְׁנוֹ
she is	היא נמצאת/קיימת	היא יֶשְׁנָה
they (masc.) are	הם נמצאים/קיימים	הם יֶשְׁנָם
they (fem.) are	הן נמצאות/קיימות	הן יֶשְׁנָן

| They say, "there is a land". | אומרים יֶשְׁנָה ארץ. |
| There is a heightened risk for heart patients to suffer a stroke. | לחולי לב יֶשְׁנוֹ סיכון מוגבר ללקות באירוע מוחי. |

6.3.4 Fixed expressions

There are other fixed expressions to which this suffix subject pronoun is used (mostly in the first person). These expressions are used extensively in post-biblical Hebrew. In Israeli Hebrew they are used in the formal registers of the language. In speech they can be found mostly in the language used for delivering formal addresses. In written form they are used in legal documents, and academic and technical discussions as well as official documents. They are used stylistically in official language.

I hereby	הִנְנִי = הנה אני
I believe/it seems to me	דּוֹמָנִי = אני משער, נדמה לי
I think, I am of the opinion	סָבוּרְנִי/סְבוּרָנִי = אני סבור

<u>Formal/legalistic announcement</u>   <u>הנני</u>

I <u>hereby</u> notify…   ...<u>הנני</u> מודיע(ה) בזאת

<u>From a formal correspondence</u>   <u>דומני</u>

<u>It seems to me</u> that you are confusing two things.   <u>דומני</u> שאתה מערבב בין שני דברים.

<u>From a legal document</u>   <u>סבורני</u>

In the light of the results of this appeal, <u>I am of the opinion</u> that each side should bear in the expenses of the appeal.   לאור התוצאות בערעור זה, <u>סבורני</u> שנכון שכל צד ישא בהוצאותיו בערעור.

6.4 Pronouns suffixed to nouns and prepositions

6.4.1 Added to singular noun forms and some prepositions

There are two sets of pronoun suffixes attached to the end of nouns or prepositions. One consists of a set of suffixes that are attached to singular nouns and to most prepositions. The other is a set of suffixes, which are attached to plural nouns and to a small number of prepositions.

For a more complete discussion of prepositions and pronominal endings, see pp. 228-235.

When pronoun suffixes are attached to nouns, they become possessive pronouns.

Pronoun suffixes attached to singular nouns

	Plural			Singular	
3rd	2nd	1st	3rd	2nd	1st
־ָם	־ְכֶם	־נוּ	־ו	־ְךָ	־ִי
־ָן	־ְכֶן		־ָהּ	־ֵךְ	

Ella, does <u>your</u> aunt live in Haifa?	‏אלה, דּוֹדָתֵךְ גרה בחיפה?
No. <u>My</u> aunt and <u>my</u> uncle live not far from Tel Aviv.	‏לא. דּוֹדִי ודוֹדָתִי גרים לא רחוק מתל-אביב.
Maccabi Petah Tiqvah will not be able to host Maccabi Haifa on Sunday in <u>its</u> stadium.	‏מכבי פתח תקווה לא תוכל לארח את מכבי חיפה ביום ראשון באיצטדיונהַ.

<u>This set of suffixes is also used for many prepositions:</u>

‏ל-, של, מ-, בשביל, עבור, את, מול, עם, אצל

He planted himself <u>across from us</u>.	‏הוא נעמד <u>מוּלנוּ</u> ולא זז.
Give <u>me</u> <u>my</u> book back.	‏החזר <u>לִי</u> את הספר <u>שֶׁלִּי</u>.
It was not easy. Believe <u>me</u>.	‏זה לא היה קל. תאמינו <u>לִי</u>.
We wanted to bring <u>him</u> back to reality.	‏רצינו להחזיר <u>אותוֹ</u> למציאות.

6.4.2 Added to plural noun forms and some prepositions
Pronoun suffixes attached to plural nouns

	Plural			Singular	
3rd	2nd	1st	3rd	2nd	1st
‏-ֵיהֶם	‏-ֵיכֶם	‏-ֵינוּ	‏-ָיו	‏-ֶיךָ	‏-ַי
‏-ֵיהֶן	‏-ֵיכֶן		‏-ֶיהָ	‏-ַיִךְ	

Ella, do <u>your parents</u> live in Haifa?	‏אלה, <u>הוֹרַיִךְ</u> גרים בחיפה?
The (its) owner of the soccer team promised that the club will not be closed as long as he is alive.	‏<u>בעליהַ</u> של קבוצת הכדורגל הבטיח שהמועדון לא ייסגר כל עוד הוא בחיים.

This set of suffixes is also used for some prepositions:

‏על, לפני, אחרי, אודות

He came <u>to us</u>.	‏הוא בא <u>אלינוּ</u>.
We heard a lot <u>about him</u>.	‏שמענו הרבה <u>עליו</u>.

6.4.3 The use of possessive pronouns
The use of pronouns as possessive suffixes is a feature of classical Hebrew, carried over to today's formal registers. In common use of Israeli Hebrew, however, this use is limited. Instead, in everyday language, the possessed noun is followed by the preposition of possession ‏שֶׁל 'of', with pronouns attached to it.

Gloss	Colloquial	Formal Register
our neighbor	השכן שֶׁלָּנוּ	שְׁכֵנֵנוּ
their friends	הידידים שֶׁלָּהֶם	יְדִידֵיהֶם

Notable exceptions are the various kinship terms that have managed to (optionally) maintain the noun + pronoun structure owing to the frequency of their use. The possessive relationship is indicated either with suffix pronouns or with a possession phrase. For instance, both אבי and אבא שלי are used in everyday speech.

| my father/my Dad | אבא שֶׁלִּי | אָבִי |
| her aunt | הדודה שֶׁלָּהּ | דּוֹדָתָהּ |

Note that even in the formal registers, one cannot add pronoun suffixes to nouns that are loan words.

| You can't fool around <u>at our office</u>. | <u>במשרד שלנו</u> לא מתבטלים. |
| Doesn't <u>your television</u> work? | <u>הטלוויזיה שלכם</u> לא עובדת? |

6.5 Demonstrative pronouns

The demonstrative pronoun is a pronoun or determiner that is used to indicate a referent's spatial, temporal or discourse location. It functions as a pronoun and as a modifier.

The demonstrative pronoun, as its name suggests, is used in some cases at the head of a sentence, as the subject. It ordinarily precedes the noun to which it refers. It points to living things or objects. Gender and number agreement with the noun to which it refers is required.

Demonstrative pronouns as an indicator of the referent's location in space and time or identity:

Masc. Sing.	this (is)	זֶה
Fem. Sing.	this (is)	זֹאת/זוֹ
Plural	these (are)	אֵלֶּה/אֵלּוּ

<u>This</u> is our <u>house</u>.	<u>זֶה</u> הבית שלנו.
<u>This</u> is not my <u>problem</u>. <u>It</u> is your problem.	<u>זֹאת</u> לא <u>הבעיה שלי</u> - <u>זֹאת הבעיה</u> שלך.
<u>These</u> are difficult <u>days</u>.	<u>אֵלֶּה</u> הם <u>ימים</u> קשים.

These were once woods, and now look at what happened to them! They were all chopped down.	אֵלּוּ היו פעם יערות - ועכשיו תסתכל מה שקרה להם! כרתו את כולם.

As a modifier, the demonstrative pronoun is part of a phrase:

I live in this house.	אני גר בבית הזה.
This problem can be solved.	ניתן לפתור את הבעיה הזאת.
These pictures are not for sale.	התמונות האלה לא למכירה.

6.5.1 Using זה for general reference

In spoken Hebrew the demonstrative pronoun זֶה 'this' can be used to refer to nouns or noun phrases, regardless of their gender and number. It is considered non-normative usage, but is used in daily informal speech.

	Normative	Colloquial
This can be a problem!	זֹאת יכולה להיות בעיה	זֶה יכול להיות בעיה!

The demonstrative pronoun זה is also used to serve as a link in a sentence that has no verb. It links the two parts of the sentence in the same way that the verb 'to be' in English links such parts, or actually separates the two parts of the sentence. The predicate that is introduced by the link זה supplies a comment to the topic, supplied by the subject of the sentence. This structure is particularly useful to separate a lengthy subject or topic from its predicate or comment.

What we are doing for him is a difficult thing.	מה שאנחנו עושים בשבילו זה דבר קשה.

In spoken Hebrew it can also be used in the past and future, just as the verb 'to be' is used to indicate the time aspect.

What we did for him was a difficult thing.	מה שעשינו בשבילו זה היה דבר קשה.
What we did for him will be a difficult thing.	מה שעשינו בשבילו זה יהיה דבר קשה.

6.5.2 Reference to contexts beyond the noun phrase

The demonstrative pronoun singular masculine זֶה is also used to refer to an entire idea or situation, or a sequence of events. These references are either specifically expressed earlier in a sentence, or a larger discourse unit, or it is part of what is generally understood from the context external to the text. In this case rather than referring to a noun or noun phrase, the pronoun stands for a larger context. In English the pronoun *it* is used to refer to such a sequence, while in Hebrew the demonstrative pronoun זֶה is used to perform the same function.

When I was invited to meetings, I always went, even though <u>it</u> was not convenient, and <u>it</u> disrupted work.	כשהזמינו אותי למפגשים, תמיד הלכתי, למרות שזֶה לא היה נוח וזֶה הפריע לי בעבודה.
If it is not <u>this</u>, then it is something else.	אם זה לא זֶה, אז זה משהו אחר.

זה can also be used to introduce an exclamatory sentence:

That's not nice!	זֶה לא יפה!
That's not what is done here!	זֶה לא מה שעושים כאן!
I don't like this at all!	זֶה לא מוצא חן בעיני!

6.5.3 Use of the feminine singular זאת for general reference

There are occasions where the feminine demonstrative pronoun זאת functions in the same manner. It is less common, and often indicates a more formal use of language.

I intend to say something to him each time that he does <u>this</u>.	אני מתכוון להעיר לו כל פעם שהוא עושה זאת.

There are certain fixed expressions where זאת is part of the expression and cannot be changed to masculine זה:

What does <u>it</u> mean? /What do you mean by this?	מה זאת אומרת?
<u>And in any case</u>, I don't think that there is no hope.	ובכל זאת, אני לא חושב שאין תקווה.

6.6 Interrogative and relative pronouns

6.6.1 The interrogative pronoun: who and what? מי ומה

The interrogative pronoun is one that is used as a question word. As in English, there is one interrogative pronoun מי that is equivalent to *who*, and another interrogative pronoun מה that is equivalent to *what*. These interrogative pronouns, as implied by their name, initiate questions, which elicit information about the subject of the sentence.

<u>Who</u> told you that there is no class today?	מִי אמר לכם שאין שיעור היום?
<u>What</u> happened to you?	מַה קרה לכם?

The interrogative pronouns can be used as question words with appropriate prepositions. The question is not about the subject of the sentence but about a prepositional complement.

<u>What</u> do you want?	מַה את רוצה?
<u>Whose</u> is this book?	שֶׁל מִי הספר הזה?
<u>What</u> did you talk <u>about</u>?	עַל מַה דיברתם?

Use in speech:

In spoken Hebrew, it is much more common to omit the direct object particle אֶת when the question word is מַה 'what', even when the question is about the object of the transitive verb:

<u>What</u> are you looking for?	(אֶת) מַה את מחפשׂת?

6.6.2 'whoever' and 'whatever'

Hebrew relative clauses modify nouns. They follow the nouns that they modify and are introduced by the subordinating particles -שֶׁ or אֲשֶׁר.

<u>The girls who</u> play soccer will go to play in Haifa.	הבנות שֶׁמשחקות כדורגל ייסעו לשחק בחיפה.
	הבנות אֲשֶׁר משחקות כדורגל ייסעו לשחק בחיפה.

When the identity of the noun is not known, the pronouns מי 'who' or מה 'what' fill the slot of the unknown noun. They are followed by the subordinating particle -שֶׁ that is an obligatory particle required for introducing relative clauses.

Whoever	...מִי שֶׁ
Anyone/everyone who	...כָּל מִי שֶׁ
Whatever	...מַה שֶׁ
Anything/everything that	...כָּל מַה שֶׁ

The following illustrations introduce sentences where nouns fill the subject and object slots, and other sentences where pronouns take the nouns' place when their identity is not known or suggest an inclusive pronoun:

1. Subject: ..ש מי 'Whoever'

<u>Subject: 'the people (who..)'</u>

<u>The people who</u> bought tickets in advance, can board the train now.

..האנשים ש<u></u>

<u>האנשים שֶׁ</u>קנו כרטיסים מראש יכולים לעלות לרכבת עכשיו.

<u>Subject: 'whoever'</u>

<u>Whoever</u> bought tickets in advance, can board the train now.

(..מי (ש<u></u>

<u>מי שֶׁ</u>קנה כרטיסים מראש יכול לעלות לרכבת עכשיו.

2. Subject: ..ש מה 'What(ever)'

<u>Object: rumors (which..)</u>

We heard about him all kinds of <u>rumors</u>, which were all true.

(..מושא: שמועות (ש<u></u>

שמענו עליו כל מיני <u>שמועות</u>, שהיו נכונות.

<u>Object: whatever</u>

<u>What(ever)</u> we heard about him was true.

(..מושא: מה (ש<u></u>

<u>מה שֶׁ</u>שמענו עליו, היה נכון.

These structures can function as subjects, as direct and indirect objects, and in prepositional phrases.

1. In a subject position

<u>Whoever</u> wants to come – can do so.

<u>כל/מי</u> שֶׁרוצה לבוא - יכול.

<u>Whatever</u> I told you is absolutely true.

<u>כל מה</u> שֶׁאמרתי לכם שריר וקיים.

2. In direct object position

I saw <u>everybody</u> I wanted to see.

ראיתי את <u>כל מי</u> שֶׁרציתי לראות.

3. In indirect object position

We spoke about <u>what</u> happened and about <u>everything </u>that we went through.

דיברנו על <u>מה</u> שַקרה ועל <u>כל מה</u> <u>ש</u>עבר עלינו.

6.7 Impersonal pronouns: something/nothing

Impersonal pronouns refer to entities that not are specifically identified. There are several ways to express an impersonal pronoun, including omitting them altogether.

<u>In a subject position</u>

<u>Someone</u> told us that the show was cancelled.

<u>מִישֶהוּ</u> אמר לנו שהההצגה בוטלה.

<u>Everyone</u> will tell you that there is no problem.

<u>כָּל אֶחָד</u> יגיד לך שאין בעיה.

<u>Everybody</u> (all) thinks that you left town.

<u>כּוּלָם</u> חושבים שעזבת את העיר.

<u>Nobody </u>knows when he will return.

<u>אַף אֶחָד לֹא</u> יודע מתי הוא יחזור.

<u>In an object position</u>

He gave your book to <u>someone</u>.

הוא נתן את הסֵפר שלך <u>לְמִישֶהוּ</u>.

We still have not heard from <u>everyone</u>.

עדיין לא שמענו <u>מִכָּל אֶחָד</u>.

They invited <u>everybody</u> to the party.

הם הזמינו <u>אֶת כּוּלָם</u> למסיבה.

Dan told <u>nobody</u> when he'd be coming back.

דן לא אמר <u>לְאַף אֶחָד</u> מתי הוא יחזור.

6.7.1 Omission of impersonal pronouns

In English indefinite pronouns can be expressed by the noun *one*, or by the pronouns *you* or *they* and sometimes *people* when they refer to an indefinite, non-specific entity. In Hebrew the subject pronoun is omitted altogether in such cases, and only the verbal predicate is present. It is a subjectless sentence that uses a third person masculine plural form of the verb (in past, present or future).

Subject	Predicate	נשוא	נושא
You	add a cup of sugar to the flour and butter mixture.	מוסיפים כוס סוכר לתערובת של הקמח והחמאה.	Ø
People	come to visit here from all corners of the world.	באים לבקר כאן מכל קצוות העולם.	Ø
They	told me that there are plenty of things to do here.	אמרו לי שיש הרבה מה לעשות כאן.	Ø
One	used to play soccer here, until the city closed the park .	היו משחקים כאן כדורגל, עד שהעירייה סגרה את הפארק.	Ø

When the predicate is a transitive verb, the passive verb is often used in English.

Subject + Predicate	נשוא	נושא
The plant <u>was closed</u> three months ago.	<u>סגרו</u> את המפעל לפני שלושה חדשים.	Ø
The stories of the first settlers <u>were not documented</u>.	<u>לא תיעדו</u> את הסיפורים של המתיישבים הראשונים.	Ø
What a pity!	חבל!	

Chapter 7
Numerals

A numeral is a word, functioning most typically as an adjective, a quantifier or a pronoun that expresses a number, and a relation to the number, such as one of the following: quantity, sequence, frequency and fraction. The following kinds of numerals will be discussed:

In terms of form and syntactic role, the main distinction within the numeral category is between 'cardinal' numbers, which are used in counting and as quantifiers of nouns, and 'ordinal' numbers, which behave like adjectives. In terms of function, however, one should distinguish between cardinal numbers used to quantify the nouns they follow, and those used in 'free counting', which refer to sequential counting.

Note
In this chapter, אי and עי are represented in the transcription only in stressed final syllables, where ['] is most likely to be heard (c.g., מֵאָה).

7.1 Free counting
Free counting involves a flow of numbers without reference to objects. Hebrew uses the feminine independent numbers in counting – see discussion of feminine and masculine numbers in the section on cardinal numbers below. Aside from being used in counting, counting numbers are also used in the following contexts:

1. <u>In naming and labeling objects</u>

Bus number 5   אוטובוס מספר חמש

6 Hertzl Street   רחוב הרצל מספר שש

2. <u>In conveying telephone numbers</u>

051-632-7894   אפס, חמש, אחת – שש, שלוש, שתיים – שבע, שמונה,

                                            תשע, ארבע

3. <u>In mathematics</u>

For various arithmetical functions, as in the following example:

  $1 + 1 = 2$ אחת ועוד אחת הם* שתיים

* In the arithmetic, הם stands for 'is/are'.

Single numbers

aḥát	אַחַת	1
shtáyim	שְׁתַּיִם	2
shalósh	שָׁלוֹשׁ	3
arbá	אַרְבַּע	4
ḥamésh	חָמֵשׁ	5
shésh	שֵׁשׁ	6
shéva	שֶׁבַע	7
shmóne	שְׁמוֹנֶה	8
tésha	תֵּשַׁע	9
éser	עֶשֶׂר	10

The zero value is conveyed by the masculine noun אֶפֶס *éfes*.

Teens

The teen numbers (11-19) are a combination of the nouns for single digits (in dependent form) and עֶשְׂרֵה- '-teen':

aḥát esrè	אַחַת עֶשְׂרֵה	11
shtéym esrè	שְׁתֵּים עֶשְׂרֵה	12
shlósh esrè	שְׁלוֹשׁ עֶשְׂרֵה	13
arbá esrè	אַרְבַּע עֶשְׂרֵה	14
ḥamésh esrè	חֲמֵשׁ עֶשְׂרֵה	15
shésh esrè	שֵׁשׁ עֶשְׂרֵה	16
shvá esrè	שְׁבַע עֶשְׂרֵה	17
shmoné esrè	שְׁמוֹנֶה עֶשְׂרֵה	18
tshá esrè	תְּשַׁע עֶשְׂרֵה	19

Numbers 20-90 take a plural form. Except for the number עֶשְׂרִים 'twenty', which is actually the plural form of 'ten', the rest of the 'tens' are the plural form of the singular. From שלוש 'three' you get שְׁלוֹשִׁים 'thirty', and so on.

esrím	עֶשְׂרִים	20
shloshím	שְׁלוֹשִׁים	30
arba´ím	אַרְבָּעִים	40
ħamishím	חֲמִשִּׁים	50
shishím	שִׁשִּׁים	60
shiv´ím	שִׁבְעִים	70
shmoním	שְׁמוֹנִים	80
tish´ím	תִּשְׁעִים	90

Single digits are added to these numbers with the conjunction 'and' -וּ to form the more complex numbers. Thus the number 'twenty-one' is expressed as 'twenty and one': עֶשְׂרִים וְאַחַת.

esrím ve-aħát	עֶשְׂרִים וְאַחַת	21
esrím u-shtáyim	עֶשְׂרִים וּשְׁתַּיִם	22
esrím ve-shalósh	עֶשְׂרִים וְשָׁלוֹשׁ	23
esrím ve-arbá	עֶשְׂרִים וְאַרְבַּע	24
esrím ve-ħamésh	עֶשְׂרִים וְחָמֵשׁ	25
esrím va-shésh	עֶשְׂרִים וָשֵׁשׁ	26
esrím va-shéva	עֶשְׂרִים וָשֶׁבַע	27
esrím u-shmoné	עֶשְׂרִים וּשְׁמוֹנֶה	28
esrím va-tésha	עֶשְׂרִים וָתֵשַׁע	29

Note
a. In normative Hebrew:
The conjunction -וְ becomes -וּ before a consonant with a 'zero *shva*', e.g. עֶשְׂרִים וּשְׁתַּיִם *esrím u-shtáyim* (*esrím ve-shtáyim* is a colloquial variant), עֶשְׂרִים וּשְׁמוֹנֶה *esrím u-shmoné* (*esrím ve-shmóne* in the colloquial, or a 'midway' compromise: *esrím u-shmóne*). The conjunction -וְ becomes -וָ before a stressed vowel, e.g., עֶשְׂרִים וָשֶׁבַע *esrím va-shéva*.

b. In spoken Hebrew:
Speakers rarely follow the practice mentioned above of changing the conjunction -וְ to its variants -וּ or -וָ in everyday Hebrew. Thus the

conjunction is usually pronounced *ve-*, regardless of the more formal rules.

Higher numbers

The noun which denotes 'hundred' is the feminine noun מֵאָה *me'á*. The noun which denotes 'thousand' is the masculine noun אֶלֶף *élef*. In combination with single digits, these nouns form the count nouns from 100 and beyond.

Hundreds

The feminine noun מֵאָה *me'á* 'a hundred' provides the base for all the numbers from 100 to 999. The dual form expressing 'two hundred' is מָאתַיִם. From 300 to 900, the hundreds are a combination of the single digit feminine numbers followed by the plural form מֵאוֹת, which follows it. Notice that the dependent form of the digits is used. (In the numbers 'three', 'seven' and 'nine', the alternate form is noticeable, as the first vowel of the independent form of the number is omitted and replaced by zero *shva* sign).

me'á	מֵאָה	100
matáyim	מָאתַיִם	200
shlósh me'òt	שְׁלוֹשׁ-מֵאוֹת	300
arbá me'òt	אַרְבַּע-מֵאוֹת	400
ħamésh me'òt	חֲמֵשׁ-מֵאוֹת	500
shésh me'òt	שֵׁשׁ-מֵאוֹת	600
shvá me'òt	שְׁבַע-מֵאוֹת	700
shmoné me'òt	שְׁמוֹנֶה-מֵאוֹת	800
tshá me'òt	תְּשַׁע-מֵאוֹת	900

To form more complex numbers with 'tens' and 'ones', the phrase starts with the highest number, which is followed by the next number in order, and ends with the 'ones'. Notice that before the last number the conjunction 'and' ו- is added, such as in the following examples:

782 שבע מאות, שמונים ושתיים

325 שלוש מאות, עשרים וחמש

Thousands

The masculine noun אֶלֶף 'a thousand' provides the base for all the numbers from 1,000 to 10,000. The dual form to express 'two thousand' is אֲלָפַיִם *alpáyim*. From 3,000 to 10,000, the thousands are a combination of the single digit masculine numbers followed by the plural form 'thousands' אֲלָפִים *alafim*, which follows it. Notice that the dependent form of the digits is used.

élef	אֶלֶף	1,000
alpáyim	אַלְפַּיִם	2,000
shlóshet alafim	שְׁלוֹשֶׁת-אֲלָפִים	3,000
arbá`at alafim	אַרְבַּעַת-אֲלָפִים	4,000
ḥaméshet alafim	חֲמֵשֶׁת-אֲלָפִים	5,000
shéshet alafim	שֵׁשֶׁת-אֲלָפִים	6,000
shiv`át alafim	שִׁבְעַת-אֲלָפִים	7,000
shmonát alafim	שְׁמוֹנַת-אֲלָפִים	8,000
tish`át alafim	תִּשְׁעַת-אֲלָפִים	9,000
aséret alafim	עֲשֶׂרֶת-אֲלָפִים	10,000

Note

If the number includes thousands and hundreds only, the conjunction 'and' is optional: 1,700 אלף שְׁבַע-מֵאוֹת or אלף וּשְׁבַע-מֵאוֹת.

Beyond ten thousand

To count thousands beyond 'ten thousand', the masculine form of the single numbers is combined with the singular form of אֶלֶף (the plural form can be used as well).

aḥád asar élef	אַחַד עָשָׂר אֶלֶף	11,000
shnéym asar élef	שְׁנַיִם עָשָׂר אֶלֶף	12,000
shloshá asar élef	שְׁלוֹשָׁה עָשָׂר אֶלֶף	13,000
arba`á asar élef	אַרְבָּעָה עָשָׂר אֶלֶף	14,000
ḥamishá asar élef	חֲמִשָּׁה עָשָׂר אֶלֶף	15,000
shishá asar élef	שִׁשָּׁה עָשָׂר אֶלֶף	16,000
shiv`á asar élef	שִׁבְעָה עָשָׂר אֶלֶף	17,000
shmoná asar élef	שְׁמוֹנָה עָשָׂר אֶלֶף	18,000
tish`á asar élef	תִּשְׁעָה עָשָׂר אֶלֶף	19,000
esrím élef	עֶשְׂרִים אֶלֶף	20,000

From 30,000 to 90,000

shloshim élef	שְׁלוֹשִׁים אֶלֶף	30,000
arba`ím élef	אַרְבָּעִים אֶלֶף	40,000
ḥamishím élef	חֲמִישִׁים אֶלֶף	50,000
shishím élef	שִׁשִּׁים אֶלֶף	60,000
shiv`ím élef	שִׁבְעִים אֶלֶף	70,000
shmoním élef	שְׁמוֹנִים אֶלֶף	80,000
tish`ím élef	תִּשְׁעִים אֶלֶף	90,000

From 100,000 to 999,999.

me'á élef	מֵאָה אֶלֶף	100,000
matáyim élef	מָאתַיִם אֶלֶף	200,000
shlósh me'òt élef	שְׁלוֹשׁ-מֵאוֹת אֶלֶף	300,000
milyón	מִילְיוֹן (ז)	1,000,000
shishá milyón	שִׁשָּׁה מִילְיוֹן	6,000,000
bilyón/milyárd	בִּילְיוֹן/מִילְיַארְד (ז)	1,000,000,000

<u>The order of numbers in the phrase:</u>

To form more complex numbers with 'hundreds', 'tens' and 'ones', the phrase starts with the highest number, which is followed by the next number in order and ends with the 'ones', the same as in English.

| שבעת אֲלָפִים, שלוש מאות, עשרים וְארבע | 7,324 |
| אֲלָפִים, מאתיים חמישים וָשש | 2,256 |

7.2 Cardinal numbers   מספרים מונים

There are two sets of cardinal numbers: masculine and feminine. Each of these sets has two subsets of independent and dependent forms of the numbers: the independent set is used in indefinite phrases, while the dependent set is used in definite phrases. In the numbers 3-10, the masculine numbers have the ‏הָ‏- ending, otherwise associated with feminine nouns.

Masculine		**Feminine**
אֶחָד	1	אַחַת
שְׁנַיִם	2	שְׁתַּיִם
שְׁלוֹשָׁה	3	שָׁלוֹשׁ
אַרְבָּעָה	4	אַרְבַּע
חֲמִשָּׁה	5	חָמֵשׁ

שִׁשָּׁה	6	שֵׁשׁ	
שִׁבְעָה	7	שֶׁבַע	
שְׁמוֹנָה	8	שְׁמוֹנֶה	
תִּשְׁעָה	9	תֵּשַׁע	
עֲשָׂרָה	10	עֶשֶׂר	

7.3 Noun phrases with cardinal numbers

Cardinal numbers combine with count nouns for the purpose of indicating the quantity of items. Except for 'one', they precede the head noun, which puts them in the same class as other quantifiers (such as כָּל, מְעַט, כַּמָּה, הַרְבֵּה) and distinguishes them from adjectives, which follow the noun they modify.

7.3.1 Use of number 'one' in numerical phrases

There is a certain redundancy in the overt inclusion of the number 'one' in a number phrase, since a singular noun, by definition and by form, is a singular entity. It makes more sense, however, if it is regarded as an adjective meaning 'single', and indeed Hebrew 'one' does behave like an adjective: in a phrase, it always follows the noun that is being counted, and has the gender features of the noun that it modifies. The number 'one' also agrees with the count-noun in its status as indefinite or definite: in an indefinite noun phrase, both count-noun and number do not have an article, while in a definite phrase, both noun and number do have a definite article.

Indefinite phrases

Masculine	זכר	Feminine	נקבה
one hat	כובע אחד	one dress	שמלה אחת

Definite phrases

Masculine	זכר	Feminine	נקבה
the one actor	השחקן האחד	the one actress	השחקנית האחת

7.3.2 Use of number 'two' and above in numerical phrases

Numerical phrases with numbers above the number 'one' are formed in a similar shape to that of [noun + noun] phrases, צירופי סמיכות. In these phrases the components combine in the following way: the number always precedes the count nouns, which, with some exceptions (particularly, in higher numbers), are plural nouns. The numerals have

the same gender features as the count nouns. When the phrases are
indefinite, the number nouns are the independent forms of the number
(with the exception of number 'two', as can be seen below). When the
number nouns are part of a definite phrase, they have the alternate
shape typical of the first noun of a סְמִיכוּת phrase.

When the number 'two' is part of an indefinite or definite phrase, it has
the form שְׁנֵי- or שְׁתֵּי- :

Indefinite phrases

Masculine	זכר	Feminine	נקבה
two boys	שְׁנֵי בנים	two girls	שְׁתֵּי בנות
two fathers	שְׁנֵי אבות	two women	שְׁתֵּי נשים

Definite phrases

Masculine	זכר	Feminine	נקבה
the two boys	שְׁנֵי הבנים	the two girls	שְׁתֵּי הבנות
the three fathers	שְׁלוֹשֶׁת האבות	the three women	שְׁלוֹשׁ הנשים

Masculine		Feminine	
Dependent form	Independent form	Dependent form	Independent form
שְׁנֵי-	שְׁנַיִם	שְׁתֵּי-	שְׁתַּיִם
שְׁלוֹשֶׁת-	שְׁלוֹשָׁה	שְׁלוֹשׁ-	שָׁלוֹשׁ
אַרְבַּעַת-	אַרְבָּעָה	אַרְבַּע-	אַרְבַּע
חֲמֵשֶׁת-	חֲמִשָּׁה	חֲמֵשׁ-	חָמֵשׁ
שֵׁשֶׁת-	שִׁשָּׁה	שֵׁשׁ-	שֵׁשׁ
שִׁבְעַת-	שִׁבְעָה	שְׁבַע-	שֶׁבַע
שְׁמוֹנַת-	שְׁמוֹנָה	שְׁמוֹנֶה-	שְׁמוֹנֶה
תִּשְׁעַת-	תִּשְׁעָה	תְּשַׁע-	תֵּשַׁע
עֲשֶׂרֶת-	עֲשָׂרָה	עֶשֶׂר-	עֶשֶׂר

Indefinite:	Five customers entered the store.	אַרְבָּעָה קונים נכנסו לחנות.
Definite:	The five customers came in together.	אַרְבַּעַת הַקונים באו ביחד.

Note

In current Hebrew the שלושת type forms are alive and well, while the
שלוש dependent ones are obsolete. Often, the שלושת type is used for
definite feminine nouns as well.

7.3.3 Definite numerical phrase beyond 10

Beyond the number 10, count nouns do not affect the form of the numeral, regardless of whether the noun is definite or indefinite.

Masculine

Indefinite:	There are <u>thirteen</u> boys in class.	יש <u>שלושה עשר</u> בנים בכיתה
Definite:	All <u>the thirteen</u> boys are friends of mine.	כל <u>שלושה עשר</u> <u>הבנים</u> חברים שלי.

Feminine

Indefinite:	There are <u>thirteen</u> girls in class.	יש <u>שלוש עשרה</u> בנות בכיתה
Definite:	All <u>the thirteen</u> girls are friends of mine.	כל <u>שלוש עשרה</u> <u>הבנות</u> חברות שלי.

7.3.4 Teen numbers – masculine and feminine

The masculine teen numbers differ in their form from feminine teen numbers (introduced in the counting section above): the first number of the compound noun is the masculine singular unit number, while the second number signifies 'teen', and its form in the masculine is עָשָׂר.

Masculine		Feminine
אַחַד עָשָׂר	11	אַחַת עֶשְׂרֵה
שְׁנֵים עָשָׂר	12	שְׁתֵּים עֶשְׂרֵה
שְׁלוֹשָׁה עָשָׂר	13	שְׁלוֹשׁ עֶשְׂרֵה
אַרְבָּעָה עָשָׂר	14	אַרְבַּע עֶשְׂרֵה
חֲמִשָּׁה עָשָׂר	15	חָמֵשׁ עֶשְׂרֵה
שִׁשָּׁה עָשָׂר	16	שֵׁשׁ עֶשְׂרֵה
שִׁבְעָה עָשָׂר	17	שְׁבַע עֶשְׂרֵה
שְׁמוֹנָה עָשָׂר	18	שְׁמוֹנֶה עֶשְׂרֵה
תִּשְׁעָה עָשָׂר	19	תְּשַׁע עֶשְׂרֵה

7.3.5 Agreement between numbers and the quantified nouns

In a numerical noun phrase, the main noun determines the choice of the gender of the number of the numeral.

Masculine	זכר	Feminine	נקבה
13 dogs	שלושה עשר <u>כלבים</u>	13 girls	שלוש עשרה <u>בנות</u>
14 days	ארבעה עשר <u>ימים</u>	14 cakes	ארבע עשרה <u>עוגות</u>

Beyond 20, only the last digit of the number agrees in gender with the noun it quantifies:

Feminine	23 companies	עשרים <u>ושלוש חברות</u>
	547 units	חמש מאות ארבעים <u>ושבע יחידות</u>
Masculine	49 books	ארבעים <u>ותשעה ספרים</u>
	365 days	שלוש מאות ששים <u>וחמישה ימים</u>

7.3.6 Numbers + pronoun suffix

The numbers 2-10 can have a plural possessive suffix added to them. By one word, which consists of a number and a pronoun suffix, one can express what takes a four-word phrase in English: 'The two of you' is rendered by the one word שְׁנֵיכֶם. The form to which the suffixes are added is a dependent form of the number: שְׁנֵי- or שְׁתֵּי and not שְׁנַיִם or שְׁתַּיִם. When the reference is to masculine nouns, or a mixed group of masculine and feminine nouns, the set of masculine numbers becomes the basis for the word, but if the reference is to feminine nouns, then the feminine number is the basis for the word. By definition, the concept is always a plural one.

<u>Numbers with plural suffixes</u>

		נקבה	זכר
the two of us		שְׁתֵּינוּ	שְׁנֵינוּ
the two of you		שְׁתֵּיכֶן	שְׁנֵיכֶם
the two of them		שְׁתֵּיהֶן	שְׁנֵיהֶם
the three of us		שְׁלוֹשְׁתֵּנוּ	
the three of you		שְׁלוֹשְׁתְּכֶן	שְׁלוֹשְׁתְּכֶם
the three of them		שְׁלוֹשְׁתָּן	שְׁלוֹשְׁתָּם

the four of us	אַרְבַּעְתֵּנוּ
the four of you	אַרְבַּעְתְּכֶן אַרְבַּעְתְּכֶם
the four of them	אַרְבַּעְתָּן אַרְבַּעְתָּם
the five of us	חֲמִשְׁתֵּנוּ
the five of you	חֲמִשְׁתְּכֶן חֲמִשְׁתְּכֶם
the five of them	חֲמִשְׁתָּן חֲמִשְׁתָּם

7.4 Ordinal numbers   מספרים סודרים

Ordinal numbers ('first, second, third') are used to indicate the order in which individual items appear. They are usually singular concepts: *the first day, the second day, the third day.*

זכר		נקבה
רִאשׁוֹן	1st	רִאשׁוֹנָה
שֵׁנִי	2nd	שְׁנִיָּה
שְׁלִישִׁי	3rd	שְׁלִישִׁית
רְבִיעִי	4th	רְבִיעִית
חֲמִישִׁי	5th	חֲמִישִׁית
שִׁישִׁי	6th	שִׁשִּׁית
שְׁבִיעִי	7th	שְׁבִיעִית
שְׁמִינִי	8th	שְׁמִינִית
תְּשִׁיעִי	9th	תְּשִׁיעִית
עֲשִׂירִי	10th	עֲשִׂירִית

In the ordinal numbers 'first' and 'second', the feminine ordinal numbers have the feminine suffix -ָה while in the numbers 3-10, the feminine ordinal numbers have the feminine suffix -ִית. Note the difference between שְׁנִיָּה 'second, f.' and שֵׁנִית 'again'.

7.4.1 Noun phrases with ordinal numbers

Ordinal numbers have gender features and function as adjectives do, and as such they follow the head nouns of the phrase. In phrases they have the same gender features as the nouns that they modify. They also reflect the indefinite or definite status of the phrase.

Indefinite phrases:

	Masculine		Feminine
a third house	בית שלישי	a first show	הצגה ראשונה

Definite phrases:

	Masculine		Feminine
the third house	הבית השלישי	the first show	ההצגה הראשונה

7.4.2 Phrases with ordinals higher than 10th

The ordinal numbers higher than 10th are formed using cardinal numbers. However, they combine with nouns as adjectives and therefore agree with the head noun in gender and in use of articles.

Dan was the eleventh customer in line.	דן היה הקונה האחד-עשר בתור.
This is the thirty-first year in which Hebrew is taught here.	זאת השנה השלושים ואחת שבה מלמדים עברית כאן.

Use of 'first' and 'last'

The noun ראשון 'first' is also paired with the noun אחרון 'last'. They are truly ordinal adjectives and as adjectives have four forms indicating both gender and number.

first	רִאשׁוֹנוֹת	רִאשׁוֹנִים	רִאשׁוֹנָה	רִאשׁוֹן
last	אַחֲרוֹנוֹת	אַחֲרוֹנִים	אַחֲרוֹנָה	אַחֲרוֹן

The first day of the week is Sunday.	היום הראשון בשבוע הוא יום ראשון.
Last but not least.	אחרון, אחרון – חביב.

7.5 Fractions   שְׁבָרִים

Partitive numbers are stated by regular nouns, which specify their fractional quality:

¼	*réva*	רֶבַע	1/2	*ħétsi/ħatsí*	חֵצִי/חֲצִי

The noun 'half' has two forms: one when it is used as an independent noun and is not combined with another noun, חֲצִי *ħétsi*, and another when it is combined with a noun as part of a phrase, -חֲצִי *ħatsí-*.

Give me a half of what you have.	*ħétsi*	תן לי חֲצִי ממה שיש לך.
Give me a half loaf of bread.	*ħatsí-*	תן לי חֲצִי כיכר לחם.

The words for 'half', 'third' and 'fourth/quarter' are masculine, while those for fractions 'fifth' through 'tenth' are feminine:

a half	*ħétsi*	חֲצִי	1/2
a third	*shlish*	שְׁלִישׁ	1/3
a fourth	*réva*	רֶבַע	1/4

| Give me a third of what you have. | תן לי שליש ממה שיש לך. |
| The time is a quarter to seven. | השעה רבע לשבע. |

a fifth	*ħamishít*	חֲמִישִׁית	1/5
a sixth	*shishít*	שִׁשִּׁית	1/6
a seventh	*shvi`it*	שְׁבִיעִית	1/7
an eighth	*shminít*	שְׁמִינִית	1/8
a ninth	*tshi`it*	תְּשִׁיעִית	1/9
a tenth	*asirít*	עֲשִׂירִית	1/10

7.6 Multiplication values

Hebrew combines the fixed form of the noun פִּי 'times' with the number. The number form is masculine; however in everyday speech the use of the feminine number in these phrases is more common.

| tenfold/ ten times as much | פִּי עֲשָׂרָה (פִּי עֶשֶׂר) |
| fourfold/ four times as much. | פִּי אַרְבָּעָה (פִּי אַרְבַּע) |

The value 'double' is expressed by the noun 'double', which has a dual ending: כְּפָלַיִם 'twice as much'.

Twice as much/double	**כְּפָלַיִם**
My book is expensive.	הספר שלי יקר.
It costs <u>twice as much</u> as your book.	הוא עולה <u>פי שניים</u> מהספר שלך.
It costs <u>double.</u>	הוא עולה <u>כפליים.</u>
It will cost you <u>five times</u> as much.	זה יעלה לך <u>פי חמישה/פי חמש.</u>

*The other number with a dual ending is שִׁבְעָתַיִם, meaning 'sevenfold'. It is a fixed idiomatic expression.

7.7 Numeric value of letters

The letters of the alphabet have number value in Hebrew. They are used in Modern Hebrew to indicate dates, days of the week, status in college (שנה א׳ is Freshman, שנה ב׳ is Sophomore, etc.), for numbering items in a list, and sometimes they are used where roman numbers are used in English to indicate page numbers.

100	ק	80	פ	10	י	8	ח	1	א
200	ר	90	צ	20	כ	9	ט	2	ב
300	ש			30	ל			3	ג
400	ת			40	מ			4	ד
				50	נ			5	ה
				60	ס			6	ו
				70	ע			7	ז

Beyond 400, letters are added up and create the higher numbers (similar to Roman numerals):

ת=400	+ ר= 200	ת״ר=600	ת=400	+ ק= 100	ת״ק=500
ת=400	+ ת= 400	ת״ת=800	ת=400	+ ש= 300	ת״ש=700

Note

The following final letters served for higher numbers, but no longer do so in contemporary Hebrew:

900 = ץ   800 = ף   700 = ן   600 = ם   500= ך

Teen numerals

The teen numbers (11-19) are expressed by combining the letters א׳-ט׳ with the letter *yod* י׳ for 10.

י״א= 11   י״ב = 12   י״ג= 13   י״ד= 14   י״ז = 17   י״ח = 18   י״ט= 19

The numbers 15, 16 are stated in terms of 9+6, and 9+7, since the combination of the letter י׳ plus either ה׳ or ו׳ includes a sequence which is used in the sacred name of God. Thus, ט״ו= 15, ט״ז = 16.

Numbers 20-90

The numbers 20-90 are expressed by combining the values of א׳-ט׳ for the single unique numbers, and the letters כ-צ for 20 to 90.

כ״א= 21   ל״ו =36   מ״ג= 43   ע״ט= 79   נ״ח = 58

Other higher numbers represented by letters

Thousands are usually represented by the apostrophe ', which is added to the letters. The apostrophe separates the thousand from the rest of the number.

5,000 = ה׳   4,000= ד׳   3,000 = ג׳   2,000=ב׳   1,000=א׳

Combining higher numbers

The principle of combining letters also works for higher numbers. If more than two letters are needed for the number, the double quotes mark " comes before the last letter.

227 = רכ״ז   508 = תק״ח   749 = תשמ״ט   5,764 = ה׳תשס״ד

7.8 Numbers in common phrases

7.8.1 Days of the week

There are two systems for the names of the days of the week: one uses the letters of the alphabet to signify the day, while the other uses the ordinal numbers following the word 'day' to signify the days of the week.

Sunday	יום ראשון	יום א׳
Monday	יום שני	יום ב׳
Tuesday	יום שלישי	יום ג׳
Wednesday	יום רביעי	יום ד׳
Thursday	יום חמישי	יום ה׳
Friday	יום שישי	יום ו׳
Saturday/Sabbath	שבת	שבת

7.8.2 Dates

Dates of the Jewish calendar are often given with the number values of the Hebrew alphabet.

Wednesday, 7th of the month of *Tevet*, 5,761   יום ד׳ ז׳ בטבת ה׳ תשס״א

The ה׳ for 5,000 is often omitted in common usage: יום ד׳ ז׳ בטבת תשס״א

The Gregorian calendar is used extensively, and the marking of the date starts with the month, day and year (day and month are in reverse order from those in English):

11/10/2002   November 10, 2002   עשרה בנובמבר, 2002   10/11/2002

7.8.3 Referring to dates

One refers to decades by using a construct phrase that combines -שְׁנוֹת 'the years of' with the various decades.

The economic crisis took place in the late 20s.	המשבר הכלכלי קרה בסוף <u>שנות העשרים</u>.

One refers to centuries by using a definite phrase (since it is regarded as a specific, known date) that combines מֵאָה 'century' with an ordinal numeral.

The 21st century started with dramatic events.	<u>המאה העשרים ואחת</u> החלה באירועים דרמטיים.

7.8.4 Numbers in telling time

The nouns that refer to time units are feminine and therefore the counting of time units is done using feminine numerals.

hour	שעה	minute	דקה	second	שנייה
7 hours	שבע שעות	5 minutes	חמש דקות	2 seconds	שתי שניות

The question is 'what hour is it?	מה השעה?
The answer starts with 'the hour is'	השעה ...

The time is six fifteen	השעה היא שש וחמש עשרה דקות.
The time is quarter past six.	השעה שש ורבע.
The time is six thirty.	השעה היא שש ושלושים דקות.
The time is half past six.	השעה שש וחצי.
The time is six forty-five.	השעה היא שש ארבעים וחמש (דקות).
The time is quarter to seven.	השעה רבע לשבע.
The time is seven exactly.	השעה היא שבע בדיוק.

Note

The 'quarter past' and 'half past' have an *a* vowel in the conjunction -וְ:
'a quarter past six' שש וָרֶבַע, 'half past six' שש וָחֵצִי .
For indicating five and ten minutes, one may alternatively use the masculine number as well, without דקות.

6:10	השעה היא שש ועשר דקות	השעה היא שש ועשרה	
8:55	השעה היא חמישה לתשע	השעה היא חמש דקות לתשע	

In numbers greater than ten, the final digit is usually feminine.

8:55	השעה היא שמונה, חמישים וחמש	השעה היא שמונה וחמישים וחמש דקות

7.8.5 Telling age

The nouns that refer to years שָׁנָה (נ.) שָׁנִים are feminine, and therefore the counting of years is done with feminine numerals. The nouns that refer to months are masculine חֹדֶשׁ (ז.) חֳדָשִׁים, and therefore the counting of months is done with masculine numerals.

The phrase of telling one's age is formed by using the noun בֶּן in all four forms to head the age phrase.

רבות	רבים	יחידה	יחיד
בְּנוֹת (x) שנים	בְּנֵי (x) שנים	בַּת (x) שנים	בֶּן (x) שנים

The questions of age and the responses are fixed expressions. They do not literally translate into the English 'how old are you?' but the message is the same. The question is expressed in Hebrew by the following phrase '[*ben/bat/bney/bnot* how many (years)] are you?' The initial head noun can be loosely translated as 'a person of'. The head noun agrees in gender and number with the person about whom such information is solicited. The noun שָׁנִים 'years' is often omitted in speech.

Questions:

Danny, <u>how old are you</u>?	דני, <u>בֶּן כמה אתה</u>!
Sarah, <u>how old are you</u>?	שרה, <u>בַּת כמה את</u>!
<u>How old are</u> your parents?	<u>בְּנֵי כמה</u> ההורים שלכם?
<u>How old are</u> the girls in your class?	<u>בְּנוֹת כמה</u> הבנות בכיתה שלכם?

Answers:

I am twenty-six.	אני בֶּן עשרים ושש.
Sarah is thirty-five.	שרה בַּת שלושים וחמש.
Our parents are fifty years old.	ההורים שלנו בְּנֵי חמישים.
The girls in class are twelve or thirteen years old.	הבנות בכיתה בְּנוֹת שתים-עשרה או שלוש-עשרה.

Fractions can be expressed by 'half' or 'a quarter' or by numbers of months:

Jonah is three and a half.	יונה בֶּן שלוש וחצי.
Leah is six and ten months.	ליאה בַּת שש ועשרה חודשים.

Chapter 8
Adjectives

Introduction: forming adjectives
8.2   Comparative and superlative adjectives
8.3   Forming adjectives by adding suffix -*i*
8.4   Nouns and adjectives of affiliation
8.5   Participles that function as adjectives
8.6   Special patterns

8.1 Introduction: forming adjectives

The adjective functions both as the modifier of a noun in a noun phrase and also functions as a non-verbal predicate. All Hebrew adjectives have four forms.

The masculine singular is considered the base form of the adjective.

	רבות	רבים	יחידה	יחיד
big, large	גְּדוֹלוֹת	גְּדוֹלִים	גְּדוֹלָה	גָּדוֹל >
private	פְּרָטִיּוֹת	פְּרָטִיִּים	פְּרָטִית	פְּרָטִי >

While the masculine singular form has no particular ending, the feminine and the plural forms all have regular endings: feminine singular ה- -*a*, ת- -*et* or -*it*; masculine plural ים- -*im*; and feminine plural ות- -*ot*.

Adjectives, whether they are noun modifiers or predicates, always take on the gender and number features of the noun they modify. While nouns don't always have predictable plural endings, which reflect their gender, adjectives always do.

	רבות	רבים	יחידה	יחיד
good friend(s)	חברות טובות	חברים טובים	חברה טובה	חבר טוב
big streets		רחובות גדולים	big street	רחוב גדול
nice women	נשים נחמדות		nice woman	אישה נחמדה

There are two ways of forming adjectives: linearly, by adding a suffix without affecting the stem (except for predictable phonetic modifications), and discontinuously, by a [root + pattern] combination. The linear derivation pattern is manifest in one formation pattern, noun+*i* (see below). Of the discontinuous adjectival patterns, there are those identical to the participles of the various verb patterns (*binyanim*), and some that are not. Regardless of the nature of derivation, adding a feminine or plural marker may result in a shift of stress in the word, and certain vowel deletions and modifications.

8.1.1 Some of the most common adjectival form groups

Certain adjective patterns keep the stem throughout all four forms. The masculine singular is considered the base form, and there are no changes in the stem itself in the other forms, but they do exhibit the suffixes that mark gender and number.

	<u>רבות</u>	<u>רבים</u>	<u>יחידה</u>	<u>יחיד</u>
secret	סוֹדִיּוֹת	סוֹדִיִּים	סוֹדִית	סוֹדִי
funny	מַצְחִיקוֹת	מַצְחִיקִים	מַצְחִיקָה	מַצְחִיק

In some patterns the feminine singular suffix is –*éCet* rather than -*á*:

dangerous	מְסֻכָּנוֹת	מְסֻכָּנִים	מְסֻכֶּנֶת	מְסֻכָּן
perfect	מֻשְׁלָמוֹת	מֻשְׁלָמִים	מֻשְׁלֶמֶת	מֻשְׁלָם

Changes to the initial vowel of the base form mark other adjective patterns. The vowel *a* of the first consonant changes to a zero; in the case where the initial consonant is א י ע י ח׳ ה׳ a *ḥataf pataḥ* accompanies it to facilitate pronunciation:

black, dark	שְׁחוֹרוֹת	שְׁחוֹרִים	שְׁחוֹרָה	שָׁחוֹר
strong	חֲזָקוֹת	חֲזָקִים	חֲזָקָה	חָזָק

8.2 Comparative and superlative adjectives
צירופי תארים של השוואה ויתרון

Adjectives may take comparative and superlative degree. The modifiers that indicate the degree are the following:

8.2.1 Comparative

The adverb יותר 'more' is added to the adjectives to form comparative constructions. The default order is for the adverb יותר to precede the adjective, although in speech it often follows it as well: יותר גדול, or גדול יותר for 'bigger'. The adverb פחות 'less' is added to the adjective to form similar constructions. The default order is the same, with the adverb פחות preceding the adjective, although in speech it often can follow the adjective.

Unlike the adjective, which in Hebrew has gender and number features, the modifier is an adverb and as such has one fixed form, which does not carry gender or number features.

sweeter/more sweet	יותר מתוק / מתוק יותר	יחיד
	יותר מתוקה/ מתוקה יותר	יחידה
	יותר מתוקים / מתוקים יותר	רבים
	יותר מתוקות / מתוקות יותר	רבות
less sweet	פחות מתוק / מתוק פחות	יחיד
	פחות מתוקה / מתוקה פחות	יחידה
	פחות מתוקים / מתוקים פחות	רבים
	פחות מתוקות / מתוקות פחות	רבות

A comparative structure by its nature involves two entities, between which a comparison is being made. The first noun phrase introduces the structure while the second noun phrase completes the proposition. The comparative adjective links the two entities by means of the particle 'than' מ-.

The new show is <u>more entertaining</u> <u>than</u> the previous one.	ההצגה החדשה <u>יותר מבדרת</u> <u>מ</u>הקודמת.
These hills are <u>less steep than</u> the ones we climbed yesterday.	הגבעות האלה <u>פחות תלולות</u> <u>מ</u>הגבעות שטיפסנו עליהן אתמול.

8.2.2 Superlative

Superlative constructions have two different forms: the adjective can be preceded by the adverb הכי *the most*, or it can be followed by the adverbial expression ביותר, which also indicates *most*.

comparative	more dangerous than	יותר מְסֻכָּן (מ)	מְסֻכָּן
superlative	the most dangerous	המְסֻכָּן ביותר	הכי מְסֻכָּן

comparative	stronger than	(מ) יותר חֲזָקָה	חֲזָקָה
superlative	the strongest	הֲחֲזָקָה ביותר	הכי חֲזָקָה

comparative	funnier	יותר מַצְחִיקִים	מַצְחִיקִים
superlative	the funniest	הַמַצְחִיקִים ביותר	הכי מַצְחִיקִים

For more information on comparative and superlative, see pp. 257-260

8.3 Forming adjectives by adding suffix *-i*

The most common way of forming new adjectives is by adding the suffix ־ִי *-i*, which stands for 'having the characteristic of', to existing words. It is a suffix that is commonly attached to nouns. Adding this suffix to a noun like אָבִיב 'spring' results in אֲבִיבִי, which means 'of spring' or 'spring-like'. This is a transparent adjective with a clear relationship to the noun from which it is derived. This formation is very common, since it only requires adding a suffix to an existing noun.

Gloss	<u>רבות</u>	<u>רבים</u>	<u>יחידה</u>	<u>יחיד</u>	<u>Noun</u>
private	פְּרָטִיוֹת	פְּרָטִיִּים	פְּרָטִית	פְּרָטִי	פְּרָט >
main	רָאשִׁיוֹת	רָאשִׁיִּים	רָאשִׁית	רָאשִׁי	ראֹש >
general	כְּלָלִיוֹת	כְּלָלִיִּים	כְּלָלִית	כְּלָלִי	כְּלָל >

Note

Notice that the stem of all forms derived from ראֹש *rósh* 'head; main item' is רָאש- *rash-*. The base form רָאש- *rash-* changes to ראֹש *rósh* when the vowel is stressed, but remains רָאש- *rash-* when it is not.

Although normally these adjectives are derived from nouns, the process of creating such adjectives is so productive, that they are also formed from bases that consist of other adjectives. For instance, טִפֵּשׁ *tipesh* 'a fool; foolish' can function as either an adjective or a noun ('a foolish person'). In this form, however, it usually refers to people, while the derived adjective טִפְּשִׁי *tipshi* 'foolish' is used to characterize an idea or an event:

<u>Base: adjective טיפש 'stupid' > טיפשי 'foolish'</u>

David is so <u>stupid</u> – all of his decisions are always <u>foolish</u>.	דוד הוא כל כך <u>טיפש</u> – כל ההחלטות שלו תמיד <u>טיפשיות</u>.

It was <u>stupid</u> to get up so early, almost in the middle of the night. Only complete <u>fools</u> do such things.

זה היה <u>טיפשי</u> לקום כל כך מוקדם, ממש באמצע הלילה. רק <u>טיפשים</u> גמורים עושים דבר כזה.

When ordinal numbers are combined in phrases they are considered adjectives and can provide the base for derivation of other adjectives. For instance, the ordinal number רִאשׁוֹן 'first' when used in its primary meaning becomes the base for a derived adjective רִאשׁוֹנִי 'primary, principal or primeval'.

<u>Base: adjective ראשון> ראשוני</u>

The <u>first</u> problem is that the work conditions are the <u>primary things</u> that need to be changed.

הבעיה <u>הראשונה</u> היא שתנאי העבודה כאן הם <u>הדברים הראשוניים</u> שזקוקים לשינוי.

There are also a few adverbs that serve as the base for new adjectives, such as מַמָּשׁ 'really' > מַמָּשִׁי 'real', or מִיָד 'immediately > מִיָדִי 'immediate'.

<u>Base: adverb מייד > מיידי</u>

There are <u>immediate</u> <u>needs</u>, for instance, it is necessary to find an apartment <u>right away</u> in a quiet neighborhood close to work.

יש <u>צרכים מיידיים</u> : למשל, צריך למצוא דירה <u>מייד</u> בשכונה שקטה וקרובה לעבודה .

8.4 Nouns and adjectives of affiliation

There is a set of derived nouns of nationality or religion that are a source for a similar set of derived adjectives. They indicate the affiliation of an individual with particular national, ethnic, or religious groups. It applies to their belonging or being identified as belonging to such a particular group. From these sets of nouns there derived adjectives. The source can be the name of a country, an ethnic or a tribal group, or a religious community. The derived nouns and the adjectives look alike, but their syntactic function is different.

Country:	Many languages are spoken in China.	בְּסִין מדברים הרבה שפות.
Derived noun:	The Chinese speak several languages.	הַסִינים מדברים מספר שפות שונות.
Derived adjective:	There are several Chinese languages.	יש כמה שפות סִיניוֹת.

The derived adjectives for the most part look the same as the derived noun. The one exception is that the masculine plural form has the extra י before the plural suffix, as can be seen in this example:

| Noun: | the diligent Japanese | היפנים החרוצים |
| Adjective: | the Japanese paintings | הציורים היפניים |

8.4.1 Nationality: denominative noun and adjective

מישראל

| Nouns: | Israeli | ישראליוֹת | ישראלים | ישראלית | ישראלי |
| Adjectives: | Israeli | ישראליוֹת | ישראליים | ישראלית | ישראלי |

Noun: Israelis   **שם: ישראלים**

Many Israelis go abroad during the holidays.

הרבה ישראלים נוסעים לחו״ל בחגים.

Adjective: Israeli   **שם תואר: ישראליים**

There are many Israeli passengers on the plane.

יש הרבה נוסעים ישראליים במטוס.

8.4.2 Ethnic group: denominative noun and adjective
From Georgia (in Central Asia)   מגרוזיה

| Nouns: | Georgian | גְרוּזִינִיוֹת | גְרוּזִינים | גְרוּזִינית | גְרוּזִינִי |
| Adjectives: | Georgian | גְרוּזִינִיוֹת | גְרוּזִינִיים | גְרוּזִינית | גְרוּזִינִי |

Noun: Georgians   **שם: גרוזינים**

The Georgians have been living in this neighborhood from the beginning of the 20th century.

הגרוזינים גרים בשכונה הזאת מתחילת המאה העשרים.

Adjective: Georgian   **שם תואר: גרוזיניים**

There are many <u>Georgian singers</u>   יש הרבה <u>זמרים גרוזיניים</u> שמשמרים
who preserve their traditional   את המוסיקה המסורתית שלהם.
music.

8.4.3 Religion: denominative noun and adjective

מ"יהדות"

<u>Nouns</u>	Jew	יְהוּדִיּוֹת	יְהוּדִים	יְהוּדִיָּה	יְהוּדִי
<u>Adjectives</u>	Jewish	יְהוּדִיּוֹת	יְהוּדִיִּים	יְהוּדִית	יְהוּדִי

Notice that in this example, both the feminine form and the masculine plural have slight differences that distinguish nouns from adjectives.

Noun: Jewish woman/Jewess   **שם: יהודיה**

In her passport it is written that she is   בדרכון כתוב שהיא <u>יהודיה</u>.
<u>Jewish</u>.

Adjective: Jewish   **שם תואר: יהודית**

She belongs to the <u>Jewish</u> faith.   היא שייכת לדת <u>היהודית</u>.

8.4.4 Predictable changes of base: noun > adjective

Some adjectives share the base of the noun with no change in vowels. If the base undergoes some changes in the process, it is because of phonologically predictable changes. When the suffix -*i* is added, the adjective's main stress moves to the suffix, and some predictable changes consequently occur in the base form:

a. Stems that do not undergo change:

1. Vowels other than *a* are not affected by reduction:	public (N) > public (Adj.)	צִבּוּר < צִבּוּרִי
2. The vowel *a* in a monosyllabic word remains:	religion > religious	דָּת < דָּתִי
3. The vowel *a* is retained in an initial closed syllable:	culture > cultural	תַּרְבּוּת < תַּרְבּוּתִי

b. Stems that undergo vowel reduction in -*i* adjective formation:

1. In an open syllable, two syllables away from the main stress, the vowel *a* is deleted:	cylinder > cylindrical security > security related	גָּלִיל < גְּלִילִי בִּטָּחוֹן < בִּטְחוֹנִי

2. When the word ends with a vowel with a final ה׳, they are both deleted:	incident > unplanned contract > contractual negation > negative	מִקְרֶה < מִקְרִי חוֹזֶה < חוֹזִי שְׁלִילָה < שְׁלִילִי
However, when the word ends with a silent א׳, that א׳ remains and 'carries' the *i*:	Bible > biblical	מִקְרָא < מִקְרָאִי
3. The final vowel historically inserted to break up a cluster (in *segolate* nouns) is deleted:	criticism > critical	בִּקֹּרֶת < בִּקָּרְתִּי

4. When the cluster of consonants is difficult to pronounce two syllables away from the stressed suffix, a short *e* replaces the zero vowel:

i. When the first consonant in the cluster is one of the consonants י׳ ל׳ מ׳ נ׳ ר׳:	location > local	מָקוֹם < מְקוֹמִי
ii. When that *a* is followed by a guttural (א׳, ה׳, ח׳, ע׳):	genius (N) > genius (Adj.)	גָּאוֹן < גָּאוֹנִי
5. When the word begins with a guttural, a *ħataf* vowel replaces the expected zero:	spring > springlike friend > friendly	אָבִיב < אֲבִיבִי חָבֵר < חֲבֵרִי

c. Some common internal vowel changes

Some internal vowel changes occur (a historical vowel may resurface with stress shift):	bear > bearlike hawk > hawklike home > homey	דֹּב < דֻּבִּי נֵץ < נִצִּי בַּיִת < בֵּיתִי

d. Changes in the suffix

When the adjective is derived from feminine nouns with an ה-ָ suffix, this suffix is replaced by -*ati*, i.e., *a* is preserved, final ה׳ changes to ת׳, and -*i* is added.	society > social fashion > fashionable problem > problematic link > vertebrate	חֶבְרָה < חֶבְרָתִי אוֹפְנָה < אוֹפְנָתִי בְּעָיָה < בְּעָיָתִי חֻלְיָה < חֻלְיָתִי

e. The suffix *-ni* is added to some monosyllabic nouns

Some adjectives add an *o* vowel to the noun base before the suffix *-ni*.	city > urban	עִיר > עִירוֹנִי
When the noun base has the vowel *a*, an extra *a* is added before the suffix *-ni*.	hand > manual	יָד > יָדָנִי

8.5 Participle forms that function as adjectives

When the form is directly related to a particular verb, adjectives are likely to be realized in the participial forms, as can be seen in the discussion of the verb system.

8.5.1 Active participle forms functioning as adjectives

The active participial forms of *pa`al, pi`el, hitpa`el, hif`il,* can also function as adjectives, normally agentive (the ones who initiate or perform the action). Such adjectives describe an action or a state characteristic of the head noun. The English counterpart of the active participles is the ending *-ing*, as in מְצַעֵר 'distressing', מְרַעֲנֵן 'refreshing'. It can often be paraphrased by 'something that is causing a state or event', as in מְצַעֵר 'distressing', i.e., 'causing distress', or מְרַעֲנֵן 'refreshing', i.e., 'causing one to become refreshed'.

			בניין פעל: צורות בינוני פועל	
just	צוֹדְקוֹת	צוֹדְקִים	צוֹדֶקֶת	צוֹדֵק
			בניין פיעל: צורות בינוני	
representative	מְיַצְּגוֹת	מְיַצְּגִים	מְיַצֶּגֶת	מְיַצֵּג
			בניין התפעל: צורות בינוני	
progressive	מִתְקַדְּמוֹת	מִתְקַדְּמִים	מִתְקַדֶּמֶת	מִתְקַדֵּם
			בניין הפעיל: צורות בינוני	
annoying	מַרְגִּיזוֹת	מַרְגִּיזִים	מַרְגִּיזָה	מַרְגִּיז

Below are examples of adjectives from each of the categories above.

The form פּוֹעֵל	Adjective		Verb
prominent	בּוֹלֵט	stand out	בָּלַט
silent	דּוֹמֵם	be silent	דָּמַם
supportive	תּוֹמֵךְ	support	תָּמַךְ

The form מְפַעֵל

The form מְפַעֵל is the most productive of all the active participles, which means that many adjectives are patterned accordingly. Its relationship to corresponding verb forms is quite transparent. The related verb is usually in *pi`el*. It also accommodates the many quadriliteral root verbal forms as the base for adjectives.

	Adjective		Verb
fascinating	מְרַתֵּק	fascinate	רִתֵּק
refreshing	מְרַעֲנֵן	refresh	רִעֲנֵן
boring	מְשַׁעֲמֵם	bore	שִׁעֲמֵם

The form מִתְפַעֵל	Adjective		Verb
convergent	מִתְכַּנֵּס	converge	הִתְכַּנֵּס
progressive	מִתְקַדֵּם	progress	הִתְקַדֵּם
adolescent	מִתְבַּגֵּר	mature	הִתְבַּגֵּר

The form מַפְעִיל	Adjective		Verb
scary	מַבְהִיל	scare	הִבְהִיל
limiting	מַגְבִּיל	limit	הִגְבִּיל
embarrassing	מֵבִיךְ	embarrass	הֵבִיךְ

8.5.2 Passive participle forms functioning as adjectives

Adjectives that are identical to the passive participle tend to be resultative adjectives, that is, a state which is a result of an action, like סגור 'closed', כתוב 'written', etc. They describe the result of a process that the subject had undergone. There are four possible sources for resultative adjectives: *pa`al* (בינוני פָּעוּל), *nif`al*, *pu`al*, and *huf`al*.

			בניין פעל: צורות בינוני פעול	
closed	סְגוּרוֹת	סְגוּרִים	סְגוּרָה	סָגוּר
			בניין נפעל: צורות רינוני	
separate	נִפְרָדוֹת	נִפְרָדִים	נִפְרֶדֶת	נִפְרָד
			בניין פועל: צורות בינוני	
dangerous	מְסֻכָּנוֹת	מְסֻכָּנִים	מְסֻכֶּנֶת	מְסֻכָּן
			בניין הופעל: צורות בינוני	
recommended	מֻמְלָצוֹת	מֻמְלָצִים	מֻמְלֶצֶת	מֻמְלָץ

Below are examples of adjectives from each of the categories above.

The form פָּעוּל	Adjective		Verb
broken	שָׁבוּר	break	שָׁבַר
open	פָּתוּחַ	open	פָּתַח
locked	נָעוּל	lock	נָעַל

The form נִפְעָל	Adjective		Verb
hidden	נִסְתָּר	be hidden	נִסְתַּר
failed	נִכְשָׁל	fail (intr.)	נִכְשַׁל
select(ed)	נִבְחָר	be chosen	נִבְחַר

The form מְפֻעָל (which, like מְפַעֵל for active participles above, is very productive, owing to the relationship to *pi`el* via *pu`al*)

	Adjective		Verb
neat, tidy	מְסֻדָּר	arrange; be arranged	סִדֵּר ; סֻדַּר
refurbished	מְשֻׁפָּץ	refurbish; be refurbished	שִׁפֵּץ ; שֻׁפַּץ
interested	מְעֻנְיָן	interest (tr.)	עִנְיֵן
state-of-the-art	מְשֻׁכְלָל	perfect; be perfected	שִׁכְלֵל

The form מֻפְעָל			
	Adjective		Verb
exaggerated	מֻגְזָם	exaggerate; be exaggerated	הִגְזִים ; הֻגְזַם
absolute	מֻחְלָט	decide; be decided	הֶחְלִיט ; הֻחְלַט
emphatic	מֻדְגָּשׁ	emphasize; be emphasized	הִדְגִּישׁ ; הֻדְגַּשׁ

8.6 Special patterns

There are other adjectival patterns, which are not as readily related to underlying verb forms as participles are. In some of them the relationship to the verb is more transparent than in others: one can readily identify the root and the verb form from which the adjective may have been derived.

8.6.1 The פָּעִיל pattern

One salient adjectival pattern whose forms can more readily be related to verb bases is פָּעִיל. In the feminine and plural forms of such adjectival forms the initial *kamats* is reduced to *shva* or to a *hataf* vowel:

Process	רבות	רבים	יחידה	יחיד
a > ø	שְׁבִירוֹת	שְׁבִירִים	שְׁבִירָה	שָׁבִיר
a stays after guttural	אֲמִינוֹת	אֲמִינִים	אֲמִינָה	אָמִין

Many recent פָּעִיל forms are equivalent to *-able* adjectives in English, which mean 'that can be …-*en*', e.g., שָׁבִיר 'fragile, breakable', i.e., that can be broken. Even if the comparable English gloss does not contain an actual *-able* suffix, it can still be shown to contain it semantically, e.g., דָּבִיק 'sticky' means 'adhesive', 'that can be glued'.

-*able* type פָּעִיל adjectives:

	Adjective		Verb
countable	סָפִיר	count	סָפַר
accessible	נָגִישׁ	approach	נִגַּשׁ
available	זָמִין	happen to be	הִזְדַּמֵּן

Other, non -*able* type פעיל adjectives:

	Adjective		Base
sensitive	רָגִישׁ	feel	הִרְגִּישׁ
direct	יָשִׁיר	straight	יָשָׁר
senior	בָּכִיר	firstborn	בְּכוֹר

8.6.2 The פַּעִיל pattern

There is also a form that sounds identical to the פָּעִיל form described above, which has a *patah* vowel as the first vowel, and in which the middle consonant has a *dagesh hazak* and is therefore geminated (lengthened) historically. However, since geminated consonants are no longer distinguishable from non-geminated ones, the two patterns are phonetically identical, except for two partial distinguishing markers: when the middle consonant is one of the following consonants: פ׳, ב׳, כ׳ it is realized as *p, b, k*. In the illustration below, the singular form is כַּבִּיר 'huge' and that stem serves the entire inflection of this group. The stem is kept in feminine and plural forms and is never reduced:

Gloss	רבות	רבים	יחידה	יחיד
huge	כַּבִּירוֹת	כַּבִּירִים	כַּבִּירָה	כַּבִּיר

Most of the adjectives that belong to this pattern group do not have transparent bases, verbal or otherwise:

violent	אַלִּים	mighty	אַדִּיר
stable	יַצִּיב	courageous	אַמִּיץ
strong, firm	תַּקִּיף	ancient, antique	עַתִּיק

There are adjectives that have a bi-consonantal base, such as חַם 'hot'. Some of them often have פָּעִיל counterparts (where *ע=י,ַ), which converts them into diminutive or 'lighter' versions of the base:

very thin	דַּקִּיק	thin	דַּק
warm	חָמִים	hot	חַם
bitterish, acrid	מָרִיר	bitter	מַר

8.6.3 The פַּעְלָן pattern

The פַּעְלָן form serves both as a noun pattern group and as an adjective pattern group.

The four forms of this adjective pattern are:

Gloss	רבות	רבים	יחידה	יחיד
diligent	שַׁקְדָּנִיוֹת	שַׁקְדָּנִים	שַׁקְדָּנִית	שַׁקְדָּן
lying; liar	שַׁקְרָנִיוֹת	שַׁקְרָנִים	שַׁקְרָנִית	שַׁקְרָן

When פַּעְלָן is interpreted as an adjective, it is likely to have a related transparent base, usually a verb.

shy	בַּיְשָׁן	be shy	הִתְבַּיֵּשׁ
stubborn	עַקְשָׁן	be stubborn	הִתְעַקֵּשׁ
conservative	שַׁמְרָן	save, conserve	שָׁמַר

Some prefer to disambiguate by using the פַּעְלָנִי form for adjectives, such as in רַגְזָנִי 'irate, bad-tempered' alongside רַגְזָן, to distinguish the adjective from noun, but most speakers do not.

8.6.4 The פָּעֵל pattern

The פָּעֵל pattern group includes adjectives that also stand for corresponding stative verbs, referring to the comparable state of being denoted by the adjective. The base form פָּעֵל has an initial *kamats* vowel. In the feminine and plural forms of such adjectival forms this *kamats* is reduced. It becomes *shva* or a *hataf* vowel:

Gloss	רבות	רבים	יחידה	יחיד
heavy	כְּבֵדוֹת	כְּבֵדִים	כְּבֵדָה	כָּבֵד
guilty	אֲשֵׁמוֹת	אֲשֵׁמִים	אֲשֵׁמָה	אָשֵׁם

A variant of פָּעֵל is the participial form of a ל״י verb: the masculine singular form ends in a *segol* vowel and a final ה׳ and the feminine singular has a *kamats* vowel and a final ה׳, while the plural forms lose both the vowel and that ה׳:

Gloss	<u>רבות</u>	<u>רבים</u>	<u>יחידה</u>	<u>יחיד</u>
hard, difficult	קָשׁוֹת	קָשִׁים	קָשָׁה	קָשֶׁה
pretty, beautiful	יָפוֹת	יָפִים	יָפָה	יָפֶה

8.6.5 The פָּעוֹל pattern

It is possible to distinguish two פָּעוֹל sub-groups: the first one maintains the *o* vowel in all the forms, but the feminine and plural forms undergo reduction of the initial *a*.

Sub-group with o throughout:

Gloss	<u>רבות</u>	<u>רבים</u>	<u>יחידה</u>	<u>יחיד</u>
close, near	קְרוֹבוֹת	קְרוֹבִים	קְרוֹבָה	קָרוֹב
big	גְּדוֹלוֹת	גְּדוֹלִים	גְּדוֹלָה	גָּדוֹל
holy	קְדוֹשׁוֹת	קְדוֹשִׁים	קְדוֹשָׁה	קָדוֹשׁ

In the second group, the initial *a* also undergoes reduction, but the second vowel in all suffixed forms is *u* instead of *o* (כְּחֻלִּים). When the *u* is stressed, which happens only in the unmarked citation form, it becomes *o* (כָּחֹל). Historically, the third root letter following *u* had to be geminated, and thus, when it is ב׳, פ׳, כ׳, it is realized as *b*, *p*, *k*, respectively. Colors and other physical characteristics prevail, as in:

o ~ u sub-group:

blue	כְּחֻלּוֹת	כְּחֻלִּים	כְּחֻלָּה	כָּחֹל
long	אֲרֻכּוֹת	אֲרֻכִּים	אֲרֻכָּה	אָרֹךְ
green	יְרֻקּוֹת	יְרֻקִּים	יְרֻקָּה	יָרֹק

Note

In colors like שָׁחוֹר 'black', אָפוֹר 'gray', etc. there is no alternation with *u*, since ר׳ cannot be geminated.

black	שְׁחוֹרֹות	שְׁחוֹרִים	שְׁחוֹרָה	שָׁחוֹר

8.6.6 The פְּעַלְעַל pattern

Some פָּעוֹל adjectives, mostly those that denote color, may undergo a reduplication process, in which the last two consonants are reduplicated: פְּעַלְעַל. It results in a new adjective that has a diminutive effect, turning 'red' into 'reddish', 'blue' into 'bluish', etc.

	פעלעל		Base פעול
pinkish	וְרַדְרַד	pink	וָרוֹד
bluish	כְּחַלְחַל	blue	כָּחוֹל
darkish	שְׁחַרְחַר	black	שָׁחוֹר

Note that the same reduplication applies if the color is realized in the פָּעָל pattern: לָבָן 'white' > לְבַנְבַּן 'whitish'.

8.6.7 Other common patterns

Pattern	Gloss				Adjective
CiCéC	blind	עִוְרוֹת	עִוְרִים	עִוֶרֶת	עִוֵּר
	deaf	חֵרְשׁוֹת	חֵרְשִׁים	חֵרֶשֶׁת	חֵרֵשׁ
CaCáC	short	קְצָרוֹת	קְצָרִים	קְצָרָה	קָצָר
	new	חֲדָשׁוֹת	חֲדָשִׁים	חֲדָשָׁה	חָדָשׁ
CaCáC	obligated	חַיָּבוֹת	חַיָּבִים	חַיֶּבֶת	חַיָּב
	mobile	נַיָּדוֹת	נַיָּדִים	נַיֶּדֶת	נַיָּד
CaCí	fresh	טְרִיּוֹת	טְרִיִּים	טְרִיָּה	טָרִי
	clean	נְקִיּוֹת	נְקִיִּים	נְקִיָּה	נָקִי
CaC	light, easy	קַלּוֹת	קַלִּים	קַלָּה	קַל
	soft	רַכּוֹת	רַכִּים	רַכָּה	רַך
CoC	good	טוֹבוֹת	טוֹבִים	טוֹבָה	טוֹב
	cheap	זוֹלוֹת	זוֹלִים	זוֹלָה	זוֹל

Chapter 9
Adverbs and adverbial expressions

9.1 Introduction

An adverb, broadly defined, is a word or a phrase that modifies a verb, an adjective, an adverb, whole clauses or sentences. Adverbs cannot modify nouns. Adverbial expressions can consist of a one-word adverb or of an adverbial phrase.

1. Modifying a verb	He <u>runs</u> <u>fast</u>.	הוא <u>רָץ מַהֵר</u>.
2. Modifying an adjective	Dan is <u>very young</u>.	דן <u>צָעִיר מְאוֹד</u>.
3. Modifying an adverb	He runs <u>very</u> <u>fast</u>.	הוא רָץ <u>מַהֵר מְאוֹד</u>.
4. Modifying a sentence	<u>Regrettably</u>, I cannot come.	<u>לְצַעֲרִי</u>, אני לא יכול לבוא.

9.2 Adverbs grouped according to form

They can be a single word adverb, functioning only as adverbs:

Single word adverbs

fast	מַהֵר	first	קֹדֶם	perhaps	אוּלַי
now	עַכְשָׁיו	here	כָּאן/פֹּה	there	שָׁם
always	תָּמִיד	thus	כָּךְ	yesterday	אֶתְמוֹל

Others have the same form as masculine singular adjectives, and can function as either adjectives or adverbs:

clear/clearly	בָּרוּר	good/well	טוֹב	early	מֻקְדָּם
hard	קָשֶׁה	nice/nicely	יָפֶה	strongly	חָזָק

Still others can function as either adverbial degree words or noun quantifiers:

very	מְאוֹד	a bit	מְעַט	much, many	הַרְבֵּה

Suffixes associated with some adverbs
Several suffixes are associated with adverbs in Hebrew.

(a) the suffix הָ- *-a* for some directional adverbs (note that stress does
not shift to the suffix, e.g., *pním ~ pníma*):

Gloss	Adverb	Gloss	Base
to town	הָעִירָה	town	(הָ)עִיר
homeward	הַבַּיְתָה	home	(הַ)בַּיִת
inward	פְּנִימָה	the inside	פְּנִים
southward	דָּרוֹמָה	south	דָּרוֹם
seaward	יָמָּה	sea, east, south	יָם, קֶדֶם, נֶגֶב

Examples

I went <u>to town</u>.	נסעתי <u>העירה</u>.
Go <u>(to) home</u>!	לך <u>הביתה</u>!
I went <u>inside</u>.	נכנסתי <u>פנימה</u>.

The directional adverbs associated with the compass are all marked by
this *-a* ending: צפונה 'northward', דרומה 'southward', מִזְרָחָה 'eastward'
and מַעֲרָבָה 'westward'.

We went <u>southward</u> towards Eilat.	נסענו <u>דרומה</u> לכיוון אילת.
You shall spread out to the west and to the east, to the north and to the south (Genesis 28:14)	וּפָרַצְתָּ <u>יָמָּה וָקֵדְמָה וְצָפֹנָה וָנֶגְבָּה</u> (בראשית כח יד)

A historical note
ימה, קדמה and נגבה are literary biblical counterparts of מערבה
'westward' etc., that designate a direction relative to its position with
respect to the Land of Israel, or to Jerusalem: the Negev region is in the
south, the Mediterranean Sea in the west, and קדמה refers either to an
ancient region east of Canaan (*kedem* = ancient?), or to the direction
one faces when praying towards Jerusalem (being before, in front).

(b) the suffix *-it* for some manner adverbs (slightly formal usage):

Gloss	Adverb	Gloss	Base
personally	אִישִׁית	personal	אִישִׁי
officially	רִשְׁמִית	official	רִשְׁמִי
temporarily	זְמַנִּית	time	זְמַן

Examples

I spoke to him <u>personally</u>.	דיברתי אתו <u>אישית</u>.
I spoke to him <u>by phone</u>.	דיברתי אתו <u>טלפונית</u>.
I am replacing him <u>temporarily</u>.	אני מחליף אותו <u>זמנית</u>.

(c) the suffix *-ot*, also for some manner adverbs, but this one can only be attached to adjectives, and is used primarily in the higher registers:

Gloss	Adverb	Gloss	Base
at length	אֲרֻכּוֹת	long	אָרוֹךְ
harshly	קָשׁוֹת	hard	קָשֶׁה

An adverb can be one word consisting of two constituents: a preposition prefixed to a noun (most commonly -בְּ 'in/with'):

Composed of two constituents			Gloss	Adverb
to+eternity	ל + הנצח	→	forever	לַנֶּצַח
in/with+care	ב + זהירות	→	carefully	בִּזְהִירוּת
in/with+quiet	ב + שקט	→	quietly	בְּשֶׁקֶט
in/with+will	ב + רצון	→	willingly	בְּרָצוֹן
to+last(ly)	ל +אחרונה	→	lately	לָאַחֲרוֹנָה
in/with+purpose	ב + כוונה	→	intentionally	בְּכַוָּנָה

An adverbial expression can be composed of other particles, such as 'negative words', which by themselves are adverbials, followed by a noun:

without will	בְּלִי רָצוֹן	unintentionally	לְלֹא כַּוָּנָה
without logic	בְּלִי שׁוּם הִגָּיוֹן	without a doubt	לְלֹא סָפֵק

It can also consist of several constituents, such as a preposition prefixed to a noun followed by an adjective:

with great care	בִּזְהִירוּת רַבָּה	with ill intention	בְּכַוָּנָה רָעָה

Adverbials can also be phrases or words that introduce an entire sentence or a clause:

first of all	רֵאשִׁית כֹּל	in the beginning	בַּהַתְחָלָה
and finally	וּלְבַסּוֹף	and in summary	וּלְסִכּוּם
to our regret	לְצַעֲרֵנוּ	fortunately	לְמַזָּלֵנוּ

Notice that in the following examples, there are actually two adverbs -
one initiates the entire sentence (and is underlined in the examples),
while the second one modifies the verb.

sentence modifier	verb modifier	תאור פועל	תאור משפט

<u>Fortunately</u> he does not <u>speak so fast</u>.   <u>למזלנו</u> הוא לא <u>מדבר כל כך מהר</u>.

sentence modifier	verb modifier	תאור פועל	תאור משפט

<u>At the beginning</u> he <u>talked very fast</u>.   <u>בהתחלה</u> הוא <u>דיבר מהר מאוד</u>.

9.2.1 Adverb or adjective?

To clarify the role of the adverb, let's compare the use of the adverb
with that of the adjective. We will find the following significant
differences:

1. The adjective changes form according to its head noun. The
agreement in gender and number with the head noun is one of the most
important structural requirements of the adjective. On the other hand,
the adverb keeps the same shape and does not change so as to agree
with any other element in the sentence or phrase. Look at the following:

He did not talk <u>fast</u>, but she did   הוא לא דיבר <u>מהר</u>, אבל גם היא לא
not talk <u>fast</u> either – neither one of   דיברה <u>מהר</u> - שניהם לא דיברו <u>מהר</u>.
them talked <u>fast</u>.

While the subject changed, from 'he' to 'she' to 'they', and the verb
form changed accordingly, the adverb did not change shape.

2. The adjective follows the noun it modifies, while the adverb follows
the verb it modifies.

Adjective	This is a <u>clear</u> chapter.	זה פרק <u>ברור</u>.
	These are <u>clear</u> directions.	אלה הוראות <u>ברורות</u>.
Adverb	He speaks <u>clearly</u>.	הוא מדבר <u>ברור</u>.
	She speaks <u>clearly</u>.	היא מדברת <u>ברור</u>.

A comparative note

In English the distinction between adverb and adjective is usually clear
since, for the most part, their forms are different, e.g., *clearly* vs. *clear*.
In Hebrew, the form of the adjective masculine singular בָּרוּר is the
same as the form of the adverb בָּרוּר, but speakers can tell which is

which by means of the two clues suggested above, agreement or its absence and position with respect to the head:

1. Observe phrases with a feminine head or a plural one. If agreement is observed (e.g., הוֹרָאוֹת בְּרוּרוֹת 'clear directions'), the modifier is an adjective; if not (e.g., הן מְדַבְּרוֹת בָּרוּר 'they (fem.) speak clearly'), it's an adverb.

2. Examine the preceding head. If it is a noun, the modifier is an adjective; if a verb, it's an adverb.

Single word adverbs

He walks <u>fast</u>.	.הוא <u>צוֹעֵד מַהֵר</u>
She eats <u>fast</u>.	.היא <u>אוכלת מַהֵר</u>
They work <u>hard</u>.	.הן <u>עובדות קָשָׁה</u>
They are learning <u>a lot</u>.	.הם <u>לומדים הַרְבֵּה</u>

Adverbial phrases

He hurt us <u>unintentionally</u>.	.הוא <u>פגע בנו בְּלִי כוונה</u>
She did everything <u>without resistance</u>.	.היא <u>עשֹתה הכל לְלֹא התנגדות</u>
They work <u>very diligently</u>.	.הם <u>עובדים בחריצות רבה</u>
They are studying <u>without a teacher</u>.	.הן <u>לומדות בלי מורה</u>

9.3 Adverbs grouped according to function

An adverb, narrowly defined, is a word belonging to a class of words that modify verbs for such categories as manner, time, place, or direction.

9.3.1 Adverbs of manner:
Adverbs that answer the question 'How?/in what manner?'
Modifying verbs

She spoke <u>quietly</u>.	.היא דיברה <u>בְּשֶׁקֶט</u>
He walked <u>slowly</u>.	.הוא הלך <u>לְאַט</u>
Did you hear <u>well</u>?	?שמעת <u>הֵיטֵב</u>

Related interrogative adverbs

<u>How</u> did you find out what happened?	?<u>אֵיךְ</u> שמעת מה קרה
<u>How</u> does one prepare a lentil stew?	?<u>כֵּיצַד</u> מכינים נזיד עדשים

9.3.2 Adverbs of time:

Adverbs that answer the question: 'When? / At what time?'

<u>First</u> she spoke and only <u>then</u> (afterwards) he spoke.	קוֹדֶם היא דיברה ורק אַחַר כָּךְ הוא דיבר.
It happened <u>only yesterday</u>.	זה קרה <u>רק אתמול</u>.
If not <u>now</u>, then <u>when</u>?	אם לא <u>עכשיו</u>, <u>אימתי</u>?

Related interrogative adverbs:

<u>When</u> did you get here?	<u>מתי</u> הגעתם לכאן?
<u>Till when</u> are you staying?	<u>עד מתי</u> אתם נשארים?

9.3.3 Adverbs of place/location:

Adverbs that answer the question: 'Where? At what place?'

We'll meet <u>up</u> in his office.	ניפגש <u>לְמַעְלָה</u> במשרד שלו.
They live <u>upstairs</u>.	הם גרים <u>לְמַעְלָה</u>.
They live <u>across</u>.	הם גרים <u>מִמּוּל</u>.

Related interrogative adverbs:

<u>Where</u> shall we meet?	<u>אֵיפֹה</u> ניפגש?

9.3.4 Adverbs of direction:

Adverbs that answer the question: 'Where to? To what place?'

We went <u>westward</u> in the direction of the sea.	נסענו <u>מַעֲרָבָה</u> לכיוון הים.
We'll go to California – we'll be going (<u>to</u>) <u>there</u> in the spring.	ניסע לקליפורניה – ניסע <u>לְשָׁם</u> באביב.
Because of the tornado threat, they went <u>down</u> to the cellar.	בגלל סכנת הטורנדו, הם ירדו <u>לְמַטָּה</u> למרתף.

Related interrogative adverbs:

<u>Where</u> are you coming <u>from</u> and <u>to where</u> are you headed?	<u>מֵאַיִן</u> אתם באים וּ<u>לְאָן</u> אתם הולכים?

9.4 Adverbs and 'degree' words

Adverbs can also be classified according to their function: some are considered 'true' adverbs, i.e. they modify verbs, while others are considered 'degree' adverbs. Degree words have a different distribution, since for the most part they modify adjectives, some adverbs and a few select verbs. They mostly modify the intensity or degree of certain qualities.

<u>adverbs</u>

The adverb modifies the verb *speaks*:

| He speaks <u>fast</u> and it is difficult to understand him. | הוא מדבר <u>מהר</u> וקשה להבין אותו. |

<u>'degree' words</u>

The 'degree' adverb modifies the adverb *fast*:

| He speaks <u>so</u> fast that it is difficult to understand him. | הוא מדבר <u>כל כך</u> מהר שקשה להבין אותו. |

Adverbs of 'degree' and 'intensity' often modify adjectives.

very	מְאֹד
so	כָּל כָּךְ
not at all	בִּכְלָל לֹא
especially	בִּמְיֻחָד

An adverb of degree that precedes an adjective is דֵי 'quite':

| He is <u>quite</u> smart. | הוא די <u>חכם</u>. |

He is talented.	הוא מוכשר.
He is <u>very</u> talented.	הוא מוכשר <u>מאוד</u>.
He is <u>so</u> talented.	הוא <u>כל כך</u> מוכשר.
He is <u>not</u> talented <u>at all</u>.	הוא <u>בכלל לא</u> מוכשר.
He is <u>especially</u> talented.	הוא מוכשר <u>במיוחד</u>.
He is <u>quite</u> talented.	הוא <u>די</u> מוכשר.

The 'degree' and 'intensity' adverbs also modify verbs that express feelings, desire, and wish, such as אוהב, שונא, רוצה, מקווה.

He <u>very much</u> likes…	הוא אוהב <u>מאוד</u>…
He wants <u>very much</u>…	הוא רוצה <u>מאוד</u>…
He hates <u>so much</u>…	הוא שונא <u>כל כך</u>…
He <u>especially</u> likes…	הוא אוהב <u>במיוחד</u>…
He <u>does not</u> like <u>at all</u>…	הוא <u>בכלל לא</u> אוהב…

Adverbs of 'degree' can also modify other adverbs that describe the degree or intensity of a particular activity.

He speaks a lot but says little.	הוא מדבר הרבה ואומר מעט.
He speaks <u>slowly</u>.	הוא מדבר <u>לאט</u>.
He speaks [<u>very</u> <u>slowly</u>].	הוא מדבר [לאט + מאוד].
He speaks [<u>so</u> <u>slowly</u>].	הוא מדבר [כל כך + לאט].
He speaks [<u>too</u> <u>slowly</u>].	הוא מדבר [יותר מדי + לאט].

He talks <u>a lot</u>.   הוא מדבר <u>הרבה</u>.
He talks [<u>a great deal</u>].   .[<u>הרבה</u> + <u>מאוד</u>] הוא מדבר
He talks [<u>so</u> much].   .[<u>כל כך</u> + <u>הרבּה</u>] הוא מדבר
He talks [<u>too</u> much].   .[<u>יותר מדי</u>] הוא מדבר

He says <u>little</u>.   .<u>מעט</u> הוא מדבר
He says [<u>very</u> little].   .[<u>מעט</u> + <u>מאוד</u>] הוא מדבר
He says [<u>too</u> little].   .[<u>מעט מדי</u>] הוא מדבר

Note

A source of confusion for many learners of Hebrew is the distinction
between הַרְבֵּה 'a lot/much' and מְאֹד 'a lot/very much'. הַרְבֵּה is a
quantifier referring to the number of times an action has taken place
(e.g., taking many trips), or to the general quantity/amount to which it
applies (e.g., eating a lot), while the intensifier מְאֹד refers to the
intensity of the action (e.g., loving a lot).
הַרְבֵּה is an adverb of degree. It is also used as a quantifier of nouns:

<u>As adverb:</u>	They read <u>a lot</u>.	.<u>הרבה</u> הם קראו
<u>As quantifier:</u>	They read <u>many books</u>.	.<u>הרבה</u> ספרים הם קראו

מְאֹד is an intensifier. It is used only with verbs that can be intensified.

<u>As adverb:</u>	We <u>very much hope</u> to hike in the mountains.	אנחנו <u>מקווים מאוד</u> .לטייל בהרים

A quantifying adverb can be used only when the verb is quantifiable.
How many times did they hike in the mountains? 'Once', 'twice', 'a
lot'.

<u>As quantifier:</u>	They <u>traveled a lot</u> abroad.	.הם <u>טיילו הרבה</u> בחו״ל
	* <s>They saw very.</s>	.*<s>הם ראו מְאֹד</s>
	They saw <u>a lot</u>.	.<u>הרבה</u> הם ראו

In English the adverb 'a lot' can be used for both הַרְבֵּה and מְאֹד. In
Hebrew they are mutually exclusive, except when one wants to further
enhance מְאֹד, and in colloquial use הַרְבֵּה מְאֹד, meaning 'an awful lot',
is used for emphasis.

As noted above, when quantifiers modify nouns, they are not considered adverbs:

A lot of money.	הַרְבֵּה כסף.
Some noise.	קְצָת רעש.
Many people.	הַרְבֵּה אנשים.

9.4.1 Adverbs that answer the question 'to what degree'?

Degree word: modifying verb

She talks too much.	היא ישנה יוֹתֵר מִדַּי.
She loved to read very much (a lot).	היא אהבה מְאוֹד לקרוא.
He ate a bit and rested a bit.	הוא אכל קְצָת ונח קְצָת.

Degree word: modifying adjective

He is a bit quiet.	הוא קְצָת שָׁקֵט.
They are quite smart.	הם דַּי נְבוֹנִים.
The food is too hot.	האוכל חַם מִדַּי.

Related interrogative adverb:

How much time did she sleep?	כַּמָּה זמן היא ישנה?
How many people were there?	כַּמָּה אנשים היו?

9.4.2 Positive and negative expressions

Adverbial positive expressions

Yes. This is indeed a serious development.	כֵּן. ההתפתחות אָכֵן רצינית.
Certainly this needs mentioning.	וַדַּאי צריך להזכיר זאת.

Adverbial negative expressions

Not here and not now.	לֹא כאן ולֹא עכשיו.
What? Are you without a coat?	מה? אתה בְּלִי מעיל?

Adverbial expressions of doubt

Not today – perhaps tomorrow.	לא היום – אוּלַי מחר.
I am worried lest they not come on time.	אני חושש שֶׁמָּא הם לא יגיעו בזמן.

9.4.3 Adverb or prepositional phrase?

After questions regarding place or time, the answer (an obligatory complement of the verb) can consist of either an adverb or a prepositional phrase that functions as an adverbial syntactically.

Place:		אֵיפֹה ניפגש?
Adverb	We'll meet <u>upstairs</u>.	(ניפגש) <u>לְמַעְלָה</u>.
Complement	We'll meet <u>at his office</u>.	(ניפגש) <u>במשרד שלו</u>.

Time:		מָתַי ניפגש?
Adverb	The meeting will be <u>tomorrow</u>.	(ניפגש) <u>מחר</u>.
Complement	The meeting will be <u>at four o'clock</u>.	(ניפגש) <u>בשעה ארבע</u>.

9.5 Sentential adverbs

The term 'adverb' suggests that adverbs modify verbs only, but as noted above, the domain of some adverbs goes beyond the verb; it can apply to the whole sentence. The adverb מהר מאוד '(very) fast' in הוא נוהג מהר מאוד 'He drives very fast' is clearly a modifier of נוהג 'drive'. But the domain of לדעתי 'in my opinion' in לדעתי, הוא נוהג מהר מדיי 'In my opinion, he drives too fast' is not the verb, nor even the whole predicate, but rather the whole sentence. If we rewrite the sentence as דעתי היא שהוא נוהג מהר מדיי 'My opinion is that he drives too fast', or 'It is my opinion that he drives too fast', we'll see that לדעתי 'in my opinion' relates to the entire sentence.

Most sentence adverbials express a point of view (that of the speaker, the writer, the subject of the sentence or another person referred to in the adverbial) regarding the sentence content, and since what they express does not form an integral part of the sentence they modify, they are often – though not necessarily – separated from it by comma intonation. The point of view can be a comment on the statement in the sentence, or it can place it in context. An adverbial such as בבקשה 'please' in תני לי שלושה כרטיסים ביציע, בבקשה 'Give me three tickets in the balcony, please' characterizes the statement as a polite request. A sentence adverbial can also serve to refer to a previous statement, e.g. כאמור 'as already noted'.

Sentence adverbials may consist of a single word, a phrase, or a clause. What is common to all is that they can be paraphrased in a manner that would expand them into full clauses, which on the surface look like the main clause to which the original sentence is subordinate. Below are some illustrations drawn from a corpus, with accompanying comments.

9.5.1 Qualifying statements of opinion

The following expressions, and others, may be used to qualify statements as constituting opinions (we will use the first person, for simplicity, but other pronouns and full nouns may be used as well):

In my opinion/according to my opinion	לְדַעְתִּי/ לְפִי דַעְתִּי
To the best of my understanding	לְפִי מֵיטַב הֲבָנָתִי
(To tell you) frankly	(לוֹמַר לְךָ) בְּכֵנוּת
To tell you the truth	לוֹמַר (לְךָ) אֶת הָאֱמֶת
Between us, confidentially	בֵּינֵינוּ
Personally	אִישִׁית

The adverbial may be expanded all the way to containing a subordinate clause with -שֶׁ, as in

As far as I understand'	עַד כַּמָּה שֶׁאֲנִי מֵבִין
As far as I know	עַד כַּמָּה שֶׁאֲנִי יוֹדֵעַ

Expressions such as לדעתי can also be located within the sentence, and they are not usually separated by commas.

1. The point of view can be that of the speaker, as in:

He is not guilty, <u>in my opinion</u>, until the court decides his guilt.	הוא אינו אשם <u>לדעתי</u> עד שבית המשפט לא יקבע את אשמתו.

2. The point of view being referred to can be that of the addressee, as in:

Rachel, <u>in your opinion</u>, is this best-seller truly a good book?	רחל, האם <u>לדעתך</u> רב-המכר הזה הוא באמת ספר טוב?

3. The point of view can also be of an entity to which the pronoun in the sentence refers to:

The Justice Department made it clear that <u>in its opinion</u> cable should not be given a license for fast internet and television broadcasts.	משרד המשפטים הבהיר כי <u>לדעתו</u> אין לתת לכבלים רשיון לאינטרנט מהיר ולשידורי טלוויזיה.

9.5.2 Evaluating a statement by expressions of regret and surprise

There are adverbial expressions of emotions such as regret or surprise that modify the entire sentence, such as:

unfortunately, regrettably	לְצַעֲרִי (הָרַב)/לְדַאֲבוֹנִי/לְמַרְבֵּה הַצַּעַר
surprisingly	לְהַפְתָּעָתִי
astonishingly	לְתַדְהֵמָתִי
disappointingly	לְאַכְזָבָתִי
luckily	לְמַזָּלִי/לְמַרְבֵּה הַמַּזָּל
what is surprising (about it) is that	הַמַּפְתִּיע בַּדָּבָר הוּא שֶׁ-/מַה שֶׁמַּפְתִּיע הוּא שֶׁ-

Here are some illustrations of the uses of these expressions:

<u>To our great regret</u>, we are not doing such good business.	לצערנו הרב, העסקים לא כל כך טובים.
<u>To my astonishment</u> I heard my name called.	לתדהמתי שמעתי שקוראים בשמי.
<u>Luckily for the driver</u>, the car did not complete the fall.	למזלו של הנהג, המכונית לא השלימה את הנפילה.

9.5.3 Is the statement true/untrue?

Adverbial expressions can be used to ascertain the truth-value of a situation or statement. They include some of the following:

of course, certainly, naturally	בֶּטַח
undoubtedly	בְּוַדַּאי/כַּמּוּבָן
it is obvious that	לְלֹא סָפֵק
as is well-known	בָּרוּר
luckily	כַּיָּדוּעַ
as expected	כַּצָּפוּי
the truth of the matter is	לַאֲמִתּוֹ שֶׁל דָּבָר
theoretically (speaking)	לַהֲלָכָה/תֵּיאוֹרֵטִית/מִבְּחִינָה תֵּיאוֹרֵטִית
formally	רִשְׁמִית/בְּאֹפֶן רִשְׁמִי
perhaps, it could be	אוּלַי
seemingly	כַּנִּרְאֶה

Here are some illustrations of the uses of these expressions:

<u>Surely</u> this is not a beginner's program.	זו <u>בטח</u> לא תוכנית למתחילים.
<u>Without a doubt</u>, it's our children who will have to pay.	<u>ללא ספק</u>, הילדים שלנו הם שיצטרכו לשלם.
Outside of Israel's territorial water, Israeli policemen <u>of course</u> have no enforcement power.	מחוץ למים הטריטוריאליים של ישראל אין <u>כמובן</u> לשוטרים ישראלים סמכות אכיפה.
<u>The truth of the matter is</u> that conditions now are quite different from what they were in the past.	<u>לאמיתו של דבר</u>, התנאים עכשיו שונים ממה שהיו בעבר.

With or without a comma?

While there is a tendency to separate the sentential adverbs from the rest of the sentence by commas, in some cases there are no such commas. Although commas do not separate בטח and כמובן in the first and third examples above, they still modify the whole sentence.

9.5.4 Introducing main propositions as subordinate clauses

Expansion to variants containing clauses with -ש is quite common:

of course, certainly, naturally	בְּטוּחַ שֶׁ-
undoubtedly	בְּוַדַּאי שֶׁ-/כַּמוּבָן שֶׁ-
as is obvious that…	בָּרוּר שֶׁ-
it is a fact that…	עֻבְדָּה שֶׁ-
it is possible that…	יִתָּכֵן שֶׁ-
it is true that…	נָכוֹן שֶׁ-

Many of the expressions above can be made negative by initiating them with the negative particle לא or אין:

it is not certain that …	לֹא בָּטוּחַ שֶׁ-
there is no doubt that …	אֵין סָפֵק שֶׁ-
it is not clear that/if	לֹא בָּרוּר שֶׁ-/אִם
it is not possible that…	לֹא יִתָּכֵן שֶׁ-
it is not true that…	לֹא נָכוֹן שֶׁ-

Here are some colloquial expressions:

really (lit. 'by my life')	בְּחַיַּי/ בְּחַיַּי שֶׁ-
it couldn't possibly be …	בַּחַיִּים … לֹא …

While structurally the adverbial expressions act as main clauses, they
do not state the main propositions. The adverbial expressions function
as modifiers of the main propositions, included in the subordinate
clauses.

<u>Some illustrations of the uses of these expressions:</u>

<u>There is no doubt that</u> there is a lot to complain about.	אין ספק שיש על מה להתלונן.
<u>Naturally</u> there is reason to be pleased.	בוודאי שיש סיבה להיות מרוצים.
<u>It is a fact that</u> many people came, in spite of the cold.	עובדה שהגיעו הרבה אנשים למרות הקור.
I <u>swear/by my life</u> I never thought of insulting you!	בחיי שלא חשבתי להעליב אתכם!

9.5.5 Placing the statement in a different or special context

The writer or speaker may wish to place the statement in the sentence
in a different or special context, introducing it as a general observation,
a request, or a deviation from the main topic.

Here are some of the expressions used for such purposes:

generally speaking	בְּאֹפֶן כְּלָלִי/בְּדֶרֶךְ כְּלָל
incidentally, by the way	אַגַּב/דֶרֶךְ אַגַּב
if you please	בְּבַקָשָׁה
with your permission	בִּרְשׁוּתְךָ/בִּרְשׁוּתְכֶם

<u>Here are some illustrations:</u>

<u>Generally speaking</u>, the company's activities will be affected by the rising costs.	באופן כללי, פעילות החברה תושפע מהתייקרות המחירים.
The CEO stated, <u>incidentally</u>, that this year also he did not expect changes.	המנכ״ל הודיע, דרך אגב, שגם השנה הוא לא מצפה לשינויים.
<u>By the way</u>, I want to add another small comment.	אגב, אני רוצה להוסיף עוד הערה קטנה.
<u>With your permission</u>, I'd like to go back to last year's report.	ברשותכם, אני רוצה לחזור לדו״ח של השנה שעברה.

9.5.6 Referencing or connecting sentence adverbials

Sentence adverbials may refer to a previous sentence or to some other context already noted, or known to the parties to the communication.

Here are some of the expressions used for such purposes:

as already noted	כָּאָמוּר
as noted above	כְּפִי שֶׁצֻיַּן לְמַעְלָה

Here are some illustrations:

As noted, the prices may change.   .כאמור, המחירים עלולים להשתנות

The CEO announced, as noted above, that he did not expect changes.   ,המנכ״ל הודיע, כפי שצוין למעלה .שהוא לא מצפה לשינויים

Sentence adverbials may also connect between sentences, not as conjunctions, but as adverbial expressions. The connections always assume a larger context, an intra-sentential one, which goes beyond the sentence.

moreover	יֶתֶר עַל כֵּן
in addition	בְּנוֹסָף לַזֶּה/לְכָךְ
in regards to, concerning	בַּאֲשֶׁר לְ-/לְנַגְבֵּי
for instance	לְמָשָׁל/לְדֻגְמָה
that is, namely	דְּהַיְנוּ
in other words	בְּמִלִּים אֲחֵרוֹת
in conclusion, to sum up	לְסַכּוּם
so	אָז
in this respect	מִבְּחִינָה זוֹ
briefly, in short	בְּקִצּוּר
if so	אִם כָּךְ/אִם כֵּן
in any case	בְּכָל זֹאת
in contrast	לְעֻמַּת זֹאת
indeed ... however ...	... אָמְנָם ... אֲבָל
on the one hand ... and on the other ...	... מִצַּד אֶחָד ... וּמִצַּד שֵׁנִי

Here are some illustrations:

We should not raise our prices; <u>moreover</u>, we must keep the quality of the product.

אסור לנו להעלות את המחירים; <u>יתר על כן</u>, אנחנו חייבים לשמור על איכות התוצר.

<u>In regards to</u> further research, it all depends on federal grants.

<u>באשר</u> למחקרים נוספים, הכל תלוי במענקים מהממשלה הפדרלית.

Dina began shopping for the trip, <u>however</u> Danny worked till the last minute.

דינה התחילה לעשות קניות לטיול, <u>לעומת זאת</u>, דני עבד עד הרגע האחרון.

It cannot be that the government, <u>on the one hand</u>, opens the market to competition, <u>and on the other hand</u>, competes with a private company.

לא ייתכן שהממשלה, <u>מצד אחד</u>, פותחת את השוק לתחרות, <u>ומצד שני</u>, מתחרה בגורם פרטי.

Chapter 10
Particles

10.1 Introduction

Particles include prepositions, conjunctions, and exclamations. While prepositions can have pronoun suffixes, conjunctions and exclamations do not. They do not change in form regardless of where they occur, and they typically have a grammatical function in the sentence.

10.2 The particle את before definite direct objects
המילית "את" לפני צירופים שמניים מיודעים

In Hebrew the prepositional-like particle את marks definite direct objects. It precedes them and links them to transitive verbs. This particle presents problems for non-native speakers for the following reasons:

a.   There is no equivalent particle in English.
b.   It is not used when the direct object is indefinite.

The definition used here for direct objects and for transitive verbs is strictly formal: a direct object is one that is not linked to its verb by a preposition (but when it is dcfinite it is preceded by the particle את). A transitive verb is likewise defined as a verb that is followed by a direct object.

Examples of indefinite direct objects:

I am reading <u>an interesting book</u>.	אני קוראת <u>ספר מעניין</u>.
The police caught <u>two robbers</u>.	המשטרה תפסה <u>שני גנבים</u>.
The children bought <u>a gift</u> for their teacher.	הילדים קנו <u>מתנה</u> למורה שלהם.

Notice that both the Hebrew and the English verbs are followed by
direct objects. No prepositions can be inserted to link the verbs to their
direct objects. The direct objects in the above examples are all
indefinite. In English, the singular noun is preceded by 'an', while the
plural noun has no article. In Hebrew there is no article for the singular
or plural indefinite nouns:

an interesting book	ספר מעניין
two robbers	שני גנבים
a gift	מתנה

The differences between Hebrew and English are present when the
direct objects are definite. In Hebrew the direct object particle אֶת
follows transitive verbs that are complemented by definite direct
objects.

Examples of definite direct objects:

I am reading <u>the interesting book</u>.	אני קוראת <u>את הספר המעניין</u>.
The police caught <u>the robbers</u>.	המשטרה תפסה <u>את הגנבים</u>.
The children bought <u>the gift</u> at the new mall.	הילדים קנו <u>את המתנה</u> בקניון החדש.

The user has to be aware of what constitutes a direct object and also has
to remember that the particle את must be inserted before such an object.
As this particle does not exist in English, it presents a problem,
especially in conversational situations when there is no time to analyze
the nature of the verb and its object.

A comparative note

Hebrew and English do not necessarily share all verbs that are
considered transitive where the object is direct. Consider the following
examples where in English the verb is transitive, while in Hebrew, a
preposition must be used to link the verb to its object and thus it is not
considered a direct object.

English: - preposition	**Hebrew: + preposition**
The principal <u>entered the classroom</u> unannounced.	המנהל <u>נכנס **לכיתה**</u> בלי להודיע מראש.
David <u>told everybody</u> to leave.	דוד <u>אמר **לכולם**</u> לצאת.
Everyone <u>left the room</u>.	כולם <u>יצאו **מהחדר**</u>.

English: + preposition   **Hebrew: - preposition**

The police <u>are searching</u> **for** witnesses to the accident.   . המשטרה <u>מחפשת עדים</u> לתאונה

A definite object is not just a noun or a noun phrase with a definite article, but also includes other nouns that are considered inherently definite: names of persons; names of geographical entities, such as countries, cities, regions; nouns with possessive suffixes and more.

An object is made definite by having one of the following features or by being one of the following entities:

<u>Definite article</u>	We'll see <u>the movie</u> tomorrow night.	. נראה <u>את הסרט</u> מחר בערב
<u>Proper name</u>	Do you know <u>Jonah Wallach</u>?	אתם מכירים <u>את יונה ולך</u>?
<u>Place name</u>	The scientists discovered <u>Sedna</u>, the 10th planet.	, המדענים גילו <u>את סדנה</u> .10-כוכב הלכת ה
<u>Nouns with possessive suffix</u>	They will put <u>their things</u> in storage.	הם ישימו <u>את חפציהם</u> .במחסן
<u>Possessive phrase</u>	We'll ask <u>our guide</u> if he has new information.	נשאל <u>את המדריך שלנו</u> . אם יש לו מידע חדש

(For a description of 'internal direct objects', see note in chapter 12, p. 289.)

When the direct object is a personal pronoun rather than a noun, the particle is merged with the pronoun suffixes. It is a definite concept.

<u>Singular</u>

אוֹתָהּ	אוֹתוֹ	אוֹתָךְ	אוֹתְךָ	אוֹתִי
her	him	you	you	me

<u>Plural</u>

אוֹתָן	אוֹתָם	אֶתְכֶן *אוֹתְכֶן	אֶתְכֶם *אוֹתְכֶם	אוֹתָנוּ
them	them	you	you	us

* In daily speech the אות- variant is also used in the plural second person suffixes.

Note

Since many learners have problems identifying a direct object and also identifying a definite direct object, it is useful to note that there are contexts where the direct object status is visible in English as well: some of the pronouns have forms that are used when they are objects, such as in *him, her, us, them.*

We saw <u>them</u> and they saw <u>us</u>.	אנחנו ראינו <u>אותם</u> והם ראו <u>אותנו</u>.
She got <u>her</u> dressed.	היא הלבישה <u>אותה</u>.
Did you see <u>him</u> in the play?	ראיתם <u>אותו</u> בהצגה?

10.3 Prepositions   מילות יחס

Prepositions indicate relationships between nouns and other components of the phrase or the sentence. Prepositions combine with other items, which function as the objects of the prepositions and form prepositional phrases. These phrases consist of a preposition and a noun, a noun phrase or a pronoun that serves to complete the phrase. Prepositions can never dangle in a sentence or a phrase – they have to be completed by nouns, noun phrases, or pronouns. Pronouns that follow prepositions are **always** attached to the prepositions, and do not appear as two separate items.

Note

A common mistake that English speakers make is to:
1. Literally translate a preposition and pronoun as two separate items:

He studies <u>with</u> <u>us</u>.	הוא למד <u>איתנו</u>.
	~~הוא למד עם + אנחנו.~~

2. Omit a noun or pronoun complement after a preposition.
Prepositions do not stand alone.

The family you asked <u>about</u> left the city.	המשפחה ששאלת <u>עליה</u> עזבה את העיר.
	~~המשפחה ששאלת <u>על</u> עזבה את העיר.~~

10.3.1 Prepositions: Form

Prepositions can be followed by either a noun (עם דן 'with Dan') or be combined with a pronominal suffix (אִתּוֹ 'with him'). Prepositions that consist of only one letter are always prefixed to nouns or pronouns and are never written as independent words.

Prepositions are also formed by more complex entities, which combine prefix prepositions with certain nouns or other prepositions into single grammatical items, such as ב+תוך 'inside' or ב+שביל 'for the sake of'.

10.3.2 One-syllable prepositions directly prefixed to nouns

The prepositions ‎ב-, ל-, כ-, which have the form of prefixes, have a *shva* that is realized as *e*. The preposition ‎מ- has an *i* vowel.

				Prepositions	
in America	*beamerika*	בָּאמריקה	in, at	*be-*	‎בְּ-
to life!	*leħáyim*	לְחיים	to	*le-*	‎לְ-
for everyone	*lekhulam*	לְכולם	for		
as a spokesman	*kedover*	כְּדובר	as	*ke-*	‎כְּ-
from Tel Aviv	*mitelaviv*	מִתל-אביב	from	*mi-**	‎מִ-*

*The form ‎מִ- is an abbreviated version of the preposition word מִן (since a ‎נ at the end of a syllable is often assimilated to the next consonant), and has achieved the status of a prefix. In texts with full vowel representation, the first consonant of the noun that follows this preposition receives a *dagesh ħazak*, to compensate for the loss of the final ‎נ of the full form of the preposition.

Prefixed to nouns that begin with a consonant cluster

When the following prepositions are prefixed to a noun that starts with a consonant cluster, the prefix *shva* vowel in ‎ב-, כ-, ל- is replaced by *i* (a *shva na`* cannot be followed by a consonant cluster, or by another *shva*):

in handwriting	*bikhtav yad*	בִּכְתב יד
for a reasonable price	*limhir savir*	לִמְחיר סביר
as one group	*kikvutsa aħat*	כִּקְבוצה אחת

The same happens when ‎ב-, כ-, ל- precede a first consonant *y* with a *shva*, except that in addition, the ‎י *y* is weakened to *i*, and the following weak *shva* is elided:

in Jericho	*be + yeriħo > biriħo*	בְּ+ יְריחו > בִּיריחו

When one of ‎ב-, כ-, ל- precedes a first consonant that is guttural with a *hataf* vowel, it takes on the color of that vowel.

in a dream	b + ħalom > baħalom	בְּ + חֲלוֹם < בַּחֲלוֹם
like a nut	k + 'egoz > ke'egoz	כְּ + אֱגוֹז < כֶּאֱגוֹז
by boat	b + 'oniya >bo'oniya	בְּ + אֳנִיָּה < בָּאֳנִיָּה

Note

These rules are often ignored in daily speech, unless the form is part of a fixed idiom. The shva e is maintained as the main vowel of the prepositions:

Normative	Colloquial	Normative	Colloquial
לִירִיחוֹ	לְירִיחוֹ	בִּכְתָב יד	בְּכְתָב יד
בָּאֳנִיָּה	בְּאֳנִיָּה	בַּחֲלוֹם	בְּחֲלוֹם

When -מ precedes one of the guttural letters א׳, ה׳, ח׳, ע׳, ר׳, the vowel of the preposition changes from *i* to *e*, which is also the case before the definite article -ה.

from a land	mi + 'erets > me'erets	מִ + אֶרֶץ < מֵאֶרֶץ
from a circle	mi+ `igul > me`igul	מִ + עִגּוּל < מֵעִגּוּל
from a man	mi+ 'adam> me'adam	מִ + אָדָם < מֵאָדָם

| from the house | mi+ habayit > mehabayit | מִ + הַבַּיִת < מֵהַבַּיִת |
| from the garden | mi+ hagina> mehagina | מִ + הַגִּנָּה < מֵהַגִּנָּה |

Note

This rule seems to be observed for the most part in daily speech. However, one can also hear the vowel *i* maintained even before gutturals and definite articles.

Normative	Colloquial	Normative	Colloquial
מֵהַבִּית	מִהַבִּית	מֵאֶרֶץ	מִאֶרֶץ

10.3.3 Prefixed to nouns with definite articles

When the prepositions ב-, כ-, ל- combine with the definite article, the ה׳ is omitted, but the *a* vowel that is part of the definite article remains: *be+ha, le+ha, ke+ha → ba, la, ka*, respectively.

Following the preposition -מ, which as note above is an abbreviation of the independent word preposition מִן, the definite article remains in its entirety: *mi+ha → meha*.

Examples

at home	*babáyit*	בַּבַּיִת	in/at the		-בְּ/בַ
to the movies	*lakolnoa`*	לַקּוֹלְנוֹעַ	to the		-לְ/לַ
for the family	*lamishpaħa*	לַמִּשְׁפָּחָה	for the		
as (the) usual	*karagil*	כָּרָגִיל	as the		כְּ/כַּ
from the sea	*mehayam*	מֵהַיָּם	from the		-מֵהַ

10.3.4 One-word prepositions

Many prepositions consist of independent words, and pronoun suffixes can be added to them.

Here is a list of some of these prepositions:

from	מִן	about	אוֹדוֹת
against	נֶגֶד	after	(אַחֲרֵי(י
around	-סָבִיב	to, toward	אֶל
until, up to	עַד	at	אֵצֶל
on, about	עַל	direct object marker	-אֶת/אֶת
next to	עַל-יַד	between, among	בֵּין
with	עִם	without	בְּלִי
of, belonging to	שֶׁל	before	לִפְנֵי
below, under	תַּחַת	through	דֶּרֶךְ
		by	מֵאֵת

Examples

They were left <u>without</u> bread or water.	הם נשארו <u>בְּלִי</u> לחם ומים.
Dan is confused <u>between</u> right and left.	דן מתבלבל <u>בֵּין</u> ימין ושמאל.
The movie is based <u>on</u> the book <u>by</u>	הסרט מבוסס <u>עַל</u> ספרו <u>שֶׁל</u>
Amos Oz.	עמוס עוז.
The book is <u>by</u> Amos Oz.	הספר הוא <u>מֵאַת</u> עמוס עוז.

10.3.5 Complex prepositions

Many prepositions consist of a combination of a prefix preposition (see above), which is combined with either nouns or other prepositions. They become one word and form a new entity. Pronoun suffixes can be added to them.

Here is a list of some of these prepositions:

in contrast with	לְעוּמַת	while, as long as	בְּעוֹד
as (+ noun)	בְּתוֹר	inside	בְּתוֹךְ
below	מִתַּחַת	for	בִּשְׁבִיל
above	מֵעַל	for	בַּעֲבוּר/עֲבוּר
opposite	מִנֶּגֶד	because of	בִּגְלַל
behind	מֵאֲחוֹרֵי	in front of	מִלִּפְנֵי
facing	מִמּוּל	instead of	בִּמְקוֹם

Examples

Two well-known architects stood <u>behind</u> (supported) the project.	שני ארכיטקטים ידועים עמדו <u>מאחורי</u> הפרוייקט.
<u>Behind them</u> was the support of two known banks.	<u>מאחוריהם</u> הייתה תמיכה של שני בנקים ידועים.
<u>As opposed to</u> some other cities, Rome is a progressive city.	<u>לעומת</u> ערים אחרות, רומא היא עיר מתקדמת.
The safe is <u>inside</u> the room.	הכספת <u>בתוך</u> החדר.
<u>Inside it</u> are documents.	<u>בתוכה</u> יש מסמכים.

Complex prepositions followed by prefixes

Many prepositions consist of a combination of prepositions, nouns, or adverbs that are followed by the monosyllabic prepositional prefixes, usually ל-, מ-. Here is a list of some of these prepositions:

beneath, below	מִתַּחַת ל-	aside from	חוּץ מ-
before	קוֹדֶם ל-	across	מֵעֵבֶר ל-
against, facing	מִנֶּגֶד ל-	around	(מ)סָבִיב ל-
excluding	מִחוּץ ל-, חוּץ מ-	above, over	מֵעַל ל-

Examples

The construction continued <u>for over</u> seven years.	הבנייה נמשכה <u>מעל לשבע</u> שנים.
<u>Aside from</u> the soup, Dan ate everything.	<u>חוץ מהמרק</u>, דן אכל את הכל.
<u>Across</u> the road was a shopping center.	<u>מעבר לכביש</u> היה מרכז קניות.
<u>Around</u> the building there were tall trees and wide lawns.	<u>מסביב לבניין</u> היו עצים גבוהים ומדשאות נרחבות.

10.3.6 Prepositions with pronoun suffixes

Here are some of the prepositions with pronoun suffixes. Notice that most of them have an ending similar to the endings added to those suffixed to singular nouns (Set A), and some have the same endings as those suffixed to plural nouns (Set B). Not all prepositions are included in the tables below.

Set A
Pronoun suffixes attached to prepositions
(Shape of possessive pronoun suffixes attached to singular nouns)

בְּ-	לְ-	שֶׁל	אֶת	
in	to	of	Direct Object	
בִּי	לִי	שֶׁלִּי	אוֹתִי	אני
בְּךָ	לְךָ	שֶׁלְּךָ	אוֹתְךָ	אתה
בָּךְ	לָךְ	שֶׁלָּךְ	אוֹתָךְ	את
בּוֹ	לוֹ	שֶׁלּוֹ	אוֹתוֹ	הוא
בָּהּ	לָהּ	שֶׁלָּהּ	אוֹתָהּ	היא
בָּנוּ	לָנוּ	שֶׁלָּנוּ	אוֹתָנוּ	אנחנו
בָּכֶם	לָכֶם	שֶׁלָּכֶם	אֶתְכֶם**	אתם
בָּכֶן	לָכֶן	שֶׁלָּכֶן	אֶתְכֶן**	אתן
בָּהֶם	לָהֶם	שֶׁלָּהֶם	אוֹתָם	הם
בָּהֶן	לָהֶן	שֶׁלָּהֶן	אוֹתָן	הן

מוּל	מִן/מִ-	בִּשְׁבִיל	עִם	עִם (אֶת)	אֵצֶל
across from	from	for	with	with	at
מוּלִי	מִמֶּנִּי	בִּשְׁבִילִי	עִמִּי	אִתִּי	אֶצְלִי
מוּלְךָ	מִמְּךָ	בִּשְׁבִילְךָ	עִמְּךָ	אִתְּךָ	אֶצְלְךָ
מוּלֵךְ*	מִמֵּךְ*	בִּשְׁבִילֵךְ*	עִמָּךְ	אִתָּךְ	אֶצְלֵךְ*
מוּלוֹ	מִמֶּנּוּ	בִּשְׁבִילוֹ	עִמּוֹ	אִתּוֹ	אֶצְלוֹ
מוּלָהּ	מִמֶּנָּה	בִּשְׁבִילָהּ	עִמָּהּ	אִתָּהּ	אֶצְלָהּ
מוּלֵנוּ	מֵאִתָּנוּ (מִמֶּנּוּ)	בִּשְׁבִילֵנוּ*	עִמָּנוּ	אִתָּנוּ	אֶצְלֵנוּ*
מוּלְכֶם	מִכֶּם	בִּשְׁבִילְכֶם	עִמָּכֶם	אִתְכֶם	אֶצְלְכֶם
מוּלְכֶן	מִכֶּן	בִּשְׁבִילְכֶן	עִמָּכֶן	אִתְכֶן	אֶצְלְכֶן
מוּלָם	מֵהֶם	בִּשְׁבִילָם	עִמָּם	אִתָּם	אֶצְלָם
מוּלָן	מֵהֶן	בִּשְׁבִילָן	עִמָּן	אִתָּן	אֶצְלָן

Note

* Notice change from *a* to *e* in the prepositions בשביל and אצל, מן.

** The second person plural forms of the direct object pronoun change their stem from אוֹת- *ot-* in the other forms to the אֶת- *et-* of the independent form.

The preposition 'with' has two sets of inflected prepositions: one is derived from the biblical form -אֶת, and the other from the alternate preposition עִם. The paradigm עִמִּי, עִמְּךָ עִמּוֹ, עִמָּה is used in the higher registers of Hebrew. In everyday speech, the alternate paradigm אִתִּי, אִתְּךָ, אִתָּךְ, אִתּוֹ, אִתָּה is the one commonly used. The independent form of the preposition is always עִם.

Historically, there were two different prepositions with the meaning of 'from'. One was derived from the preposition מֵאֵת, and the other from the preposition מִן.

מֵאֵת	מֵאִתִּי, מֵאִתְּךָ, מֵאִתָּךְ, מֵאִתּוֹ, מֵאִתָּה	מֵאִתָּנוּ, מֵאִתְּכֶם/ן, מֵאִתָּם/ן
מִן	מִמֶּנִּי, מִמְּךָ, מִמֵּךְ, מִמֶּנָּה, מִמֶּנּוּ	מֵאִתָּנוּ (מִמֶּנּוּ), מִכֶּם/ן, מֵהֶם/ן

In contemporary use, the stem of מִן is used in most of the forms, and it has a couple of separate sub-stems, מִמֶּנ- and מִמ/מֵ (in both cases, the נ of מִן is fully assimilated). The מֵאֵת forms are rarely used, except for מֵאִתָּנוּ, which is used more frequently than מִמֶּנּוּ, most likely because this form of first person plural is identical to the third person singular, masculine.

Set B
Pronoun suffixes attached to prepositions
(Shape of possessive pronoun suffixes attached to plural nouns)

בִּלְעֲדֵי	עַל יְדֵי	עַל	אֶל	
without	by	on/about	toward	
בִּלְעָדַי	עַל יָדַי	עָלַי	אֵלַי	*אני*
בִּלְעָדֶיךָ	עַל יָדֶיךָ	עָלֶיךָ	אֵלֶיךָ	*אתה*
בִּלְעָדַיִךְ	עַל יָדַיִךְ	עָלַיִךְ	אֵלַיִךְ	*את*
בִּלְעָדָיו	עַל יָדָיו	עָלָיו	אֵלָיו	*הוא*
בִּלְעָדֶיהָ	עַל יָדֶיהָ	עָלֶיהָ	אֵלֶיהָ	*היא*
בִּלְעָדֵינוּ	עַל יָדֵינוּ	עָלֵינוּ	אֵלֵינוּ	*אנחנו*
בִּלְעֲדֵיכֶם	עַל יְדֵיכֶם	עֲלֵיכֶם	אֲלֵיכֶם	*אתם*
בִּלְעֲדֵיכֶן	עַל יְדֵיכֶן	עֲלֵיכֶן	אֲלֵיכֶן	*אתן*
בִּלְעֲדֵיהֶם	עַל יְדֵיהֶם	עֲלֵיהֶם	אֲלֵיהֶם	*הם*
בִּלְעֲדֵיהֶן	עַל יְדֵיהֶן	עֲלֵיהֶן	אֲלֵיהֶן	*הן*

מֵעַל	מִתַּחַת	אוֹדוֹת	מֵאַחֲרֵי	לְפְנֵי
above	below	about	behind	before
מֵעָלַי	מִתַּחְתַּי	אוֹדוֹתַי	מֵאַחֲרַי	לְפָנַי
מֵעָלֶיךָ	מִתַּחְתֶּיךָ	אוֹדוֹתֶיךָ	מֵאַחֲרֶיךָ	לְפָנֶיךָ
מֵעָלַיִךְ	מִתַּחְתַּיִךְ	אוֹדוֹתַיִךְ	מֵאַחֲרַיִךְ	לְפָנַיִךְ
מֵעָלָיו	מִתַּחְתָּיו	אוֹדוֹתָיו	מֵאַחֲרָיו	לְפָנָיו
מֵעָלֶיהָ	מִתַּחְתֶּיהָ	אוֹדוֹתֶיהָ	מֵאַחֲרֶיהָ	לְפָנֶיהָ
מֵעָלֵינוּ	מִתַּחְתֵּינוּ	אוֹדוֹתֵינוּ	מֵאַחֲרֵינוּ	לְפָנֵינוּ
מֵעֲלֵיכֶם	מִתַּחְתֵּיכֶם	אוֹדוֹתֵיכֶם	מֵאַחֲרֵיכֶם	לִפְנֵיכֶם
מֵעֲלֵיכֶן	מִתַּחְתֵּיכֶן	אוֹדוֹתֵיכֶן	מֵאַחֲרֵיכֶן	לִפְנֵיכֶן
מֵעֲלֵיהֶם	מִתַּחְתֵּיהֶם	אוֹדוֹתֵיהֶם	מֵאַחֲרֵיהֶם	לִפְנֵיהֶם
מֵעֲלֵיהֶן	מִתַּחְתֵּיהֶן	אוֹדוֹתֵיהֶן	מֵאַחֲרֵיהֶן	לִפְנֵיהֶן

Note

Normally the preposition 'without' in its independent form is בלי, followed by a noun, as in בלי תקווה 'without hope', but it uses the variant independent form בלעדי- when a pronoun suffix is attached to it, as in בלעדיך 'without you'.

Look for vowel changes in the stem of many of the second and third person plural forms, which take place because of the shift of stress to the last syllable.

David's parents did not hear <u>about us</u>, but we heard <u>about them</u>.	ההורים של דוד לא שמעו <u>עלינו</u>, אבל אנחנו שמענו <u>עליהם</u>.
We stood in line <u>ahead of them</u>, and <u>ahead of us</u> stood many others.	עמדנו בתור <u>לפניהם</u>, ו<u>לפנינו</u> עמדו עוד הרבה אנשים.
Everything was made possible <u>by them</u>, since they stood <u>behind him</u> and supported all his efforts.	הכל התאפשר <u>על ידיהם</u>, כי הם עמדו <u>מאחריו</u> ותמכו בכל מאמציו.

10.3.7 Prepositions with nouns, adjectives, and verbs

Prepositions are sometimes so firmly wedded to other words that they have practically become idiomatic expressions. This occurs in three categories: nouns, adjectives, and verbs. Although the former two are usually verb-related, they will be introduced first, before we embark on a fuller discussion of verb-and-preposition collocations.

Nouns and prepositions

If a noun and a verb share the same root and semantic features, they often take the same preposition. For instance, the noun אֱמוּנָה 'belief' shares the same root and base meaning with the verb לְהַאֲמִין בּ- 'to believe (in)'. The preposition follows the noun as well as the related verb and links the object to either one.

Here is a list of nouns with prepositions that link the objects to them:

Noun		Verb	
belief in	אֱמוּנָה בּ-	believe in	לְהַאֲמִין בּ-
success in	הַצְלָחָה בּ-	succeed in	לְהַצְלִיחַ בּ-
expertise in	הִתְמַחוּת בּ-	specialize in	לְהִתְמַחוֹת בּ-
devotion to	הִתְמַסְּרוּת לְ-	devote self to	לְהִתְמַסֵּר לְ-
voting for	הַצְבָּעָה בְּעַד	vote for	לְהַצְבִּיעַ בְּעַד

Adjectives and participles with prepositions

An adjective derived from a verb usually takes the same preposition as the verb. Here is a list of adjectives and participles with prepositions that link the objects to them:

Adjective		Verb	
interested in	מְעוּנְיָן בּ-	be interested in	לְהִתְעַנְיֵן בּ-
married to	נָשׂוּי לְ-	get married to	לְהִנָּשֵׂא לְ-
proud of	גֵּאֶה בּ-	be proud of	לְהִתְגָּאוֹת בּ-
similar to	דּוֹמֶה לְ-	be similar to	לְהִדָּמוֹת לְ-
belonging to	שַׁיָּךְ לְ-	belong to	לְהִשְׁתַּיֵּךְ לְ-
confident in	בָּטוּחַ בּ-	trust in	לִבְטֹחַ בּ-

Ruth's daughter is so much <u>like her</u> <u>mother</u>.	הבת של רות כל כך <u>דומה לאמא</u> <u>שלה</u>.
These books don't <u>belong to us</u>.	הספרים האלה לא <u>שייכים לנו</u>.
He is so <u>sure of himself</u>.	הוא כל כך <u>בטוח בעצמו</u>.

Verbs and prepositions

Some transitive verbs are followed directly by a direct object, and some are linked to their object by certain obligatory prepositions.

A comparative note

There is no predictable equivalence between the combination of verbs and prepositions in Hebrew and their equivalents in English. This is a nearly arbitrary feature that must be learned.

trust in	בָּטַח בְּ-	give up	וִתֵּר עַל
be proud of	הִתְגָּאָה בְּ-	rely on	סָמַךְ עַל
fall in love with	הִתְאַהֵב בְּ-	think about	חָשַׁב עַל
damage, hurt	פָּגַע בְּ-	overcome	הִתְגַּבֵּר עַל

part from	נִפְרַד מִ-	bother	הִפְרִיעַ לְ-
be impressed by	הִתְפַּעֵל מִ-	need	הִזְדַּקֵּק לְ-
retire from/ leave	פָּרַשׁ מִ-	yearn for	הִשְׁתּוֹקֵק לְ-
be excited by	הִתְרַגֵּשׁ מִ-	become	הָפַךְ לְ-

approach	הִתְקָרֵב אֶל	accept	הִשְׁלִים עִם
accompany	הִתְלַוָּה אֶל	confront	הִתְמוֹדֵד עִם
intend, refer	הִתְכַּוֵּן אֶל	argue with	הִתְוַכֵּחַ עִם
turn to, address	פָּנָה אֶל	marry	הִתְחַתֵּן עִם

It is difficult to <u>accept</u> the situation.	קשה <u>להשלים עם</u> המצב.
Don't <u>bother</u> us! We are busy.	אל <u>תפריע לנו</u>! אנחנו עסוקים.
We are <u>overcoming</u> the difficulties.	אנחנו <u>מתגברים על</u> הקשיים.
Dan <u>married</u> Dana.	דן <u>התחתן עם</u> דנה.
Don't <u>come near</u> us!	אל <u>תתקרבו אלינו</u>!

One verb with several prepositional phrases

It is possible for one verb to occur in a sentence with the several prepositions that link it to its different objects. Each of the objects has a different function in the sentence.

We did not agree <u>with</u> David <u>about</u> the prices in his work proposal.	לא הסכמנו <u>עם</u> דוד <u>על</u> המחירים בהצעת העבודה שלו.
We demonstrated <u>with</u> the workers <u>against</u> the closing of the plant.	הִפְגַּנּוּ <u>עִם</u> הפועלים <u>נֶגֶד</u> סגירת המפעל.
The teacher spoke <u>with</u> the students <u>about</u> the material that will be on the test.	המורה דיבר עם התלמידים <u>על</u> החומר שיהיה במבחן.

Meaning – combined verbs and prepositions

The meanings of some verbs are determined by the combination of
those verbs with different prepositions and objects. Here are some
examples of how verbs' meanings can be determined by the preposition
that follows them. In most cases the meanings are related but not
identical:

go to the office	לגשת אל המשרד
go to (visit) friends	לגשת לחברים
take tests	לגשת לבחינות
turn right at the corner	לפנות ימינה בפינה
address someone	לפנות אל מישהו
turn to the mayor (for advice, help)	לפנות אל ראש העיר
It all depends on your decision.	.הכל תלוי בהחלטה שלך
The laundry is hanging on the line in the yard.	.הכביסה תלויה על החבל בחצר
contact the committee members	להתקשר אל חברי הועד
get in touch by phone	להתקשר בטלפון/טלפונית
become attached to friends	להתקשר לחברים
visit/pay a visit to relatives	לבקר קרובי משפחה
visit in/go to see all the museums in town	לבקר בכל המוזיאונים בעיר
rely on experts' opinions	לסמוך על דעות של מומחים
support the falling wall	לסמוך את הקיר המתמוטט
bring the books to the library	להביא את הספרים לספריה
bring about good results	להביא לתוצאות טובות
point at someone	להצביע על מישהו
vote for someone	להצביע בעד מישהו
agree/concur with the expressed opinions	להסכים לדעות שהובעו
consent/comply with the parents not to go out alone late at night	להסכים עם ההורים לא לצאת לבד מאוחר בערב

10.3.8 Prepositions in context

As mentioned above, the choice of prepositions is determined by a number of factors, including the type of link being provided, the relationship between the items, and prescribed prepositions for time and location. As in English, certain verbs are followed by certain prepositions that give them their full meaning.

Here are examples of verbs followed by prepositions in Hebrew, while the English takes no preposition before the object.

He approached <u>us</u>.	הוא התקרב <u>אלינו</u>.
Do the children bother <u>you</u>?	הילדים מפריעים <u>לכם</u>?
It is necessary to accept <u>the situation</u>.	צריך להשלים <u>עם המצב</u>.

The preposition of possession שֶׁל

The preposition שֶׁל is used exclusively in expressions of possession.

Singular

שֶׁלָּהּ	שֶׁלּוֹ	שֶׁלָּךְ	שֶׁלְּךָ	שֶׁלִּי
her/s	his	your/s	your/s	my/mine

Plural

שֶׁלָּהֶן	שֶׁלָּהֶם	שֶׁלָּכֶן	שֶׁלָּכֶם	שֶׁלָּנוּ
their/s	their/s	your/s	your/s	our/s

Locators of place and time

Many prepositional phrases serve to specify space or time.

Space	In every place, in the sea, on land or in the air, there is a way to communicate.	בכל מקום: בים, ביבשה או באוויר, יש דרך ליצור קשר.
Time	I am free at any time, in the morning or the evening.	אני פנוי בכל שעה, בבוקר או בערב.

Prepositions of Location: *in, at,* and *on* -בְּ

The most common preposition that indicates location is the prefix -בְּ. It can be translated as 'in' or 'at' and at times by 'on' or 'by' '(a mode of transportation).

in/at/by   -ב

He sleeps <u>in</u> his bed.   הוא ישן <u>ב</u>מיטה שלו.

She is staying <u>at</u> home today.   היא נשארת <u>ב</u>בית היום.

There is no smoking <u>on</u> the plane.   אסור לעשן <u>ב</u>מטוס.

Will you be traveling <u>by</u> train or <u>by</u> bus?   תיסעו <u>ב</u>רכבת או <u>ב</u>אוטובוס?

Prepositions of location: *on* על

The preposition of location 'on' על indicates being on or on top of a specific surface. (It also functions as a preposition that indicates the content of some transmitted message: the story is about his childhood. Obviously, in this particular instance it does not indicate location. Several prepositions have more than one function and meaning).

on (a surface)   על

The blanket is <u>on the sofa</u>.   השמיכה <u>על הספה</u>.

The clothes are <u>on the floor</u>.   הבגדים <u>על הרצפה</u>.

The coat is <u>on the chair</u>.   המעיל <u>על הכיסא</u>.

The notebook is <u>on the desk</u>.   המחברת <u>על השולחן</u>.

Prepositions of time: *at,* and *on* ב-

As in prepositions of location, the most common preposition that indicates time is the prefix -ב. It can be translated into English as 'in', 'at', and at times by 'on', or is absent in English.

at, on, by   -ב

He arrived <u>at seven in the evening</u>.   הוא הגיע <u>בשבע בערב</u>.

He arrived <u>on time</u>.   הוא הגיע <u>בזמן</u>.

There were elections <u>last year</u>.   היו בחירות <u>בשנה שעברה</u>.

In some words the concept of time is inherent, and therefore there is no need for a preposition at all.

<u>Yesterday</u> was Dan's birthday.   יום ההולדת של דנה היה <u>אתמול</u>.

<u>Now</u> is the time for many changes.   <u>עכשיו</u> הגיע הזמן להרבה שינויים.

<u>This year</u> there are interesting programs.   <u>השנה</u> יש תוכניות מעניינות.

Preposition of direction אֶל/ל–

The preposition ל-/אֶל signifies an orientation toward a goal or a destination. It usually follows verbs of movement.

Directional: to/into/toward

Dina went up <u>to</u> the third floor.

דינה עלתה <u>אל</u> הקומה השלישית
(או : לַקומה השלישית).

The sand washed <u>into</u> the water.

החול נסחף <u>אל</u> המים.

The group made progress <u>toward</u> the goal.

הקבוצה התקדמה <u>אל</u> המטרה.

When the destination is a full noun, the preposition -ל may often be used as well:

Goal: noun phrase

David returned <u>to</u> his house.

דוד חזר <u>אל</u> ביתו/דוד חזר <u>לביתו</u>.

However, if the destination is a pronoun, only אֶל is allowed:

Goal: expressed by pronoun.

David left his family last year, but he returned <u>to them</u> this year.

דוד עזב את משפחתו בשנה שעברה, אבל
הוא חזר <u>אליהם</u> השנה.

The preposition מִן or its abbreviated version -מ signifies movement or orientation from a goal or a destination. It usually follows verbs of movement, but can also follow nouns.

Directional: from

Dina went <u>out of</u> the house.

דינה יצאה <u>מהבית</u>.

This is the road <u>from</u> Tel Aviv to Haifa.

זאת הדרך <u>מתל</u>-אביב לחיפה.

The preposition of location/position: אֵצֶל

The preposition אֵצֶל can be roughly translated as 'at (somebody's place)'. It implies that the object is a person, and the location – which is associated with the person – is understood and can be further specified. It is similar to the French preposition *chez*, which also signifies someone's place (of residence or work). For instance, the phrase 'at David's' is conveyed by אצל דוד, which can be further expanded by אצל דוד במשרד 'at David's office', or אצל דוד בבית 'at David's home'.

Notice that the prepositions -אֶל and -אֵצֶל are complementary. While both convey a location or a destination associated with a person, they follow different types of verbs: אֶל follows directional verbs, whereas אֵצֶל accompanies situational or stative verbs.

<u>Directional</u>

We went <u>to their place</u> for a short visit.   .נסענו <u>אליהם</u> לביקור קצר

<u>Locational</u>

We were <u>at their place</u> for three days.   .היינו <u>אצלם</u> שלושה ימים

Prepositions following verbs expressing stationary position

Verbs of stationary position indicate a continuous position with no change in motion.

The cat is sitting <u>on</u> the rug.   .החתול יושב <u>על</u> השטיח

The doctor is <u>in</u> his office.   .הרופא נמצא <u>ב</u>משרד שלו

My relatives are <u>at</u> my parents'.   .הקרובים שלי <u>אצל</u> ההורים שלי

Some verbs of motion indicate a continuous, almost always circular movement, within a specific location:

The cat is running around <u>in the </u>yard.   .החתול מתרוצץ <u>ב</u>חצר

The children are roaming <u>in our neighborhood.</u>   הילדים מסתובבים <u>אצלנו</u> <u>בשכונה</u>.

My relatives are walking <u>around town</u>.   .הקרובים שלי מטיילים <u>בעיר</u>

However, most verbs of motion indicate a movement toward another location:

The cat ran away <u>to</u> the neighbors.   .החתול ברח <u>אל</u> השכן

The children went <u>to</u> the beach.   .הילדים הלכו <u>לים</u>

My relatives drove <u>to</u> the new mall.   .הקרובים שלי נסעו <u>לקניון</u> החדש

Cause and effect relationship

Prepositions, as well as verbs, convey either the completion of an action, or the point or the position of the subject as a result of that action. This distinction helps us understand how directional and locative prepositions are related: they stand in the relationship of cause and effect.

Verbs of movement: cause

He jumped <u>into</u> the pool.   .הוא קפץ <u>לבריכה</u>

She fell <u>into</u> the water.   .היא נפלה <u>למים</u>

They drove <u>to</u> the mall.   .הם נסעו <u>לקניון</u>

Dan went <u>to</u> his relatives.   .דן <u>הלך</u> <u>אל</u> הקרובים שלו

They came <u>to us</u>.   .הם באו <u>אלינו</u>

Position of subject: effect

He is <u>at</u> the pool.	.הוא <u>ב</u>בריכה
She is <u>in</u> the water.	.היא <u>ב</u>מים
Dan was <u>at</u> his relatives.	.דן היה <u>אצל</u> הקרובים שלו
They were <u>at our place</u>.	.<u>הם היו אצלנו</u>

10.3.9 Prepositions expressing relational position
In relation to object: inside (of) לְתוֹךְ, בְּתוֹךְ into

He entered <u>into</u> (inside) the building.	.הוא נכנס <u>לתוך</u> הבניין
He is sitting <u>inside</u> the Jacuzzi.	.הוא יושב <u>בתוך</u> הג׳קוזי
They are standing <u>inside</u> the fountain.	.הם עומדים <u>בתוך</u> המזרקה

In relation to object: outside (of) מחוץ ל

He is standing <u>outside</u> the building.	.הוא עומד <u>מחוץ</u> לבניין
He is sitting <u>beside</u> the pool.	.הוא יושב <u>מחוץ</u> לבריכה
They are standing <u>outside</u> the restaurant.	.הם עומדים <u>מחוץ</u> למסעדה

In relation to object: in front (of) מִלְפְנֵי /לִפְנֵי

<u>In front of me</u> I see mountains.	.<u>מלפני</u> אני רואה הרים
<u>In front of</u> the house there is a garden.	.<u>מלפני</u> הבית יש גינה
The library is <u>in front of</u> the Physics Bldg.	.הספרייה <u>לפני</u> בניין הפיסיקה

In relation to object: behind מֵאֲחוֹרֵי

The pool is <u>behind</u> the house.	.הבריכה <u>מאחורי</u> הבית
We live <u>behind</u> the store.	.אנחנו גרים <u>מאחורי</u> החנות
I am standing <u>behind him.</u>	.<u>אני עומד מאחוריו</u>

In relation to object: across from/facing מול/מְמוּל ל-

Our office is exactly <u>across from you</u>.	.המשרד שלנו בדיוק <u>ממולכם</u>
<u>Facing</u> the house is a big park.	.<u>ממול</u> לבית יש פארק גדול
It's not on this side - it is <u>across the way</u>.	.זה לא בצד הזה – זה <u>ממול</u>

In relation to object: next to עַל יַד

Who lives <u>next to you</u>?	?מי גר <u>על ידכם</u>
The movie theater is <u>next to</u> the bookstore.	.הקולנוע <u>על יד</u> חנות הספרים
There is a restaurant <u>next to</u> the hotel.	.יש מסעדה <u>על יד</u> המלון

10.4 Prepositional phrases or adverbs?

By definition, prepositions link to nominal entities (nouns, noun phrases or pronouns), whereas adverbs, which modify verbs, adjectives, other adverbs, or sentences, do not. The difference can best be demonstrated by comparing forms that originated from the fusion of prepositions and nouns into derived 'atomic' adverbs of location, with prepositional phrases in which similar forms function as prepositions linking to a following noun or a noun phrase:

Prep Phrase	They are standing <u>outside the house</u>.	הם עומדים <u>מחוץ לבית</u>.
Adverb	They are standing <u>outside</u>.	הם עומדים <u>בחוץ</u>.
Prep Phrase	He is <u>inside the building</u>.	הוא <u>בתוך הבניין</u>.
Adverb	He is <u>inside</u>.	הוא נמצא <u>בפנים</u>.
Prep Phrase	The office is <u>under the residential floor</u>.	המשרד <u>מתחת לקומת המגורים</u>.
Adverb	The office is downstairs.	המשרד נמצא <u>למטה</u>.
Prep Phrase	The store is exactly <u>above the supermarket</u>.	החנות בדיוק <u>מעל לסופרמרקט</u>.
Adverb	The store is <u>upstairs</u>, on the second floor.	החנות <u>למעלה</u>, בקומה השנייה.

Because the forms in the left column are prepositions, they must be followed by a nominal entity, personal pronouns included (e.g. ,בתוכו מעליו). The borderline between prepositions and adverbs, however, is not always clear. Below are two particles, בְּמֶשֶׁךְ and בְּעוֹד, that are regarded as adverbs by some, but at the same time function as prepositions.

10.4.1 Prepositions of duration: for/during/while בְּמֶשֶׁךְ

The preposition בְּמֶשֶׁךְ 'during' is a preposition that refers to duration of time.

for/during	**בְּמֶשֶׁךְ**
<u>During school</u>, he also worked.	<u>במשך הלימודים</u>, הוא גם עבד.
<u>For four years</u>, the family lived in the South.	<u>במשך ארבע שנים</u> המשפחה גרה בדרום.

10.4.2 Preposition 'in + time unit' בְּעוֹד

The preposition בְּעוֹד 'in (a certain amount of time)', which is always followed by a time phrase, indicates an expectation of a period of time in the future.

in + time unit	בְּעוֹד
He will meet us <u>in an hour</u>.	הוא יפגוש אותנו <u>בעוד שעה</u>.
School will end <u>in a week</u>.	הלימודים יסתיימו <u>בעוד כשבוע</u>.
An Iranian delegation will undertake a historical visit the United States <u>in a few weeks</u>.	משלחת איראנית תצא <u>בעוד כמה</u> <u>שבועות</u> לביקור היסטורי בארה"ב.

10.4.3 Combination of prepositions מ- עד 'from-until/up to'

These prepositions indicate an ongoing time period that started or is to start at a given time and will last till a specific time. The preposition עַד 'until' can be preceded by a conjunction וְעַד 'and until'. When it introduces a clause it is linked to it by the relative particle -שֶׁ.

from – until/up to	מ – עד
We waited for you <u>from</u> seven <u>till</u> midnight. Where were you?	חכינו לך <u>מ</u>שבע <u>עד</u> חצות. איפה היית?
Dr. Wolf works <u>from</u> 9 a.m. <u>till</u> 1 p.m. at his office, and <u>from</u> 4 p.m. <u>till</u> 10 p.m. he works at the hospital.	ד"ר וולף עובד <u>מ</u>תשע בבוקר <u>עד</u> אחת בצוהריים במשרד שלו, ו<u>מ</u>ארבע <u>עד</u> עשר הוא עובד בבית החולים.
Attorney Ayalon worked on this case from the beginning of this year <u>and until</u> she completed her obligation a week ago.	עורכת הדין איילון עבדה על התיק הזה <u>מ</u>תחילת השנה הזאת <u>ועד</u> <u>ש</u>היא סיימה את תפקידה לפני שבוע.

10.5 Coordinating conjunctions   מילות חיבור

A coordinating conjunction links words, phrases, or clauses. Coordinating conjunctions join single words, or they may join groups of words, but they must always join similar elements: e.g., noun + noun, verb phrase + verb phrase, sentence + sentence.

Coordinating conjunctions

and	-וְ
or	אוֹ
if	אִם
but, however; too, also	אַף, גַם
however	אֲבָל, אַךְ
only	רַק, אַךְ
except, but	אֶלָא
indeed, surely	אָכֵן
indeed, in truth	אָמְנָם
and however	וְאִלוּ
because	כִּי

Notes on the conjunction -ו and the vowels attached to it:
The conjunction -ו is pronounced *ve-* in most cases, and in everyday speech in virtually all cases, except for set expressions.

In normative Hebrew, however, the following rules apply:
- -ו is pronounced *ve-* in most cases, but before the consonants ב/ב, ו, מ, פ/פ it is pronounced *u.*
  Example: *bayit umishpakha*   בית ומשפחה
- -ו is pronounced *u* also before a consonant cluster or before any *shva* vowel.
  Example: *drom utsfon tel aviv*   דרום וצפון תל-אביב
  Example: *hi tavo utedaber itkhem*   היא תבוא ותדבר אתכם
- -ו is pronounced *vi-* before the consonant י with a *shva* (the *shva* and the *y* are elided).
  Example: *telaviv virushalayim*   תל-אביב וירושלים
- -ו is pronounced with a vowel that echoes a following *ħataf:*
  Examples: *limudim va`avoda*   לימודים וַעֲבוֹדה
  'emet ve'emuna   אמת וֶאֱמוּנה
- -ו is pronounced *va-* before a stressed vowel.
  Examples: *kaftor vaféraħ*   כפתור וָפֶרַח
  bayit vagan   בית וָגָן

The various coordinative conjunctions not only coordinate units in the sentence, but also set these units in a special relationship to one another.

Noun + noun

Inclusion:

We have season tickets to the theater <u>and</u> the opera.

יש לנו כרטיסי-מנוי [לתיאטרון <u>וְ</u>לאופרה].

Exclusion:

We have season tickets <u>only</u> to the theater <u>but not</u> to the opera.

יש לנו כרטיסי מנוי [<u>רק</u> לתיאטרון ולא לאופרה].

Verb + verb

Inclusion:

Dan walks to work <u>and</u> runs after work.

דן הולך ברגל לעבודה <u>וְ</u>רָץ אחרי העבודה.

Exclusion:

Dan walks <u>but</u> does not run.

דן הולך ברגל <u>וְ</u>לא רָץ.

Sentence + sentence

Neutral:

Dan wanted to sit in the balcony, <u>and</u> Dina wanted to sit in the orchestra.

דן רצה לשבת ביציע, <u>וְ</u>דינה רצתה לשבת באולם.

Differing attitudes:

Dan wanted to go, <u>but</u>/<u>however</u> Dina wanted to stay home.

דן רצה ללכת, <u>אבל</u>/<u>ואילו</u> דינה רצתה להישאר בבית.

Inclusion:

Dan wanted to sit in the balcony, <u>and</u> Dina <u>also</u> wanted to sit there.

דן רצה לשבת ביציע, <u>וגם</u> דינה רצתה לשבת שם.

Cause:

Dan bought tickets for Dina, because she <u>too</u> wanted to go to the show.

דן קנה כרטיסים בשביל דינה, כי <u>גם</u> היא רצתה ללכת להצגה.

10.5.1 Correlative conjunctions

Correlative conjunctions are used in pairs. Like the coordinate conjunctions they join similar elements. When joining singular and plural subjects, the subject closest to the verb determines whether the verb is singular or plural.

Both:

<u>Both</u> my brother and my sister play the guitar.

<u>גם</u> אחי <u>וגם</u> אחותי מנגנים בגיטרה.

Either/or:

You have a choice: <u>either</u> to sit at
home, <u>or</u> to go with us to visit Shlomit.

יש לכם ברירה – <u>או</u> לשבת בבית
<u>או</u> לבוא איתנו לבקר את שלומית.

Not only but also:

<u>Not only</u> my brother, <u>but also</u> my
father plays basketball.

<u>לא רק</u> אחי <u>אלא גם</u> אבי משחק
כדורסל.

Two nouns in opposition:

Dan told Rina to buy tickets <u>not</u> in the
orchestra <u>but only</u> in the balcony.

דן אמר לרינה לקנות כרטיסים,
<u>לא</u> באולם, <u>אלא</u> ביציע.

Two verbs in opposition:

Dan does <u>not</u> drive <u>but rather</u> walks.

דן <u>לא</u> נוהג <u>אלא</u> הולך ברגל.

Opposition:

Dina <u>really</u> wanted to take a taxi,
<u>however</u> Dan wanted to walk.

<u>אומנם</u> דינה רצתה לנסוע במונית,
<u>אבל</u> דן רצה ללכת ברגל.

Condition + result:

<u>If</u> you <u>really</u> insist, <u>then</u> we'll all walk
to the theater.

<u>אם אכן</u> אתם עומדים על כך, <u>אז</u>
כולנו נלך ברגל לקולנוע.

10.6 Subordinators   מילות שעבוד

Subordinators (subordinating conjunctions) are essential in introducing
subordinating clauses. Some of them are adverbs that act like
conjunctions, and all are placed at the front of the clause. The
subordinate clause can come either before or after the main clause.
Subordinators are usually single words, but there are also a number of
multi-word subordinators that function like a single subordinating
conjunction. They can be classified according to their use in regard to
time, cause and effect, opposition, or condition.

Subordinators

that/which	-שֶׁ
that/which	אֲשֶׁר
that + object complement clause	-כִּי/שֶׁ
after + clause	-אַחֲרֵי שֶׁ
since/because + clause	-מִכֵּיוָן שֶׁ/מִפְּנֵי שֶׁ
	-מִשּׁוּם שֶׁ
while	-כַּאֲשֶׁר/כְּשֶׁ
in spite of/that + clause	-לַמְרוֹת שֶׁ

even though	אֲפִילוּ אִם/אִם כִּי
	עַל אַף שֶׁ-/אַף עַל פִּי שֶׁ-
instead of + clause	בִּמְקוֹם שֶׁ-
while + clause	בְּעוֹד שֶׁ-
as long as + clause	כָּל עוֹד שֶׁ-
before + clause	לִפְנֵי שֶׁ-
in order that	כְּדֵי שֶׁ-/עַל מְנַת שֶׁ-
if (condition)	אִם
if/if not (condition)	לוּ/לוּלֵא

He said <u>that</u> they were not coming.	הוא אמר <u>ש</u>הם לא יבואו.
It was reported <u>that</u> the thieves <u>who</u> were caught were children.	נמסר <u>כי</u> הגנבים <u>ש</u>נתפסו היו ילדים.
We'll eat <u>after</u> the concert is over.	נאכל <u>אחרי ש</u>הקונצרט ייגמר.
<u>Since</u> we are going out this evening, we can't meet.	<u>מכיוון ש</u>אנחנו יוצאים הערב, לא נוכל להיפגש.
<u>While</u> we were in town, we ate at the Indian restaurant.	<u>כאשר/כשהיינו</u> בעיר, אכלנו במסעדה ההודית.
<u>Even though</u> you think so, it's not true.	<u>אפילו אם</u> את חושבת כך, זה לא נכון.
<u>In spite of the fact that</u> we have already seen the movie, we are ready to see it again.	<u>למרות ש</u>ראינו כבר את הסרט, אנחנו מוכנים לראות אותו שוב.
<u>Instead of</u> everyone coming at six, we'll ask some to come at eight.	<u>במקום ש</u>כולם יבואו בשש, נבקש מכמה לבוא בשמונה.
<u>As long as</u> he is not about to change his mind, we won't help him.	<u>כל עוד ש</u>הוא לא משנה את דעתו, לא נעזור לו.

10.7 Exclamation particles   מילות קריאה

Exclamation particles are special words that serve to emphasize a statement. They are used as declamatory devices, to call attention to statements being made or to express surprise.

There are two main exclamation particles: הנה! הרי! They are both used mostly in the more formal register, particularly when the pronoun suffixes are added.

1. Behold! Here, here is! הִנֵּה!

This particle is used mostly to point at something that is in near proximity:

Finally! Here is the house!   !סוף, סוף! הַנֵּה הבית

It can also be used to point at an object/person in a particular situation:

And here we are - in the middle of   וְהִנֵּה אנחנו - באמצע המדבר - ואין
the desert with no living soul   נפש חיה בסביבה.
around.

2. Why (for emphasis); indeed!; you see הֲרֵי

This particle is used mostly for emphasis:

Why, he always talks nonsense.   .הֲרֵי הוא תמיד מדבר שטויות

But you have been told what to do.   .הֲרֵי כבר הסבירו לכם מה לעשות

Both these particles can have personal pronoun suffix subjects added to them. They are usually used in the higher, more formal language registers and in classical literature.

הִנֵּה with personal pronouns

Here I am	הִנְנִי = הִנֵּה אני
Here you are	הִנְךָ = הנה אתה
Here you are	הִנֵּךְ = הנה את
Here he is	הִנּוֹ = הנה הוא
Here she is	הִנָּהּ = הנה היא
Here we are	הִנֵּנוּ = הנה אנחנו
Here you are	הִנְּכֶם = הנה אתם
Here you are	הִנְּכֶן = הנה אתן
Here they are	הִנָּם = הנה הם
Here they are	הִנָּן = הנה הן

Example from Biblical Hebrew:

And he said unto him, "Abraham", and he said: "<u>Here I am</u>" (Genesis 22: 1).	וַיֹּאמֶר אֵלָיו, אַבְרָהָם וַיֹּאמֶר <u>הִנֵּנִי</u>. (בראשית כב: א)

Examples from medical literature:

The examination of blood pressure <u>is</u> a routine examination.	בדיקת לחץ דם <u>הֶנָּה</u> בדיקה שגרתית.

Example from legal literature:

Since <u>I am</u> over 110 years of age, an Israeli citizen and since <u>I am</u> of sound mind ...	הואיל <u>וְהִנֵּנִי</u> למעלה מגיל שמונה עשרה שנים, אזרח ישראל והואיל <u>וְהִנֵּנִי</u> שקול בדעתי, ...

הֲרֵי with personal pronouns

I am indeed	הֲרֵינִי = הרי אני
You are indeed	הֲרֵיךָ = הרי אתה
You are indeed	הֲרֵיךְ = הרי את
He is indeed	הֲרֵיהוּ = הרי הוא
She is indeed	הֲרֵיהִי = הרי היא
We are indeed	הֲרֵינוּ = הרי אנחנו
You are indeed	הֲרֵיכֶם = הרי אתם
You are indeed	הֲרֵיכֶן = הרי אתן
They are indeed	הֲרֵיהֶם = הרי הם
They are indeed	הֲרֵיהֶן = הרי הן

Examples from rabbinic literature:

The emperor heard the lady of the house anxiously asking her husband: "Nevertheless, <u>he is indeed but</u> a human being!"	שמע הקיסר את בעלת-הבית שואלת בחשש את בעלה: "בכל-זאת, <u>הֲרֵיהוּ</u> אדם!"

She said to him, "<u>I am hereby</u> consecrated to you, for <u>I am hereby</u> a wife to you".	אמרה לו, <u>הֲרֵינִי</u> מקודשת לך, <u>הֲרֵי אֲנִי</u> לך לאישה.

Example from a contract:

<u>I hereby</u> promise to pay the full tuition for the summer course/s for which I have registered.	<u>הֲרֵינִי</u> מתחייב/ת לשלם את מלוא שכר הלימוד עבור קורס/י סימסטר הקיץ אליהם נרשמתי.

Chapter 11
Noun phrases

11.1 Introduction to noun phrases   מבוא לצירופים שמניים

A noun phrase consists of a single noun (indefinite or definite), which can have additional components modify it. A single noun can have an article added to it or a pronoun suffixed to it and remain a single word, or independent words can be added to it as modifiers. The noun itself is viewed as the head of the phrase. It is the central item in the phrase. The other added components expand the meaning of the head noun or particularize it. The additional components can be articles, adjectives, demonstrative pronouns, numerals, other modifying nouns, prepositions with pronouns, relative clauses, or gerunds and infinitives that function as nouns.

The noun phrase can function as a subject, a nominal predicate, a direct or indirect object, or within larger constituents (e.g., within a prepositional phrase or a sentential adverb, etc.). Here are some illustrations of the most basic positions:

<u>Subject</u>	These <u>dogs</u> are old.	.הכלבים האלה זקנים
<u>Predicate</u>	Shunra is a <u>cute cat</u>.	.שונרא הוא חתול חמוד
<u>Direct object</u>	Where did you buy <u>this dog</u>?	איפה קניתם את הכלב הזה?
<u>Indirect object</u>	They went for a walk <u>with their dogs</u>.	הם יצאו לטייל עם הכלבים שלהם.

11.1.1 Indefinite noun phrases

There is no indefinite article in Hebrew. Nouns that have no article are indefinite.

Tell me, do you have (any) <u>tickets</u> for the show?	תגיד לי, יש לך כרטיסים להצגה?

It is possible to add the number אחד/אחת 'one' to a singular noun, to indicate a similar notion to 'one object/an object'.

I only have <u>one ticket</u>.	.יש לי רק כרטיס אחד
There is only <u>one restaurant</u> in which he is willing to eat.	יש רק מסעדה אחת שהוא מוכן לאכול בה.

11.1.2 Definite noun phrases

All nouns, with the exception of proper names, can become definite. In the example below both speaker and listener know what tickets are being referred to. The context as well as the formal addition of a definite article makes the noun 'tickets' definite in the second sentence.

I bought tickets for the show.	.קניתי כרטיסים להצגה
<u>The tickets</u> are in the box office.	.הכרטיסים בקופה

11.2 Noun phrase: [noun + adjective]

When a phrase consists of a linear combination of a noun and an adjective, the noun is the head of the phrase and thus is referred to as the *head noun* of the phrase. The gender and number features, and the definite/indefinite status of the head noun, are reflected in the form of the adjective that follows it. The matching of features is known as agreement.

Gender agreement

<u>Masc. Sing.</u>	You can see <u>the new movie</u> at the theater in the mall.	.אפשר לראות את <u>הסרט החדש</u> בקולנוע בקניון
<u>Fem. Sing.</u>	The <u>new show</u> begins this evening.	.<u>ההצגה החדשה</u> מתחילה הערב

Number agreement

<u>Singular and plural</u>	There is <u>one new waiter</u> and <u>five old waiters</u> in our restaurant.	יש <u>מלצר אחד חדש</u> וחמישה <u>מלצרים ותיקים</u> במסעדה שלנו.

Definite/indefinite agreement

When the head noun is indefinite, the entire phrase is indefinite. When the head noun is definite, the entire phrase is definite. The definite article is added to both the noun and the adjective: <u>הסרט החדש</u> 'the new movie'.

<u>Indefinite</u>	There is <u>a new show</u> at the Cameri Theater.	יש <u>הצגה חדשה</u> בתיאטרון הקאמרי.
<u>Definite</u>	I heard that <u>the new show</u> is worth seeing.	שמעתי שכדאי לראות את <u>ההצגה החדשה</u>.

Comparative Notes

1. The word order in the Hebrew phrase is the reverse of that in the English phrase, where the adjective is in first position and the noun is in second position. 'A big building' is literally *building big* בניין גדול, and 'a new library' is literally *library new* ספרייה חדשה.

2. In English the adjectives have only one form, and do not reflect any number and gender features. The same is not true for Hebrew, where four forms reflect all the above features.

3. In English the entire definite phrase is introduced by the definite article. In Hebrew the article is attached to several components of the phrase: the noun and the adjectives that follow it.

<u>The</u> big building > <u>the</u> building + <u>the</u> big	<u>הבניין הגדול</u>
<u>The</u> new municipal center > <u>the</u> center + <u>the</u> city + <u>the</u> new	<u>המרכז העירוני החדש</u>

The [noun + adjective] phrase can also occupy the predicate position in a verbless sentence. Past and future tenses are indicated by the addition of the verb 'to be'.

Present	This is a <u>sad</u> <u>story</u>.	זה <u>סיפור עצוב</u>.
Past	This was an <u>interesting</u> <u>act</u>.	זאת <u>היתה פעולה מעניינת</u>.
Future	These will be <u>important</u> <u>events</u>.	אלה <u>יהיו אירועים חשובים</u>.

Note

The predicate phrase is indefinite as a rule. There can be some contexts in which the predicate phrase is definite:

Indefinite	His story is <u>a sad story</u>.	הסיפור שלו <u>סיפור עצוב</u>.
Definite	This is <u>his sad story</u>.	זה <u>הסיפור העצוב שלו</u>.

The adjective is an optional component of the noun phrase. The noun can always function without the adjective in a viable sentence; the adjective cannot constitute a viable phrase by itself.

A (nice) <u>woman</u> came for the   <u>אישה</u> (נחמדה) באה להתראיין לעבודה.
job interview.

The same sentence is not viable without the head noun:

~~*Nice showed up for the interview.~~   ~~* נחמדה באה להתראיין.~~

The exception to this rule is when adjectives function as predicates in verbless sentences such as in the following example:

This woman is <u>nice</u>.   האישה הזאת <u>נחמדה</u>.

The use of the adjective as a predicate is seen by some as an abbreviation of the use of a full noun phrase:

This woman is a <u>nice woman</u>.   האישה הזאת <u>אישה נחמדה</u>.

11.2.1 Phrases with more than one adjective

There are noun phrases with a string of two adjectives or more. When more than one adjective is involved, the relationship between them and the noun head can be of two kinds. In one, the conjunction -ו 'and' is attached to the final adjective, and a comma is inserted after the first adjective and after subsequent ones, except for the last adjective, the one that is preceded by the conjunction. The two, three etc. adjectives are of equal status with respect to the head:

a big house	בית גדול
a new, big house	בית גדול וחדש
a beautiful, new, big house	בית גדול, חדש ויפה

11.2.2 Agreement in gender and number with the head noun

When an adjective accompanies a noun the gender is marked by the overt features, which are part of the adjective forms. Gender in adjectives is always marked transparently, which often is not the case in nouns. The suffixes of the adjectives are regular: the feminine singular is marked by -ָה or -ת, the masculine plural ending is -ים and the feminine plural ending is -ות.

Note

Notice how in the following examples, the masculine plural noun ending is either *-im* or *-ot*, while the masculine plural adjective always ends in *-im*.

Masculine plural noun suffix –ot		Masculine plural noun suffix –im	
<u>רבים</u>	<u>יחיד</u>	<u>רבים</u>	<u>יחיד</u>
חלו<u>נות</u> גבו<u>הים</u>	חלון גבוה	שחק<u>נים</u> טו<u>בים</u>	שחקן טוב
tall windows	a tall window	good players	a good player

Similarly, notice how in the following examples, the feminine plural noun ending is either *-im* or *-ot*, while the feminine plural adjective always ends in *-ot*.

Feminine plural noun suffix –im		Feminine plural noun suffix –ot	
<u>רבות</u>	<u>יחידה</u>	<u>רבות</u>	<u>יחידה</u>
ער<u>ים</u> גדו<u>לות</u>	עיר גדו<u>לה</u>	ברי<u>כות</u> קטנו<u>ת</u>	ברי<u>כה</u> קטנ<u>ה</u>
big cities	a big city	small pools	a small pool

Note

One way in which a learner can find out the gender of a noun is when it is part of a noun phrase that includes an adjective. The form of the adjective overtly indicates the gender of the noun it modifies. In a phrase such as עיר קטנה 'a small city', while עיר does not have an overt feminine feature, the adjective does, and thus identifies the noun as feminine.

11.3 Comparative and superlative adjective phrases

11.3.1 Comparative phrases צירופי השוואה/יתרון

A comparison can be made between two items of the same class. Adjectives can be used to compare two nouns in regard to some quality they possess.

Suspense movies are <u>more</u> <u>interesting</u> than romantic movies.	סרטי מתח <u>יותר</u> <u>מעניינים</u> <u>מ</u>סרטים רומנטיים.
This movie is <u>less</u> <u>interesting</u> <u>than</u> the one we saw yesterday.	הסרט הזה <u>פחות</u> <u>מעניין</u> <u>מ</u>הסרט שראינו אתמול.

11.3.2 Forming a comparative adjectival structure

1. The adverbs יוֹתֵר 'more' or פָּחוֹת 'less' are the first items that are added to an adjective when two entities are compared. They usually precede the adjective: יוֹתֵר טוב 'better (more good)' or פָּחוֹת טוב 'worse (less good)'.

2. The two components being compared have to be linked to make the comparison. The link to the second noun/noun phrase follows the adjective, and the equivalent of the English adverb 'than' is represented in Hebrew either by ‑מ or by מֵאֲשֶׁר.

An example is presented here, for a comparison between the performance of Student A and that of Student B (in the right to left order of the Hebrew structure):

Item 2	Than	Adjective	More/less	Item 1
תלמיד ב'	מ/מֵאֲשֶׁר	טוב	יוֹתֵר	תלמיד א'
תלמיד א'	מ/מֵאֲשֶׁר	טוב	פָּחוֹת	תלמיד ב'

Note

1. In common use the word order of the comparative adjective phrase can be changed: גדול יותר or יותר גדול 'larger'. It does not change the meaning of the phrase.

2. The adverbs of comparison יותר and פחות can be intensified by adding adverbs of degree or intensification: הַרְבֵּה יותר, קְצָת יותר.

Such phrases consist of the following parts (in the order of their appearance):

1. Adverb of degree, such as הרבה/קצת 'a lot/a bit'
2. Adverb of comparison יותר/פחות
3. Adjective
4. Providing the link מ/מאשר

A <u>lot</u> <u>more</u> important than	...הרבה <u>יותר</u> חשוב מ
A <u>bit</u> <u>more</u> important than	...קצת <u>יותר</u> גדול מ
A <u>lot</u> <u>less</u> serious than	..הרבה <u>פחות</u> רציני מ
A <u>bit</u> <u>less</u> scary than	..קצת <u>פחות</u> מפחיד מ

11.3.3 Superlative phrases   צירופי הפלגה

Meaning

Adjectives are not absolute values. Their quality or intensity can be evaluated by their status within a group of nouns they modify. A person can be the tallest in a certain group, or the tallest in the world.

The superlative adjective is a form of an adjective used to express the highest or most intense degree of the quality being attributed. The label 'superlative' does not suggest a value judgment, but a position on the spectrum of a particular quality, e.g., between the least hot and hottest:

הֲכִי פחות חם		הֲכִי חם
- <_____	חם_____	> +

Form: most

There are two ways to form superlative adjectives:

1. One way to form a superlative adjective is to add the adverb בְּיוֹתֵר 'most' to modify the adjective. The adjective is usually definite and ביותר follows it:

| This is the <u>most</u> <u>frightening</u> movie | זה הסרט <u>המפחיד</u> <u>בְּיוֹתֵר</u> שראיתי אי |
| I have ever seen. | פעם. |

2. The second option is the preferred form in speech and it is the one in which the degree adverb הֲכִי is used to express the superlative. It also means 'the most'. It precedes the adjective. The adverb הכי is considered to include the feature of definiteness, and therefore the adjective does not have a definite article.

| This is the <u>most</u> <u>frightening</u> movie | זה הסרט <u>הכי</u> <u>מפחיד</u> שראיתי אי |
| I have ever seen. | פעם. |

Since adverbs have a fixed form, the gender and number features of the adjective they modify do not influence them:

the <u>most</u> serious	<u>הכי</u> רציני	<u>הרציני ביותר</u>
	<u>הכי</u> רצינית	<u>הרצינית ביותר</u>
	<u>הכי</u> רציניים	<u>הרציניים ביותר</u>
	<u>הכי</u> רציניות	<u>הרציניות ביותר</u>

Form: 'least'

The adverb 'the least' is also a superlative of sorts. It describes an extreme at the other end of the spectrum. A person can be described not as the tallest but rather as the least tall. In Hebrew there is no term for 'least', and it is expressed by combining two adverbs הֲכִי פָּחוֹת to form a new adverbial phrase that precedes the adjective.

the <u>least</u> serious	<u>הכי פחות</u> רציני
	<u>הכי פחות</u> רצינית
	<u>הכי פחות</u> רציניים
	<u>הכי פחות</u> רציניות

As mentioned earlier, the positive or negative values are not determined by the adverbs, but rather semantically, by the adjective. The adverb הֲכִי פָּחוֹת refers only to the degree or intensity.

<u>Positive</u>	The <u>least</u> dangerous	<u>הכי פחות</u> מסוכן
<u>Negative</u>	The <u>least</u> tasty	<u>הכי פחות</u> טעים
<u>Neutral</u>	The <u>least</u> known	<u>הכי פחות</u> ידוע

11.3.4 Too much or not enough?

Adjectives can also be modified to indicate either excessive or too little intensity, degree or amount. To indicate excessiveness, the degree adverb מִדַּי is used. It too can be used for either end of the scale, יותר מִדַּי 'too excessive', or פחות מִדַּי 'too little'.

There are variant forms to express excess. The adverb מִדַּי by itself can follow the adjective without adding יותר (פחות מדי cannot be abbreviated in such a manner). In informal speech the word order can be changed to an adjective followed by מִדַּי. 'Too hot' can be expressed by מִדַּי חם or by חם מִדַּי.

The soup is <u>too hot</u>.   .המרק <u>מדי חם</u>

.המרק <u>חם מדי</u>

.המרק <u>יותר מדי חם</u>

.המרק <u>חם יותר מדי</u>

To express the notion of 'less than expected', or 'not enough', in addition to פָּחוּת מִדַּי, the adverbial expression לֹא מַסְפִּיק 'not enough' can modify the adjective.

The soup is <u>not hot enough</u>.   .המרק <u>לא מספיק חם</u>

.המרק <u>לא חם מספיק</u>

Or by paraphrasing it:

The soup is <u>too cold</u>.   .המרק <u>קר מדי</u>

More illustrations:

This book is <u>too difficult</u>   .הספר הזה <u>יותר מדי קשה</u>

.הספר הזה <u>קשה מדי</u>

.הספר הזה <u>מדי קשה</u>

The photos are <u>not clear enough</u>.   .הצילומים <u>לא מספיק ברורים</u>

.הצילומים <u>פחות מדי ברורים</u>

11.4 Apposition noun phrases   צירופי תמורה

An apposition is a construction consisting of two or more adjacent nouns or noun phrases that have identical referents, each of which could potentially be independent of the other. In the following example both החבר שלי and יונתן refer to the same person.

<u>My friend</u> <u>Jonathan</u> decided to   <u>החבר שלי</u> <u>יונתן</u> החליט להצטרף
join us.   .אלינו

When the two nouns or noun phrases appear side by side, referring to the same entity, they are without a preposition or a conjunction to connect them. In phrases of apposition each of these nouns has to be able to function as an independent unit and if we omit one of the two, the syntactic structure will still be intact.

<u>My friend</u> decided to join us.   .<u>החבר שלי</u> החליט להצטרף אלינו

<u>Jonathan</u> decided to join us.   .<u>יונתן</u> החליט להצטרף אלינו

Apposition phrases can fill the subject slot, the predicate slot, or the object slot, or follow prepositions.

Noun + Name Apposition Phrase (both function as subject)

The <u>city</u> (of) <u>Haifa</u> is in the North.   .<u>העיר חיפה</u> נמצאת בצפון

Noun + Noun Apposition Phrase (both function as predicate)

Israel is <u>a member state</u> in the UN.   .ישראל היא <u>מדינה חברה</u> באו״ם

Noun + Name Apposition Phrase (both function as object)

We received a letter from <u>the</u>   .קיבלנו מכתב <u>מהמנהל דן עדן</u>
<u>director, Dan Eden.</u>

The slots in the apposition phrase can be filled by either single nouns or by noun phrases.

Noun + Name Apposition Phrase

<u>Prime Minister David Ben-Gurion</u>   <u>ראש הממשלה דוד בן-גוריון</u> הכריז
declared the independence of the   .על עצמאותה של מדינת ישראל
State of Israel.

First noun phrase as head of entire phrase

<u>The Prime Minister</u> declared the   <u>ראש הממשלה</u> הכריז על עצמאותה של
independence of the State of   .מדינת ישראל
Israel.

Name phrase as head of entire phrase:

<u>David Ben-Gurion</u> declared the   <u>דוד בן-גוריון</u> הכריז על עצמאותה של
independence of the State of   .מדינת ישראל
Israel.

11.5 Construct phrases (noun + noun)   צֵירוּפֵי סְמִיכוּת

There are noun phrases composed of two or three nouns in a dependent relationship. The relationship may be of possession, or of some other nature. The first noun is the head noun, or nucleus of the phrase, and the second noun functions as the attribute of the first noun:

Gloss	Literal translation	סמיכות
a press conference	*a party of journalists*	מסיבת עיתונאים
a vegetable store	*a store for vegetables*	חנות ירקות
party members	*members of a political party*	חברֵי מפלגה

Note

The relationship between these nouns is different from that of apposition. The nouns concerned are not (potentially) independent, but bound to one another in a formal way and also by meaning. The term צֵירוּפֵי סמיכות 'construct phrases' is used to refer to such [noun + noun] phrases.

11.5.1 Types of construct phrases

Three types of phrases are considered to be in a סמיכות relationship, expressed by three different structures:

צירופי סמיכות :

1	Ordinary (bound) construct	סְמִיכוּת רְגִילָה (דְבוּקָה/חֲבוּרָה)
2	Separated construct	סְמִיכוּת מְפֹרֶקֶת/פְּרוּדָה
3	Double construct	סְמִיכוּת כְּפוּלָה

In many cases all three structures can be used to convey the same meaning, but their formation is slightly different. Here is an example of three options of forming such construct phrases:

Gloss	Construct phrase	Construct type
The emperor's clothes	בִּגְדֵי הקיסר	1. סמיכות רגילה
	הַבְּגָדִים של הקיסר	2. סמיכות מפורקת
	בְּגָדָיו של הקיסר	3. סמיכות כפולה

In this section we will deal mostly with the ordinary construct phrase, and the double construct phrase. The separated construct phrase is dealt with in more detail in this chapter in the discussion of phrases of possession.

Since the meanings of these different construct phrases are identical, the choice of which of these structures to use is often a matter of style. In common use, speakers frequently opt for the separated construct, i.e. the possession prepositional phrase הבגדים של הקיסר 'the clothes of the emperor'. In the written mode and in mid-higher registers of speech, language users commonly use the double construct בגדיו של הקיסר

(literally: 'his clothes of the emperor', where 'his' refers to the following noun: 'emperor'). Since in frequent kinship terms, speakers do use forms with possessive suffixes in daily speech, e.g., אָבִיו 'his father', אִשְׁתּוֹ 'his wife', double construct expressions containing such terms are found in everyday usage as well, e.g., אִשְׁתּוֹ שֶׁל חיים 'Hayyim's wife', אָבִיו של מיכאל 'Michael's father' (For a detailed description of possessive pronoun suffixes, see Chapter 6 – Pronouns). The ordinary construct בְּגְדֵי הקיסר is more frequently found in higher registers of formal Hebrew, or in fixed expressions.

11.5.2 Construct phrases: form and meaning
Forms and underlying structures of ordinary סמיכות
The two parts of the construct phrase are perceived in traditional grammar as having a dependency relationship. The head noun is considered dependent on the noun or nouns that follow it, and is known as שֵׁם נִסְמָךְ, literally 'supported noun'. By the same token, the second noun, the modifier, is considered the supporter, and is known as שֵׁם סוֹמֵךְ, literally 'a supporting noun'.

Definite and indefinite construct phrases
In indefinite construct phrases, both נִסְמָךְ and סוֹמֵךְ are indefinite:

2 noun phrase	a bank director	מנהל בנק
3 noun phrase	a bank workers' organization	ארגון עובדי בנק

In definite construct phrases only the last noun of the סמיכות has a definite article:

2 noun phrase	<u>the</u> bank director	מנהל הַבנק
3 noun phrase	the bank workers' organization	ארגון עובדי הַבנק

The head noun השם הנסמך may be the same as the independent form, but in many cases has a variant form, which displays an overt indication of its syntactic position and function.

Singular > Plural
To change a construct phrase to plural, the first noun, the *head noun*, undergoes a change in number. The second noun does not change.

Gloss	סמיכות	Head noun
a coffeehouse	בֵּית קָפֶה	בַּיִת (ז) (בֵּית-)
coffeehouses	בָּתֵי קָפֶה	בָּתִּים (בָּתֵי-)

| a Sabbath meal | סְעוּדַת שַׁבָּת | סְעוּדָה (נ) (סְעוּדַת-) |
| Sabbath meals | סְעוּדוֹת שַׁבָּת | סְעוּדוֹת (סְעוּדוֹת-) |

The dependent noun: changes in shape

In many noun classes there is a predictable change of shape of the first noun of the סְמִיכוּת, resulting from its being assigned a lower degree of stress than the second noun. In the examples below, in one phrase the first noun stands alone, and has an independent form, and in the second phrase it is part of a [noun + noun] phrase and undergoes some change.

This is an immigrant problem.	זאת בְּעָיַת מהגרים.	<	זאת בְּעָיָה של מהגרים.
The literature classes are interesting.	שִׁעוּרֵי הַסִּפְרוּת מעניינים.	<	הַשִּׁעוּרִים לספרות מעניינים.
This is our study (=our work room).	זה חֲדַר העבודה שלנו.	<	זה החֶדֶר שבו אנחנו עובדים.

Some changes in form in the שם נסמך are predictable:

1. In feminine singular nouns ending in ‐ָה‐ ‐*a*, such as בְּעָיָה, the final ending changes in the following way: ‐ה < ‐ת‐. The vowel sign changes from *kamats* to *patah*, but it is pronounced the same.

שִׁירָה > שִׁירַת‐	שׂמְלָה > שׂמְלַת‐	פִּינָה > פִּינַת‐	ילְדָה > יַלְדַת‐
שירת ברבור	שׂמלת משי	פינת רחוב	ילדת חלום
swan song	silk dress	street corner	dream girl

2. In masculine plural nouns that end in ‐*im*, such as שִׁעוּרִים, the final ‐ם is omitted and the vowel is changed to ‐*ey*: שִׁעוּרִים > שִׁעוּרֵי‐. Some stem vowels are subject to change as well (Note changes in the plural of *segolate* nouns, Chapter 5).

צוֹפִים > צוֹפֵי‐	חַיָּלִים > חַיָּלֵי‐	סְפָרִים > סִפְרֵי‐	יְלָדִים > יַלְדֵי‐
צוֹפֵי ים	חַיָּלֵי בדיל	סִפְרֵי לימוד	יַלְדֵי בית ספר
sea scouts	lead soldiers	textbooks	school kids

3. It is also predictable that feminine plural nouns ending in ‐וֹת, such as תַּלְמִידוֹת, will not undergo any change at the end of the word, though vowels may change within the stem, as a result of stress shift.

4. In general, vowel changes in the first noun of a סמיכות phrase result from stress shift. The primary stress of the phrase falls on the stressed vowel of the last noun, and the stress of the first one is reduced to secondary stress. Consequently, unstressed vowels in the first noun are weakened or deleted altogether. Thus, in the noun בָּנוֹת 'girls', the first vowel *a* is omitted, and the noun is now -בְּנוֹת *bnot-*, such as in the phrase בְּנוֹת שֵׁשׁ עֶשְׂרֵה 'sixteen years old': *banót > bnòt shésh esrè*.

No change in form		Internal vowel change	
רַקְדָנִים	נַגָנוֹת	בָּנִים	בָּנוֹת
רַקְדָנֵי ג'אז	נַגָנוֹת כִּנּוֹר	בְּנֵי שְׁמוֹנֶה עֶשְׂרֵה	בְּנוֹת שֵׁשׁ עֶשְׂרֵה
jazz dancers	violin players	18 years old	16 years old

Construct noun 1, שם נסמך undergoes internal changes:

Gloss		Plural		Singular
thing	דִּבְרֵי-	דְּבָרִים	דְּבַר-	דָּבָר
language	שְׂפוֹת-	שָׂפוֹת	שְׂפַת-	שָׂפָה
memory	זִכְרוֹנוֹת-	זִכְרוֹנוֹת	זִכְרוֹן-	זִכָּרוֹן

Construct noun 1, שם נסמך, does not undergo internal changes:

Gloss		Plural		Singular
hammer	פַּטִּישֵׁי-	פַּטִּישִׁים	פַּטִּישׁ-	פַּטִּישׁ
carpenter	נַגָרֵי-	נַגָרִים	נַגַר-	נַגָר
map	מַפּוֹת-	מַפּוֹת	מַפַּת-	מַפָּה

Note: although the first vowel here is also *a*, it is unaffected because of the following *dagesh ḥazak*, which 'protects' it from reduction.

Types of construct phrase heads

The head of the construct phrase can be of a number of different categories:

1. The head can be a noun: לֶקֶט (שֶׁל שִׁירָה מְתוּרְגֶּמֶת)

Phrase: a translated poetry <u>anthology</u>   [לֶקֶט שירה] מתורגמת

2. The head can be a noun-quantifier: רוֹב (הַסְּפָרִים)

Phrase: <u>most/the majority</u> of his books   [רוֹב הספרים] שלו

3. The head can be an adjective: יְפֵה (תוֹאַר)

Phrase: a <u>good looking</u> guy   בחור [יְפֵה תואר]

4. The head can be a participle: (של המכשיר) **הַמַּפְעִיל**

Phrase: the <u>operator</u> of this tool   [<u>מַפְעִיל</u> המכשיר] הזה

5. The head can be a prefix word:

Phrase: When I was a kid, I loved to ride   כשהייתי ילד אהבתי
             a <u>tri</u>cycle.   לרכוב על [<u>תְּלַת</u>-אוֹפָן.]

Underlying propositions of construct phrases

Many construct phrases can be restated by means of a sentence or a prepositional phrase. These structures are perceived to be the underlying propositions of the phrase.

1. Paraphrase of a possessive relationship:

<u>Sentence</u>	The immigrants have a problem.	.למהגרים יש בְּעָיָה
<u>Prepositional phrase</u>	a problem of immigrants	בְּעָיָה של מהגרים
<u>סמיכות</u>	an immigrants' problem	בְּעָיַת מהגרים

2. Paraphrase of a purpose relationship:

<u>Sentence</u>	The beaches are for bathing.	.החופים הם לרחצה
<u>Prepositional phrase</u>	beaches for bathing	חופים לרחצה
<u>סמיכות</u>	bathing beaches	חופֵי רחצה

11.5.3 Semi compounds bound phrases > compound nouns

There are many fixed expressions of bound construct phrases, which have achieved an almost fused word or compound noun status. Most of them cannot be taken apart and cannot be paraphrased by the comparable split structures, as the parts do not mean the sum of the two nouns:

Gloss	Split structure	סמיכות
synagogue	בית של כנסת	בֵּית כְּנֶסֶת
school	בית של ספר	בֵּית סֵפֶר
lawyer	עורך של דין	עוֹרֵךְ דין
mayor	ראש של עיר	ראש עיר

However, while they have become one semantic unit, they still maintain the two separate components in writing. They also maintain the syntactic characteristics of construct phrases: the head noun determines the gender and number of the phrase, and when the phrase is definite, the definite article precedes the second noun: בית הכנסת, עורך הדין, ראש העיר. Some of these phrases are undergoing a change of status to becoming true compound nouns when they begin to be written as one word, and when the unit is treated grammatically as one word, such as having the definite article prefixed to the new compound word. It occurs informally at first in daily speech, when speakers begin to use such compounds, as in הַבֵּית-סֵפֶר, or in דִין-הָעורך. It eventually gets reflected in writing, when first, the two separate words בֵּית סֵפֶר are written as a hyphenated phrase, בֵּית-סֵפֶר. In informal writing, בֶּן-אָדָם 'human being' is often represented as בֶּנְאָדָם, and occasionally even בֶּנָדָם, to reflect everyday pronunciation. The continuously changing status of these noun combinations can also be seen in the free variation choices of עורך הדין שלנו side by side with הָעורך-דין שלנו, with the latter becoming much more common in use, but still perceived by some as substandard. In all the above structures the plural form maintains the סמיכות two noun structure: בתֵי ספר, עורכֵי דין, בנֵי אדם.

In the final step of the process of becoming a single unit, the two components of this structure become one word. For instance, the combination of basketball began as two separate words כַּדּור סַל, but now they have become one word, כַּדּורסַל, like their English counterparts. The combination סוף שָבועַ 'week end' is well on its way to becoming one unit, סוֹפְשָבועַ, both in speech and in writing. For instance, the daily newspaper *Maariv* has a special weekend section called סוֹפְשבועַ. However, the plural form maintains the סמיכות the two noun structure סופֵי שבוע 'weekends'.

11.5.4 Meanings of construct phrases
When the components of the construct phrase combine they often create a new concept. The meaning of the new unit depends partially on the kind of association there is between the nouns. The structure is not totally open, as there are semantic restrictions on what appropriate combinations there can be. To form a construct phrase from a noun such as חוֹף (ז) 'shore/beach', it needs to be complemented by a noun that refers to a body of water, the purpose it serves, or the name of a particular beach.

| Eilat beach | חוֹף אֵילַת | seashore | חוֹף יָם |
| river bank | חוֹף נָהָר | swimming beaches | חוֹפֵי רַחֲצָה |

Some of the main groups, classified in terms of their semantic relationship between the nouns, are listed here:

1. Connection of possession:

| סמיכות | public funds | כַּסְפֵּי הציבור |
| Paraphrase | funds that belong to the public | כְּסָפִים ששייכים לציבור |

| סמיכות | the club members | חַבְרֵי המועדון |
| Paraphrase | the members that belong to the club | הַחֲבֵרִים ששייכים למועדון |

2. Connection of material - made from/of:

| סמיכות | a silk dress | שִׂמְלַת משי |
| Paraphrase | a dress made from silk | שִׂמְלָה עשויה ממשי |

| סמיכות | a paper tiger | נְמֵר נייר |
| Paraphrase | a tiger made from paper | נָמֵר עשוי מנייר |

3. Connection of function - for the purpose of:

| סמיכות | a cargo plane | מְטוֹס הובלה |
| Paraphrase | a plane for carrying cargo | מָטוֹס מיועד להובלה |

| סמיכות | a bedroom | חֲדַר שֵׁינה |
| Paraphrase | a room for sleeping | חֶדֶר מיועד לשינה |

4. Connection of location - comes from/is located at:

| סמיכות | laboratory animals | חַיּוֹת מעבדה |
| Paraphrase | the animals in the laboratory | חַיּוֹת שנמצאות במעבדה |

| סמיכות | the city streets | רְחוֹבוֹת העיר |
| Paraphrase | the streets of the city | הָרְחוֹבוֹת בעיר |

5. Connection of time:

| סמיכות | the summer vacation | חופְשַׁת הקיץ |
| Paraphrase | the vacation during the summer | הַחוּפְשָׁה בזמן הקיץ |

| סמיכות | a ten o'clock snack | אֲרוּחַת עשר |
| Paraphrase | a snack at ten o'clock | אֲרוּחָה בשעה עשר |

6. Cause and effect:

סמיכות	battle/shell shock	הֶלֶם קרב
Paraphrase	shock cause by battle	הֶלֶם שנגרם על ידי קרב

סמיכות	altitude sickness	מַחֲלַת גבהים
Paraphrase	sickness caused by high altitudes	מַחֲלָה שנגרמת על ידי גבהים

7. Connection to actor:

סמיכות	howling of jackals	יְלָלוֹת תנים
Paraphrase	the howling jackals make	יְלָלוֹת שמייללים תנים

סמיכות	a court's decree	צַו בית המשפט
Paraphrase	a decree made by the court	הַצַו שבית המשפט פסק

8. Connection to object of action:

סמיכות	respect for elders	כיבוד הורים
Paraphrase	respect given to elders	הַכָּבוֹד שנותנים להורים

סמיכות	children's education	חִינוך ילדים
Paraphrase	education given to children	הַחִינוך שנותנים לילדים

9. Connection of quantity/measure, or of vessel containing matter:

סמיכות	a milk bottle	בַּקְבּוּק חלב
Paraphrase	a bottle that contains milk	בַּקְבּוּק שמכיל חלב

סמיכות	a fruit basket	סַל פֵּירוֹת
Paraphrase	a basket containing fruit	סַל שמכיל פֵּירוֹת

Note

Some combinations are ambiguous and can be interpreted in two different ways, with two different underlying structures:

סמיכות	a wine glass	כוס יין
Paraphrase 1	a glass that contains wine	כוס שמכילה יין
Paraphrase 2	a glass for wine (a type of glass)	כוס ליין

Adjectival phrases can be created out of construct phrases. The nucleus of such a phrase is usually an adjective in a נִסְמָךְ form, and thus may have a variant dependent form, followed by a noun, to which it directly relates and to which it provides some kind of attribution. For instance, 'golden-haired' is in Hebrew literally 'golden as to hair' זְהוֹב שֵׂיעָר. These are bound phrases that cannot be taken apart.

10. Connection of descriptive adjective:

סמיכות	good-hearted	טוֹב לֵב
Paraphrase	he has a good heart	יש לו לב טוב

סמיכות	experienced/with experience	בַּעֲלַת ניסיון
Paraphrase	she has experience	יש לה ניסיון

סמיכות	unprecedented	חֲסַר תקדים
Paraphrase	it has no precedence	אין לו תקדים

סמיכות	good-looking/handsome	יְפֵה תואר
Paraphrase	with good looks	עם מראה חיצוני יָפֶה

11.5.5 Construct phrase modified by adjectives

The construct phrase can be further modified by an adjective. It can be definite or indefinite.

In the indefinite phrase, both nouns appear without an article. If the phrase is modified by an adjective, the adjective has no article either. (Adjectives in these phrases modify the head noun of the phrase).

	2. תואר	1. צירוף סמיכות
an old school	ישן	בית ספר (ז)
a veteran Knesset member	ותיקה	חברת כנסת (נ)
splendid office buildings	מפוארים	בנייֵני משׂרדים (ז.ר.)

In definite phrases, only the second noun has the definite article attached to it. It makes the entire phrase definite. If there is an adjective that modifies the phrase, a definite article is also prefixed to it.

the old school	הַישן	בבית הַספר

When the two nouns have the same gender and number, and the adjective reflects that gender and number, it is at times ambiguous which of the nouns is being modified.

	2. תואר	1. צירוף סמיכות	Option 1
	חשוב	מְנַהֵל משׂרד	an <u>important</u> office <u>manager</u>
	גדולה	בירת מדינה	a <u>large</u> state <u>capital</u>
	חדשים	מְעוֹנוֹת סטודנטים	<u>new</u> students' <u>dormitories</u>

3. תואר	2. שם	1. שֵם	Option 2
חשוב	משׂרד	מנהל	a manager of an <u>important</u> office
גדולה	מדינה	בירת	a capital of <u>a large</u> state
חדשים	סטוּדֶנטים	מבחֵני	exams of <u>new</u> students
כחולות	חולצות	חבילות	parcels of <u>blue</u> shirts

11.5.6 Word order in phrases with סמיכות

Construct as part of possessive phrases

The construct phrase can be part of a possessive phrase. The construct phrase can be viewed as constituting one unit that fills the slot of the head noun, and the possessive preposition with a noun or pronoun is added to it. The phrase is usually definite (see above rules of possessive noun phrases). The סמיכות phrase functions as the head noun, and the preposition of possession של follows, complemented by a noun or a pronoun suffix.

2. של +	1. סמיכות	
שלי	בית הספר	my school
של ישראל	עיר הבירה	the capital city of Israel

סמיכות with possessive prepositions and adjectives

The סמיכות phrase can have an adjective that modifies it. In this case the order of the three components is as follows:

3. של	2. תואר	1. סמיכות	
<u>שלי</u>	הישן	בית הספר	my old school
<u>של עכּוֹ</u>	הצרות	סמטאות העיר	the narrow alleys of Akko

A comparative note

Compare the word order in English and in Hebrew in the following:

our beautiful capital city.   עיר הבירה היפה שלנו

our +(beautiful + [city + capital]).   ([עיר הבירה] + היפה) + שלנו)

1. The first and most notable difference is the word order. In English the order of the components is the reverse from that in Hebrew.

2. There is no definite article in the entire English phrase. The possessive pronoun at the head of the phrase makes the entire phrase definite.

3. There are two definite articles in Hebrew: the first prefixed to the second noun of the סמיכות phrase and the second prefixed to the adjective.

11.5.7 Double construct phrase   סמיכות כפולה

The double construct phrase is known as such because it consists of two possessive structures, one with a possessive pronoun, another with שֶׁל, both referring to the same 'possessor'.

The actor's election as state governor	בחירתוֹ של הַשחקָן למושל
brought up many questions.	המדינה העלתה שאלות רבות.

A pronoun suffix is added to the possessed noun בחירה, yielding בחירתוֹ 'his election'. The suffix shares the same number and gender as the possessor noun השחקן 'the actor' and anticipates its occurrence. The possessor השחקן is then mentioned, following the preposition של. This structure is <u>exclusive to third person</u> suffixes only. The formal restriction is that it must have a pronoun suffixed to the noun, i.e., בחירתוֹ, and cannot be paraphrased by a prepositional phrase הבחירה שלוֹ. The other restriction involves the use with the third person exclusively.

A comparison between an ordinary construct and a double construct:

1. Ordinary construct

the king's clothes	clothes of + the king	בְּגְדֵי המלך

2. Double construct

the king's clothes	[his clothes] + of [the king]	בְּגָדָיו של המלך

The following tables display examples of the double construct phrases with singular and plural nouns and pronoun suffixes:

Singular Noun + Prepositional Phrase

the director's house	של המנהל	בֵּיתוֹ	הַבַּיִת של המנהל
the (f.) teacher's son	של המורָה	בְּנָהּ	הַבֵּן של המורָה
our parents' house	של ההורים	בֵּיתָם	הַבַּיִת של ההורים
the girls' room	של הבנות	חַדְרָן	הַחֶדֶר של הבנות

Plural Noun + Prepositional Phrase

David's sons	של דויד	בָּנָיו	הַבָּנִים של דָויד
Ahuva's sons	של אהובה	בָּנֶיהָ	הַבָּנִים של אהובה
our friends' sons	של החברים שלנו	בְּנֵיהֶם	הַבָּנִים של החברים
my relatives' sons	של הקרובות שלי	בְּנֵיהֶן	הַבָּנִים של הקרובות

11.5.8 Semantic restrictions of the possessor noun

The possessor noun, i.e. the second noun of such a phrase, has to be a noun with features that enable it to have a possessive or pseudo-possessive relationship with another noun. It is most often a person, or a group or an institution that represents people, or an animal or a fictional character that is endowed with such qualities.

Possessive:

the judge's wife	אִשְׁתּוֹ של השופט	הָאִשָּׁה של השופט	אֵשֶׁת השופט

Pseudo-possessive:

the nation's pride	גַּאֲוָתוֹ של העם	הַגַּאֲוָה של העם	גַּאֲוַת העם

It cannot be an inanimate object, which has no such semantic features. In such an underlying relationship between the two nouns the double construct expression cannot be used.

bedroom	~~חדרה של השינה~~	הַחֶדֶר לשינה	חֶדֶר + שינה
golden earrings	~~עגיליו של הזהב~~	הָעֲגִילִים מזהב	עֲגִילִים + זהב

11.5.9 Strings of three-nouns סמיכות

There are construct phrases where the string of nouns consists of three nouns: the first noun is the head of the phrase and it is modified by another construct phrase. When the phrase is made definite, the definite article is attached to the last noun and it makes the entire phrase definite.

the eve of [the World War].	ערב [מִלְחֶמֶת העולם]

A three-noun string of the סמיכות noun phrase can have an adjective added to it. The adjective follows all the nouns, regardless of which one it modifies.

on the eve of World War <u>II</u> (=<u>the second</u>)	ערב מלחמת העולם <u>השנייה</u>
<u>elementary</u> school children	תלמידי בתי ספר <u>יסודיים</u>

The adjective can modify the head noun, or it can modify the second or even the third noun. If the nouns have different gender and number features, the form of the adjective helps identify which noun component of the phrase is being modified.

<u>Masculine singular adjective modifies the first noun</u>

The new member of the Labor party.   חֲבֵר מִפְלֶגֶת העבודה החדש.

- <u>the new member</u> of   <u>החבר החדש</u> של
- the Labor party.   מפלגת העבודה

<u>Feminine singular adjective modifies the second noun</u>

The member of the present Labor party   חבר מפלגת העבודה הנוכחית

- the member of   החבר של
- <u>the present Labor party</u>   <u>מפלגת העבודה הנוכחית</u>

A comparative note

In English, the three-noun string sequence is usually separated and rendered by a prepositional phrase, with the adjective preceding the specific noun it modifies:

the new <u>pilots</u> of the <u>El Al planes</u>   <u>טייסי מטוסי אל-על</u> החדשים

In Hebrew the three nouns appear contiguously whereas in English the phrase is broken up by the preposition 'of' and the adjective is next to the noun it modifies. The sequence *the new El Al plane pilots* would be very awkward and considered ungrammatical.

When all the nouns of the סמיכות have the same number and gender, the adjective can modify all of them and it is not clear which one is being modified. This is the case in the following example, where the feminine singular adjective can modify any one of these three nouns, all of which are feminine singular: אוניברסיטה/ תזמורת /מנצחת

the new university orchestra   מנצחת תזמורת האוניברסיטה
conductor   החדשה

There are three possible readings to the sentence above:

the new conductor of the university orchestra	<u>המנצחת החדשה</u> של התזמורת של האוניברסיטה
the conductor of the new orchestra of the university	המנצחת של <u>התזמורת החדשה</u> של האוניברסיטה
the conductor of the orchestra of the new university	המנצחת של התזמורת של <u>האוניברסיטה החדשה</u>

The three-noun sequence is normally broken in such cases, to clarify which noun is being modified by the adjective.

Quantifiers in סמיכות noun phrase

Quantifiers can modify one of the components of the construct phrase:

a state of <u>all its citizens</u>	מדינת <u>כל אזרחיה</u>
<u>the two</u> labor <u>organizations</u>	<u>שני ארגוני</u> הפועלים

11.6 Phrases of possession

Phrases of possession have an underlying sentential structure. המכונית שֶׁלִּי 'my car', for instance, implies the underlying sentence יֵשׁ לִי מכונית 'I have a car', and reflects that relationship of possession. One noun refers to what is possessed, in this case 'the car', and the other noun refers to whoever possesses it, in this case 'I'.

The possessed noun is the head noun (the noun being modified), and the possessor noun is the modifier. In the illustration below, the head noun is החנות 'the store' and the modifier answers the question של מי החנות? 'Whose store is it?'

Possessor	of	Possessed	Gloss	Possession phrase
ההורים	של	החנות	the parents' store	החנות של ההורים
הם	של	החנות	their store	החנות שלהם

A comparative note

The word order is different in Hebrew and in English. In English the possessor precedes the possessed: 'my car', while in Hebrew the word order is reversed: המכונית שלי.

11.6.1 Possessive noun phrases: options

Possessive noun phrases can be formed in the following ways:

1. A noun that indicates what is being possessed, followed by the preposition שֶׁל, which is followed by the possessor noun.

3	**2**	**1**		**3**	**2**	**1**
Possessor	of	Possessed		Possessor	of	Possessed
שולה	של	האח		שמואל	של	ההורים
	Shula's brother				Shmuel's parents	

2. A pronoun can substitute for the possessor noun, and it is suffixed to the preposition של: הַחֲנוּת שֶׁלּוֹ 'his store'.

3. A possessive personal pronoun can also be suffixed to the possessed noun. In such a case there is no need for the preposition of possession: אֲחוֹתוֹ 'his sister'.

There are several categories of nouns, to which the possessive pronoun suffix cannot be added, such as most nouns of foreign origin, for instance הַהִיסְטוֹרְיָה שֶׁלָּנוּ 'our history' rather than הִיסְטוֹרִיתֵּנוּ*, which is not permissible. Certain classes of words actually **favor** the noun + pronoun option, notably kinship terms.

For a discussion of possessive personal pronouns see pp. 169-170.

Regular phrases of possession are usually definite in Hebrew. Definite status has to be either indicated by a definite article, by a noun with a pronoun suffix, or even by a proper name:

Definite article	Dan's friends	החברים של דן
Pronoun ending	his friends	חבריו
Proper name	our Dan	דן שלנו

Possessive noun phrases can be also indefinite. The meaning of the indefinite phrase is different from that of the definite phrase of possession. Rather than the more general הַחֲבֵרָה שלי 'my friend', the meaning of the indefinite phrase חֲבֵרָה שלי is 'a friend of mine/one of my friends'.

Indefinite phrases

<u>A friend of mine</u> lives in town.	חברה <u>שלי</u> גרה בעיר.
<u>Some friends of mine</u> live in town.	חברות <u>שלי</u> גרות בעיר.

11.6.2 Word order in possessive noun phrases

When the possessed noun of the phrase is modified by an adjective, the constituents of the possessive noun phrases are organized in one of the following two ways:

1. The noun and adjectives come first and then are followed by the prepositional phrase of possession.

	<u>של + שם/כ"ג</u>	<u>תואר</u>	<u>שם</u>
his oldest daughter	<u>שֶׁלּוֹ</u>	הבכורה	הבת
Dan's old friends	<u>של דן</u>	הוותיקים	הידידים

2. The possessive can precede the adjectives only if it is attached to the noun itself as a suffix pronoun.

	<u>תואר</u>	<u>שם + כ"ג</u>
his oldest daughter	הבכורה	בתו
his old friends	הוותיקים	יְדִידָיו

11.7 Phrases with demonstrative pronouns

Demonstrative pronouns belong to the class of specific determiners. They are usually part of a definite phrase and follow a noun with which they agree in gender and number, as adjectives do (which is why some refer to them as demonstrative adjectives). There are two sets of demonstrative pronouns: one that indicates or points to an object of close proximity in place or time, and one that indicates a reference to another place or time or to a different set of events.

Demonstrative Pronouns

a close time or place	This book is not mine.	<u>הספר הזה</u> הוא לא שלי.
	This library is new.	<u>הספרייה הזאת</u> חדשה.
	These books belong to the library.	<u>הספרים האלה</u> שייכים לספרייה.

a distant time or place	That book is David's.	<u>הספר ההוא</u> הוא של דוד.
	That library was too small.	<u>הספרייה ההיא</u> הייתה קטנה מדיי.
	Those books are too expensive.	<u>הספרים ההם</u> יקרים מדיי.

Demonstrative pronouns

| a close time or place | this/these | הַזֶּה, הַזֹּאת, הָאֵלֶּה |
| a distant time or place | that/those | הַהוּא, הַהִיא, הָהֵם, הָהֵן |

11.7.1 Demonstrative pronouns of close proximity

When the demonstrative pronoun is used to modify a noun, it functions as a regular adjective does. It follows the rules of syntax, which apply to adjectives, in that it occupies the same position as that of an adjective, and follows the rules of word order, gender and definiteness agreement of the adjective in a noun phrase.

<u>Masculine singular</u>

| + Adjective | The new book is not mine. | הספר החדש הוא לא שלי. |
| + Demonstrative | This book is not mine. | הספר הזה הוא לא שלי. |

<u>Feminine singular</u>

| + Adjective | The new library is excellent. | הספרייה החדשה מצוינת. |
| + Demonstrative | This library is excellent. | הספרייה הזאת מצוינת. |

<u>Masculine plural</u>

| + Adjective | The new buildings are very tall. | הבניינים החדשים גבוהים מאוד. |
| + Demonstrative | These buildings are very tall. | הבניינים האלה גבוהים מאוד. |

<u>Feminine plural</u>

| + Adjective | The new villas are very expensive. | הוילות החדשות יקרות מאוד. |
| + Demonstrative | These villas are very expensive. | הוילות האלה יקרות מאוד. |

The phrases where nouns are accompanied by demonstrative pronouns are definite in form as well as in meaning. With few exceptions, the definite article is prefixed to both the noun and the demonstrative pronoun: הבית הַזֶּה, האישה הַזֹּאת, האנשים הָאֵלֶּה. However, such phrases can also be constructed with a noun and a demonstrative pronoun without the use of the definite article, i.e., בַּיִת זֶה, אישה זאת, אנשים אֵלֶּה, and still remain definite. The difference is stylistic only.

<u>With definite article</u>	<u>Without definite article</u>
<u>בדף הזה</u> נעשה שימוש במסגרות.	<u>בדף זֶה</u> נעשה שימוש במסגרות.

'Frames are being used in this page'.

The variation of the phrase without a definite article can be found in formal speech and in written texts.

A comparative note

The use of the definite article with demonstrative pronouns (treating it as if it were an adjective) is not limited to Hebrew. It is a feature shared with Phoenician, Aramaic, and Classical Arabic.

11.7.2 Demonstrative pronouns of remote proximity

The function of the remote demonstrative is to relate the noun to a place and time remote from the speaker's environment. The remote reference can also be to a particular segment or object in the context of a text (anaphora), which can be found in relative proximity.

There are two singular demonstrative pronouns of remote proximity and two plural ones. They are composed of the definite article and the third person pronoun.

<u>רבות</u>	<u>רבים</u>	<u>יחידה</u>	<u>יחיד</u>
הָהֵן	הָהֵם	הַהִיא	הַהוּא
those	those	that	that
ha-hén	*ha-hém*	*ha-hí*	*ha-hú*

The phrases where nouns are accompanied by demonstrative pronouns are definite in form as well as in meaning.

Masculine singular

this	This house is small.	הבית הַזֶּה קטן.
that	That house is big.	הבית ההוא גדול.

Feminine singular

this	This library is near.	הספרייה הַזֹּאת קרובה.
that	That library is far.	הספרייה ההיא רחוקה.

Masculine plural

| these | These buildings are near. | .הבניינים האלה קרובים |
| those | Those buildings are far. | .הבניינים ההם רחוקים |

Feminine plural

| these | These stores are near. | החנויות האלה קרובות. |
| those | Those stores are far. | .החנויות ההן רחוקות |

A historical note

The demonstrative pronoun had a number of historical variants, some
of which survived in the higher registers of Modern Hebrew.

All three variants of close proximity demonstratives can be found in
Israeli Hebrew, but הָאֵלּוּ belongs to a somewhat higher register, and
הַלָּלוּ is somewhat higher than הָאֵלּוּ.

There are also variants among the remote proximity ones. Biblical
Hebrew had a relatively rare הַלָּזֶה 'that', as in הנה בעל החלומות הַלָּזֶה בא
'Behold, here comes that master of dreams'. Sometimes both masculine
and feminine singular forms may be shortened to הַלָּז (which is the only
variant Mishnaic Hebrew uses). Both are restricted to use in a highly
literary register, and for all practical purposes are considered obsolete.

<u>רבים-רבות</u>	<u>יחידה</u>	<u>יחיד</u>
הַלָּלוּ	הַלֵּזוּ	הַלָּז/הַלָּזֶה
hallálu	*hallezú*	*halláz/hallazé*
these/those	this/that	this/that

On the eve of the holy Sabbath <u>this event</u> occurred.	.בערב שבת קודש היה <u>המעשה הלז</u>
Who is <u>that</u> man walking in the field?	מי <u>האיש הלזה</u> ההולך בשדה?
<u>This land</u>, once desolate, has become like the garden of Eden. (Ezekiel, Chapter 36: 35)	<u>הארץ הלזו</u> הנשמה היתה כגן עדן (יחזקאל ל״ו : ל״ה)

In biblical Hebrew, one only finds אֵלֶּה or הָאֵלֶּה 'these', or the shortened variant הָאֵל. Mishnaic Hebrew, while still maintaining הָאֵלֶּה, prefers the variant הָאֵלּוּ, and introduces a third one, הַלָּלוּ as in:

| We light <u>these</u> candles to commemorate the miracles and wonders | הנרות הללו אנו מדליקין על הניסים ועל הנפלאות. |

The most frequently used, in speech as well as in writing, is the demonstrative pronoun הַלָּלוּ, which, as mentioned, is used with the meaning of either 'these' or 'those'. It depends on the context as to which meaning is given to the deictic, close or remote proximity in time and place. The demonstratives הַלָּז, הַלֵּזוּ, הַלָּלוּ can also function as stand-alone items. The most commonly used is הַלָּז, which stands for 'that person' and not just 'that'.

| Who is <u>that person</u> who set himself up as the barometer for morality and justice? | מי זה <u>הלז</u> ששם את עצמו כברומטר המוסר והצדק? |

| <u>That person</u> was also in Spain and worked on a topic of philosophy about Plato. | <u>הלז</u> גם היה בארץ ספרד ועבד שם בעניין פילוסופי על אודות אפלטון. |

11.8 Prepositional phrases

An extensive discussion of prepositional phrases can be found in Chapter 10. A short summary is included here.

Prepositional phrases consist of a preposition followed by a noun, a noun phrase or a pronoun.

Prep + Noun	David went walking with <u>friends</u>.	דוד יצא לטייל <u>עם חברים</u>.
Prep + Noun phrase	David went walking with <u>his friends</u>.	דוד יצא לטייל <u>עם החברים שלו</u>.
Prep + pronoun suffix	David went walking with <u>them</u>.	דוד יצא לטייל <u>אתם</u>.

11.9 Numerical and quantifier phrases

Noun phrases with numerals or quantifiers are discussed extensively in chapter 7. A short summary is included here.

11.9.1 Numerical + noun

The number *one*, when it combines with another noun to form a phrase, always <u>follows the noun</u> that is being counted, since it is conceived of as an adjective. Since it functions as an adjective, it has the gender features of the noun that it modifies. The number noun also agrees with the head noun in its status as indefinite or definite.

Indefinite phrases:

	Masculine זכר		Feminine נקבה
one hat	כּוֹבַע אֶחָד	one dress	שִׂמְלָה אַחַת

Indefinite phrases:

	Masculine זכר		Feminine נקבה
the one actor	הַשַּׂחְקָן הָאֶחָד	the one actress	הַשַּׂחְקָנִית הָאַחַת

Numerical phrases with numbers above the number 1 are formed in a similar shape to that of [noun + noun] phrases, צירופי סמיכות. In these phrases the components combine in the following way: the numerals always precede the count nouns, which, with some exceptions (particularly, in higher numbers), are plural nouns. The numerals have the same gender features as the count nouns. When the phrases are indefinite, the number nouns are independent forms of the number (with the exception of number *two*). When the number nouns are part of a definite phrase, they have the alternate shape typical of the first noun of a סמיכות phrase. When the number *two* is part of an indefinite or definite phrase, it has a variant form: שְׁתַּיִם ~ שְׁתֵּי- and שְׁנֵי- ~ שְׁנַיִם.

Indefinite phrases:

	Masculine זכר		Feminine נקבה
two boys	שְׁנֵי בנים	two girls	שְׁתֵּי בנות

Definite phrases:

	Masculine זכר		Feminine נקבה
the two boys	שְׁנֵי הבנים	the two girls	שְׁתֵּי הבנות

Numerals 2-10 that combine with nouns in phrases:

<u>Indefinite:</u>	They have three cute children.	יש להם שְׁלוֹשָׁה ילדים נחמדים.
<u>Definite:</u>	Their three children all study here.	כל שְׁלוֹשֶׁת הילדים שלהם לומדים כאן.

11.9.2 Quantifier + noun

Noun phrases can consist of a quantifier followed by the head noun. Since the modification is only of quantity, quantifiers are not considered adjectives, and – possibly to differentiate them from adjectives – they precede the head noun, as a rule. Numbers (numerals) may **also** be regarded as quantifiers, which is why they also preceded the (head) noun.

Most of the students came to class.	רוֹב התלמידים הגיעו לשיעור.
Only some of the students arrived.	רק חֵלֶק מהתלמידים הגיעו.
Many students came to the demonstration.	הַרבֵּה סטודנטים הגיעו להפגנה.
Only a few students came to the demonstration.	רק כַּמָה סטודנטים הגיעו להפגנה.

11.10 Noun phrases with determiners

Determiners consist of a small class of words, which accompany nouns and mark their status of being definite or indefinite or in some other way determine aspects of the identity of the noun. There are several classes of determiners and most of them precede the noun and their presence is totally dependent on the noun. A few follow nouns. Determiners cannot occur in isolation.

The most common determiner is the definite article, discussed in the introductory section above.

11.10.1 Determiners that precede nouns

There is another type of determiner, which in English is expressed by 'that same…' It is similar in meaning to the use of the demonstrative pronoun that is distant in time or place, האיש הַהוּא 'that man'. The particle used for the direct object with third person pronoun ending is also used to express the pronoun modifier 'that same'. Unlike the phrase האיש הַהוּא, where the pronoun fills the same slot as an adjective does, in these phrases the determiner precedes the noun and agrees with it in gender and number. It is usually followed by a definite noun, but can also be followed by an indefinite noun, to form a noun phrase.

אוֹתָן הנשים	אוֹתָם האנשים	אוֹתָהּ האישה	אוֹתוֹ האיש
אוֹתָן נשים	אוֹתָם אנשים	אוֹתָהּ אישה	אוֹתוֹ איש
those same	those same	that same	that same
women	men	woman	man

The use of such phrases always implies the presence and a prior use of the noun to which the modifier 'that same' refers to. The phrase can be a subject slot or function as part of an object in the sentence.

I met a charming man in the movies. Later I met <u>the same man</u> in the library.	בקולנוע פגשתי איש מקסים. מאוחר יותר, פגשתי (את*) <u>אוֹתוֹ האיש</u> בספריה.
<u>That same woman</u>, about whom I told you, is our librarian.	<u>אוֹתָהּ האישה</u> שעליה סיפרתי לך, היא הספרנית שלנו.

* In normative Hebrew, an את אותו sequence is not allowed, however in speech it is commonly used.

Other determiners that follow nouns are אֵיזֶה/אֵיזְשֶׁהוּ 'some kind of', כָּל 'any, every', כָּל מִינֵי 'all kinds of'.

	Some people	Some woman	Some man
Normative use	אֵילוּ אנשים/נשים	אֵיזוֹ אישה	אֵיזֶה איש
Common use	אֵיזֶה אנשים/נשים	אֵיזֶה אישה	אֵיזֶה איש
		אֵיזוֹשֶׁהִי אישה	אֵיזֶשֶׁהוּ איש

The bicycle was just left in <u>some place.</u>	סתם השאירו את האופניים ב<u>איזה מקום.</u>
The stories are supposed to reflect reality in <u>some kind of way</u>.	הסיפורים אמורים ב<u>איזשהו אופן</u> לשקף את המציאות.
One has to set <u>some kind of system</u> of rules.	מוכרחים לקבוע <u>איזושהי מערכת</u> כללים.

Note

The adverbials איזה, איזו have an additional function. They are used as interrogatives, meaning 'what (kind of)', or 'which one'?

<u>Which</u> book did you buy?	אֵיזֶה ספר קנית?
<u>To what</u> show are you going?	לְאֵיזוֹ הצגה אתם הולכים?

Phrases with adverbials -כָּל 'every/each' and (ל־א) אַף/שום 'none'

The adverb -כָּל followed by an indefinite singular noun has the function of a determiner, and means 'each/every'.

<u>Each student</u> has to turn in a paper at the end of the term.	<u>כל תלמיד</u> חייב להגיש את העבודה בסוף הסימסטר.
<u>Every woman athlete</u> trains here.	<u>כל ספורטאית</u> מתאמנת כאן.

Negation is stated by the determiners אַף/שום with the negative as part of the sentence.

<u>No students</u> turned in a paper on time.	<u>אף תלמיד לא</u> הגיש את העבודה בזמן.
There were <u>no incidents</u> of violence on campus.	<u>לא</u> היו <u>שום מקרים</u> של אלימות בקמפוס.

When the adverb -כָּל precedes a plural definite noun it also functions as a determiner or a quantifier.

<u>All the students</u> have to turn in a paper at the end of the term.	<u>כל התלמידים</u> חייבים להגיש את העבודה בסוף הסימסטר.
<u>All the athletes</u> were chosen by a committee.	<u>כל הספורטאים</u> נבחרו על ידי ועדה.

The combined expression כָּל מִינֵי means 'all kinds of', and it too precedes the noun and functions as a determiner.

I did not come because I had <u>all kinds of problems</u>.	לא באתי כי היו לי <u>כל מיני בעיות</u>.

11.10.2 Determiners that follow nouns

There is an additional set of determiners, which is expressed in English by כָּזֶה 'such a ...' These determiners combine two components: the adverb -כְּמוֹ/כ 'like' and the pronoun 'this/these', resulting in their conflation into one word כָּזֶה. The structure of the noun phrase in which such a determiner is used consists of a definite article followed by the particle -כ, conflated to -כָּ, where the *a* vowel is the result of a reduced

definite article כָּ < כְּ+הָ. These are inherently indefinite phrases, even
though the determiner includes the remnant of a definite article.

Like the demonstrative pronouns this determiner has three forms: two
singular and one plural, determined by the preceding noun.

	Noun phrase	Paraphrase
such a man	אִישׁ כָּזֶה	= כְּמוֹ הָאִישׁ הזה
such a woman	אישה כָּזֹאת	= כְּמוֹ הָאישה הזאת
such people	אנשים כָּאֵלֶה	= כְּמוֹ הָאנשים האלה
such women	נשים כָּאֵלֶה	= כְּמוֹ הנשים האלה

such a crisis	משבר <u>כמו המשבר הזה</u> מסוכן מאוד.	משבר כזה מסוכן מאוד.
such problems	צריך לטפל בבעיות <u>כמו הבעיות האלה.</u>	צריך לטפל בבעיות כאלה.
such a good worker	קל למצוא עובדות, אבל עובדת שהיא טובה <u>כמו העובדת הזאת</u> קשה למצוא.	עובדת טובה כזאת קשה למצוא.

Sometimes the determiner appears without the noun, but implies the
presence of either an impersonal noun or something that has already
been referred to earlier in the text.

| such ones | <u>כמו האנשים האלה</u> יש הרבה אנשים בכפר. | כאלה יש הרבה אצלנו בכפר. |

11.10.3 Noun + subordinate clause modifier

Instead of modifying the head noun with an adjective, a whole clause
may substitute for it, fulfilling more or less the same function. The
clause must, of course, contain a reference to the head, either manifest
or hidden:

The invitation that <u>you sent</u> arrived.	ההזמנה <u>ששלחתם</u> הגיעה.
The girl <u>I met last week</u> does not want to see me any more.	הבחורה <u>שפגשתי בשבוע שעבר</u> לא רוצה לראות אותי יותר.
The woman who <u>entered the store</u> did not recognize me.	האישה <u>שנכנסה לחנות</u> לא הכירה אותי.
The writer <u>we talked about</u> yesterday published a new book.	הסופר <u>שדיברנו עליו</u> אתמול הוציא ספר חדש.

11.11 Gerunds and infinitives in noun phrases

Since some verbal expressions – in particular, the gerund (שֵׁם הַפְּעוּלָה) and the infinitive (שֵׁם הַפֹּעַל) – can act as nouns, these also can form the nucleus of a noun phrase. And as verbal expressions are formed from verbs, they can also take direct objects and can be modified by adverbs. A gerund phrase or infinitive phrase, then, is a noun phrase consisting of a verbal noun, its modifiers (both adjectives and adverbs), and its objects:

Gerund phrase	Swimming in the sea is our main pastime.	שׂחִייה בַּים היא העיסוק העיקרי שלנו.
Gerund phrase	David plans to arrive on time for course registration.	דוד מתכונן להגיע בזמן להרשמה לקורס.
Infinitive phrase	To hike in the mountains is all he wants to do.	לטייל בהרים זה כל מה שהוא רוצה לעשות.
Infinitive phrase	The love of his life is to travel and to travel endlessly.	אהבת חייו זה לנסוע ולנסוע בלי סוף.

Chapter 12
Verb phrases

12.1 Introduction to verb phrases

A variety of verb phrases are discussed in this chapter. A verb phrase consists of a verb, which functions as the main component of a phrase, and some additional components. As the main component of a phrase, we refer to that verb as the *head* verb of the phrase. The other components added to it expand the meaning of the head noun or particularize it. The additional components can be noun phrases or prepositional phrases that function as objects, or they can be other verbs that modify the meaning of the *head* verb. The verb phrase functions as the predicate of a sentence.

It is possible to classify verb phrases according to the structural components. The primary distinction made below is between verbs with different complements, and compound verbs.

12.2 Verb phrases [verb + object]

The central component of the predicate is most often a verb. Adjuncts can be appended to add information either to the predicate or to the entire sentence:

The following are the main structures of such verb phrases:

Verb phrase: verb form

The birdwatcher <u>got up</u> at dawn.   הצפר קָם עם שחר.

Verb phrase: verb + noun phrase (object)

The birdwatcher <u>brought</u> <u>binoculars</u>.   הצפר הֵבִיא מִשְׁקֶפֶת.

Verb phrase: verb + obligatory prepositional phrase (indirect object)

The birdwatcher <u>joined</u> (attached   הצפר הִצְטָרֵף לקבוצת מטיילים.
himself <u>to</u>) <u>a group of hikers</u>.

12.2.1 Verbs + direct objects

The direct object follows a transitive verb with the particle את when the
object is definite:

An object is made definite by having or being one of the following:

<u>Definite article</u>	They have not yet met <u>the neighbors</u>.	הם עוד לא פגשו <u>את</u> <u>השכנים</u>.
<u>Proper name</u>	They met <u>Dina</u> in the store.	הם פגשו <u>את דינה</u> בחנות.
<u>Place name</u>	They saw <u>London</u>.	הם ראו <u>את לונדון</u>.
<u>With possessive</u> <u>suffix</u>	They met <u>our parents</u>.	הם פגשו <u>את הורינו</u>.
<u>Possessive phrase</u>	They met <u>Rina's daughter</u>.	הם פגשו את הבת של רינה.

The direct object links with the verb without any prepositions or particles
when it is indefinite:

<u>Indefinite object</u>	They met <u>friends</u> at the coffeehouse.	הם פגשו <u>חברים</u> בבית הקפה.

In all of the above the object is obligatory, since the verb is not complete
without it: הם פגשו ... 'they met ...' is not complete without an object.

Note

In Hebrew there is an additional expansion of the verb by the verbal
noun, which is sometimes referred to as מושא פנימי 'internal object': a
verbal noun, which comes in object position as part of the expanded verb
phrase, and is of the same root as the verb it modifies. In form, it is like
English *fight a fight*, but its meaning is different. For the most part it is a
stylistic device that is used for emphasis. In English this expanded phrase
is translated by a verb, or by an appropriate phrase, such as 'make a
decision', or 'make an investment'.

<u>Internal direct object</u>	
They <u>advanced</u> the program in a meaningful way.	הם <u>קידמו</u> את התוכנית <u>קידום</u> ניכר.
They <u>made</u> serious <u>investments</u> in this project.	הם <u>השקיעו השקעות</u> רציניות בפרוייקט.
You <u>made a</u> bold <u>decision</u>!	החלטתם החלטה נועזת!

12.2.2 Verbs + obligatory prepositional phrases (indirect objects)

There are a number of verbs that have an obligatory preposition. When the preposition is obligatory, it is followed by an object, a nominal entity, which is a noun, a noun phrase or a pronoun. The citation form of the verb includes that preposition as a related part of the verb (see additional discussion in Chapter 10).

In the examples below notice that where Hebrew requires an obligatory preposition to link a verb with an object, in English the verb often links to its object without any preposition.

Gloss	Verbs and prepositions	
Dan bumped into the stone and fell.	דן נתקל באבן ונפל.	נִתְקַל ב-
How can you betray all of your principles?	איך אתה יכול לבגוד בכל העקרונות שלך?	בָּגַד ב-
The host hurt the feelings of the guest.	המנחה פגע ברגשות של האורח.	פָּגַע ב-
When will you help us get ready for the party?	מתי תעזרו לנו להכין את המסיבה?	עָזַר ל-
Listen to what is being said to you.	הקשיבו למה שאומרים לכם.	הִקְשִׁיב ל-
Don't take away from the value of the things we agreed on.	אל תגרע מערך הדברים שהסכמנו עליהם.	גָּרַע מ-

Some verbs have two meanings: one without an obligatory preposition, and one with an obligatory preposition.

Non-Obligatory Complement

stand (on a chair)	(על הכיסא)	עָמַד

Obligatory preposition with object

insist on, stand by	דעתו	עָמַד עַל

The children <u>stood</u> <u>on</u> the stage.	הילדים <u>עמדו</u> <u>על</u> הבמה.
The parents <u>insisted</u> that he come home on time.	ההורים <u>עמדו</u> <u>על</u> כך שהוא יבוא הביתה בזמן.

A comparative note

Some English verbs have a similar requirement, but the preposition following an English verb is not necessarily identical to the Hebrew preposition following an equivalent verb.

Identical preposition	rely on	סָמַךְ עַל
	trust in	בָּטַח ב-
	believe in	הֶאֱמִין ב-
Different preposition	bump into	נִתְקַל ב-
	look at	הִסְתַּכֵּל עַל
No preposition	influence	הִשְׁפִּיעַ עַל
	cause	גָּרַם ל-

12.3 Compound verb phrases

Compound verb phrases are phrases of two (or at times more) verbs, which combine into single phrases with one verb finite, i.e., in tense, and the second a verb in the infinitive mood. However, when discussing these verb phrases, it is important to distinguish between two main groups. In the first one the two verbs constitute one unit, which functions as one predicate. The first verb is an auxiliary verb and the second one is the infinitive form of the main verb.

They <u>could not open</u> the door.   הם <u>לא יכלו לפתוח</u> את הדלת.

In the other category two verbs are joined in a similar manner: the first is a finite verb and the second is an infinitive. But unlike the expanded verb phrase, in this case each verb forms a separate predicate. Essentially, the two-verb combination is a 'shortcut' version of two separate statements. The verbs of this verb phrase can be discontinuous, i.e., some other item can come between the two:

They <u>convinced</u> us <u>to open</u> the door.   הם <u>שכנעו</u> אותנו <u>לפתוח</u> את הדלת.

We shall refer to the first category as 'expanded verbs' and to the second one as 'two-kernel verb phrases'. Thus, although externally, the two types of phrases look alike, since they have one finite verb and one infinitive verb, their underlying structure is different. Following is a discussion of these two classes of verb phrases.

12.3.1 Expanded verb phrases.

As described above, expanded verb phrases include two verbs: the first is a finite verb (verb in tense), while the second one is an infinitive. The first verb functions as an auxiliary to the second verb, and the combination of the two is considered one expanded verb. The second verb serves as the *head* of the verb phrase; the function of the first (auxiliary) verb is to indicate the tense, and in some way to modify the meaning of the head verb. The two verbs do not constitute separate

kernels of separate underlying predicates. These verbs can be divided
into categories by the type of function they perform.

Aspectual function: initiating, continuing and ending the process

The first of the two verbs in these types of verb phrases are, for the most
part, verbs of initiating, continuing and finishing a process. The second
verb is the main verb, while the first verb indicates the stage of the
process.

he spoke	הוא דיבר
he <u>started</u> <u>speaking</u>	הוא התחיל לדבר
he <u>continued</u> <u>speaking</u>	הוא המשיך לדבר
he <u>stopped</u> <u>speaking</u>	הוא הפסיק לדבר

The above phrases have words in sequence, that cannot be taken apart or
be discontinuous. They function as one unit.

Note

Most of these modifying verbs, which constitute the first verb of the
expanded verb phrase, can also function in other contexts as main verbs.

1. Main Verb: להפסיק את 'interrupt'

Don't <u>interrupt</u> <u>me</u> while I am speaking.   .אל <u>תפסיק אותי</u> כשאני מדברת

<u>Compare with use in expanded verb phrase:</u>
להפסיק + שם פועל   'stop/cease'
He <u>stopped</u> <u>talking</u> to me.   .הוא <u>הפסיק לדבר</u> איתי

2. Main Verb (Colloquial use): להתחיל עם 'start with/get involved with'

I did not <u>start</u> <u>with</u> <u>her</u> – she started   אני לא <u>התחלתי איתה</u>, היא התחילה
with me.   .איתי

<u>Compare with use in expanded verb phrase:</u>
להתחיל + שם פועל   'begin/start'
Dan <u>started</u> <u>studying</u> Hebrew when   דן <u>התחיל ללמוד</u> עברית כשהוא היה בן
he was five.   .חמש

3. Main verb: לגמור (את) 'finish/complete'

He <u>finished</u> all the food that was in   .הוא <u>גמר את</u> כל האוכל שהיה במקרר
the refrigerator.

Compare with use in expanded verb phrase:

לגמור + שם פועל 'complete/end'

He <u>finished</u> eating an hour ago.   .הוא <u>גמר לאכול</u> לפני שעה

Truncated predicates

These verbs can sometimes be used without the second verb, when it is not specifically mentioned in the immediate phrase but is alluded to somewhere else in the immediate or shared context. In this case it is considered a truncated phrase, as the main verb is only implied.

Context: conversation

| V1+V2 | When did he start working for you? | ?מתי הוא התחיל לעבוד אצלכם |
| Missing V2 | He started in September. | .הוא התחיל בספטמבר |

Context: a narrative passage

| Verb 'tell' missing in sentence 2 | He told us all about what happened to him. He went on and on, and did not stop till everyone fell asleep. | הוא סיפר לנו את כל מה שקרה לו. הוא המשיך והמשיך ולא הפסיק עד שכולם נרדמו. |

Verbs with quantifier adverbial notions

They often either quantify or qualify the action that the verb denotes:

he spoke	הוא דיבר
he spoke a lot	הוא הִרְבָּה לדבר
he spoke a little	הוא הִמְעִיט לדבר

Paraphrasing with adverbs:

הוא הרבה לדבר = הוא דיבר הַרְבֵּה

הוא מיעט/המעיט לדבר = הוא דיבר מְעַט

הוא הֵיטִיב לדבר = הוא דיבר יפה/טוב

Verbs with time adverbial notion

he came	הוא בא
he came early	הוא הִקְדִּים לבוא
he came late	הוא אֵחֵר לבוא

Paraphrasing with adverbs:

הוא הקדים לבוא = הוא בא מוקדָם

הוא אחר לבוא = הוא בא מְאוחָר

Verbs with manner adverbial notions

he came	הוא בא
he came fast	הוא מיהר לבוא
he hurried to finish	הוא הזדרז לסיים

Paraphrasing with adverbs:

הוא מיהר לבוא = הוא בא מהר

הוא הזדרז לסיים = הוא סיים מהר

12.3.2 Chain (catenative) verb phrases

Support role: verbs that combine with a following non-finite verb are often called catenative verbs (where the term 'catenative' means 'chaining'). This term includes verbs like להתחיל 'start', להמשיך 'keep/continue', לעזור 'help'. The catenative verb can support not only one infinitive, but also a chain of infinitives. This chain of verbs forms a sequence of infinitives.

Chain verb phrases:

He began to talk.	הוא התחיל לדבר.
He also began to laugh.	הוא התחיל גם לצחוק.
He started disrupting.	הוא התחיל להפריע.

Expanded verb phrases with a chain of non-finite verbs:

He began talking, laughing and disrupting.	הוא התחיל לדבר, לצחוק ולהפריע.
He kept talking, laughing and disrupting.	הוא המשיך לדבר, לצחוק ולהפריע.

Note that the catenation is not limited to a series of separate infinitives; it can also be hierarchical:

He started learning (lit. lo learn) to write at the age of six.	הוא התחיל ללמוד לכתוב בגיל שש.

'Learning to write' is one expanded verb, further expanded into 'beginning to learn to write'.

12.3.3 Verb phrase: finite verb + finite verb

A few expanded verb phrases consist of a combination of auxiliary verbs, such as המשיך 'continue/keep doing', שב/חזר 'did again', that serve as modifying verbs to a main verb, which unlike all previous ones is in finite (i.e., in tense) rather than in the infinitive form.

He <u>retold</u> the same story.   הוא <u>חזר וסיפר</u> את אותו הסיפור.

She kept disrupting.   היא המשיכה והפריעה .

These verb sequences can be paraphrased by adverbs of repetition and continuation:

He told the same story lots of   הוא חזר וסיפר = הוא סיפר את

times.   הסיפור הרבה פעמים.

She disrupted again and again.   היא המשיכה והפריעה = היא הפריעה

     שוב ושוב.

The two verbs that make up the expanded verb phrase of repetition and continuity share the same tense. The auxiliary verb refers to aspects of the process, its continuity or repetition, while the second verb is the main verb, the action itself.

<u>Verb 1</u>		<u>Verb 2</u>	<u>Verb 2</u>		<u>Verb 1</u>
repeated	and	told	סיפר	ו	חזר
continued	and	disrupted	הפריעה	ו	המשיכה

A comparative note

The translation of the auxiliary verb into English is often rendered by an adverb (e.g., *again and again*), or by a verb in tense followed by an infinitive or gerund, or by a prefix (e.g. *re-*), rather than by an auxiliary verb, as in the following sentence:

She <u>re-emphasizes</u> (<u>comes back</u>   היא <u>שבה ומדגישה</u> את החשיבות של

and <u>emphasizes</u>) the importance of   המשימה.

the task.

     <u>שבה ומדגישה</u> = מדגישה שוב ושוב

He will <u>rewrite</u> <u>again</u> <u>and</u> <u>again</u>   הוא <u>יחזור ויכתוב</u> עד שהוא יהיה

until he is satisfied with the results.   מרוצה מהתוצאות.

     <u>יחזור ויכתוב</u> = יכתוב עוד מספר פעמים

12.3.4 Two-kernel verb phrases

So far, we have dealt with compound verbs that constitute true fusion of an auxiliary verb and a main verb into one expanded verb. But as noted above, there are cases in which the two component verbs may be regarded as two separate predicates of more-or-less equal weight. It was suggested that the formal criterion by which one distinguishes between auxiliary verbs and modifying ones described here is whether the underlying structure can be restated as two separate sentences, or is one single structure, even in the underlying structure. Consider the following:

| Compound verb phrase: | Dan <u>decided</u> <u>to become</u> a professional tennis player. | דן <u>החליט</u> <u>להיות</u> שחקן טניס מקצועי. |

It is clear that the underlying structure has two component sentences:

| S1 | Dan decided [something]. | דן הֶחליט [משהו]. |
| S2 | Dan will be a professional player. | דן יהיה שחקן מקצועי. |

The sentence can also be paraphrased as a complex sentence with a main clause and a subordinate clause:

| Dan decided that he is going to be a professional player. | דן החליט ש + הוא יהיה שחקן מקצועי. |

The subjects of the two propositions do not need to be identical. When the object of the first verb is expressed and specified, it can function as the subject of the second verb. In such cases the verb phrase includes two verbs, which are not necessarily contiguous. Both the underlying base sentences and the paraphrase as a complex sentence suggest that each component verb can be viable on its own.

He <u>asked</u> his friends <u>to lock up</u> the office.	הוא <u>ביקש</u> מחבריו <u>לנעול</u> את המשרד.
S1	He asked [something] of his friends.	הוא ביקש [משהו] מחבריו.
S2	His friends will lock the office.	חבריו ינעלו את המשרד.

This sentence can also be paraphrase as a complex sentence with a main clause and a subordinate clause:

| He asked of his friends that + they will lock the office. | הוא ביקש מחבריו ש + הם יִנְעֲלו את המשרד. |

The same cannot be shown with the typical expanded verb we discussed earlier. Observe the following:

| Expanded Verb Phrase | The snow <u>started falling</u> early in the morning. | השלג <u>התחיל לרדת</u> לפנות בוקר. |

A sentence like this cannot be shown to have an underlying structure of two separate clauses, because doing do would not capture its meaning – it does not say that the snow started and the snow fell; rather, it speaks of the time of its initiation. Nor can it be paraphrased by a main and subordinate clause, since there is no way of subordinating either verb in an embedded clause. There is but one predicate and one *head* verb, the infinitive. The verb הִתְחִיל is just a modifier of the head verb and does not function here as a verb with an equal status.

12.4 Grouping verb phrases by semantic considerations

There are many groups of verbs that can be part of a compound verb phrase. Some form one predicate unit, while others consist of a combination of two separate predicates (as discussed above). Here are some of the many semantic categories that can be observed in compound verbs:

<u>Initiation, continuity and cessation</u>

She <u>started</u> crying.	היא <u>התחילה</u> לבכות.
He <u>continued</u> playing.	הוא <u>המשיך</u> לנגן.

<u>Modifying main verb – auxiliary verb has an adverbial function.</u>

They <u>hurried</u> to finish the task.	הם <u>מיהרו</u> לסיים את המשימה.
You came <u>early.</u>	<u>הקדמת</u> לבוא.

<u>Trial, success and failure</u>

He <u>tried</u> to move the piano.	הוא <u>ניסה</u> להזיז את הפסנתר.
He <u>succeeded/managed</u> to move the piano.	הוא <u>הצליח</u> להזיז את הפסנתר.

<u>Attitude</u>

He <u>hates </u>working here.	הוא <u>שונא</u> לעבוד כאן.
They <u>prefer</u> working here.	הן <u>מעדיפות</u> לעבוד כאן.

<u>Wish/desire</u>

We <u>don't want</u> to go home.	אנחנו <u>לא רוצים</u> ללכת הביתה.
Dana <u>aspires</u> to become president.	דנה <u>שואפת</u> להיות נשיאה.

<u>Promise/enabling</u>

They <u>promised</u> to help us.	הם <u>הבטיחו</u> לעזור לנו.
They <u>made it possible</u> for us to move the furniture.	הם <u>אפשרו</u> לנו להזיז את הרהיטים.

<u>Planning/consideration</u>

We <u>are considering</u> skipping class.	אנחנו <u>חושבים</u> לא לבוא לשיעור.
The city <u>is getting ready</u> to remove the snow.	העיר <u>נערכת</u> לנקות את השלג.

<u>Skill/capability</u>

He does not <u>know how</u> to drive.	הוא לא <u>יודע</u> לנהוג.

12.5 Modal verbs

Modal verbs modify main verbs by expressing such modalities as necessity, possibility, expectation, wish, desire and the like, reflecting the attitudes and beliefs of the speaker. Many modal verbs function as auxiliary verbs and combine with main verbs to form verb phrases. Like the initial verbs in phrases described above, the modal verbs are finite, while the main verbs are in the infinitive mood.

You <u>should</u> be helping us.	אתם <u>צריכים</u> לעזור לנו.
He <u>is supposed</u> to come today.	הוא <u>אמור</u> לבוא היום.
He <u>cannot</u> get here on time.	הוא <u>לא יכול</u> להגיע בזמן.
He <u>is likely</u> to stay here a couple more days.	הוא <u>עשוי</u> להישאר כאן עוד יומיים.
He <u>might</u> invite too many guests.	הוא <u>עלול</u> להזמין יותר מדי אורחים.

For a discussion of modal verbs and their function, see Chapter 13.

12.6 Habitual aspect phrases

The habitual aspect expresses the occurrence of an event or state as characteristic of a period of time. While in English it is conveyed by the auxiliary verb *used to*, in Hebrew it is expressed by the use of the past tense of היה, followed by the present tense form of the main verb.

The boy <u>used to play</u> the piano every afternoon.	הילד <u>היה מנגן</u> בפסנתר כל יום אחר הצוהריים.

The verb *to be* is conjugated in all the forms of the past tense, and the main verb has the four forms of the present tense. The participle form reflects agreement in form with the subject of the verb phrase:

<u>Gloss</u>	<u>Feminine Singular</u>	<u>Masculine Singular</u>
I used to play	הייתי מְנַגֶּנֶת	הייתי מְנַגֵּן
you used to play	הָיִית מְנַגֶּנֶת	הָיִיתָ מְנַגֵּן
he/she used to play	היא הייתה מְנַגֶּנֶת	הוא היה מְנַגֵּן

<u>Gloss</u>	<u>Feminine Plural</u>	<u>Masculine Plural</u>
we used to play	היינו מְנַגְּנוֹת	היינו מְנַגְּנִים
you used to play	הייתן מְנַגְּנוֹת	הייתם מְנַגְּנִים
they used to play	הן היו מְנַגְּנוֹת	הם היו מְנַגְּנִים

12.7 Subjunctive: would have/could have

In Hebrew, the subjunctive mood typically signals that the proposition with which it is associated is non-actual and nonfactual. The meanings that are associated with this mood in Hebrew are wish or desire and possibility. The structure is identical to that described in the phrases of habitual action: the verb היה (conjugated in the appropriate person) with the present tense form of the main verb.

Subjunctive: wish and desire   היה + רוצה

The boy <u>would have liked</u> to play the piano.	הילד <u>היה רוצֶה</u> לנגן בפסנתר.
I <u>would have loved</u> to play.	<u>הייתי רוצֶה</u> לנגן.
You <u>would have loved</u> to sing.	<u>היית רוצֶה</u> לשיר.
She <u>would have loved</u> to dance.	היא <u>הייתה רוצֶה</u> לרקוד.

Subjunctive: possibility   היה + יכול

I <u>could have</u> danced all night.	<u>הייתי יכולה</u> לרקוד כל הלילה.
My brother <u>could have</u> played.	אחי <u>היה יכול</u> לנגן.
You <u>could have</u> sung.	<u>הייתן יכולות</u> לשיר.
They <u>could have</u> danced.	הם <u>היו יכולים</u> לרקוד.

For more discussion, see p. 311, and see similar structures in hypothetical conditions, pp. 360-362.

Chapter 13
Modal verbs and expressions

13.1 Introduction to modality

The expression of modality discloses the speaker's attitudes towards a variety of events and characters transmitted through an assortment of propositions. It involves the modification of propositions by the introduction of such notions as possibility, impossibility, expectation, permission, request, necessity, contingency, intention, willingness, wish, and desire.

An example of a proposition:

Every day David <u>returns</u> home at seven.	דוד <u>חוזר</u> הביתה כל יום בשבע.

This statement can be modified in the following ways with modal expressions:

David <u>can return</u> home at seven.	דוד <u>יכול לחזור</u> הביתה בשבע.
David <u>cannot return</u> home at seven.	דוד <u>לא יכול לחזור</u> הביתה בשבע.
David <u>has to return</u> home at seven.	דוד <u>צריך לחזור</u> הביתה בשבע.
David <u>is supposed to return</u> home at seven.	דוד <u>אמור לחזור</u> הביתה בשבע.

13.1.1 Types of modality

There are two types of modals in Hebrew:

1. Modal verbs, which are 'auxiliary' verbs, and are used in conjunction with main verbs to modify their meaning. They combine in their finite form with the infinitive form of main verbs:

David <u>has to</u> return home at seven.	דוד <u>צריך</u> לחזור הביתה בשבע.

2. Modal impersonal expressions are used to modify the meaning of the main proposition by adverbial expressions that initiate the entire proposition. The modal expressions are followed with main verbs in the infinitive.

It is <u>necessary</u> to return home on time.   .צָרִיךְ לחזור הביתה בזמן

13.2 Modal verb phrases

Modal verbs are conjugated in the present tense, and as such have four participial forms grouped by gender and number. Some modal verbs have more than one meaning and function in a number of situations. The modal verbs can be classified according to the meanings they convey and the functions they perform:

13.2.1 Obligation

The modal verbs צריך, מוכרח, חייב are used to express obligation. The choice of one of the modals over another is a matter of degree: the general expression of obligation is the modal verb צריך 'has to', a stronger meaning of 'must' is carried by מוכרח, and חייב is the strongest expressions, literally meaning 'obliged'.

	<u>רבות</u>	<u>רבים</u>	<u>יחידה</u>	<u>יחיד</u>
have (to), ought	צְרִיכוֹת	צְרִיכִים	צְרִיכָה	צָרִיךְ
have to, should	מֻכְרָחוֹת	מֻכְרָחִים	מֻכְרָחָה	מֻכְרָח
be required/obliged (to)	חַיָּבוֹת	חַיָּבִים	חַיֶּבֶת	חַיָּב

Everyone <u>has to</u> come on time.   .כולם צְרִיכִים לבוא בזמן
We <u>must</u> go to the library.   .אנחנו מוכרחים ללכת לספריה
Everybody <u>is required</u> to hand in his   כולם חייבים להגיש את העבודה
or her work in a week.   .בעוד שבוע

13.2.2 Possibility   יכול/עשוי/עלול

The notion of the possibility of things happening is conveyed by these three verbs: יכול, עשוי, עלול. While יכול conveys possibility, עשוי brings in the notion of likelihood, a positive assessment of possibility, while עלול has a negative nuance, meaning that this is a possibility the speaker hopes does not come true. עלול is therefore used almost exclusively with verbs which have negative connotations, or with negative statements.

	רבות	רבים	יחידה	יחיד
may be able to	יְכוֹלוֹת	יְכוֹלִים	יְכוֹלָה	יָכוֹל
may, could	עֲשׂוּיוֹת	עֲשׂוּיִים	עֲשׂוּיָה	עָשׂוּי
might, liable to	עֲלוּלוֹת	עֲלוּלִים	עֲלוּלָה	עָלוּל

Dana <u>can</u> be hired here, if there will be a job.	דנה <u>יכולה</u> להתקבל לעבודה כאן, אם תהיה משרה פנויה.
Dana <u>may/is likely</u> to be hired here since she has suitable qualifications.	דנה <u>עשויה</u> להתקבל לעבודה כאן כי יש לה כישורים מתאימים.
Dana <u>might not</u> be hired here because she does not have enough experience.	דנה <u>עלולה לא</u> להתקבל לעבודה כאן, כי אין לה מספיק ניסיון.

13.2.3 Ability/capability   יכול/מסוגל

The modal verbs יכול and מסוגל are used to express ability (in the sense of being able to physically or mentally do something, or knowing how to do something), as distinguished from possibility.

	רבות	רבים	יחידה	יחיד
can; be capable of	יְכוֹלוֹת	יְכוֹלִים	יְכוֹלָה	יָכוֹל
be able to	מְסֻגָּלוֹת	מְסֻגָּלִים	מְסֻגֶּלֶת	מְסֻגָּל

Dan is <u>capable of</u> driving, but he does not have a driver's license.	דן <u>יכול</u> לנהוג אבל אין לו רשיון נהיגה.
You are very tired; are you sure that you <u>are able to/can</u> drive?	אתה מאוד עייף, אתה בטוח שאתה <u>מסוגל</u> לנהוג?/שאתה <u>יכול</u> לנהוג?

13.2.4 Permission/request   יכול

The modal verb יכול is used to express a request or asking for permission, as well as possibility and capability.

Request

Can I ride with you?	אני <u>יכול</u> לבוא אתכם?
May we ride with you? Do you have space?	אנחנו <u>יכולים</u> לנסוע אתכם? יש לכם מקום?

Permission

Of course you can come with us.	כמובן שאתם <u>יכולים</u> לבוא איתנו.
<u>May</u> I go?	אני <u>יכול</u> ללכת?
You <u>may</u> go. It is already after eight.	אתה <u>יכול</u> ללכת. כבר אחרי שמונה.

13.2.5 Expectation/probability   אמור/צריך/צפוי

The modal verbs אמור, צריך are used to express expectation.   The
primary meaning of the modal verb צריך is that of obligation, but it can
be used to express expectation.   The modal verb צפוי, which also means
'expected to', is used less often.

	רבות	רבים	יחידה	יחיד
supposed to	אֲמוּרוֹת	אֲמוּרִים	אֲמוּרָה	אָמוּר
expected to	צְפוּיוֹת	צְפוּיִים	צְפוּיָה	צָפוּי
is about	עֲתִידוֹת	עֲתִידִים	עֲתִידָה	עָתִיד
is about to	עוֹמְדוֹת	עוֹמְדִים	עוֹמֶדֶת	עוֹמֵד

They <u>are expected</u> to get here in ten minutes.	הם <u>אמורים</u> להגיע עוד עשר דקות.
The bus <u>should/is expected</u> to get here exactly at eight.	האוטובוס <u>צריך</u> להגיע לכאן בדיוק בשמונה.
The bus <u>is about</u> to arrive any moment.	האוטובוס <u>עומד</u> להגיע כל רגע.
A big surprise <u>is expected</u> for everyone: the bus will arrive on time.	<u>צפויה</u> לכולם הפתעה גדולה: האוטובוס יגיע בזמן.

Expectations

Our parents <u>should</u> come on time.	ההורים <u>צריכים</u> להגיע בזמן.
Our parents <u>are expected</u> to come on time.	ההורים <u>אמורים</u> להגיע בזמן.
Our parents <u>are supposed</u> to come on time.	ההורים <u>צריכים/אמורים</u> להגיע בזמן.

13.2.6 Action about to take place (עתיד, עומד, צפוי)

We <u>are about</u> to offer him to become a partner in the business.	אנחנו <u>עומדים</u> להציע לו להיות שותף בעסק.
The plant <u>is about/expected</u> to bring large profits.	המפעל <u>עתיד</u> להביא רווחים רבים.

Anticipated action

About 100 guests are <u>likely/anticipated</u> to come.	כ-100 אורחים <u>צפויים</u> להגיע.

Note

The *pa'ul* verb form צָפוּי 'expected/predictable' can also be used as a predicative adjective.

This was <u>expected/predictable</u>.   .זה היה <u>צפוי</u> מראש

13.2.7 Readiness and willingness

The four present tense forms of the verb מוכן 'be ready' can be used as modal verbs. They combine the meaning of 'ready' and 'willing'.

The verb עָרוּךְ can also be used as a modal verb, meaning 'ready' or 'set up for'.

	רבות	רבים	יחידה	יחיד
be ready/willing	מוּכָנוֹת	מוּכָנִים	מוּכָנָה	מוּכָן
be set/ready	עֲרוּכוֹת	עֲרוּכִים	עֲרוּכָה	עָרוּךְ

The company <u>is ready</u> to return the money to you.   .החברה <u>מוכנה</u> להחזיר לך את הכסף

The school <u>is all set</u> to receive all of the new pupils.   בית הספר <u>ערוך</u> לקבל את כל התלמידים החדשים.

Note

The *pa'ul* verb form עָרוּךְ 'set' and the *huf'al* present tense form מוכן have additional meanings. As main verbs they can be used as predicative adjectives:

The table is <u>set</u> for the holiday meal.   .השולחן <u>ערוך</u> לארוחת החג

The meal is <u>ready</u>.   .הארוחה <u>מוכנה</u>

13.2.8 Planning and intentions

Verbs of planning can be fully conjugated in all tenses. With the exception of להתכונן 'get ready', which is truly a modal verb, the others can serve as main verbs, as well as express modality when they are combined with an infinitive verb.

	רבות	רבים	יחידה	יחיד
plan, get ready	מִתְכּוֹנְנוֹת	מִתְכּוֹנְנִים	מִתְכּוֹנֶנֶת	מִתְכּוֹנֵן
intend	מִתְכַּוְּנוֹת	מִתְכַּוְּנִים	מִתְכַּוֶּנֶת	מִתְכַּוֵּן
make plans/plan	מְתַכְנְנוֹת	מְתַכְנְנִים	מְתַכְנֶנֶת	מְתַכְנֵן

Dan <u>is getting ready</u> to move.	דן <u>מתכונן</u> לעבור דירה.
He <u>does not intend</u> to cause damage.	הוא <u>לא מתכוון</u> לגרום נזק.
Dan <u>is planning</u> to finish his dissertation in June.	דן <u>מתכנן</u> לסיים את הדיסרטציה שלו ביוני.

Note

All three above-mentioned verbs can also function as main verbs:

Dan <u>is preparing</u> for the test.	דן <u>מתכונן</u> למבחן.
He <u>did not mean</u> it.	הוא <u>לא התכוון</u> לזה.
Dan <u>is planning</u> the graduation party.	דן <u>מתכנן</u> את מסיבת הגמר.

13.2.9 Expressing wish or desire

To express wish or desire, the verb היה 'to be' in its past tense conjugations combines in a subjunctive-like way with verbs of wish or desire to indicate such meanings.

Verb of wish/desire	I <u>want</u> to come tonight.	אני <u>רוצה</u> לבוא הערב.
Subjunctive use	I <u>would love</u> to come tonight.	<u>הייתי רוצה</u> מאוד לבוא הערב.
Impossible wish	We <u>would have liked</u> to come tonight, but we cannot.	<u>היינו רוצים</u> לבוא הערב, אבל אנחנו לא יכולים.

For more on the subjunctive see page 299.

13.3 Impersonal modal expressions

There are modal impersonal expressions, which also combine with the main verb in the infinitive to express modality:

13.3.1 Modal expression + infinitive

1. <u>Obligation/necessity</u>

| It is necessary to reach the beach by car. | <u>צריך</u> להגיע לחוף במכונית. | צָרִיךְ |
| It is not necessary to walk (there). | <u>לא צריך</u> ללכת ברגל. | לא צָרִיךְ |

2. <u>Possibility</u>

| It is possible to reach the beach by bus. | <u>אפשר</u> להגיע לחוף באוטובוס. | אֶפְשָׁר |
| It is impossible to reach it by car. | <u>אי אפשר</u> להגיע לשם ברכב. | אִי אֶפְשָׁר |

3. Permission

It is alright to stay here till midnight.	מוּתָּר להישאר כאן עד חצות.	מֻתָּר
It is forbidden/not allowed to leave the computers on.	אסור לעזוב את המחשבים דלוקים.	אָסוּר

13.3.2 Modal expression + subordinate clause

Some of these expressions are combined with the linking particle -שֶׁ to introduce the main clause:

4. Possibility

It could be that we'll make it on time.	יכול להיות שנגיע בזמן.	יָכוֹל להיות ש-
It might be that we won't make it on time.	ייתכן שלא נוכל להגיע בזמן.	יִתָּכֵן ש-

5. Plausibility

It is plausible that we'll have enough time.	סביר שיהיה לנו מספיק זמן.	סָבִיר ש-
It stands to reason that we'll have enough time to do everything.	מתקבל על הדעת שיהיה לנו מספיק זמן לעשות הכל.	מִתְקַבֵּל על הַדַעַת ש-

6. Desirability

It is recommended/a good idea that everyone be present.	רצוי שכולם יהיו נוכחים.	רָצוּי ש-
It is important that everyone be present.	חשוב שכולם יהיו מוכנים.	חָשׁוּב ש-

13.4 Temporal aspects in modality

Most modal expressions are in the present tense, however there are contexts where past and future are also used.

13.4.1 Modal verbs: past and future

Some of the modal verbs exist as participles only, while others can be fully conjugated. In order to express the past and the future tenses in verbs that only have participial forms, the verb היה 'to be' in its appropriate tense, gender, number and person features combines with these modal verbs to indicate the temporal aspect.

They <u>are obliged</u> to pack.	הם <u>חייבים</u> לארוז.	בינוני
They <u>were obliged</u> to pack.	הם <u>היו חייבים</u> לארוז.	עבר
They <u>will be obliged </u>to pack.	הם <u>יהיו חייבים</u> לארוז.	עתיד

Other verbs have a full conjugation and the finite form of the modal verb is conjugated in the appropriate tense.

I <u>am planning</u> to host them.	אני <u>מתכונן</u> לארח אותם.	בינוני
I <u>planned</u> to host them.	<u>התכוננתי</u> לארח אותם.	עבר
<u>We'll plan</u> to host them.	<u>נתכונן</u> לארח אותם.	עתיד

Other verbs can have either structure:

I <u>need/have</u> to host them.	אני <u>צריך</u> לארח אותם.	בינוני
I <u>needed/had</u> <u>הייתי צריך</u> לארח אותם.	<u>הצטרכתי</u> לארח	עבר
to host them.	אותם.	

No combination with היה in the future:

I'll <u>have to</u> host them.	<u>אצטרך</u> לארח אותם.	עתיד

13.4.2 Verb or participle?
1. Modal verbs have the forms of present participles:

אמור, עשוי, עלול, צפוי, חייב, מוכן, ערוך

Past and future are indicated by the auxiliary verb היה, which is part of the modal phrase and indicates the temporal aspect.

2. A few modal verbs are conjugated in all tenses:

צריך, יכול, מתכונן

The temporal aspect of the modal phrase is indicated by the modal verb.

3. There are modal verbs that can appear either in a participle form with the verb היה 'to be' as tense indicator, or in their full conjugation in the appropriate tenses, in addition to the present participles. The two main verbs are צריך and יכול.

The present tense of צריך and יכול is irregular, and has parallels in adjectival patterns.

בינוני:	בינוני:
יָכוֹל, יְכוֹלָה, יְכוֹלִים, יְכוֹלוֹת	צָרִיךְ, צְרִיכָה, צְרִיכִים, צְרִיכוֹת

The verb לְהִצְטָרֵךְ is conjugated in its past and future tenses in the *hitpa`el* conjugation. יכול is in *pa`al*, but note that its future forms follow the *hif`il* conjugation for roots with initial י (or medial ו/י).

עבר: יכל			עבר: הצטרך	
רבים	**יחיד**		**רבים**	**יחיד**
יָכֹלְנוּ	יָכֹלְתִּי		הִצְטָרַכְנוּ	הִצְטָרַכְתִּי
יְכָלְתֶּם	יָכֹלְתָּ		הִצְטָרַכְתֶּם	הִצְטָרַכְתָּ
יְכָלְתֶּן	יָכֹלְתְּ		הִצְטָרַכְתֶּן	הִצְטָרַכְתְּ
הם יָכְלוּ	הוּא יָכֹל		הם הִצְטָרְכוּ	הוּא הִצְטָרֵךְ
הן יָכְלוּ	הִיא יָכְלָה		הן הִצְטָרְכוּ	הִיא הִצְטָרְכָה

עתיד: יוכל			עתיד: יצטרך	
רבים	**יחיד**		**רבים**	**יחיד**
נוּכַל	אוּכַל		נִצְטָרֵךְ	אֶצְטָרֵךְ
תּוּכְלוּ	תּוּכַל		תִּצְטָרְכוּ	תִּצְטָרֵךְ
תּוּכְלוּ	תּוּכְלִי		תִּצְטָרְכוּ	תִּצְטָרְכִי
הם יוּכְלוּ	הוּא יוּכַל		הם יִצְטָרְכוּ	הוּא יִצְטָרֵךְ
הן יוּכְלוּ	הִיא תּוּכַל		הן יִצְטָרְכוּ	הִיא תִּצְטָרֵךְ

13.4.3 Are הצטרך and היה צריך identical in meaning?

In the past tense, in everyday speech speakers use the phrase that combines היה and צריך much more often than they use the conjugated form of להצטרך, which is often reserved for more formal speech. They mean the same and are a matter of style, left to the speaker's choice.

We <u>had to</u> finish the project.	<u>היינו צריכים</u> לסיים את הפרוייקט.
We <u>needed/had</u> to stay in the library till ten.	<u>הצטרכנו</u> להישאר בספריה עד עשר.

In the future tense, the conjugated verb is used most often, especially when followed by an infinitive.

We <u>will have to</u> pack this evening, because we are leaving early in the morning.	<u>נצטרך</u> לארוז עוד הערב, כי אנחנו יוצאים מוקדם בבוקר.

The verb להצטרך has an infinitive form and an imperative form, but the imperative is not used, since it has no practical application.

Note

The verb צריך is also a transitive main verb, and as such it means 'need', and is not a modal verb. It is followed by a direct object.

The children need help.	הילדים צריכים עזרה.
The children needed help.	הילדים היו צריכים עזרה.
The children will need help.	הילדים יהיו צריכים עזרה.

13.4.4 Are יכולתי and הייתי יכול identical in meaning?

In the past tense the verb יכול means 'could/was able to'.

I could have eaten in the cafeteria, but I did not feel like it. יכולתי לאכול בקפטריה, אבל לא היה לי חשק.

Do you think that he can come on time? אתה חושב שהוא יכול להגיע בזמן?

I think that he is able to, but he does not want to. אני חושב שהוא יכול, אבל הוא לא רוצה.

When יכול is combined with the verb היה it usually conveys the meaning of an unrealizable act, 'could have done something' (but this is no longer a possibility).

We could have come, if we had not been so busy. היינו יכולים לבוא, לולא היינו כל כך עסוקים.

In the future tense, the conjugated verb is used most often:

We will not be able to come, since we have other plans. לא נוכל לבוא, כי יש לנו תוכניות אחרות.

Comparative notes

The verb יכל has no imperative or infinitive forms. There is no direct way to express 'to be able to'. It has to be expressed indirectly:

1.After an expression of wish for the future, 'to be able to' is translated as 'to have an opportunity to':

You want to be able to do everything: ride a bike, swim, and sail.

*You want that you'll have an opportunity to do everything: ride a bike, swim, and sail. אתם רוצים שתהיה לכם אפשרות לעשות הכל: לרכב על אופניים, לשחות ולשוט במפרשית.

2. If 'to be able to' is in a past tense context, it is translated by a hypothetical conditional, with the expression 'have an opportunity to':

It would have been nice <u>to be able</u> to be there together.

It would have been nice <u>if it had</u>   היה נחמד <u>לו הייתה אפשרות</u> להיות
<u>been possible</u> to be there together.   שם ביחד.

3. If 'to be able to' is part of a future projection, it is translated by a future conditional, with the expression 'have an opportunity to':

It would be so great <u>to be able to go</u> on a trip to Australia.
'to be able to' is translated by a future conditional.

It would be so great <u>if we</u> can go   זה יהיה ממש כיף <u>אם נוכל</u> לנסוע
on a trip to Australia.   לטייל באוסטרליה.

4. There are times where 'to be able to' is omitted altogether:

I'd like <u>to be able</u> to come – but I am not sure that I'll be free.

<u>I'd like to come</u> – but I am not   <u>הייתי רוצה לבוא</u>, אבל אני לא בטוחה
sure that I'll be free.   שיהיה לי זמן.

13.4.5 Tense indication in modal expressions

Modal expressions always require the verb היה for past and future tense markings.

Impersonal modal expressions can also be transformed to past and future tenses:

It is forbidden to sit here.	אסור לשבת כאן.	בינוני
It was forbidden to sit there.	היה אסור לשבת שם.	עבר
It will be forbidden to sit there.	יהיה אסור לשבת שם.	עתיד

These expressions can be stated in the positive or negative in the past and in the future tenses:

positive	<u>It was possible</u> to get there by bus.	<u>אפשר היה</u> להגיע לשם באוטובוס.
negative	<u>It was impossible</u> to get there by bus.	<u>אי אפשר היה</u> להגיע לשם באוטובוס.

13.5 Modality expressed by phrases with היה
13.5.1 The subjunctive use with 'wish' and 'desire'

To express wish or desire, verbs with that lexical meaning (want, wish, desire, hope) can be used with a finite verb in a verb phrase. Another possibility is the use of a combination with 'to be' in the past tense in its entire conjugation.

Verbs of wish/desire

Verb of wish/desire	I <u>want</u> to come tonight.	אני <u>רוצה</u> לבוא הערב.
Verb of hope	I <u>hope</u> to come tonight.	אני <u>מקווה</u> לבוא הערב.

Combination of היה + רוצה

Subjunctive use	I <u>would love</u> to come tonight.	<u>הייתי רוצה</u> מאוד לבוא הערב.
Impossible wish	<u>We would have liked</u> to come tonight, but we cannot.	<u>היינו רוצים</u> לבוא הערב, אבל אנחנו לא יכולים.

13.5.2 The modal phrase היה + יכול

The addition of the verb היה in the past tense to the modal verb יכול creates a number of additional nuances of meaning. The following sentences will consider the modal verb יכול as used with an infinitive in an assertion, and the various nuances when combined with the past tense of היה יכול, from consideration of a real possibility to consideration of a possibility that is no longer valid.

Assertion

I <u>can</u> come to swim.	אני <u>יכול</u> לבוא לשחות.

Considering the possibility

I <u>could</u> come to swim.	<u>הייתי יכול</u> לבוא לשחות.

Any number of possibilities:

'I could have, but I did not' is expressed by this היה + יכול combination. The rest of the context of the situation is used to assign to this phrase its precise meaning, whether it should be read as an existing possibility, or whether it should be considered an unrealized one.

Considering alternatives

I <u>could</u> be swimming in the pool now, but instead I am stuck in the office.

<u>הייתי יכול</u> לשחות בבריכה, אבל במקום זה אני תקוע במשרד.

Possibility no longer valid

I <u>could have been swimming</u> at the pool instead of working in the office.
I <u>could have swum</u> at the pool but I did not have enough time.

<u>הייתי יכול/יכולתי לשחות</u> בבריכה במקום לעבוד במשרד.
<u>הייתי יכול לשחות</u> בבריכה, אבל לא היה לי מספיק זמן.

Comparative notes

1. In Hebrew the sentence הייתי יכול לשחות בבריכה can have two possible readings: (1) the first reading is that of an option that is available for the speaker: 'I could be swimming in the pool (if only I wanted to/took the time to do it)'. The speaker is contemplating that option. (2) The second possible context in which this utterance could be used is in a situation in which something could have been realized but was not. 'I could have been swimming in the pool (but I did not)'. The full context of the utterance provides the reading of that sentence.

In English this is made clear to the reader/listener since there are various choices for expressing the past subjunctive: 'I could be swimming', 'I could have swum', 'I could have been swimming'; in Hebrew, however, all of those are indicated by the one expression הייתי יכול לשחות.

2. Unlike English, Hebrew does not have passive modal sentences. What is expressed by passive verbs in English is expressed by the modal verbs followed by a transitive main verb in Hebrew.

Subjectless sentence: Expression of need

The room <u>should be</u> cleaned once a day. (Literally, 'it is necessary to clean the room once a day').

<u>צריך</u> לנקות את החדר פעם ביום.

Subjectless sentence: Instruction

The room <u>should be</u> cleaned now!

<u>צריך</u> לנקות את החדר עכשיו!

Subjectless sentences: invalid or unfulfilled condition

The room <u>should have been</u> fixed yesterday.	<u>היה צריך</u> לסדר את החדר כבר אתמול.
The room <u>should have been</u> fixed, but nobody was there to fix it.	<u>צריך היה</u> לסדר את החדר, אבל לא היה מי שיסדר אותו.

13.5.3 Unfulfilled expectations

They <u>should have</u> come two hours ago, but we have not heard from them yet.	הם <u>היו צריכים</u> להגיע לפני שעתיים, אבל עדיין לא שמענו מהם.
Our parents <u>were supposed/expected</u> to arrive at midnight, but they got here only at four in the morning.	ההורים <u>היו צריכים</u> להגיע בחצות, אבל הם הגיעו רק בארבע בבוקר.

Chapter 14
Clauses and sentences

14.1 Introduction

The sentence is the maximal unit of syntax, while the minimal units that compose it are individual words. The major constituents of sentences are the subject and predicate phrases that join to construct a sentence. These constituents combine not only in a linear order, but also in a hierarchical and layered manner.

a. A linear arrangement:

The parents registered their kids
for gym classes.

ההורים רשמו את הילדים לשיעורי
התעמלות.

b. A hierarchical, layered structure:

The sentence is represented here by a simplified graphic tree illustration, reflecting the division into the two main parts of the sentence:

ההורים רשמו את הילדים לשיעורי התעמלות

Predicate **Subject**

רשמו את הילדים לשיעורי התעמלות ההורים

רשמו   את הילדים   לשיעורי התעמלות

In addition, it is useful to have a description of the syntactic units that constitute the sentence not only in the traditional terms of subject and predicate, but also in terms of the composition of its constituents: a noun phrase and a verb phrase.

Each phrase has a head, also referred to as the nucleus that represents the entire phrase. It also can have dependent elements that provide additional information. Thus in the sentence above the core noun of the noun phrase ההורים 'the parents' constitutes the head, and the core verb of the verb phrase רשמו 'registered' constitutes the head. The 'dependent' components of the head noun are usually referred to as the attributes, while the 'dependent' components of the verb phrase that accompany the verb nucleus, are usually referred to as objects and adjuncts.

Types of phrases
The major (phrasal) sentence constituents:
Noun phrase (NP) צירוף שמני (צ״ש)
Verb phrase (VP) צירוף פועלי (צ״פ)
Adjective phrase, functioning as an attribute (AdjP) צירוף תואר (צ״ת)
Prepositional phrase, functioning as an adjunct (PP) צירוף יחס (צ״י)

The phrases can also be identified by their syntactic function:
Subject phrase צירוף נושאי
Predicate phrase צירוף נשואי

Types of sentences
There are two main categories of sentences identified by the content of their predicate:
Verbal sentences משפטים פועליים
Nominal sentences משפטים שמניים

14.2 Verbal sentences   משפטים פועליים

Verbal sentences are defined by their predicate. Those with a predicate that consists of a verb as its nucleus are considered verbal sentences. The main verb can be in tense, or part of a verb phrase where it appears in an infinitive form, or part of a verb phrase with a subject suffix or prefix, or without a subject.

David <u>works</u> at the electric company.	דוד <u>עובד</u> בחברת החשמל.
David can <u>work</u> for his father.	דוד יכול <u>לעבוד</u> אצל אבא שלו.
We <u>worked</u> for David's Dad.	<u>עבדנו</u> אצל אבא של דוד.
<u>Work</u> and don't waste time!	<u>עבדו</u> ואל תתבטלו!

14.2.1 Verbal sentences without subjects

There are two main types of verbal sentences without subjects:

1. Imperative sentences   משפטי ציווי

By the nature of their meaning, imperative sentences do not include subjects. They are used to give orders or directives to a second party, which is present. Their form, therefore, reflects the person being addressed.

David, go home!	דוד, לך הביתה!
Rina, get out of here!	רינה, צאי מכאן!
David and Rina, close the door!	דוד ורינה, סגרו את הדלת!

2. Impersonal sentences   משפטים סתמיים

There are sentences where the subject is not expressed overtly, but rather is implied. There are others where the subject is impersonal.

1. Verbs in sentences without a subject are always in the third person masculine plural, and can be in the present, past or future. In English such impersonal subjects are expressed by *they, one, you,* or by the verb being in the passive voice. A similar general impersonal subject is assumed and implied, though not expressed, in Hebrew.

(One) does not <u>talk</u> in the library.	בספריה לא <u>מדברים</u>.
The danger to the environment <u>was</u> not <u>known</u> then.	לא <u>ידעו</u> אז על הסכנה לסביבה.
If (you) <u>do</u> what (you) should, the situation will improve.	אם <u>יעשו</u> מה שצריך, המצב ישתפר.

b. Another way of expressing a sentence without an overt subject is to have a passive verb in the third person, masculine singular. In English this type of subject is usually expressed by the pronoun *it* (sometimes called 'a dummy *it*', since it does not refer to any particular object or event).

It was agreed on to fire the striking workers.	הוסכם על פיטור העובדים השובתים.
It was decided to hire new workers.	הוחלט לשכור עובדים חדשים.

c. There are sentences that consist of fixed expressions that lack a grammatical subject. They usually describe a state of being or an emotional state, such as 'It is hot' חם or 'It is sad' עצוב. In Hebrew these expressions usually consist of adjectives in the third person masculine. In English such sentences start with an impersonal subject *it*.

It is not easy to study Hebrew.	לא קל ללמוד עברית.
It is important to know what is new.	חשוב לדעת מה חדש.
It is cold outside.	קר בחוץ.

To include the logical subject in statements such as עצוב 'it is sad', or קר 'it is cold', and explain who is sad, or who is cold, these stative expressions are followed by a prepositional phrase with ל- 'to', to which a noun or a pronoun suffix are attached. That noun or pronoun suffix can be said to be the logical subject of the sentence, but not its grammatical subject.

is it hot to you? → Are you hot?	חם לכם?
it is sad for Ron → Ron is sad.	עצוב לרון.
it is known to me → I am aware.	ידוע לי.

A comparative note

As seen in the examples above, in English similar sentences are, for the most part, not thought of as impersonal sentences. However, there are sentences where the 'dummy' pronoun *it* supplies an impersonal subject, both the logical and grammatical.

It is difficult for us to remember everything.	קשה לנו לזכור את הכל.
It is important for everyone to come on time.	חשוב לכולם לבוא בזמן.

d. The subject in impersonal sentences can also be overtly expressed by an impersonal pronoun:

Somebody told me this story.   .מִישֶׁהוּ סיפר לי את הסיפור הזה

Anybody could have known this.   .כָּל אֶחָד היה יכול לדעת את זה

14.3 Nominal sentences   משפטים שמניים

Nominal sentences are sentences whose predicate does not have a verb. The predicate has as its nucleus a noun, an adjective, a prepositional phrase, or an adverbial expression. In the present tense there is no verb 'is' or 'are' and no tense indication. The future and past tenses are usually indicated by the verb היה 'be' in their appropriate conjugated form. At times the verb היה 'be' is also present in the moods. Other verbs of being or becoming, such as נהיה, נעשה or הפך ל , can be used as well.

The major types of nominal sentences are: equational sentences, existential sentences and sentences of possession.

14.4 Equational sentences   משפטי זיהוי

Equational sentences are defined by the composition of their predicate. The predicate consists of a noun phrase, an adjective, or a prepositional phrase, such as:

This movie is an animated film.   .הסרט הזה סרט מצוייר

The audience's response is not surprising.   .התגובה של הקהל לא מפתיעה

Women are from Venus and men are from Mars.   .נשים מנוגה וגברים ממאדים

14.4.1 The copula (link)   האוגד

Equational sentences separate the subject and predicate by means of a copula (אוֹגֵד), which is the link between the two items. In the present tense it consists of third person personal pronouns. The copula usually agrees in gender and number with the head noun of the subject phrase. It may be regarded as equivalent to the English copula verb 'to be' in the present tense.

The new movie is an animated film.   .הסרט החדש הוא סרט מצוייר

The audience's response is not at all encouraging.   התגובה של הקהל היא בכלל לא .מעודדת

Women <u>are</u> from Venus and men <u>are</u> from Mars. נשים <u>הן</u> מנוגה וגברים <u>הם</u> ממאדים.

The past and future אוגד is a finite verb form of 'to be' in the third person, and it usually agrees in gender and number with the subject of the sentence.

The old movie <u>was</u> a Western. הסרט הישן <u>היה</u> מערבון.

The audience's response <u>will be</u> very positive. התגובה של הקהל <u>תהיה</u> חיובית.

His family <u>was</u> very rich. המשפחה שלו <u>הייתה</u> עשירה מאוד.

In the first and second person of equational sentences there is no copula in the present tense.

3rd person   Avi Katz is a doctor. אבי כץ הוא רופא.

1st person   I am also a doctor. גם אני רופא.

However, when the predicate is definite, in everyday speech even first or second person can have a third person copula that separates between the subject and the predicate:

3rd person   Who is the doctor here? מי הוא הרופא כאן?

1st person   I am the doctor here. אני <u>הוא הרופא</u> כאן/אני הרופא כאן.

In sentences in the past and future tenses the verb 'be' serves all persons.

3rd person   Rina Bar was a party member. רינה בר הייתה חברה במפלגה.

2nd person   Were you also a party member? גם את היית חברה במפלגה?

The negation of a nominal sentence consists of the negative particle לא. In the present tense, the existential expression אֵין can be used with a personal pronoun suffix.

The house <u>is not</u> new. הבית <u>לא</u> חדש.

הבית <u>הוא לא</u> חדש.

הבית <u>אינו</u> חדש.

The house <u>was not</u> new. הבית <u>לא היה</u> חדש.

14.4.2 Predicate: prepositional phrase or adverbs

When the predicate of a nominal phrase is a prepositional phrase, the prepositional phrase has a fixed form and is not affected by any of the other constituents of the sentence.

Predicate: prepositional phrase

Haifa is in northern Israel.	בצפון ישראל.	היא	חיפה
The article was about the economic situation.	על המצב הכלכלי.	הייתה	הכתבה
The interview will be in your office.	במשרד שלך.	יהיה	הראיון

Predicate: adverb

The meeting is tomorrow.	מחר.	היא	הפגישה
The restaurant was there.	שם.	הייתה	המסעדה
The interview will be here.	כאן.	יהיה	הראיון

When the prepositional phrase or adverb marks location, the copula can be changed to the verb נמצא '(is/are) located'.

The café is on the beach.	על שפת הים.	נמצא	בית הקפה
The restaurant is downtown.	במרכז העיר.	נמצאת	המסעדה
The offices are located here.	כאן.	נמצאים	המשרדים

14.4.3 The demonstrative pronoun as copula

A clause that begins with an infinitive or a question word or with a subordinating particle can constitute the subject of a sentence. The copula in this configuration is usually the demonstrative pronoun and not the subject pronoun.

1. Head of sentence: infinitive phrase

In this type of sentence the infinitive phrase, functioning as a gerund, replaces the noun phrase:

<u>Climbing</u> (to climb) mountains <u>is</u> Dan's main hobby.	<u>לטפס</u> על הרים <u>זה</u> התחביב העיקרי של דן.
<u>Meeting</u> (to meet) local people <u>is</u> the purpose of the tourists.	<u>לפגוש</u> אנשים מקומיים <u>זאת</u> המטרה של התיירים.

2. Head of sentence: whatever/whoever מה ש/מי ש

This type of sentence is introduced by a question word followed by the
particle -ש, which introduces the opening clause.

<u>What</u> he told you <u>is</u> just not true.	<u>מַה</u> שהוא סיפר לכם <u>זֶה</u> פשוט לא נכון.
<u>Whoever</u> did not do his job, <u>were</u> not the people who work here, <u>it was</u> the director.	<u>מִי</u> שלא עשה את שלו <u>זֶה</u> לא <u>הָיוּ</u> האנשים שעובדים כאן, <u>זֶה הָיָה</u> המנהל.

3. Head of sentence: (the fact) that... ...ש (זה)

This type of sentence is introduced by the subordinating particle -ש
followed by an opening clause. This subordinating particle can be
preceded by זה, similar to the use of the phrase 'the fact (that)' in
English.

<u>That fact that</u> he has not been working for a year is a surprising thing.	<u>זֶה</u> שהוא לא עובד כבר שנה <u>זֶה</u> דבר מפתיע.
<u>That</u> he has not been working for a year is a fact.	<u>שֶ</u>הוא לא עובד כבר שנה <u>זֹאת</u> עובדה.

As the subject of such sentences is a clause and not a nominal entity, it
has no number or gender features. In such instances it is the predicate
of the sentence that determines the type of the אוגד, which does not
consist of an independent subject pronoun but of the masculine or
feminine form of the demonstrative pronoun. The past and future tenses
are handled by the verb 'to be' conjugated in the appropriate form that
agrees with the predicate.

14.4.4 Linking verbs
a. Verbs of becoming

In addition to copulas like the verb היה 'to be' and the pronouns
(personal and demonstrative) that may work as alternatives to it, there
exist copula-like auxiliary verbs whose main function is also to connect
between the subject and predicate, but which add some 'verb-like'
quality to the relationship between the two that goes beyond merely
stating identity or quality. The most common involve a change-of-state,
or 'becoming', as in the following:

The policeman Erez <u>became</u> a sergeant this week.	השוטר ארז <u>הפך</u> השבוע לַסָמָל.
Ephraim <u>has become</u> a good-looking boy.	אפריים גדל <u>ונהיה</u> בחור נאה.
With (the passing of) time, he <u>became</u> the Governor's right hand man.	עם הזמן הוא <u>נעשה (ל)</u>יד ימינו של המושל.

b. Verbs describing state and change of state

The linking verbs can describe various stages of being, becoming, and remaining:

They <u>were</u> our very good <u>friends</u>.	הם <u>היו החברים</u> הטובים שלנו.
They <u>became</u> our very good <u>friends</u>.	הם <u>נהיו החברים</u> הטובים שלנו.
They <u>remained</u> our very good <u>friends</u>.	הם <u>נשארו החברים</u> הטובים שלנו.

c. Verbs or perception

In addition to the verbs of 'becoming' or those describing a state, there are also verbs or perception that can be used to link a subject and its predicate. They have to be completed by adverbs, adjectives, or other nouns.

Predicate of Clause 2: adverb

The main verbs of perception are נראה 'seem' or נשמע 'sounds'.
They are often completed by the adverbs טוב 'good', or רע 'bad'. The adverb does not change its shape regardless of the gender or number of the subject.

Aliza doesn't look bad.	עליזה <u>נראית</u> לא רע.
It does not sound good.	זה לא <u>נשמע</u> טוב.

Predicate of Clause 2: adjective

It is possible to consider the verb and its complement as consisting of two separate propositions. In this case the adjective or noun following the verb of perception agrees with the subject in gender and number.

You seem -	אתם נראים -
You are sad.	אתם עצובים.

The two clauses are fused into one by omitting the subject of the second clause, which is redundant, and combining the two clauses.

<u>Combined into a sentence</u>

Why do you <u>seem</u> so <u>sad</u>?	למה אתם <u>נראים</u> כל כך <u>עצובים</u>?

This drama sounds -	- הדרמה הזאת נשמעת
This drama is very melodramatic.	הדרמה הזאת מלודרמטית מאוד.
<u>Combined into a sentence:</u>	
This drama <u>sounds</u> very melodramatic.	הדרמה הזאת <u>נשמעת מלודרמטית</u> מאוד.

There are other verbs of this type where the copulative element goes well beyond the mere subject-predicate relationship.

Dan is <u>considered/regarded</u> as an excellent interviewer.	דן <u>נחשב למראיין</u> מצוין.

14.5 Existential sentences משפטי קיום

The predicate of existential sentences is the existential expression יֵשׁ 'there is/are' or its negation אֵין 'there is/are not'. It points to the existence or the state of the subject.

<u>There is</u> a pool in the backyard.	<u>יש</u> בריכה בשכונה.
<u>There is no</u> big yard, but there is a nice garden.	<u>אין</u> חצר גדולה, אבל יש גינה נחמדה.

In the present tense, the existential expressions do not have number and gender features. They are used for all subjects, be they masculine or feminine, singular or plural:

There is an organized tour of the area.	יש טיול מאורגן בסביבה.
There is no matinee today.	אין הצגה יומית היום.
There are settlements in the south.	יש יישובים בדרום.
There is no news today.	אין חדשות היום.

Past and future: 'to be' + agreement features

When these sentences are in the past or future, the verb 'to be' is used in the third person. The verb forms in the past and future, unlike the existential expression, have features of gender and number. If the subject is masculine singular, the verb form is the third person singular היה, if the subject is feminine singular, the verb form is הייתה, and when the subject is plural, the verb form is היו.

<u>There is</u> a new nightclub in town.	<u>יש</u> מועדון לילה חדש בעיר.
<u>There were</u> rumors in the air.	<u>היו</u> שמועות באוויר.
<u>There won't be</u> another such chance.	<u>לא תהיה</u> עוד הזדמנות כזאת.

14.6 Sentences of possession   משפטי קניין

Sentences of possession describe the relationship between two objects. The function of the objects can be described as 'possessor' and 'possessed'. The relationship between these objects is not necessarily that of actual ownership; it can be one of having certain qualities or characteristics.

The actual process for creating sentences of possession can be described as the putting together of the following components:

1. Starting with an existential expression: 'there is/there are' יֵשׁ (or its negative)
2. Adding the subject of the existential expression, such as 'interesting books' ספרים מעניינים

We now have an existential sentence:
There are interesting books.   .יש ספרים מעניינים

3. What is needed is information about who has the interesting books. This information is added by means of a prepositional phrase, consisting of the preposition ל- and a noun/noun phrase or a pronoun suffix of the possessor.
4. We now have a sentence of possession:
<u>Dan</u> has interesting books.   .יש <u>לדן</u> ספרים מעניינים

We can identify the two main nominal entities as:
<u>Possessed item</u>: 'interesting books'   <u>Possessor</u>: 'Dan'

The 'possessed' item is the <u>grammatical subject</u> of the sentence, and the 'possessor' is part of the prepositional phrase. This is counter-intuitive for English speakers, since the possessor of the object is not in the subject position. In English, one simply follows the rules of other verbal sentences: 'Dan (subject) + has (verb) + a book (direct object)'. Dan is the possessor, and he constitutes the logical and grammatical subject of the sentence. In Hebrew there is no verb that expresses the notion of 'to have'. The statement of possession is therefore conveyed by other means, as seen above. 'Dan has a book' is literally expressed by a statement of this nature: *'There is to Dan a book',* or *'a book exists (belonging) to Dan'.*

A comparative note

In English many inanimate objects can be the subjects of sentences of possession, but their Hebrew counterparts are usually locative complements of existential expressions in existential sentences.

This house has a pool.	יש בבית הזה בריכה.
The town does not have many parks.	אין בעיר הרבה גנים.

14.6.1 Sentences of possession in present tense

The present tense of a sentence of possession is indicated by the predicate existential expressions יֵשׁ 'there is/there are' and its negative counterpart אֵין 'there isn't/there aren't'. These existential expressions do not have gender or number features. They are used whether the noun is masculine or feminine, singular or plural.

He has some friends in Tel Aviv.	יש לו חברים בתל-אביב.
This (f.) student has lots of work.	יש לסטודנטית הזאת הרבה עבודה.
Dan has no friends in Tel Aviv.	אין לדן חברים בתל-אביב.

14.6.2 Past and future: 'to be' + agreement features

When these sentences are in the past or future, the verb 'to be' is used in the third person. The agreement in number and gender is with the head noun of the subject (the 'possessed' noun).

<u>He had</u> some <u>friends</u> in Tel Aviv.	<u>היו לו חברים</u> בתל-אביב.
Dan <u>had</u> <u>no opportunity</u> to travel.	<u>לא הייתה</u> לדן <u>הזדמנות</u> לטייל.
<u>Will</u> you <u>have</u> <u>time</u> to come and help me?	<u>יהיה</u> לך <u>זמן</u> לבוא לעזור לי?
<u>I won't have</u> a <u>problem</u> helping you.	<u>לא תהיה</u> לי <u>בעיה</u> לעזור לך.

14.6.3 Possession is not necessarily ownership

To indicate true ownership, it is also possible to use the adjective שַׁיָּךְ and the preposition -ל. This phrase is equivalent to the English 'belongs to'.

This computer <u>belongs to</u> everyone – it is not just yours.	המחשב הזה <u>שייך לכולם</u> – הוא לא רק שלך.
This car does not <u>belong to me</u>.	המכונית הזאת לא <u>שייכת לי</u>.
These fields <u>belong to</u> the agricultural station.	השדות האלה <u>שייכים לחווה</u> החקלאית.
All the laboratories <u>belong to</u> the government.	כל המעבדות <u>שייכות לממשלה</u>.

The past and future of such sentences are indicated by adding the verb 'to be' in the appropriate tense.

The coat <u>used to belong</u> to my big brother.

המעיל <u>היה שייך</u> לאחי הגדול.

One day all of this <u>will belong</u> to you.

יום אחד הכל <u>יהיה שייך</u> לך.

There is a difference in meaning between יש לדן ספרים מעניינים 'Dan has interesting books', and הספרים האלה שייכים לדן 'These books belong to Dan'. While the first sentence indicates possession, it does not necessarily indicate ownership.

14.6.4 Word order

When the 'possessor' is a pronoun, the word order is fixed:

<u>He</u> has some friends in Tel Aviv.

יש <u>לו</u> חברים בתל-אביב.

When the 'possessor' is a full noun or a noun phrase, there are two possible orderings. The word order can also follow the one above, with the existential statement initiating the sentence:

<u>My family</u> has relatives in Haifa.

יש <u>למשפחה שלי</u> קרובים בחיפה.

The other option – when a full noun or a noun phrase is involved – is for the 'possessor' to initiate the same sentence as the topic, followed by the rest of the information in the sentence.

<u>My family</u> has relatives in Haifa.

<u>למשפחה שלי</u> יש קרובים בחיפה.

Less commonly, if one really wishes to focus attention on the possessor as the topic of the sentence, one can front it further: In the example below, the topic of the sentence is 'my family', and the comment about the family is that it has some relatives in Tel Aviv.

<u>My family</u>, <u>it</u> has relatives in Haifa.

<u>המשפחה שלי</u>, יש <u>לה</u> קרובים בחיפה.

14.6.5 Sentences of possession with indefinite subjects

Notice that all the examples and explanations above had indefinite subjects.

I have <u>a class</u> right now.

יש לי <u>שיעור</u> עכשיו.

Dan has <u>problems</u> at work.

לדן יש <u>בעיות</u> בעבודה.

Who does not have <u>problems</u> at work?

למי אין <u>בעיות</u> בעבודה?

The main point of a sentence with an indefinite subject is to transmit new information about the existence of a certain item and its relationship to its possessor.

14.6.6 Possessive sentences with definite subjects

The situation is more complex when the subject is definite. The normative rules governing sentences of possession with definite subjects are the same as the ones that govern sentences with indefinite subjects.

Expected normative use (rarely in practice):

<u>Indefinite Subject:</u>	I have new books.	.יש לי ספרים חדשים
<u>Definite Subject:</u>	I have <u>the</u> new <u>books</u>	יש לי <u>הספרים</u> החדשים
	that you gave me.	.שנתת לי

Common use

In common use speakers avoid using definite subjects in possessive sentences. They tend to endow the existential expression of possession יש ל- with a verbal quality. As such it assumes the status of a transitive verb. Thus 'the possessed' item takes on a new role of a direct object, as is indicated by the introduction of the definite accusative marker את, which only precedes a definite direct object.

I have <u>the book</u> that you gave me.	.יש לי <u>את הספר</u> שנתת לי
We don't have <u>the money</u> for the	אין לנו <u>את הכסף</u> בשביל
tickets.	.הכרטיסים

Another strategy to avoid using יש לי הספרים שנתת לי is to paraphrase the sentence הספרים שנתת לי הם אצלי 'the books that you gave me are at my place', i.e. 'I have them'.

Those who insist that the use of את is ungrammatical, still have to contend with the problem in such utterances as 'I have it', where a direct object pronoun takes the place of the subject noun. Such a sentence can be expressed **only** with the addition of the direct object marker את with the appropriate pronoun suffix: אותו/אותה/אותם/אותן

Do you have <u>the book</u> that I gave you?	?יש לך <u>את הספר</u> שנתתי לך
Sorry, but I don't have <u>it</u>.	.מצטער, אבל אין לי <u>אותו</u>

14.6.7 Sentences of possession in the past and future

In the past and future tenses, the verb להיות is inserted to indicate tense, but unlike the existential expressions יש/אין, the verb forms do include gender and number features that reflect the features of the grammatical subject, and thus are subject to agreement with it. The agreement is not that simple or obvious, as the subject that governs such rules **follows** the verbal expression. Note that all the verb forms are in the third person, regardless of who the 'possessor' is. Also, in the past and future tenses the negative particle לא is used for negation of the expressions of possession.

Past tense statements
Gender and Number of 'possessed' objects

Masc. Sing.	We had a <u>class</u> today.	היה לנו שיעור היום.
Fem. Sing.	He had no <u>plan</u> for this evening.	לא הייתה לו תוכנית לערב.
Plural	He had <u>many problems</u> at work.	היו לו בעיות בעבודה.

Future tense statements
Gender and Number of 'possessed' objects

Masc. Sing.	We won't have a <u>class</u> today.	לא יהיה לנו שיעור היום.
Fem. Sing.	He'll have a <u>plan</u> for this evening?	תהיה לו תוכנית לערב?
Plural	He won't have <u>any problems</u> at work.	לא יהיו לו בעיות בעבודה.

The possessed noun, which is the grammatical subject of the sentence, determines the gender and number features, and unlike English, the verb never reflects the person features of the possessor. This is a frequent source of errors for speakers of English, where the possessor is the grammatical as well as the logical subject of sentences of possession.

A fairly common mistake made by non-native speakers is to work in a 'translation mode' and start the sentence with the possessor as the subject:

Masculine, singular   I had a class today   <u>הייתי לי שיעור היום</u>.

The correct verbal form is determined by the noun 'class' and not by a subject pronoun, such as 'I'.

Masculine, singular   I had a <u>class</u> today   <u>היה לי</u> שיעור היום.

The position of adverbs and subordinate clauses

Adverbs or subordinate clauses (such as time clauses) in sentences of possession can initiate a sentence of possession or come at the end of the sentence.

<u>When we studied</u> we had many friends.   <u>כשלמדנו</u> היו לנו הרבה חברים.

We had many friends <u>when we studied</u>.   היו לנו הרבה חברים <u>כשלמדנו</u>.

Cancellation of gender and number features in colloquial speech

Agreement features of gender and number are sometimes cancelled in colloquial spoken Hebrew. Sentences of possession include the verb היה/יהיה with no gender or number features, even when the subject is feminine or plural. This variant is particularly common in casual or rapid speech, and only when the verb comes before the subject. It is important to emphasize that this is not an option in written Hebrew, nor in standard or more formal speech.

<u>Normative</u>

I once <u>had</u> such a car.   <u>הייתה לי</u> פעם <u>מכונית</u> כזאת.

We'll <u>have</u> some new <u>workers</u> in the plant.   <u>יהיו לנו עובדים</u> חדשים במפעל.

<u>Substandard but common colloquial use</u>

I once had such a car.   היה לי פעם מכונית כזאת.

We'll have some new workers in the plant.   יהיה לנו עובדים חדשים במפעל.

14.6.8 No infinitive in sentences of possession

Possessive expressions (היה ל- ,יש, etc.) do not have an infinitive mood. Appropriate paraphrases have to be found, and the message has to be stated in other ways. This is done often through the use of subordinate clauses in the future tense. At other times, the idea can be conveyed through an impersonal modal verb.

I hope <u>to have</u> a dog.

<u>Paraphrase:</u>   I hope that <u>I will have</u> a dog.   אני מקווה <u>שיהיה לי</u> כלב.

One needs <u>to have</u> a lot of money.

<u>Paraphrase:</u>   <u>One needs</u> a lot of money, if one   <u>צריך</u> (שיהיה) הרבה

wants an apartment in town.   כסף, אם רוצים דירה

בעיר.

14.6.9 Sentences of possession with expanded subjects

A clause that begins with an infinitive, or a question word, can also constitute the subject of a sentence of possession. As such it has no number or gender features, and the verb in the past and future has the form of the masculine singular.

I have something to tell you.   יש לי משהו להגיד לך.

I have nothing more to say to you.   אין לי יותר מה להגיד לך.

Did you have somewhere to live?   היה לכם איפה לגור?

David will not have anybody to talk to.   לדוד לא יהיה עם מי לדבר.

14.7 Elliptical sentences   משפטים חסרים

An elliptical sentence is one in which some component of the sentence is lacking, but can be figured out from the context or from syntactic clues. The general assumption is that the speaker and the listener share a common background, or a context, and therefore can fill the gaps.

There can be overt clues that point to the missing element. In a sentence like הגענו 'we have arrived', for instance, the subject pronoun אנחנו 'we' can easily be reconstructed from the pronominal residue at the end of the verb form itself, נו-:

We got there only after seven.   הגענו לשם רק אחרי שבע.

In a sentence which has two verbal clauses, the subject need not be repeated in the second clause as it can be reconstructed from the earlier mention:

Moshe had breakfast and went to   משה אכל ארוחת בוקר והלך

work.   לעבודה.

The same is true of gaps in parallel structures: in the following example, it suffices for the verb שותה to appear in the first sentence;

repeating it in the following parallel structure would have been superfluous:

Dan drinks coffee, and Dina cold tea. .דן שותה קפה, ודינה תה קר

In a conversational situation, the response to a question is often lacking part of the sentence:

Where were you? ?איפה הייתם

In the library. .בספריה

There are other cases, where the sentence consists of an interjection, warning or sending a message to someone who may be in the proximity of the speaker:

Sit down, please! לשבת בבקשה   Quiet! !שקט

Elliptical sentences can also consist of general statements that express the speaker's opinion/feeling regarding the world around him/her, or his/her experience:

(It is) suffocating	מחניק	All right, OK	בסדר/טוב
(It is) hard for me	קשה לי	(It's a) pity	חבל
(It is) boring	משעמם	Great!	נהדר

In most cases, these sentences consist of predicates, or comments, providing the new information the speaker/writer wishes to impart. The hidden subject, usually an *it*-type one (e.g. זה נהדר 'It is great!') is self evident and redundant.

While sentences, on the whole, include all minimally required syntactic components; there are occasions in which one of the required syntactic components is missing. Some elliptical sentences lack the predicate. Such sentences tend to occur in such contexts as news headlines, greetings, or advertisements:

News headline   כותרת בעיתון
A petition to the Supreme Court: : עתירה לבג״ץ
Converting the beaches to pay-   הפיכת חופי הרחצה לחופים בתשלום -
beaches – a blight to the state   מכת מדינה
Missing component in parentheses
A petition (was presented) to the   .הוגשה) עתירה לבג״ץ)
Supreme Court.

Converting the public beaches to pay-beaches (constitutes) a blight to the state.	הפיכת חופי הרחצה לחופים בתשלום (מהווה) מכת מדינה.

<u>A birthday greeting</u>	<u>ברכה ליום הולדת</u>
To darling Tamar	לתמר החמודה
Lots of joy	הרבה שמחה
Lots of love	הרבה אהבה
And most important: health	הכי חשוב : בריאות
Mom, Dad and your brothers	אמא, אבא והאחים

<u>Missing component in parentheses</u>	
(we wish you) a lot of joy, lots of love, and most important health, (greeting is from) Mom, Dad and your brothers	(אנחנו מאחלים לך) הרבה שמחה, אהבה והכי חשוב בריאות, (מ)אמא, אבא והאחים

<u>Advertisement</u>	<u>פרסומת</u>
NetAction.	נטאקשון.
Fantastic sales!	מכירות פיצוץ!
Group purchasing in wholesale prices.	קנייה קבוצתית במחיר סיטונאי.

<u>Missing component in parentheses</u>	
There (are) fantastic sales.	(יש) מכירות פיצוץ.
Group purchasing (is available/possible) in wholesale prices.	קנייה קבוצתית (אפשרית) במחיר סיטונאי.

14.8 Classification of sentences by function

Sentences can also be classified according to their function and content. Some are used for making statements, others pose questions, while others issue directives, and some include exclamations of surprise, or convey excitement. They have illocutionary functions, and describe different aspects of language performance.

The following is the traditional categorization of sentences by the function that they perform:

Declarative sentences   משפטי חיווי (הגד)

Declarative sentences make factual statements or describe situations or impressions. Such sentences usually end with a period.

We bought a small house outside town.	קנינו בית קטן מחוץ לעיר.
Our house is surrounded by woods.	הבית שלנו מוקף בחורשות.

Interrogative sentences   משפטי שאלה

Interrogative sentences pose questions. They are initiated by question words or ones that require a yes/no answer, and can end with rising intonation at the end of the sentence indicating a question. They usually end with a question mark.

Where did you buy a house?	איפה קניתם בית?
Is it a new house?	זה בית חדש?

Imperative sentences   משפטי ציווי

Imperative sentences issue directives (commands, instructions, requests, prohibitions etc.). They usually end with an exclamation mark. They can have imperative verb commands, or infinitive forms.

Sit down, please!	שבו בבקשה!
Be seated, please!	נא לשבת!
Turn around!	אחורה פנה!
Smoking is not allowed!	אסור לעשן!
No smoking!	לא לעשן!

Exclamatory sentences   משפטי קריאה

Exclamatory sentences have an emotive or attitudinal meaning. They are usually subjectless sentences, often initiated by an adverbial expression, and at times consist of one word only. They usually end with an exclamation mark.

How you have grown!	כמה שגדלת!
Great!	יופי!
What a true catastrophe!	איזה אסון אמיתי!

14.9 Classification of sentences by structure

The three main groups of sentences are presented in a short summary, and each will then be discussed separately.

1. Simple sentences   משפטים פשוטים

Simple sentences include one subject and one predicate. They are usually composed of a noun phrase and a verb phrase or a verbless predicate. Each sentence includes one proposition.

Shakespeare is considered the most important playwright.	שקספיר נחשב למחזאי החשוב ביותר.
Hanoch Levin and Nissim Alloni are the important Israeli playwrights of the 20th century.	חנוך לוין ונסים אלוני הם המחזאים הישראליים החשובים של המאה העשרים.

2. Coordinate/compound sentences   משפטים מאוחים (מחוברים)

Coordinate sentences include two or more separate and independent clauses that are usually linked by conjunctions.

The well-known author received many international awards, <u>however</u> he did not win the Nobel Prize for Literature.	הסופר הידוע זכה בפרסים בינלאומיים, <u>אולם</u> הוא לא זכה בפרס נובל לספרות.
We were exhausted, <u>but</u> we arrived in time for Dad's birthday party.	היינו עייפים, <u>אבל</u> הגענו בזמן לחגיגת יום ההולדת של אבא.

3. Complex sentences   משפטים מורכבים

Complex sentences include one independent clause and at least one subordinate clause.

You knew that they could not come.	הרי ידעתם שהם לא יוכלו לבוא.

Some sentences are compound-complex, that is, they have more than one independent clause and at least one dependent clause:

After the party was over, my grandfather claimed that he knew about the party, but we think that it was truly a surprise.	אחרי שהמסיבה נגמרה, סבא שלי טען שהוא ידע על המסיבה, אבל אנחנו חושבים שזאת הייתה באמת הפתעה.

14.10 Simple sentences   משפטים פשוטים

A simple sentence consists of one independent clause, such as:

We drove from Tel Aviv to Haifa in less than an hour.	נסענו מתל-אביב לחיפה בפחות משעה.

A simple sentence is composed minimally of the following components: a subject and a predicate. Each of the main components of the simple sentence can have variants.

1. The subject can be a single noun, a pronoun or a noun phrase, and more rarely can also be a clause (in which case the sentence is no longer simple – see section on complement clauses below, p 340):

<u>The road</u> from Tel Aviv to Haifa is in good condition.	<u>הכביש</u> מתל-אביב לחיפה הוא במצב טוב.
<u>That I drive</u> from Tel Aviv to Haifa is not surprising – I work there.	<u>שאני נוהגת</u> מתל אביב לחיפה, זה לא מפתיע – אני עובדת שם.
<u>Driving</u> from Tel Aviv to Haifa is not something special.	<u>לנהוג</u> מתל אביב לחיפה, זה לא משהו מיוחד.

2. Verbs may have complements that are obligatory, and others that are optional.

They <u>drive</u> too fast.	הם <u>נוהגים</u> מהר מדי.
He will <u>meet with</u> the advisor tomorrow afternoon.	הוא <u>ייפגש עם</u> היועץ מחר אחר הצוהריים.

3. There are also simple sentences that are elliptical sentences, i.e. one of its main components may be omitted.

(They) feed the animals twice a day.	<u>מאכילים</u> את החיות פעמיים ביום.

14.10.1 'Inclusive' sentences   משפטים כוללים

As noted above, the simple sentence basically states one proposition. It consists of one clause, in contrast to the coordinate and complex sentences that have more than one.

Ariel and Tamar bought ice cream at a stand on the beach.	אריאל ותמר קנו גלידה בקיוסק על חוף הים.

However, because the statement above has two separate entities as its subject, it can be stated by two simple sentences:

Ariel bought ice cream.   אריאל קנה גלידה.
Tamar bought ice cream.   תמר קנתה גלידה.

Because some of the content of each proposition is identical to that of the other, the respective subjects can be combined into one, and the sentence can be expanded in this manner:

 Ariel and Tamar bought ice cream.   אריאל ותמר קנו גלידה.

The question that is posed is whether a sentence that includes coordinated phrases, such as two or more subjects, or two or more predicates, or several other items of the same syntactic category and level, should be still considered a simple sentence. The answer is often 'yes', since the sentence still constitutes one main proposition: הם קנו גלידה. However, in traditional Hebrew grammar it is often viewed as a separate sub-category, and referred to as משפט כולל, an 'inclusive' sentence, with an underlying structure of two separate propositions. Here are more illustrations:

Shmuel and Neta had coffee.   שמואל ונטע שתו קפה.
<u>Two subjects:</u>
Shmuel drank coffee.   שמואל שתה קפה.
Neta drank coffee.   נטע שתתה קפה.

They drank coffee and ate cake at   הם שתו קפה ואכלו עוגה בבית הקפה.
the café.
<u>Two verbs</u>
They drank coffee.   הם שתו קפה.
They ate cake.   הם אכלו עוגה.

Waiter, bring me coffee and cake.   מלצר, הבא לי קפה ועוגה.
<u>Two direct objects</u>
Bring me coffee!   הבא לי קפה!
Bring me cake!   הבא לי עוגה!

Waiter, bring (to) me and (to) my   מלצר, הבא לי ולאשתי קפה ועוגה!
wife coffee and cake.

<u>Two indirect objects</u>

| Bring (to) me coffee and cake. | !הבא לי קפה ועוגה |
| Bring (to) her coffee and cake. | !הבא לה קפה ועוגה |

The coordination is on the phrase level, but on the sentence level there is a good case to make that there is but one main proposition and therefore the sentences can be viewed as simple sentences, with expanded phrases.

14.11 Coordinate/compound sentences   משפטים מאוחים/מחוברים

Coordinate sentences, also referred to as compound sentences, are sentences that include more than one independent clause. A conjunction often joins the two or more separate sentences. There can also be some relationship between the component sentences, which is indicated by the type of conjunction that joins them. What distinguishes the coordinate sentence is the fact that it comprises of two syntactic structures of the same level, two independent sentences that are joined into one longer sentence, while each one remains intact.

| David and Leah went to the movies, <u>and</u> their children stayed home. | דוד ולאה הלכו לקולנוע וַהילדים שלהם נשארו בבית. |

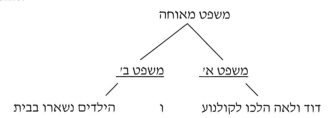

Here are some of the conjunctions that link independent sentences and define their mutual relationship:

<u>Choice</u>	<u>ברירה</u>	<u>Addition</u>	<u>תוספת</u>
or	אוֹ	and	-וְ
either... or	אוֹ ...אוֹ	also	גַּם
		as well	גַּם... וְגַם
		too	אַף

Conclusion	<u>מַסְקָנָה</u>	Opposition	<u>עִימוּת</u>
therefore	לָכֵן/וְלָכֵן	but	אֲבָל
consequently	לְפִיכָךְ	however	אוּלָם
as a result	אִי לְכָךְ	but	אַךְ
		nevertheless	אִם כִּי
		nonetheless	בְּכָל זֹאת

<u>Illustrations:</u>

More than 4000 students gave up their summer vacation this year, <u>and</u> they attend school every morning.	יותר מ-4,000 תלמידים ויתרו השנה על החופש הגדול, ומתייצבים מדי בוקר בבית הספר.
Yoni returned late, <u>but</u> Dalia came back early.	יוני חזר מאוחר, <u>אבל</u> דליה הגיעה מוקדם.
He knew it would hurt us, <u>but</u> he did it <u>anyhow</u>.	הוא ידע שזה יפגע בנו, <u>ובכל זאת</u> הוא עשה את זה.
There is a water shortage, and <u>consequently</u> everyone is asked to save water between 1-5 p.m.	יש מחסור במים, <u>ולפיכך</u> כולם מתבקשים לחסוך במים בין 1-5 אחה"צ.
We are not tired at all, <u>so therefore</u> we plan to go out and have a good time this evening.	אנחנו בכלל לא עייפים, <u>ולכן</u> אנחנו מתכוננים לצאת לבלות הערב.

14.12 Complex sentences   משפטים מורכבים

Complex sentences contain one independent clause and at least one dependent clause (clauses that cannot stand alone as sentences). Unlike compound sentences, a complex sentence contains clauses that are not equal. Consider the following examples:

<u>Simple sentence</u>	<u>משפט פשוט</u>
I was given tickets for the show. I don't feel like going.	נתנו לי כרטיסים להצגה. לא מתחשק לי ללכת.
<u>Compound sentence</u>	<u>משפט מאוחה (מחובר)</u>
I was given tickets for the show, <u>but</u> I don't feel like going.	נתנו לי כרטיסים להצגה, <u>אבל</u> לא מתחשק לי ללכת.
<u>Complex sentence</u>	<u>משפט מורכב</u>
<u>Even though</u> I was given tickets for the show, I don't feel like going.	<u>למרות</u> <u>ש</u>נתנו לי כרטיסים להצגה, לא מתחשק לי ללכת.

In the first example, there are two separate simple sentences:

‫1. נתנו לי כרטיסים להצגה. 2. לא מתחשק לי ללכת.‬

The second example joins them together into a single sentence with the coordinating conjunction, but both parts could still stand as independent sentences. Both sentences are equal, and it is difficult to tell which is more important:

‫1. נתנו לי כרטיסים להצגה אבל 2. לא מתחשק לי ללכת.‬

In the third example, the first clause is incomplete, or a dependent clause, and has to be completed:

‫1. למרות שנתנו לי כרטיסים להצגה, _____.‬

When a subordinating conjunction, such as למרות ש, initiates the first clause, it becomes clear that the fact that you were given tickets is less important than, or is subordinate to, the fact that you do not want to go.

14.12.1 Subordinate clauses   ‫פסוקיות משועבדות‬

A subordinate clause is usually introduced by a subordinating element such as a subordinating conjunction or relative pronoun. The subordinate clause depends on the rest of the sentence for its full meaning, and thus cannot stand alone. It must always be attached to a main clause that completes the meaning. The subordinate clauses include a wide range of clauses that will be discussed in the following segments. They can expand the noun phrases or the verb phrases to which they are joined with a variety of subordinating conjunctions.

The following diagram is that of a subordinate clause that expands the noun phrase, which serves as a subject:

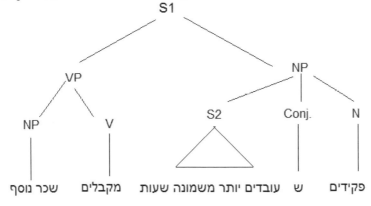

The diagram below is of a verb phrase that includes a subordinate clause that serves as the verb complement.

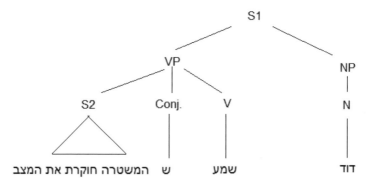

Note

The main clause is traditionally labeled משפט עיקרי (literally translated as 'main sentence'), and the subordinate clause is labeled either משפט טפל (secondary sentence) or משפט משועבד (subordinate sentence). We shall refer to the clause as פסוקית and to the full sentence as משפט.

14.13 Complement clauses   פסוקיות משלימות

Some subordinate clauses function as noun phrase substitutes, expanding an object, a subject, or a predicate into clauses. They are called 'complement' clauses because they constitute noun phrase substitutes, expanded into clauses, which complement verbs or other predicates. Such subordinate clauses can be classified into three categories:

Subject

Subject clause	The person who toils on the eve of the Sabbath, will eat on the Sabbath.	מִי שטרח בערב שבת, יאכל בשבת.
Noun phrase	The 'toiler' on the Sabbath eve, will eat on the Sabbath.	הטורח בערב שבת, אוכל בשבת.
Subject clause	What you heard from Dan is not true.	מה ששמעת מדן, איננו נכון/זה לא נכון.
Noun phrase	The rumors are not true.	השמועות אינן נכונות.

When the predicate is an adverbial expression, the subject clause usually follows the predicate.

<u>Subject clause</u>	It is possible that he won't get here tomorrow.	ייתכן שהוא לא יגיע מחר.

Here is the underlying structure:

<u>Subject clause</u>	That he won't be coming	שהוא לא יגיע
<u>Predicate</u>	Is possible	ייתכן

2. Predicate clause   פסוקית נשוא

A clause may also substitute for the predicate, as in

The question is what will happen tomorrow.	השאלה היא, מה יקרה מחר.

The two component sentences are:

<u>Main clause</u>	The question is [something]	השאלה היא [משהו]
<u>Predicate clause</u>	What will happen tomorrow	מה יקרה מחר

The abstract [something] is replaced by the predicate clause. It is also possible to front the predicate clause by a simple change in the order of the components:

<u>Transformation:</u>

What will happen tomorrow is the question.	מה יקרה מחר, זאת השאלה.

One may substitute the verb in tense by an infinitive, and similarly front the predicate clause:

The question is, what to do with him.	השאלה היא, מה לעשות אתו.

<u>Transformation:</u>

What to do with him, that is the question.	מה לעשות אתו, זאת השאלה.

3. Object clause   פסוקית מושא

A subordinate object clause serves as the direct object in the sentence. Its function is to expand verbs of saying/intention/thinking/desiring. It becomes clearer when one compares a complement clause as an object with a noun phrase serving in the same grammatical role:

Direct object

<u>Comp. clause</u>	He heard <u>that an accident occurred.</u>	.הוא שמע <u>שקרתה תאונה</u>
<u>Noun phrase</u>	He heard <u>the news</u>.	.הוא שמע <u>את החדשות</u>

The complement object clause is initiated by the subordinating particle -ש, while the noun phrase direct object is initiated by the accusative particle את.

This is the underlying structure of the sentence with the object complement clause:

<u>Main clause</u>	He heard [something]	[הוא שמע [משהו
<u>Object clause</u>	An accident occurred	[קרתה תאונה]

In order to form a complex sentence out of these two clauses, the abstract 'something' is replaced by the whole object clause, and the subordinate clause is preceded by the complementizer 'that', which is normally -ש. In higher registers it can be replaced by כי. The subjects of the two sentences are different הוא/תאונה, and the object sentence is unchanged and is preceded by the conjoining particle.

After verbs of 'wish' or 'desire', when the subjects of the two sentences are identical, the subject of the second clause is omitted, and the infinitive form of the verb is used.

I want to eat.   .אני רוצה לאכול

The underlying structure reveals two separate clauses, while the surface structure has an expanded verb phrase 'want...to eat':
Here is the underlying structure:

<u>Main clause</u>	I want [something]	[אני רוצה [משהו
<u>Subordinate object clause</u>	I will eat	[אֲנִי אֹכַל]

When the subjects are different the use of the infinitive is no longer an option.

I want you to eat (lit. I want that you will eat).   .אני רוצה שאתה תאכל

Note

Since in English the (different) subject of the second clause becomes an object, English speakers tend to make the following mistake: ~~אני רוצה~~ ~~אותך לאכול~~, which is not an option in Hebrew.

Expansion of direct objects

There are also complex sentences that consist of two clauses, where the second clause describes the state of, or the activity of, the object of the first clause, in the same time frame of reference:

Clause 1	I saw <u>Ronit</u>.	ראיתי את רונית.
Clause 2	<u>Ronit</u> was dancing.	רונית רקדה.

Ronit is the object in the first clause, and the subject in the second clause. The two occur simultaneously. The second clause can be used as the modifier of the direct object (or possibly as an adverbial adjunct of the main verb), in the following manner:

Conflating the two clauses and omitting the redundant occurrence of Ronit.

I saw <u>Ronit</u>.	ראיתי את רונית.
(Ronit) was dancing.	(רונית) רקדה.

Combining the two clauses with a time subordinator.

I saw <u>Ronit</u>.	ראיתי את רונית.
While (Ronit) was dancing.	כש(רונית) רקדה.

Changing the verb form to a participle and omitting the time subordinator.

I saw <u>Ronit dancing</u>.	ראיתי את <u>רונית רוקדת</u>.

Notice that the gender and number feature of the participle agree with the noun of the direct object:

We heard <u>them</u> <u>laughing</u>.	שמענו <u>אותן</u> <u>צוחקות</u>.
We caught <u>them</u> <u>breaking</u> into the car.	תפסנו <u>אותם</u> <u>פורצים</u> למכונית.
He found <u>the girl</u> <u>trembling</u> with fear.	הוא מצא את <u>הילדה</u> <u>רועדת</u> מפחד.

14.14 Attributive clauses   פסוקיות לוואי

An attributive clause is a subordinate clause that modifies any noun. It
serves the same function as an adjective in that it adds information to
the head noun.

NP: noun + adjective   צ"ש: שם + תואר

The new books are very   הספרים החדשים יקרים מאוד.
expensive.

NP: noun + attributive clause   צ"ש: שם + פסוקית לוואי

The books I bought yesterday are   הספרים שקניתי אתמול יקרים מאוד.
very expensive.

The underlying structure of the second sentence contains two basic
clauses: a main clause and an attributive clause.

The books are expensive.   הספרים יקרים מאוד.
I bought books yesterday.   קניתי אתמול ספרים.

Notice that there is a common element to both the main clause and the
attributive clause, and that is the noun ספרים 'books' that is referred to
in both clauses. This feature characterizes all relative clauses (see
below). However, not all attributive clauses are relative clauses and
some attributive clauses may not have a reference in the main clause.
Consider the following:

NP: noun + adjective   צ"ש: שם + תואר

The awful rumor troubled me.   השמועה הנוראית הטרידה אותי.

NP: noun + attributive clause   צ"ש: שם + פסוקית לוואי

The rumor that thousands of   השמועה שיפוטרו אלפי עובדים
workers will be laid off troubled   הטרידה אותי.
me.

The underlying structure of the second sentence contains two basic
clauses:

The rumor bothered me.   השמועה הטרידה אותי.
Thousands of workers will be laid off.   אלפי עובדים יפוטרו.

Notice that unlike the ספרים 'books' example above, in this one the
main and the subordinate clause do not share any common nominal
entities. They are two separate clauses. The attributive clause completes

the noun by adding information to it. As we can see, attributive clauses can be relative clauses when they have a co-referent in the main clause, or they can be a subordinate but not a relative clause when they do not have a co-referent in the main clause.

14.15 Relative clauses   **פסוקיות זיקה**

A relative clause is a subordinate clause that modifies any noun in the main clause, but also shares a co-referent with the main clause, or has a trace or 'echo' of that noun that is co-referential. As a noun modifier, it is attributive, i.e., can be thought of as being equivalent to an adjective.

When the verb in the relative clause is finite, the clause is generally introduced by -ש, אשר or -ה. The relative particle -ה can only be used before present tense participles.

1. When the subjects of the two clauses are identical

The man **who** is standing by the door is my brother.

האיש **ש**עומד ליד הדלת הוא אחי.
האיש **אשר** עומד ליד הדלת הוא אחי.
האיש **ה**עומד ליד הדלת הוא אחי.

Notice that each sentence has two clauses: a main clause, and a relative clause. Both share the subject, in this case, but the subject is not repeated in the relative clause, as it has already been introduced in the sentence earlier and therefore its presence is redundant.

Main clause	A man is standing by the door.	איש עומד ליד הדלת.
Relative clause	That man is my brother.	האיש הוא אחי.

The noun preceding the relative clause, which is co-referential with the same noun within the relative clause, is called the antecedent.

A comparative note

While English relative pronouns like *who* are used to link such clauses, in Hebrew the relative particle -ש (or its variants) introduces the relative clause.

2. When the object of the relative clause is a direct object

Main clause	I have a commitment to the public.	יש לי מחויבות ל[ציבור]
Relative clause	I represent the public.	אני מייצג [את הציבור]

There are a number of ways of linking the two clauses together, to form the complex sentence 'I have a commitment to the public that I represent':

a. Instead of repeating the object twice, the second object phrase is replaced by the direct object marker את with a pronoun suffix, which reflects the gender and number of the object.

1. יש לי מחויבות לציבור שאותו אני מייצג.

b. There is another option, which is to initiate the relative clause with the relative particle -ש, keep the clause order intact, and place the object with the direct object pronoun at the end:

2. יש לי מחויבות ל**ציבור** שאני מייצג **אותו**.

c. A third option, when the co-referential is a direct object, is to delete it when the two clauses are merged into one complex sentence:

3. יש לי מחויבות ל**ציבור** שאני מייצג.

3. When the object of the relative clause is an indirect object

When the noun in the subordinate clause is an indirect object, following a preposition, the pronominal residue is obligatory since the preposition cannot stand on its own:

The paper on which (that on it) the book   הנייר שעליו הודפס הספר הוא
was printed is of a high quality.   באיכות גבוהה.

Main clause	The paper is of a high quality.	[הנייר] הוא באיכות גבוהה.
Relative clause	The book was printed on the paper.	הספר הודפס על [הנייר].

Note that the preposition plus pronoun עליו 'on it' does not have to occur at the beginning of the clause:

הנייר שהספר הודפס עליו הוא באיכות גבוהה.

The paper on which the book was printed is of the best quality.

14.15.1 Relative suffix pronouns   הכינוי המוסב

Relative clauses whose objects are linked to their verbs by prepositions maintain the prepositions but replace the full nouns by pronoun suffixes, which agree in gender and number features with the nouns to which they refer. No preposition can be left 'dangling;' in Hebrew they are complemented by suffixes echoing the noun, while in English the preposition is followed by the relative pronouns, such as *which*, *whom*, or *that*.

הַבַּיִת שֶׁבּוֹ גרנו היה במרכז העיר.

התערוכות שֶׁבָּהֶן ביקרתי היו מעניינות.

Other examples

The <u>bench</u> <u>on which</u> we sat.	<u>הספסל שעליו</u> ישבנו.	ישבנו על הספסל.
The <u>notebook</u> <u>in which</u> we wrote.	<u>המחברת שבה</u> כתבנו.	כתבנו במחברת.
The <u>friend</u> <u>to whom</u> we phone.	<u>החבר שאליו</u> טלפנו.	טלפנו אל החבר.
The <u>man</u> <u>with whom</u> we met.	<u>האיש שאתו</u> נפגשנו.	נפגשנו עם האיש.
The <u>teacher</u> about whom we talked.	<u>המורה שעליה</u> דיברנו.	דיברנו על המורה.
The <u>children</u> <u>whom</u> we saw.	<u>הילדים שאותם</u> ראינו.	ראינו את הילדים.

14.15.2 Restrictive relative clauses   פסוקיות זיקה מצמצמות

Before it is modified, any noun potentially refers to the whole class of nouns in the universe that it designates. Thus, on its own and without any modification, the noun משוררים 'poets', for instance, refers to the class of all poets. One result of modification is that it restricts the domain of the noun from the whole class to a sub-class. Thus the phrase משוררים צעירים 'young poets', narrows down the scope from the class of all poets to the sub-class of those who are young. Simple adjectival modifiers generally restrict the domain of the head noun in this manner.

Restrictive relative clauses function in a similar manner as modifiers within the expanded noun phrase structure:

We met students who came from a variety of countries.	פגשנו תלמידים שבאו מארצות שונות.

The relative clause restricts the antecedent noun in the main clause from the whole class of students to those who came from a variety of countries.

The contrast between restrictive and non-restrictive

It is not always clear whether the relative clause is restrictive or not, and inability to make the distinction may cause ambiguity. For instance:

Young poets who publish on the Internet are read by many readers.	משוררים צעירים שמפרסמים באינטרנט נקראים על ידי הרבה קוראים.
Young poets, who publish on the Internet, are read by many readers.	משוררים צעירים, שמפרסמים באינטרנט, נקראים על ידי הרבה קוראים.

The first example is restrictive. It states that many readers read young poets who publish on the Internet. The inserted relative clause restricts the domain from all young poets to those who publish on the Internet, implying that there are other young poets who do not. The second example is non-restrictive and it states that young poets in general are read by many, adding as an 'aside' that they generally publish on the Internet. The 'aside' is signaled by breaks in intonation, which are symbolized by commas separating the relative clause from the rest of the sentence. The comma intonation suggests that the relative clause is a non-restrictive 'afterthought', i.e., that in general, young poets (i.e. essentially **all** of them, the whole class) publish on the Internet.

There are three formal features that can clarify the distinction between the two types of clauses:
1. The comma signs that distinguish between the two types of clauses. Only the non-restrictive relative clause is initiated and completed with comma signs and thus signals its special 'afterthought', non-restrictive meaning.
2. Added modifiers: 'only' for the restrictive clauses, and 'all' for the non-restrictive ones.
3. Adding something like 'by the way' or 'I want to add' to identify the non-restrictive clause.

Only young poets who publish on the Internet are read by many readers.	רק משוררים צעירים שמפרסמים באינטרנט נקראים על ידי הרבה קוראים.
All young poets, who publish on the Internet, are read by many readers.	כל המשוררים הצעירים, שמפרסמים באינטרנט, נקראים על ידי הרבה קוראים.
Young poets, who, by the way, publish on the Internet, are read by many readers.	משוררים צעירים,שדרך אגב, מפרסמים באינטרנט, נקראים על ידי הרבה קוראים.

14.16 Adverbial clauses   פסוקיות אדוורביליות

Adverbial clauses usually substitute for adverbs. There are a variety of such adverbial clauses, and most of them are preceded by a meaningful particle and the subordinator -ש that introduces the adverbial clause.

Time adverb	We returned <u>early</u>.	חזרנו <u>מוקדם</u>.
Time clause	We returned <u>before the sun set</u>.	חזרנו <u>לפני שהשמש שקעה</u>.

14.16.1 Time clauses   פסוקיות זמן

There are a variety of time subordinators, and the choice of a particular one for a particular meaning is usually determined by register.

These clauses usually answer the following questions:

'when'? 'since when'? 'till when?'		מתי? ממתי? עד מתי?
Meaning	Variant (higher register)	Subordinator
when	כַּאֲשֶׁר, בְּשָׁעָה שֶ-, בְּעֵת שֶ-	כְּשֶ-, בִּזְמַן שֶ-
before	בְּטֶרֶם, קֹדֶם שֶ-	לִפְנֵי שֶ-
after	לְאַחַר שֶ-	אַחֲרֵי שֶ-
since	מִשֶּ-	מֵאָז (שֶ-), מִזְּמַן שֶ-
until	עַד אֲשֶׁר	עַד שֶ-
while	בְּעוֹד, בְּשָׁעָה שֶ-	בִּזְמַן שֶ-
as long as	כָּל עוֹד	כָּל זְמַן שֶ-

Here are some examples for the use of time clauses:

I wasn't at home <u>when she arrived</u>.	לא הייתי בבית <u>כשהיא הגיעה</u>.
Main clause I wasn't at home.	לא הייתי בבית.
Time clause She arrived.	היא הגיעה.

<u>Before he turned to politics</u>, he was the National bank manager.	<u>לפני שפנה לפוליטיקה</u>, הוא היה מנהל הבנק הלאומי.
Main clause He was the bank's director.	הוא היה מנהל הבנק הלאומי.
Time clause He turned to politics.	הוא פנה לפוליטיקה.

Some time clauses contain gerunds instead of finite verbs, usually in the higher registers:

<u>Upon immigrating to Israel</u>, he changed his name.	<u>בעלותו לישראל</u> הוא שינה את שמו.

This sentence can be paraphrased with the substitution of a finite verb for the gerund and a change in order of the sentence components:

He changed his name <u>when he immigrated to Israel</u>.	הוא שינה את שמו <u>כשהוא עלה לישראל</u>.

14.16.2 Location/place clauses   פסוקיות מקום

There are a variety of location subordinators, and the choice of a particular one for a particular meaning is usually determined by register.

These clauses usually answer the questions:

'where?' 'from where?' 'to where?'	איפה, מאיפה, לאן?

Register/context	Meaning	Subordinator
common use	where	שֶׁבּוֹ/שֶׁבָּהּ/שֶׁבָּהֶם/שֶׁבָּהֶן
high register		בְּמָקוֹם שֶׁ
use of adverb		שָׁם
high register	where/wherever	בַּאֲשֶׁר
colloquial, sub-standard		אֵיפֹה שֶׁ*
standard	to where/ever	לְכָל מָקוֹם שֶׁ
colloquial, sub-standard		לְאָן שֶׁ*

Common use

I'll go with you <u>wherever you wish (to go)</u>	אני אבוא איתך <u>לאן שתרצי (ללכת)</u>

Main clause	I will come with you [to any place]	אני אבוא איתך [לכל מקום]
Links	Where[ever]	[לאן] ש
Location Clause	You want to go [there]	את רוצה ללכת [לשם]

Higher register

| Wherever (at the place where) repentants stand, even the most righteous are not allowed to stand | במקום שבעלי תשובה עומדים, צדיקים גמורים אינם יכולים לעמוד. |

| Main clause | The most righteous are not allowed to stand (in the place) | צדיקים גמורים אינם יכולים לעמוד ב[מקום] |
| Location | Repentants stand (in the place) | בעלי תשובה עומדים ב[מקום] |

14.16.3 Manner clauses   פסוקיות אופן

There are a variety of manner subordinators, and the choice of a particular one for a particular meaning is usually determined by specific meaning or by register.

These clauses usually answer the questions:
'how?' 'in what way?'   איך? באיזה אופן? באיזו דרך?

Register/context	Meaning	Subordinator
common use	like	כְּמוֹ ש
		כְּפִי ש
	thus/so that	כָּךְ ש
higher register	just like	כְּשֵׁם ש
common use	as if	כְּאִלּוּ (ש)
common use	in a manner that	בְּאֹפֶן ש/בְּדֶרֶךְ ש

| I spoke to him directly, as I spoke to everyone. | דיברתי אתו ישירות , כמו שדיברתי עם כולם/כפי שדיברתי עם כולם. |

<u>Main clause</u>	I spoke to him directly	דיברתי אתו ישירות
<u>Links</u>	as/in the same manner as	כמו ש/כפי ש
<u>Manner clause</u>	I spoke to everyone.	דיברתי עם כולם

<u>Here are other illustrations</u>

A painting has to be presented <u>so that</u> its hues will be captured by the viewer.	ציור יש להציג <u>כד ש</u>גווניו ייקלטו על ידי המסתכל.
I felt <u>as if</u> someone else was speaking from within me.	הרגשתי <u>כאילו ש</u>מישהו אחר מדבר מתוכי.
<u>Just as</u> you found it difficult, I too had difficulties.	<u>כשם ש</u>היה לכם קשה, גם לי היו קשיים.

14.16.4 Comparative clauses   פסוקיות השוואה

Sentences can include two statements between which a comparison is made. The statement in the main or primary clause is compared with a statement in a secondary or relative clause position. The main clause expresses the comparison by means of the adverbs יוֹתֵר 'more' or פָּחוֹת 'less', and the two are linked by either the expression מֵאֲשֶׁר 'than' or by the expression מִמַּה ש 'than what…' (The use of מֵאֲשֶׁר is considered a bit more formal).

David reads <u>much better than</u> he writes.	דוד קורא הרבה <u>יותר טוב מאשר</u> הוא כותב. / דוד קורא הרבה <u>יותר טוב ממה ש</u>הוא כותב.

<u>Main clause</u>	David reads well.	דוד קורא טוב
<u>Comparative link</u>	much more than	הרבה יותר...מאשר/ הרבה יותר...ממה ש...
<u>Subordinate clause</u>	He writes.	הוא כותב.

The comparison is always done in reference to the primary or main clause. The order of the clauses can be changed and the comparison stated in the negative rather than the positive, thus changing the point of reference. However, the proposition essentially stays the same.

David writes less well than he reads.	דוד כותב <u>פחות טוב מאשר</u> הוא קורא.

The subject of the two sentences is identical in the first example, but it can be a comparison between two clauses whose subject is not identical. Since the two sentences share the predicate, it is possible to omit it in the subordinate clause.

Dr. Levy contributed <u>more than</u> Dr. Cohen.	‏ד״ר לוי תרם <u>יותר מאשר</u> ד״ר כהן (תרם)/ ‏ד״ר לוי תרם <u>יותר ממה ש</u>ד״ר כהן תרם.

<u>Main clause</u>	Dr. Levi contributed	‏ד״ר לוי תרם
<u>Comparative link</u>	more than	‏יותר...מאשר/
		‏יותר...ממה ש...
<u>Subordinate clause</u>	Dr. Cohen (contributed)	‏ד״ר כהן (תרם).

The superlative is expressed either by one sentence where the adverb is preceded by הֲכִי 'the most' or through a comparative structure where the subordinate clause makes the comparison with everybody else, מִכֻּלָּם 'than everybody/anyone else'.

David ran <u>the fastest.</u>	‏דוד רץ <u>הכי מהר</u>.
David runs <u>faster than</u> anybody.	‏דוד רץ <u>יותר מהר מכולם</u>.
Dr. Levy contributed <u>the most.</u>	‏ד״ר לוי תרם <u>הכי הרבה</u>.
Dr. Levy contributed <u>more than</u> anybody.	‏ד״ר לוי תרם <u>יותר מכולם</u>.

A comparative note

In English the expression 'more than' provides the link of comparison between two clauses. In Hebrew the equivalent expression is either יותר..מאשר or יותר ממה ש.. . It is never just יותר מ. Common mistakes of non-native speakers are sentences such as:

‏*דוד קורא יותר משהוא כותב דוד קורא יותר טוב מהוא* /*כותב*

The Hebrew options are:

‏דוד קורא יותר טוב מאשר הוא כותב/ דוד קורא יותר טוב ממה שהוא כותב.

14.16.5 Cause clauses   פסוקיות סיבה

Cause clauses are ones that give the reason or cause for the proposition stated in the main clause. They are usually oriented to the present conditions or past events. There are a variety of cause subordinators, and the choice of a particular one for a particular meaning is usually

determined by register. These clauses usually answer the following
questions:

'why'? 'for what reason'? 'because of what?'	למה/מדוע, מאיזו סיבה, בגלל מה, בזכות מה?

Register/context	Meaning	Subordinator
common use	because	מִפְּנֵי ש
common use	since	מִשּׁוּם ש
common use		מִכֵּיוָן ש
common use		מֵאַחַר ש
higher register		הוֹאִיל ו
higher register		הֱיוֹת ו/ש
does not initiate a sentence, only a second clause		כִּי
used in colloquial		בִּגְלַל ש

The shop did not have a security guard <u>since it is relatively small</u>.	החנות לא הייתה מאובטחת <u>מפני שהיא קטנה יחסית.</u>

<u>Main clause</u>	The shop did not have a security guard	החנות לא הייתה מאובטחת
<u>Links</u>	since	מפני ש
<u>Cause clause</u>	it is relatively small.	היא קטנה יחסית.

Notes on word order
Cause clauses often follow the main clause:

We did not go to the concert <u>because</u> there were no tickets.	לא הלכנו לקונצרט <u>היות ו</u>לא היו כרטיסים.

But they can also introduce the sentence:

<u>Since</u> they have no car, they'll walk.	<u>מכיוון ש</u>אין להם מכונית, הם ילכו ברגל.

The particle כִּי can only introduce the relative clause following the
main clause:

The company spokeswoman claims that no damage has been caused, <u>since</u> the two preparations contain the same active ingredients.	דוברת החברה טוענת שלא נגרם כל נזק, <u>כִּי</u> שני התכשירים מכילים את אותם חומרים פעילים.

14.16.6 Consequence clauses   פסוקיות תוצאה

While the main clause can describe a situation or an action, the result clause supplies information on the consequences of such situations or actions. Result clauses are usually introduced by כָּך שֶ- 'so that'. These clauses usually answer such questions as:

'for what purpose?' 'so that what would happen?'	?לאיזו מטרה? כדי שמה יקרה
Our company wants the legislation to pass <u>so that</u> it can own all the radio stations.	,החברה שלנו רוצה שהחוק יעבור <u>כך ש</u>כל תחנות הרדיו יהיו שלנו.

<u>Main clause</u>	Our company wants the legislation to pass	החברה שלנו רוצה שהחוק יעבור
<u>Links</u>	so that	כך ש
<u>Result clause</u>	It can own all the radio stations.	כל תחנות הרדיו יהיו שלנו.

Another illustration

Not enough signatures were collected for the petition, <u>so that it did not make it to the courthouse</u>.	לא נתקבלו מספיק חתימות לעתירה, <u>כך שהעתירה לא הגיעה לבית המשפט</u>.

14.16.7 Intent clauses   פסוקיות תכלית

Intent or purpose sentences combine two clauses – a main clause and a purpose relative clause. The main clause provides the information about the action, while the purpose clause adds information about the purpose for which such action is about to be taken. These clauses usually answer the questions:

'for what?' 'for what need?'	?לְשֵם מה, לאיזה צורך, בשביל מה

Register/context	Meaning	Subordinator
common use	so that	כְּדֵי ש
higher register	in order that	עַל מְנַת ש

Sarah called her friends, <u>so that they'll all go to vote</u>.	שרה טלפנה לחבריה, <u>כדי שכולם ילכו להצביע</u>.

<u>Main clause</u>	Sarah called her friends	שרה טלפנה לחבריה
<u>Links</u>	so that/in order that	כדי ש
<u>Purpose Clause</u>	they will all go to vote.	(הם) ילכו להצביע.

<u>Some more examples:</u>

The Tel Aviv city hall opened an investigation <u>in order to</u> clarify the situation.	עיריית תל-אביב פתחה בחקירה <u>על מנת</u> לברר את המצב.
<u>In order to</u> enable the elderly to also participate in the voting, we supplied transportation for whoever wanted.	<u>כדי ש</u>גם הקשישים יוכלו להשתתף בהצבעה, סיפקנו תחבורה לכל מי שרצה.
<u>For</u> the draft bill <u>to be</u> approved in the Knesset plenum, they need the support of 80 members.	<u>על מנת ש</u>ההצעה תאושר במליאת הכנסת, יש צורך בתמיכה של 80 חברים.

14.16.8 Concession clauses   פסוקיות ויתור

Concession sentences combine two clauses – a main clause and a concession relative clause. The main clause provides the information about a situation or action while the concession clause adds information that goes against expectations or even against logic.

Register/context	Meaning	Subordinator
common use	in spite of	לַמְרוֹת ש
higher register	although	אַף עַל פִּי
higher register	even though	עַל אַף ש
higher register		אַף כִּי
higher register		אַף ש
colloquial use		אֲפִלוּ ש

Dan moved to work in Haifa, <u>even though</u> his family stayed in Tel Aviv.	דן עבר לעבוד בחיפה, <u>למרות שהמשפחה שלו נשארה בתל-אביב</u>.

Main clause	Dan moved to work in Haifa	דן עבר לעבוד בחיפה
Links	even though	למרות ש
Concession Clause	His family stayed in Tel Aviv.	המשפחה שלו נשארה בתל-אביב.

Here are some examples using some of the other subordinators

| Although he was not born in Israel, he speaks fluent Hebrew, including slang. | למרות שלא נולד בארץ, הוא מדבר עברית רהוטה, כולל סלנג. |

| The photography is good, even though the plot is boring. | הצילום טוב, אף על פי שהעלילה משעממת. |

| Although the suspects' identity is known, they were not detained. | על אף שזהותם של החשודים ידועה, הם לא נעצרו. |

| In spite (of the fact) that I was offered a raise, I did not agree to stay. | אפילו שהציעו לי העלאה במשכורת, לא הסכמתי להישאר. |

14.17 Conditional sentences   משפטי תנאי

There are two types of conditional sentences: ones that express real conditions, and ones that express hypothetical conditions that could have been or that constitute imagined counterfactual conditions. Both types of conditional sentences have similar structures – they constitute sentences consisting of two clauses:

1) The if-clause: a subordinate clause, initiated by such particles as אם or לו 'if', which states the condition.
2) The result clause: the main clause that specifies the consequences.

14.17.1 Real conditional sentence   משפט תנאי קיים

The real conditional sentence (also referred to as valid conditional sentence) is a structure used for stating possibilities in the present or in the future. The likelihood that the condition will be realized is as good as that it will not be.

1. Stating future possibilities

| [If I have enough money], I'll buy a new car. | [אם יהיה לי מספיק כסף], אקנה מכונית חדשה. |

The building blocks of such a sentence are:

initiator	If	אם
condition	I'll have enough money	יהיה לי מספיק כסף
result	I'll buy a new car	אקנה מכונית חדשה

The main clause states what will happen if the condition stated in the subordinate clause is realized. If the condition refers to a possible future event, both main clause and subordinate clause have verbs in the future tense.

A comparative note

While in the Hebrew conditional sentence the tense sequence is: (if) future + future, in English, such a sentence has the following tense sequence: (if) present + future.

2. Stating general truths or scientific facts

A real conditional sentence can be used for making general statements with no particular time reference. In such cases the present tense is used in both clauses of the conditional sentence.

[If there is not enough rain], the water   [אִם לא יורדים מספיק גשמים],
level of the Sea of Galilee drops.   מפלס הכינרת יורד.

The building blocks of such a sentence are the following:

initiator	If	אם
condition	There is not enough rain	לא יורדים מספיק
		גשמים
result	The water level of the Sea of Galilee drops	מפלס הכינרת יורד

Note

Conditional sentences stating general truths can also be initiated by the time subordinator כש- 'when' (this is true for both Hebrew and English).

When there is not enough rain, the   כְּשלא יורדים מספיק גשמים
water level of the Sea of Galilee drops.   מפלס הכינרת יורד.

Some real conditional clauses may also be in the past tense. They involve speculation of what the result of the condition was.

If the train came on time, they
already left for home.

אם הרכבת הגיעה בזמן, הם כבר נסעו
הביתה.

Common real conditional clause subordinators

Register/context	Meaning	Subordinator
common use	if	אִם
all registers	in case that	בְּמִקְרֶה שֶׁ-
higher register	as long as	בְּמִדָּה שֶׁ-
higher register		בְּמִדָּה וְ-
higher register		בְּאִם
common use		כָּל עוֹד
common use		כָּל זְמַן שֶׁ-
common use	with exclusion	וּבִלְבָד שֶׁ-
high register	unless	אֶלָּא אִם כֵּן

Further illustrations:

History will not forgive him <u>if</u> he
does not exhaust the prospect for
peace.

ההיסטוריה לא תסלח לו <u>אם</u> לא ימצה
את הסיכוי לשלום.

<u>In case</u> the value of the dollar
goes down, The Israel Bank will
have to step in.

<u>במקרה שֶׁ</u>ערך הדולר ירד, בנק ישראל
ייאלץ להתערב.

We cannot help him, <u>as long as</u> he
is not aware of his condition.

אנחנו לא יכולים לעזור לו, <u>כל זמן</u>
<u>שֶׁ</u>הוא לא מודע למצבו.

They are willing to pay a lot <u>so</u>
<u>long as</u> the children get accepted to
this school.

הם מוכנים לשלם הרבה <u>ובלבד</u>
שהילדים יתקבלו לבית הספר הזה .

14.17.2 Counterfactual conditional sentence

משפט תנאי בטל

The counterfactual conditional sentence (also referred to as
'hypothetical' or 'contrary-to-fact') is a structure used for stating
possibilities that are no longer realizable, or imaginary ones where
there is no likelihood that they will be realized. Usually, both the
subordinate and the main clause have compound verb phrases which

include היה in the past tense and a main verb in the present tense. (For the full conjugation of such verb phrases see Chapter 12, page 289).

1. Stating possibilities that did not materialize

Here is an example of an unreal conditional sentence about an opportunity that no longer can be realized.

[Had the architect planned properly], the workers would have finished the job long ago.	[אם הארכיטקט היה מתכנן כראוי], הפועלים היו גומרים את העבודה מזמן.

The building blocks of such a sentence are the following:

initiator	If	אם
condition	the architect would have planned properly,	הארכיטקט היה מתכנן כראוי,
result	the workers would have finished the job long ago	הפועלים היו גומרים את העבודה מזמן.

The logical conclusion is that since the architect had not planned properly, the workers have not finished the job yet. The counter situation is an established fact. The hypothetical sentence discusses a situation that had been possible in the past but the opportunity is no longer there and therefore is impossible to realize.

2. Stating imaginary conditions

The unreal conditional clause can also refer to the realm of the imaginary. There are conditional clauses that involve speculations that are contrary to our known factual world.

Had the Ice Age not put an end the dinosaurs, they might have existed today.	לו תקופת הקרח לא הייתה שמה קץ לדינוזאורים, אולי הם היו קיימים גם היום.

Verbal and nominal clauses in hypothetical sentences
1. Verbal predicate in conditional clauses

When the unreal conditional clause has a main verb, then its verb phrase, as mentioned above, consists of the verb היה and a main verb in the present tense.

Had you let us know about the event earlier, we would have come.

אם הייתם מודיעים לנו על האירוע מראש, היינו באים.

The main verbs are clearly evident in the conclusion. The fact is: You did not let us know and we did not come.

לא הודעתם לנו ולא באנו.

In the conditional clause (but not in the result clause) it is possible to use a verb in the (simple) past tense (rather than the compound verb phrase). The particles לו and אִלּוּ rather than אם, are used in such cases, as they contain the notion of unreal condition.

Had you let us know about the event earlier, we would have come.

אילו הודעתם לנו על האירוע מראש, היינו באים.

2. Non-verbal predicate in conditional clauses

When the unreal conditional clause is a nominal clause and its predicate does not have a verb, the linking verb היה functions as the tense indicator, and is there when the tenses are past or future.
Look at the following example:

Two main clauses provide the propositions for real and unreal conditional clauses.

| Possession | I have money | יש לי כסף |
| Equational | The car is mine | המכונית שלי |

Real conditional sentence

If I have money, the car will be mine.

אם יהיה לי כסף, המכונית תהיה שלי.

Unreal conditional sentence

If I had had money, the car would have been mine.

לו היה לי כסף, המכונית כבר היתה שלי.

Here is a further example of an unreal conditional sentence with verbless clauses. It is an old popular proverb, used metaphorically to mean 'this could never happen/has no chance of happening'.

<u>If</u> my grandmother <u>had wheels</u> she <u>would have been</u> a bus.		<u>לו היו</u> לסבתא שלי גלגלים, היא <u>הייתה</u> אוטובוס.
<u>initiator</u>	If	לו
<u>condition</u>	My grandmother had wheels	היו לסבתא שלי גלגלים
<u>result</u>	She would have been a bus.	היא הייתה אוטובוס.

There are also negative hypothetical conditions, in which the main clause could hypothetically apply only if the conditional clause were not true. Their subordinators all contain the sequence לא 'no, not':

<u>Had</u> Guttenberg <u>not invented</u> the printing press, the world would have looked completely different today.	<u>לולא המציא</u> גוטנברג את מכונת הדפוס, העולם היה נראה היום אחרת לגמרי.

The negative hypothetical conditional particle אלמלא, can also state a condition with a noun phrase rather than an entire clause:

<u>Were it not</u> for Guttenberg and his printing press, the world would have looked completely different today.	<u>אלמלא</u> גוטנברג ומכונת הדפוס שלו, העולם היה נראה היום אחרת לגמרי.

Common hypothetical conditional clause subordinators
These subordinators, other than אם, include as part of their meaning the hypothetical sense.

Register/context	Meaning	Subordinator
all registers	if	אִם
all registers	if/had…	לוּ
all registers	if/had…	אִלוּ
all registers	had not…	לוּלֵא
higher register	were it not (for)	אִלְמָלֵא

A historical note
לו is a form from biblical Hebrew, whereas אילו is used more often in post-biblical Hebrew.

14.18 Integrated sentence   המשפט המשולב
In actual texts, as well as in conversation, different types of clauses and sentences come together, to form entities, which add sentences and clauses to each other, and/or embed them within each other.

It is hard to assume that anybody would
discontinue medical treatment because
s/he has read a newspaper report.

קשה להניח שמישהו יפסיק
טיפול רפואי משום שקרא
כתבה בעיתון.

This sentence has one main clause and two clauses – an object complement clause and a reason clause:

<u>Main clause</u>	It is difficult to assume (that)	קשה להניח (ש)
<u>Object Complement</u> <u>Clause</u>	[Someone] will stop medical treatment [for a certain reason].	[מישהו] יפסיק טיפול רפואי [מסיבה מסוימת].
<u>Reason Clause</u>	because he read a newspaper report.	משום שהוא קרא כתבה בעיתון.

Chapter 15
Language in context

15.1 Introduction

Many grammars consider the sentence as the maximal linguistic unit for discussion. Thus sentences are often discussed and described as separate, independent entities ('context free'), rather than parts of larger units of text. Language in context has to be considered beyond the domain of the individual sentence. It is usually a sequence of sentences (or utterances), which combine into a coherent unit, organized around a particular topic of discussion.

Language in context has its own rules. Ordinary word order and fully and well-constructed sentences give way to different language arrangements, dependent on a host of pragmatic considerations. Language utterances get their meaning not only from their formal structures, but also from the various communicative situations and contexts in which they are used, as well as from cultural conventions unique to each language. Communicative acts are conveyed in a variety of language registers by agreed upon language codes, prescribed by different communities of speakers in an array of communicative and social situations. It is important to view meaning not only through dictionary values and morphological or syntactic structures, but also as integral parts of larger texts and contexts.

The terms 'text' and 'discourse' שִׂיחַ are often used interchangeably to refer to language beyond individual sentences. Although 'text' is more closely associated in our minds with written materials, and 'discourse' with naturally occurring language, emphasizing conversation and social interaction, the distinction is generally no longer drawn today. Similarly, the analysis of larger-than-sentence units may be referred to as either discourse or text analysis. In the context of this chapter we shall refer to all sequences of language by the general term 'text'.

This chapter contains a discussion of some of the uses of Hebrew for communication purposes, both within and beyond the sentence structure, in a variety of communicative situations, and with various transformations affecting the shape of the message (such as direct and indirect speech).

15.2 Sentence or utterance?

A sentence, in the more technical sense of the word, is a syntactic unit that is part of a text, but one that can also be discussed in isolation. An utterance is a unit of discourse, which is an actual performance of speech or writing. We will be using the general term 'sentence' to cover both sentences and utterances.

The sentence הוא לא מבין עברית can be understood in the following ways:
1. as an item of information:
He does not understand Hebrew.   .הוא לא מבין עברית

2. as a question
Doesn't he understand Hebrew?   ?הוא לא מבין עברית

3. as an expression of surprise or disbelief
He (really) does not understand Hebrew?   ?הוא לא מבין עברית

4. as an expression of annoyance:
Doesn't he understand Hebrew? (meaning: I   ?הוא לא מבין עברית
stated it clearly enough; how come he doesn't
understand?)

5. <u>with emphasis on a particular component</u> of the sentence, which will give it a focus (see section 15.4), such as:

Focusing on הוא:

<u>He</u> does not understand Hebrew (but I do).

<u>הוא</u> לא מבין עברית.

Focusing on מבין:

He does not <u>understand</u> Hebrew (but he likes the sound of it).

הוא לא <u>מבין</u> עברית.

Focusing on עברית:

He does not understand <u>Hebrew</u> (but he does understand <u>Arabic</u>).

הוא לא מבין <u>עברית</u>.

Some sentences consist of one-word exclamations:

Really!?	<div dir="rtl">באמת!!</div>
So what now??	<div dir="rtl">אז מה עכשיו??</div>
We'll see!	<div dir="rtl">נראה!</div>

15.3 Topic and comment

A topic is the component of the sentence that states what the sentence is about. The rest of the sentence is considered to be the comment on that topic. The topic and comment are concerned with the content of the sentence, its meaning and not necessarily its structure. It is another way of looking at the sentence, other than its syntactic structure.

Syntactic considerations: Subject

The subject is the noun phrase which the predicate comments on or tells something new about, but its identity is established by a formal syntactic criterion: agreement with the predicate, regardless of whether it is a verb, a noun, or an adjective. Here are some illustrations of grammatical subjects that determine the gender and number features of the predicate.

<u>The City</u> <u>built</u> two new schools.	<div dir="rtl"><u>העירייה</u> <u>בנתה</u> שני בתי ספר חדשים.</div>
<u>The mayor</u> <u>is</u> a businessman.	<div dir="rtl"><u>ראש העיר</u> <u>הוא</u> איש עסקים.</div>
<u>Many mayors</u> today <u>are</u> very <u>young.</u>	<div dir="rtl">הרבה ראשי ערים היום <u>צעירים</u> מאוד.</div>

For agreement rules, see pp. 253-256.

Content (semantic) considerations: Topic

Consider a sentence where the speaker supplies new information regarding an entity whose identity has already been established by the context:

<u>This movie</u> has already been seen by many Israelis./ Many Israelis have already seen this movie.	.את <u>הסרט הזה</u> כבר ראו הרבה ישראלים

The topic of the sentence is את הסרט הזה 'this movie', since this is what is being talked about and its identity is already known. The speaker wants to convey the new information that many have already seen the movie and that is what is regarded as the comment. While the **grammatical subject** is 'many Israelis', the **topic** is 'this movie', and כבר ראו 'have already seen' is the **comment** on the topic. In English the passive voice conveys this message best, and thus 'this movie' is moved to the front of the sentence and serves as both topic and subject. Such use of the passive for the purpose of topicalization is not acceptable in Hebrew.

The underlying topic-comment structure

Normally, the topic of the sentence is present at the beginning of a sentence and is identical to its subject.

<u>Many Israelis</u> saw this movie. .הרבה ישראלים ראו את הסרט הזה

One way to draw attention to the object of the sentence is to move it to the front of the sentence, and change the word order.

We have already seen <u>this movie</u>. .את הסרט הזה כבר ראינו

Another way, involving stronger emphasis, is not only to move the topic to the front, but also leave a 'trace' of it (a pronoun) in the comment, so that on its own, the comment constitutes a full whole clause. The topic is then separated from its comment by a comma:

<u>This movie</u>, we've already seen it. .הסרט הזה, כבר ראינו אותו

A sentence in which a constituent has been topicalized is called משפט ייחוד. The term is usually used to refer to cases of topicalization in which a pronoun trace is left in the comment component.

Note

1. A topic that has been fronted, particularly when separated by a comma, may be paraphrased in English by 'as for', as in: 'As for this movie, we have already seen it'. A comma is most likely to occur when a pronominal trace is left behind in the comment.

2. When a definite direct object is fronted, the accusative marker את is moved along with it:

We have already heard <u>your story</u>. (lit.   <u>את הסיפור שלך</u> כבר שמענו.
Your story, we have already heard it
before.)

The same is true when a preposition is present:

We have a good experience <u>with this</u>   <u>עם החברה הזאת</u> היה לנו ניסיון
<u>company</u>. (lit. With this company, we   טוב בעבר.
have had good experience in the past.)

Categories other than nouns can be topicalized. Thus, an adverb can be a topic. In the second sentence of the following example, the adverb is topicalized:

<u>Not a single tourist</u> remained here   <u>אף תייר</u> כבר לא נשאר פה עכשיו.
by this time.

A fronting of the adverbial expression:

<u>By this time</u> not a single tourist   <u>עכשיו</u> כבר לא נשאר פה אף תייר.
remained here.

Once עכשיו is fronted, it is clearly marked as the topic, and the rest of the sentence is the new information, the comment.

An infinitive (functioning here as a gerund) can serve as a topic as well:

<u>Working</u> is not exactly fun.   <u>לעבוד</u> זה לא בדיוק כייף.

Consider another illustration:

<u>This man</u>, who is he?   <u>האיש הזה</u>, מי הוא?

A sentence such as ?האיש הזה, מי הוא 'This man, who is he?' can be conceived as being uttered in the context of attending a large social gathering, pointing to a particular person, and asking for new information: 'who is he?' In other words, האיש הזה 'this man' is the topic, מי הוא 'who is he' is the comment. Fronting האיש הזה clarifies its topic role.

15.4 Focus and topic

Moving an element to the front of the sentence to clearly mark it as a topic is one kind of focusing, but its purpose is to identify the topic, not to contrast it. A more general type of focusing, discussed earlier in section 15.2 above, refers to the emphasis placed on one constituent or another in the sentence, usually for the purpose of distinguishing it from possible others. It is also typically characterized by stronger-than-usual stress. As shown above, any component of the sentence can be contrastively focused. One should remember that it can also be found at the beginning of the sentence, in which case it is identified not only by mere fronting (i.e., topicalization), but also by emphatic stress, intended to contrast.

Here are some illustrations:

To Italy we are willing to go in the summer, but not to India.

לאיטליה אנחנו מוכנים לנסוע בקיץ,
אבל לא להודו.

I spoke to him, not to you.

אליו דיברתי, לא אליך.

The focus may also be signaled by words such as רק 'only', אפילו 'even':

Only with the supervisor am I willing to speak.

רק עם האחראי אני מוכן לדבר.

Even at his best friends' place he does not feel at home.

אפילו אצל החברים הכי טובים שלו
הוא לא מרגיש בבית.

15.5 Deixis: reference to person, time and location

Another manner of viewing the text from a particular vantage point is that of deixis (i.e. reference by means of an expression relative to the situation). It is the function of a deictic word or expression within the sentence to specify its reference to a given situation. It helps anchor the text and clarify it in terms of the vantage point. Deictic words such as 'here' and 'now' are interpreted in relationship to the situation that is being referred to. A speaker is typically the deictic center of his or her own references.

Illustration of the use of deictic words in a conversation:

The situation: someone knocking at the door. Speaker A tries to establish the references and speaker B adds information.

Person	Who is <u>this</u>?	א : מי <u>זה</u>?
	It's <u>I</u>.	ב : <u>אני</u>!
Location	What are you doing <u>here</u>?	א : מה אתה עושה <u>כאן</u>?
	I came to visit.	ב : באתי לבקר.
Time	<u>Now</u>?	א : <u>עכשיו</u>?
	If not now, then <u>when</u>?	ב : אם לא עכשיו, <u>אימתי</u>?

The conversation rendition assumes the present tense of the speakers (but not of the reader of this text).

When the context being established is not in a conversational setting but in a text being heard or read, the references are not always as clear. Here is an excerpt from a short story, where the vantage point is a little girl who is lost and the deictic references are both to the space around her at this point in the story and also to her regular space: her home.

<u>story</u> <u>space</u>	The little girl looked <u>around</u> <u>her</u> with desperation.	הילדה הקטנה הסתכלה <u>סביבה</u> בְּיֵאוּש.
<u>home</u> <u>location</u>	"If you tell me where you live, I can help you go home".	״אם תגידי לי איפה את גרה אני יכולה לעזור לך לחזור <u>הביתה</u>״.
	"I live at <u>Dad and Mom's</u> <u>home</u>".	״אני גרה <u>בבית של אבא ואמא</u>״.
	"And do you know the name of <u>your street</u>?"	״ואת יודעת מה שֵׁם <u>הרחוב</u> <u>שלך</u>?״

The segments from the story assume that the events happened in the past, as the story's expository segments are told in the past, but it also builds a conversation between two speakers that takes place in that situation and uses a rendition of a present tense in the story. The discussion centers on the attempts to locate the girl's home, in contrast to her being lost in another location.

15.5.1 The person deixis

1. The person deixis is a reference to the participant's role as a referent. Person deixis is commonly expressed by pronouns.

In the conversation above, the first and second persons are both present, so the reference is clear.

| Speaker 1 | If <u>you</u> tell <u>me</u> where you live, <u>I</u> can help you go back home. | אם תגידי <u>לי</u> איפה <u>את</u> גרה <u>אני</u> יכולה לעזור לך לחזור הביתה. |
| Speaker 2 | <u>I</u> live at my Dad and Mom's home. | <u>אני</u> גרה בבית של אבא ואמא. |

The third person is assumed not to be present, and therefore the pronoun has to have a reference either in the text itself, or has to be known to others from another context.

| Third person | <u>The little girl</u> looked <u>around her</u> in desperation. For many hours <u>she</u> had been standing in the street. | <u>הילדה הקטנה</u> הסתכלה <u>סביבה</u> בְּיֵאוּש. כבר המון המון שעות <u>היא</u> עמדה ברחוב. |

Pronouns do not have to be subject pronouns; they can be attached to other words and function in other capacities (e.g., possessive).

| 2nd person | And do you know the name of <u>your</u> street? | "ואת יודעת מה שֵם הרחוב <u>שלך</u>?" |

15.5.2 Time deixis

Time deixis is reference to time relative to a temporal reference point. Typically, this point is the moment of utterance, or it can be a point of time to which the speaker refers (usually a time adverbial expression).

Temporal adverbs:

• **now / then**

| "Mother! You don't know what happened! I thought I got lost and <u>then</u> this fairy found me and ..." | "אמא! את לא יודעת מה קרה! חשבתי שהלכתי לאיבוד <u>ואז</u> הפֵּיָה הזאת מצאה אותי ו..." |

I was with my Mom but <u>then</u> she met a friend of hers and started talking to her and I was terribly bored.

הייתי עם אמא שלי אבל <u>אז</u> היא פגשה חברה שלה והתחילה לדבר איתה והיה לי נורא נורא משעמם.

- **yesterday / today / tomorrow/other time adverbs**

The audacious robbers emptied the safes' room <u>last weekend</u> in the 'Diamond Center' in the heart of the diamond dealers' quarter.

הפורצים הנועזים רוקנו <u>בסוף השבוע</u> את חדר הכספות של "מרכז היהלומים" בלב רובע היהלומנים.

Change of tense (is not fully reflected in the English translation)

You <u>don't know</u> how <u>long I have been looking</u> for you! <u>I have been looking</u> for you for half an hour in every store on this street!

את לא <u>יודעת</u> כמה <u>חיפשתי</u> אותך! כבר חצי שעה אני <u>מחפשת</u> אותך בכל חנות וחנות ברחוב!

15.5.3 Place deixis

The place reference localizes both the speech participants and narrated participants in space. It is a reference to a location relative to the position of a participant in the speech event, typically the speaker.

- **here /there** in relation to the participant

Yaeli's mother turned to <u>the chair where the woman had been sitting</u>, but the woman was no longer <u>there</u>.

אמא של יעלי הסתובבה אל <u>הכיסא שעליו ישבה האישה</u>, אבל האישה כבר לא הייתה <u>שם</u>.

- **to the right/left** of the participant

<u>To my left</u> sat a man who did not seem familiar to me.

<u>משמאלי</u> ישב אדם אחד שלא נראה לי מוכר.

- **above/below** the participant

<u>From up above</u> the voices of the celebrators were heard.

<u>מלמעלה</u> נשמעו הקולות של החוגגים.

- **from there/to here,** i.e. to the participants

The letter reached <u>us</u> only yesterday.

המכתב הגיע <u>אלינו</u> רק אתמול.

15.6 Direct and indirect speech   דיבור ישיר ודיבור עקיף
15.6.1 Direct speech

Hebrew, like English, can convey quotes directly or indirectly. Direct speech is very simple: the exact words of the original speaker are quoted, and are usually delimited with double quotes, as in:

The manager said, "I need the report this evening".	המנהל אמר : "אני צריך את הדו"ח עוד הערב".
Lisa replied, "No problem!"	עליזה ענתה : "אין בעיה!"

However, in literary texts, direct speech is often conveyed without any quote marks, and is understood as such from the context. A comma often separates the quote from the rest of the text.

The director opened the door for me and said with a smile, Good morning, Malka, come in.	הבמאי פתח לי את הדלת ואמר בחיוך, בוקר טוב מלכה, היכנסי.
She mumbled in her sleep, why are we going so slowly?	היא מלמלת מתוך שינה, למה נוסעים כל כך לאט?

Verbs which report/declare speech

say, speak, utter	אמר ל
tell, relate, recount	סיפר
add, supplement (saying)	הוסיף
announce, make known	הודיע
declare, state publicly	הכריז
answer, rejoin	ענה
reply, respond	השיב
claim, assert, proclaim	טען
proclaim, state	הצהיר

Verbs which convey attitude to speech

rebuke, reproach	גער
scold, admonish	נזף ב
encourage	עודד

Verbs of manner of speech

shout, yell	צעק
whisper	לחש
mumble	מלמל

Here is an illustration of the use of such verbs in a joke:

בדיחה עם פעלי אמירה :

Dan came to class half an hour after
the bell. The teacher <u>scolded</u> him:
"Why were you so late"?
Dan <u>answered</u> her: "You yourself
<u>said to us</u> that it is never too late to
study".

דן הגיע לשיעור חצי שעה אחרי
הצלצול.
המורה <u>נזפה בו</u> : "מדוע איחרת כל
כך"?
<u>ענה</u> לה דן : "את בעצמך <u>אמרת לנו</u>
שלעולם לא מאוחר ללמוד".

15.6.2 Indirect speech

Indirect speech is reported speech that is presented with some grammatical modifications, and not as it was uttered by the original speaker. When we turn direct speech into indirect speech, we link the two clauses by ש-, or in more formal speech, particularly in writing, by the particle כי. Like 'that' in English, this subordinating conjunction introduces reported speech. The first and second person pronouns are replaced by third person pronouns and the discourse is removed from the immediate proximity to a more distant one. Hebrew differs from English in that in Hebrew there are no changes in the tenses of the speech being reported and no special forms for 'future-in-the-past' (such as *will* into *would*). In most cases the reporting verb is in the past tense, introducing what someone has already said.

Examples of no change in tenses (compare with the English rendition):

Indirect speech	Direct Speech
רוני <u>אמר</u> שהוא <u>אוהב</u> שוקולד. ←	רוני <u>אמר</u> : "אני <u>אוהב</u> שוקולד".

Roni <u>said that</u> he <u>loves</u> chocolate.

רוני <u>אמר</u> שהוא <u>היה הולך</u> לראות סרטים כל שבוע. ←	רוני אמר : "<u>הייתי הולך</u> לראות סרטים כל שבוע".

Roni <u>said that</u> he <u>used to go</u> to see movies every week.

רוני <u>אמר</u> שהוא <u>כבר ראה</u> את הסרט. ←	רוני אמר : "<u>כבר ראיתי</u> את הסרט הזה".

Roni <u>said that</u> he <u>had already seen</u> the movie.

חברי הכנסת <u>אמרו</u> שלא <u>ישנו</u> את   ←   חברי הכנסת: "לא <u>נשנה</u> את
הצבעתם כל עוד לא <u>יתקבלו</u> עובדות   הצבעתנו כל עוד לא <u>יתקבלו</u> עובדות
חדשות.   חדשות".

The Knesset members <u>said that</u> they <u>would not change</u> their vote as long as no new facts were submitted.

Examples of change in person (same as in English):

Indirect speech		**Direct Speech**
רונית אמרה <u>שהיא</u> אוהבת את כל המחזות של שקספיר.	←	רונית אמרה: <u>אני</u> אוהבת את כל המחזות של שקספיר.
רונית אמרה לדן <u>שהוא</u> יכול ללכת <u>איתם</u> לתיאטרון.	←	רונית אמרה לדן: "<u>אתה</u> יכול ללכת <u>איתנו</u> לתיאטרון".

15.6.3 Indirect speech: interrogatives

There are two types of questions: one is about the entire proposition of the sentence, and the other is about a particular component in the sentence. A question can also be part of reported speech, either direct or indirect. It is usually introduced by the verb שאל (את) 'asked', as in the following sentence: רונית שאלה את דן אם <u>הוא</u> רוצה לבוא <u>איתם</u> לתיאטרון.

Question about the entire statement

A question about the entire statement demands a yes/no answer, as it is about its truth-value. In Hebrew no question word is necessary to initiate this type of question. What indicates that this is a question rather than a statement is a question mark at the end of the sentence, or raising of the tone at the end of the sentence. The question word הַאִם can be used optionally to indicate the question status of the sentence. Unlike English, there is no auxiliary verb (such as 'do' or 'be') that accompanies the main verb to indicate a question. Notice that in reporting a question there is no change in tense, only in person.

רונית שאלה את דן אם <u>הוא</u> רוצה   ←   רונית שאלה את דן: "(<u>האם</u>) אתה
לבוא <u>איתם</u> לתיאטרון.   <u>רוצה</u> לבוא איתנו?"

Ronit asked Dan if he   Ronit asked Dan: "<u>Do</u> you <u>want</u>
<u>wanted</u>/<u>would like</u> to come   to come with us?"
with them to the theater.

Question about a component in the statement

The second type of question is initiated by a question word and is about one particular component of the sentence. In indirect speech that question word is maintained and changes involve person (as already discussed above).

דן שאל את רונית מתי <u>הם</u> מתכוננים ללכת לתיאטרון.	←	דן שאל את רונית: "מתי <u>אתם</u> מתכוננים ללכת לתיאטרון?"
החברים שלנו שאלו אותנו למה לא <u>באנו</u> אתמול.	←	החברים שלנו שאל אותנו: "למה לא <u>באתם</u> אתמול?"

15.6.4 Place and time: changes from close to remote references

In addition to changes in persons in indirect speech, references to time and place also change. The changes are in proximity – from a close to a more remote reference: 'here' often changes to 'there', 'in this place' to 'in that place', 'now' to 'then' and 'today' to 'on that day', etc.

Examples of change in time and place:

רונית רצתה לדעת אם יש <u>שם</u> חנויות טובות.	←	רונית שאלה: "יש <u>כאן</u> חנויות ספרים טובות?"
דן רצה לדעת אם מתחשק לרונית ללכת לשתות קפה <u>באותו רגע</u>.	←	דן שאל את רונית: "מתחשק לך ללכת לשתות קפה <u>עכשיו</u>?"
המנהל אמר שהוא זוכר את <u>האיש ההוא</u> ושהוא היה <u>שם</u> כבר פעמיים.	←	המנהל אמר: "אני זוכר את <u>האיש הזה</u>. הוא היה <u>כאן</u> כבר פעמיים".

There are several reporting verbs that can be used to introduce indirect speech:

Dan <u>said</u> <u>that</u> he does/did not feel well.	דן <u>אמר</u> <u>שהוא</u> לא מרגיש טוב.	אמר
Dan <u>told</u> <u>that</u> he had been to the doctor and had tests.	דן <u>סיפר</u> <u>שהוא</u> היה אצל הרופא ועשו לו בדיקות.	סיפר
He <u>added</u> <u>that</u> the doctor did not know why he did not feel well.	הוא <u>הוסיף</u> <u>שהרופא</u> לא יודע למה הוא לא מרגיש טוב.	הוסיף

הודיע	דן <u>הודיע</u> <u>ש</u>הוא מבטל את המסיבה שתכנן.	Dan <u>announced</u> <u>that</u> he was cancelling the party.
הודיע	דן <u>הודיע</u> <u>ל</u>בעל הבית שלו <u>ש</u>הוא מתכונן לעבור דירה.	Dan <u>notified</u> his landlord <u>that</u> he was planning to move.
הכריז	הוא <u>הכריז</u> <u>כי</u> לא יהיו כל שינויים במדיניות הכלכלית של הממשלה.	He <u>declared</u> <u>that</u> there wouldn't be any changes in the government's economic policy.
השיב	לשאלות של העיתונאים הוא <u>השיב</u> <u>כי</u> אין לו מה להוסיף.	He <u>responded</u> to the questions of the journalists <u>that</u> he had nothing to add.
ענה	הוא <u>ענה</u> <u>ש</u>אם יהיה לו משהו חדש לומר, הוא יודיע לכולם.	He <u>answered</u> <u>that</u> if he would have something new to say, he would let everyone know.
עמד על כך	הוא <u>עמד</u> <u>על כך</u> <u>ש</u>לא ישנה את דעתו.	He <u>insisted</u> <u>that</u> he would not change his mind.
טען	הוא <u>טען</u> <u>ש</u>אין מקום להמשיך במסיבת העיתונאים.	He <u>maintained</u> <u>that</u> there was no reason to go on with the press conference.
הצהיר	הוא <u>הצהיר</u> בפומבי <u>כי</u> החלטותיו נעשו אחרי שיקולים רבים.	He <u>declared</u> publicly <u>that</u> his decisions were made after a great deal of consideration.

15.7 Language registers   **משלבים**

A particular level of usage is referred to as a register. What characterizes a register is either a community of speakers, or the circumstances in which language is spoken. Each person has more than one language register he/she resorts to. One may use a formal, elevated style of language to deliver a speech, or talk in an informal style to acquaintances and relatives, and speak in a particular colloquial style when getting together with a sports team they belong to.

The normative usage that most Hebrew speakers conceive of as correct is the formal register, used in a variety of formal contexts (lectures, radio news delivery, written texts etc). Here are some examples of choices made in formal and informal registers of Hebrew:

Choice of negative in present tense

	Informal	Formal
He is <u>not</u> thinking of coming.	הוא <u>לא</u> חושב לבוא.	הוא <u>אינו</u> חושב לבוא.

Choice of vocabulary

	Informal	Formal
Tell him to wait.	<u>תגיד</u> לו לחכות.	<u>אמור</u> לו לחכות.

Choice of tense/verb form

	Informal	Formal
Tell him to wait.	<u>תגיד</u> לו לחכות.	<u>הגד</u> לו לחכות.

A sample of a longer text, is a letter to the editor of the newspaper *Maariv* about an incident at work that led to dismissal from work. The writer uses formal language to discuss his situation, as he perceives that both the public platform and the gravity of the situation demand more formality. For comparison, we have rephrased it as it might be spoken in an informal context.

Two possible renditions of a letter to the editor

Informal	Formal
האשימו אותי בזה שגרמתי נזק לרכב של החברה ואמרו לי שאני חייב שיבדקו אותי בפוליגרף, ואם לא, יפטרו אותי. הפוליגרף מצא שאני לא אמרתי את האמת ופיטרו אותי, למרות שאני לא גרמתי שום נזק. האם זה חוקי?!	הואשמתי בגרימת נזק לרכב של החברה וחייבו אותי להיבדק בפוליגרף, או שאפוטר. הפוליגרף מצא שאיני דובר אמת ופוטרתי, למרות שלא גרמתי כל נזק. האם זה חוקי?!

15.7.1 Making choices: the literary register

Until recently, literature tended to use a higher-than-average formal register, but nowadays many authors often incorporate or deliberately choose to use a variety of language registers, including less formal language.

Literary register choice: colloquial informal language

חברה שלי חושבת שאני פְרָיֶיר, שתמיד דופקים אותי, שיש לי פרצוף דורש. לפני חודש, איך שהשתחררנו מהצבא, נסענו לטיול באמריקה והיא אומרת שגנבו אותי בכרטיסים. היא גם חושבת שאני רזה מדי. אבל דווקא בקשר לזה, היא אומרת, אין לה כעסים עלי, כי זה לא בשליטתי.

(Opening segment from *"How To Make A Good Script Great"* by Etgar Keret**)**

Literary register choices: mixing registers

Here is the last stanza of a poem written for children, that mixes both children's and colloquial registers as one of its poetic devices:

אני אוהב

אני אוהב את אימא ואת אבא גם
ואת שולה הגננת ואת הדודה מרים
אני אוהב את סבא ואת סבתא אני אוהב את אחותי
אבל הכי הכי הרבה אני אוהב אותי.

(משיר של יהונתן גפן)

There are several colloquial registers. When talking to family members speakers make some different choices than the ones they use when speaking either to neighbors and friends, or to colleagues or to total strangers. There are speech norms at work and at play. Adults may speak differently to children. Teenagers often have their own language codes and tend to address their contemporaries differently from the way they address their parents, teachers or other figures of authority. All of the above and many more situations determine choice of vocabulary, style, tone of voice, choice of language strategy, degree of directness and formality.

Here are some illustrations:

Direct	Sit here!	!שבו כאן
Polite	Please, sit down.	!תשבו בבקשה
Formal polite (but insistent)	Sit down, if you please.	!נא לשבת

| Polite suggestion | You may sit. | .אתם יכולים לשבת |
| Indirect suggestion | You don't have to stand. | .אתם לא צריכים לעמוד |

15.7.2 Register and metaphor

One should not take it for granted that the use of metaphors automatically identifies a text as belonging to the literary register; slang makes extensive use of metaphors as well, and speakers whose speech typically belongs to one register may cross over to the other: when it is done in jest, or to impress with familiarity with the opposite register, or to achieve a special effect.

Here are some metaphor groups that are used to the same semantic end in the two diametrically opposed registers, the literary register and slang.

Meaning of both	Slang metaphor	Literary Metaphor
beat someone up	; נתן ליטוף ; השכיב ; קימט ; כִּסֵחַ ; דפק/ניפֵּח לו את הצורה	; הנחית מתנת יד ; הגביה/הניף ידו (על) ; הראהו (את) נחת זרועו ; הפליא בו את מכותיו
suffer greatly	אכל חצץ ; אכל קש	שבע מרורים ; שתה את כוס התרעלה עד תומה
be in love (with)	; משוגע (על) ; דלוק/נדלק (על) ; קרוע/נקרע (על) ; גנוב/נגנב (על) ; הרוס (על) ; נטרף (על) ; מורעל (על) ; נעול (על) ; שפוט	נפשו קשורה בנפשה ; נטה לבו אחרי... ; דבקה נפשו ב...

Note that slang is not a corruption of language; it is a separate legitimate register within the colloquial range, usually restricted to particular social classes or age groups, making a conscious effort to distinguish themselves from the 'conventional' broader society.

15.7.3 Borrowing of expressions

There are many popular metaphorical expressions and idioms that were borrowed from other languages and have entered the Hebrew vocabulary:

afraid of one's own shadow	מפחד מהצל של עצמו
tail between the legs	עם הזנב בין הרגליים
eat like a horse	אוכל כמו סוס
the ball is in your court	הכדור במגרש שלך
break the ice	לשבור את הקרח
cut corners	לעגל פינות
get on someone's nerves	לעלות על העצבים
keep a low profile	לשמור על פרופיל נמוך
from the horse's mouth	מפי הסוס
give me a ring (call me)	תן לי צלצול

15.8 Genres of text   סוגות של טקסט

The variety of existent texts that are delivered in various channels of communication differ from one another in their structure and organization. It is therefore helpful to attempt to classify them according to their organization, their characteristics and their overall purpose. Texts that are more formal, professional, ceremonial and cultural, or intended for mass consumption, tend to have a more structured and formulated organization. Among such texts are legal contracts, scholarly articles, media news, prayers and blessings, recipes and others. The more individual texts, such as personal letters, informal conversations, op-ed articles, fictional works, are less formulated.

Texts can be classified into genres on the basis of the intent of the communicator. Each of these genres can be described as having an overall purpose of (1) information, (2) entertainment, (3) persuasion and influence, and (4) aesthetics.

The following text genres can be considered in the context of the overall purposes described listed above:

Text genre	Communicator's intent is to
Narrative	Tell about a sequence of events (historical, contemporary, fictional tale, folk tale, drama etc.)
Procedural	Give instructions on how to do something (technical information on how to operate a new gadget, directions on what to do on a test, stage directions etc.)

Expository   Explain something (such as a scholarly
              article, a science textbook, political
              address, religious sermon etc.)
Descriptive   List the characteristics of something
              (description of a medical or scientific
              procedure, technical description,
              descriptions of fictional or real
              characters, descriptions of landscape,
              poetic descriptions etc.)

The list above is by no means an exhaustive one, or the only way to classify genres of texts, but covers some common categories.

15.9 Cohesion and coherence of text

The texture of any given discourse unit is reflected by a number of external devices as well as internal organization and logic that give the text its cohesion and coherence.

Text coherence (consistency and logic of the text)

The logical and rhetorical relationships between propositions constitute the coherence of a text. There can be two propositions that have no common elements that unite them, except for the fact they appear in sequence. In this case, a temporal relationship may exist between them or a cause and effect relationship. For instance, the following sentences suggest such a way of putting two propositions together:

1. Hurricane Isabel reached the state of North Carolina in the United States in the past hours.	1. סופת ההוריקן ״איזבל״ הגיעה לחופי מדינת קרוליינה הצפונית בארה״ב בשעות האחרונות.
2. More than 300 thousand people in North Carolina and Virginia left their homes for fear of the damage caused by the hurricane.	2. יותר מ-300 אלף איש בקרוליינה הצפונית ובווירג׳יניה פינו את בתיהם מחשש מפגיעת ההוריקן.

We can say that there is both a temporal and a causal relationship between these two sentences. The first states the fact that the hurricane arrived, and the second describes the consequences that occurred once the storm arrived. Coherence, then, is the content connecting these sentences to each other.

Text cohesion (unity and structural organization)

In addition to the coherence of a text content-wise, there are external signals in the superstructure of the text that provide the connectivity or the cohesion of the text. Most of them are grammatical (although the notion of cohesion may also be extended to the lexicon), and are generally manifest in the use of referencing devices and of connectives, such as וְאוּלָם 'however' below:

1. The hurricane winds are likely to get to the speed of 105 kilometers per hour.	1. רוחות ההוריקן עשויות להגיע למהירות של 105 קמ״ש.
2. <u>However,</u> the main worry concerns the damage that will be caused by the flooding brought about by the storm that is expected to create waves, 12 feet high.	2. <u>ואולם</u> הדאגה העיקרית היא מהנזק שייגרם משיטפונות הסופה, שאמורה ליצור גלים בגובה של 12 רגל.

Referencing and co-referencing contribute to text cohesion by building a system of participants, places, objects, time, and other features within the larger text unit.

Reference may be to an entity that is not mentioned anywhere in the text proper, but which is understood in the broader context; e.g., in the context of a discussion of a particular company one may find the following sentence:

<u>The President</u> has no idea what is going on.	ל<u>נשיא</u> אין מושג מה קורה.

The reference is clearly to the president of the company, even though this fact is not mentioned overtly.

In most cases, however, the reference is established by co-referencing one occurrence of an entity with another one; often it is in the form of a pronoun.

<u>Danny</u> will not come tonight. <u>He</u> is very busy.	<u>דני</u> לא יבוא הערב. <u>הוא</u> עסוק מאוד.
<u>Danny</u>: "Hello Ruth. <u>I</u> am not coming tonight".	<u>דני</u>: ״הלו רות, <u>אני</u> לא בא הערב״.

Ruth: "but <u>you</u> said that <u>you</u> would come".   ".רות : " אבל <u>אתה</u> אמרת ש<u>תבוא</u>"

When a reference points back to an occurrence of a referent earlier in the text, the linkage/relationship is called *anaphora*. There are a few cases, particularly in literary texts, when the reference occurs *before* the referent is specifically identified. Such subsequent appearance of the referent is called *cataphora*.

Examples of cataphora

Sentence 1: general reference to 'a suspect'

The Tel Aviv police detained <u>a suspect</u> in the deadly running over of a 17-year-old young woman on the Tel Aviv promenade two weeks ago.

משטרת תל אביב עצרה <u>חשוד</u> בדריסתה למוות של הצעירה בת ה-17 בטיילת בתל אביב לפני שבועיים.

Sentence 2: specific mention of the suspect's name, age, place, and history

<u>The suspect, Avi Yaakobi, a 33-year-old ex-con from Petah Tikva,</u> is suspected of having driven without a license and trying to hide facts connected to the accident.

<u>החשוד, אבי יעקובי, אסיר לשעבר בן 33 מפתח-תקווה</u>, חשוד שנהג ללא רשיון וניסה להסתיר ראיות הקשורות לתאונה.

15.10 Language in context: sample texts

Language in use is not organized in the same way as a sequence of independent sentences, all of which are formally correct, but may or may not have any meaningful clear relationship between them. Language in use always has a context, a style and other features which give it the cohesion, coherence and style, demonstrated by its organization and structure, which follow many of the language behavioral rules described earlier in the chapter.

The two main styles of larger units of discourse are the conversation and the narrative, or 'story' type of discourse.

15.10.1 Conversations

One of the most difficult tasks for a learner of Hebrew or any other foreign language, is trying to participate in a conversation, understand the intent of speakers, the rules of taking turns in a conversation (sometimes totally ignored), how to address strangers and how to address family and close friends, and what conventions are required by different social situations.

In listening and comprehension, it is important to consider and determine the following factors:

- How the participants take turns
- How they construct their utterances across turns
- How participants identify and repair communication problems
- How conversation works in different conventional settings

Sample 1: Rendition of a conversation

(From a simulation of a conversation in a written text. The setting is home, and the conversation takes place in intimate circumstances, between a mother and a daughter):

"Tikva'le, come, I warmed up some vegetable soup for you, come and taste".	״תקווה׳לה, בואי, חיממתי קצת מרק ירקות, בואי תטעמי״.
"No, Mom, I don't feel like it".	״לא, אמא, לא בא לי״.
"Come on, just a tiny drop of soup, it's hot".	״בואי, בואי, רק טיפה׳לה מרק, זה חם״.
"Mom, I ate at the university".	״אמא, אכלתי באוניברסיטה״.
"OK, OK, but only a little bit of soup, it's nothing, it's all water".	״טוב, טוב, אבל רק קצת מרק, זה כלום, זה הכול מים״.
"I don't want to".	״אני לא רוצה״.

Sample 2: from a newspaper interview

(From an interview with the then Labor Party Minister of Education, Yossi Sarid. The style is quasi-formal and utterances are full sentences. Response is directed at the question posed.)

"In the Labor Party they say that you are still considering running for Prime Minister".	״במפלגת העבודה אומרים שאתה עדיין חושב על ריצה לראשות הממשלה״.
"No, I don't believe that I can be elected, not in the present situation. I don't see such a	״לא, אני לא חושב שאני יכול להיבחר, לא בסיטואציה הנוכחית. אני לא רואה אפשרות כזו. אני מכיר את המבנה של

possibility. I know the structure of
Israel, and cannot see how enough
opposition support me to be PM".

ישראל, ולא רואה איך מספיק ניגודים
תומכים בי כדי שאהיה לראש
ממשלה".

15.10.2 Narratives

A narrative discourse is an account of events, usually in the past, that
employs verbs of speech, motion, and action to describe a series of
events that are contingent one on another, and that typically focuses on
one or more performers of actions.

Some of the features of narratives are:
1. Events are organized chronologically.
2. First or third person pronoun forms are used.
3. The text is oriented around a specific agent or agents.

Here are some common categories of narratives:

Folk tales
Stories about real or imagined events, often containing supernatural
elements.

Historical events
Stories or accounts about the social and political history of the world
and its contacts with the rest of the world.

Mythology
Stories explaining origins, natural phenomena, or social and religious
customs, often involving the supernatural.

Personal experience
Accounts of significant events in the life of the narrator or the
community.

Sample text 3: Rendition of a folk tale:

האמת

היה פַּעַם אדם שרצה להכיר את הָאֱמֶת. היה אומר לאשתו הַשְׁכֵּם וְהַעֲרֵב: "הייתי
רוצה פעם אחת לפגוש את האמת, לשׂוֹחֵחַ איתה, להכּיר אותה פנים אל פנים..."
"מה אתה מבַלבֵּל לי את המוֹחַ. אתה רוצה להכּיר את האמת? מִצְדִי, לֵך תחַפֵּשׂ
אותה, דַּבֵּר אתה. מה אתה רוצה ממני?!"
והוא באמת יצא לדרך. עזב הכל - אישה, ילדים. יצא לחפש את האמת. עלה הרים
וירד גבעות, חיפש את האמת לאורך החופים, בנבכֵי היערות. חיפש אותה בכפרים
קטנים, חיפש אותה בערים גדולות, ויום אחד, על ראשוֹ של הָר, תַּאֲמינו או לא,

בְּתוֹךְ מְעָרָה, הוּא מצא את האמת. הָאמת הָיתה אישה זקֵנה, כְּפוּפַת גֵו, שְׂעָרה
שֵׂיבָה וְעוֹרָה צָפוּד וצהוֹב כְּקלָף. אך בשעה שדִיבּרה היה קוֹלָהּ צָלוּל וזַךְ כמים,
וְהוּא ידע שזאת האמת. שנה ויום שָׁהָה בְּמחִיצָתָהּ, ושמע מפִּיהָ את כל מה שהיה
בְּפִיהָ לומר לו.

כַּעֲבוֹר שנה החליט האיש לשוב לבֵיתו. לפנֵי שנפרד ממנה אמר לה : "גבִירתי
האמת, את לימדת אותי כל כך הרבה. אני עכשיו חוזר לבֵיתי. אוּלַי יש משהו
שאני יכול לעשות למַעֲנֵךְ?" האמת חשבה לרגע, הֵרִימה אֶצבַּע גרומה ורועדת
ואמרה לו : "כֵּן. כאשר תשוב לשם ותספר עָלַי, אל תא'מַר שאני זקֵנה וּבָלָה. אֱמוֹר
להם כי אני יפה וצעירה...״

Partial analysis

This short simple tale incorporates various language and discourse devices mentioned in this chapter. They give it the shape of a text, rather than being a sequence of sentences. The choice of vocabulary, the choice not to repeat the subject within the paragraph, as it is obvious, the word order and more, all characterize this as a coherent and cohesive text. Included are a few comments to highlight the reading of the text, and to accentuate the fact that sentences within a larger text take on a different shape to help contour the text and give it its flow. The character Truth is referred to as האמת, as generic abstract nouns use the definite article to get the same effect as English does with capital letters.

Comments	Text
Title of the story "Truth"	**האמת**
Comments	**Text**
Conventional beginning of a folk tale: verb and adverb precede subject.	היה פַּעם אדם שרצה להכיר את הָאֱמֶת.
Once upon a time there was a man who wanted to get to know the truth/ Truth.	
Subject not repeated and use of habitual aspect:	היה אומר לאשתו הַשְׁכֵּם וְהַעֲרֵב :
(He) used to say to his wife morning and night:	

Use of direct speech, and modality
– expressions of wish:
*"I would love to meet Truth, if
only once, and speak with her and
get to know her face to face..."*

"הייתי רוצה פעם אחת לפגוש את
האמת, לשׂוֹחֵחַ איתה, להכיר אותה
פנים אל פנים..."

The addressee is the wife, and there
is no need to mention this, as the
context is clear. Her response starts
with a comment and a question:
*"Why are you driving me crazy?
You want to get to know Truth?"*

"מה אתה מבַלבֵּל לי את המוֹחַ. אתה
רוצה להכיר את האמת?

It continues with a suggestion and a
direction addressing his wish:
*"As far as I am concerned, go
ahead and look for her, talk to her.
What do you want from me?"*

מִצְדִי, לֵךְ תחַפֵּשׂ אותה, דַבֵּר אתה.
מה אתה רוצה ממני?"

A narrative sequence: the subject is
not repeated after the first sentence
in this sequence and a verb starts
each new sentence.
*And indeed he went on his way. Left
everything – wife, children. Went
out to seek the truth along shores, in
the heart of forests. Searched for
her in small villages, looked for her
in big cities,*

והוא באמת יצא לדרך. עזב הכל -
אישה, ילדים. יצא לחפש את האמת.
עלה הרים וירד גבעות, חיפש את
האמת לאורך החופים, בנבכֵי
היערות. חיפש אותה בכפרים
קטנים, חיפש אותה בערים גדולות,

A break in the sequence includes
addressing the reader:
*And one day, at the top of a
mountain, believe it or not, inside a
cave, he found Truth.*

ויום אחד, על ראשׂו של הָר, תאֲמינו
או לא, בתוך מערָה, הוא מצא את
האמת.

Descriptive passage:
*Truth was an old woman, bent, her
hair gray and her skin as wrinkled*

האמת היתה אישה זקֵנה, כפופַת
גֵו, שׂערה שֵׂיבָה ועוֹרָהּ צָפוּד וצהוב

and as yellow as parchment. But when she spoke her voice was clear and pure like water, and he knew that she was Truth.	כְּקְלָף. אַךְ בשעה שדיברה היה קוֹלָהּ צָלוּל וְזַךְ כמים, והוא ידע שזאת האמת.

Expository passage – focus on time and omission of subject:
A year and a day he stayed in her company, and heard from her what she had to say to him.	שנה ויום שָׁהָה בְּמְחִיצָתָהּ, ושמע מפיה את כל מה שהיה בְּפִיהָ לומר לו.

Time adverb begins the sentence, and word order changes to verb in tense + subject: + infinitive of expanded verb:
After a year the man decided to return to his home.	כַּעֲבוֹר שנה החליט האיש לשוב לבֵיתוֹ.

Concluding dialogue (use of direct speech). Subject A (the protagonist) is not mentioned, as his identity, is known from the earlier part of the text. Before he parted from her, he said to her: *"Lady Truth, you taught me so much. I am now returning to my home. Is there something I could do for you?"*

לפנֵי שנפרד ממנה אמר לה : "גבירתי האמת, את לימדת אותי כל כך הרבה. אני עכשיו חוזר לבֵיתי. אולַי יש משהו שאני יכול לעשות למַעֲנֵךְ?"

The second speaker, Truth, takes her turn. The choice of words is from a high language register:
Truth thought for a moment, lifted a thin and shaking finger and said to him: "Yes. When you get back there and tell about me, don't tell them that I am an old, worn out woman. Tell them that I am beautiful and young ..."

האמת חשבה לרגע, הֵרִימה אֶצבּע גרומה ורועדת ואמרה לו : "כן. כאשר תשוב לשָׁם ותספר עָלי, אל תֹאמַר שאני זקֵנה וּבָלָה. אֱמֹר להם כי אני יפה וצעירה..."

Appendix 1: verb tables

Note: In most conjugations other than regular שְׁלֵמִים, only deviations from the שְׁלֵמִים will be listed.

בניין: פָּעַל

בניין: פָּעַל
גזרה: שלמים, אֶפְעֹל
שורש: ש-מ-ר
שם פועל: לִשְׁמֹר
מקור: שָׁמוֹר, שְׁמֹר

	עבר	עתיד	ציווי
אני	שָׁמַרְתִּי	אֶשְׁמֹר	
אתה	שָׁמַרְתָּ	תִּשְׁמֹר	שְׁמֹר
את	שָׁמַרְתְּ	תִּשְׁמְרִי	שִׁמְרִי
הוא	שָׁמַר	יִשְׁמֹר	
היא	שָׁמְרָה	תִּשְׁמֹר	
אנחנו	שָׁמַרְנוּ	נִשְׁמֹר	
אתם	שְׁמַרְתֶּם	תִּשְׁמְרוּ	שִׁמְרוּ
אתן	שְׁמַרְתֶּן	תִּשְׁמְרוּ	שִׁמְרוּ
הם/ן	שָׁמְרוּ	יִשְׁמְרוּ	
(אתן/הן)		(תִּשְׁמֹרְנָה)	(שְׁמֹרְנָה)

הווה	
יחיד	שׁוֹמֵר
יחידה	שׁוֹמֶרֶת
רבים	שׁוֹמְרִים
רבות	שׁוֹמְרוֹת

בניין: פָּעַל
גזרה: שלמים, אֶפְעַל
שורש: ל-מ-ד

עתיד			
אני	אֶלְמַד	*אנחנו*	נִלְמַד
אתה	תִּלְמַד	*אתם*	תִּלְמְדוּ
את	תִּלְמְדִי	*אתן*	תִּלְמְדוּ
הוא	יִלְמַד	*הם/ן*	יִלְמְדוּ
היא	תִּלְמַד	*(אתן/הן)*	(תִּלְמַדְנָה)

ציווי			
אתה	לְמַד	*את*	לִמְדִי
אתם	לִמְדוּ	*אתן*	(לְמַדְנָה)

בניין: פָּעַל, פ׳ גרונית א׳
שורש: א-ס-פ
שם פועל: לֶאֱסֹף

עתיד			
אני	אֶאֱסֹף	*אנחנו*	נֶאֱסֹף
אתה	תֶּאֱסֹף	*אתם*	תַּאַסְפוּ
את	תַּאַסְפִי	*אתן*	תַּאַסְפוּ
הוא	יֶאֱסֹף	*הם/ן*	יַאַסְפוּ
היא	תֶּאֱסֹף	*(אתן/הן)*	(תֶּאֱסֹפְנָה)

עבר	
אתם	אֲסַפְתֶּם
אתן	אֲסַפְתֶּן

ציווי	
אתה	אֱסֹף
אתן	(אֱסֹפְנָה)

	עתיד			בניין : פָּעַל , פ׳ גרונית ה׳ ע׳ (ח׳)		
נַעֲבֹד	אנחנו	אֶעֱבֹד	אני	שורש : ע-ב-ד		
תַּעַבְדוּ	אתם	תַּעֲבֹד	אתה	שם פועל : לַעֲבֹד		
תַּעַבְדוּ	אתן	תַּעַבְדִי	את		ציווי	עבר
יַעַבְדוּ	הם/ן	יַעֲבֹד	הוא	עֲבֹד	אתה	אתם עֲבַדְתֶּם
(תַּעֲבֹדְנָה)	(אתן/הן)	תַּעֲבֹד	היא	(עֲבֹדְנָה)	אתן	אתן עֲבַדְתֶּן

	עתיד			בניין : פָּעַל , פ׳ גרונית ח׳ (some)		
נַחְבֹּשׁ	אנחנו	אֶחְבֹּשׁ	אני	שורש : ח-ב-שׁ		
תַּחְבְּשׁוּ	אתם	תַּחְבֹּשׁ	אתה	שם פועל : לַחְבֹּשׁ		
תַּחְבְּשׁוּ	אתן	תַּחְבְּשִׁי	את		ציווי	עבר
יַחְבְּשׁוּ	הם/ן	יַחְבֹּשׁ	הוא	חֲבֹשׁ	אתה	אתם חֲבַשְׁתֶּם
(תַּחְבֹּשְׁנָה)	(אתן/הן)	תַּחְבֹּשׁ	היא	(חֲבֹשְׁנָה)	אתן	אתן חֲבַשְׁתֶּן

	עתיד			בניין : פָּעַל , פ׳ גרונית א׳ נחה		
נֹאכַל	אנחנו	אֹכַל	אני	שורש : א-כ-ל		
תֹּאכְלוּ	אתם	תֹּאכַל	אתה	שם פועל : לֶאֱכֹל		
תֹּאכְלוּ	אתן	תֹּאכְלִי	את		ציווי	עבר
יֹאכְלוּ	הם/ן	יֹאכַל	הוא	אֱכֹל	אתה	אתם אֲכַלְתֶּם
(תֹּאכַלְנָה)	(אתן/הן)	תֹּאכַל	היא	(אֱכֹלְנָה)	אתן	אתן אֲכַלְתֶּן

	הווה		עתיד			בניין : פָּעַל , ע׳ גרונית		
שׁוֹאֲלִים	אנחנו		תִּשְׁאֲלִי	את		שורש : שׁ-א-ל		
שׁוֹאֲלוֹת	אתם		תִּשְׁאֲלוּ	אתם		שם פועל : לִשְׁאֹל		
			יִשְׁאֲלוּ	הם/הן			ציווי	עבר
						שַׁאֲלִי	את	היא שָׁאֲלָה
						שַׁאֲלוּ	אתם/ן	הם/הן שָׁאֲלוּ

	הווה			בניין : פָּעַל , לה״פ גרונית ח׳		
שׁוֹלַחַת	יחידה	שׁוֹלֵחַ	יחיד	שורש : שׁ-ל-ח		
				שם פועל : לִשְׁלֹחַ		

בניין : פָּעַל , ע׳ גרונית
שורש : ג-ב-ה
שם פועל : לִגְבֹּהַ

הווה		עתיד	
גָּבֹהַ	יחיד	אֲגְבַּה	אני
גְּבוֹהָה	יחידה	תִּגְבַּה	אתה
גְּבוֹהִים	רבים	יִגְבַּה	הוא
גְּבוֹהוֹת	רבות	תִּגְבַּה	היא
		נִגְבַּה	אנחנו

עבר			ציווי	
הוא	גָּבַה	אתה	גְּבַה	
היא	גָּבְהָה	אתם	גִּבְהוּ	

בניין : פָּעַל , חסרי פ״י
שורש : י-ש-ב
שם פועל : לָשֶׁבֶת

	עתיד		
נֵשֵׁב	אנחנו	אֵשֵׁב	אני
תֵּשְׁבוּ	אתם	תֵּשֵׁב	אתה
תֵּשְׁבוּ	אתן	תֵּשְׁבִי	את
יֵשְׁבוּ	הם/ן	יֵשֵׁב	הוא
(תֵּשַׁבְנָה)		תֵּשֵׁב	היא

ציווי				
אתה	שֵׁב	את	שְׁבִי	
אתם	שְׁבוּ	אתן	(שֵׁבְנָה)	

בניין : פָּעַל , נחי פ״י
שורש : י-ר-ש
שם פועל : לָרֶשֶׁת

	עתיד		
נִירַשׁ	אנחנו	אִירַשׁ	אני
תִּירְשׁוּ	אתם	תִּירַשׁ	אתה
תִּירְשׁוּ	אתן	תִּירְשִׁי	את
יִירְשׁוּ	הם/ן	יִירַשׁ	הוא
(תִּירַשְׁנָה)		תִּירַשׁ	היא

ציווי				
אתה	יְרַשׁ	את	יְרְשִׁי	
אתם	יִרְשׁוּ	אתן	(יְרַשְׁנָה)	

בניין : פָּעַל , חסרי פ״נ
שורש : נ-פ-ל
שם פועל : לִפֹּל

	עתיד		
נִפֹּל	אנחנו	אֶפֹּל	אני
תִּפְּלוּ	אתם	תִּפֹּל	אתה
תִּפְּלוּ	אתן	תִּפְּלִי	את
יִפְּלוּ	הם/ן	יִפֹּל	הוא
(תִּפֹּלְנָה)		תִּפֹּל	היא

ציווי				
אתה	נְפֹל	את	נִפְלִי	
אתם	נִפְלוּ	אתן	(נְפֹלְנָה)	

בניין : פָּעַל
גזרה : נחי ע״ו
שורש : ק-ו-מ
שם פועל : לָקוּם
מקור : קוֹם, קוּם

ציווי	עתיד	עבר	
	אָקוּם	קַמְתִּי	אני
קוּם	תָּקוּם	קַמְתָּ	אתה
קוּמִי	תָּקוּמִי	קַמְתְּ	את
	יָקוּם	קָם	הוא
	תָּקוּם	קָמָה	היא

הווה			עבר	עתיד	ציווי
		אנחנו	קַמְנוּ	נָקוּם	
יחיד	קָם	אתם	קַמְתֶּם	תָּקוּמוּ	קוּמוּ
יחידה	קָמָה	אתן	קַמְתֶּן	תָּקוּמוּ	קוּמוּ
רבים	קָמִים	הם/ן	קָמוּ	יָקוּמוּ	
רבות	קָמוֹת	(אתן/הן)		(תָּקֹמְנָה)	(קֹמְנָה)

בניין: פָּעַל
גזרה: נחי ע"י
שורש: ש-י-ם
שם פועל: לָשִׂים
מקור: שׂוֹם, שִׂים

		עבר	עתיד	ציווי
	אני	שַׂמְתִּי	אָשִׂים	
	אתה	שַׂמְתָּ	תָּשִׂים	שִׂים
	את	שַׂמְתְּ	תָּשִׂימִי	שִׂימִי
	הוא	שָׂם	יָשִׂים	
	היא	שָׂמָה	תָּשִׂים	

הווה			עבר	עתיד	ציווי
		אנחנו	שַׂמְנוּ	נָשִׂים	
יחיד	שָׂם	אתם	שַׂמְתֶּם	תָּשִׂימוּ	שִׂימוּ
יחידה	שָׂמָה	אתן	שַׂמְתֶּן	תָּשִׂימוּ	שִׂימוּ
רבים	שָׂמִים	הם/ן	שָׂמוּ	יָשִׂימוּ	
רבות	שָׂמוֹת	(אתן/הן)		(תָּשֵׂמְנָה)	(שֵׂמְנָה)

In modern Hebrew the so-called 'doubled roots', which have identical second and last root consonants, are conjugated as regular verbs, however, historically there was a separate special conjugation, which has some residues in current Hebrew:

בניין: פָּעַל
גזרה: כפולים (ע"ע)
שורש: ח-נ-נ
שם פועל: לָחֹן
מקור: חָנוֹן, חֹן

		עבר	עתיד	ציווי
	אני	חַנּוֹתִי	אָחֹן	
	אתה	חַנּוֹתָ	תָּחֹן	חֹן
	את	חַנּוֹת	תָּחֹנִּי	חֹנִּי
	הוא	חָנַן	יָחֹן	
	היא	חָנְנָה	תָּחֹן	

הווה			עבר	עתיד	ציווי
		אנחנו	חַנּוֹנוּ	נָחֹן	
יחיד	חוֹנֵן	אתם	חַנּוֹתֶם	תָּחֹנּוּ	חֹנּוּ
יחידה	חוֹנֶנֶת	אתן	חַנּוֹתֶן	תָּחֹנּוּ	חֹנּוּ
רבים	חוֹנְנִים	הם/ן	חָנְנוּ	יָחֹנּוּ	
רבות	חוֹנְנוֹת	(אתן/הן)		(תָּחֹנָּה)	(חֹנָּה)

ציווי	עתיד	עבר		בניין : פָּעַל
	אֶקְרָא	קָרָאתִי	אני	גזרה : נחי ל"א
קְרָא	תִּקְרָא	קָרָאתָ	אתה	שורש : ק-ר-א
קִרְאִי	תִּקְרְאִי	קָרָאת	את	שם פועל : לִקְרֹא
	יִקְרָא	קָרָא	הוא	מקור : קָרוֹא, קָרֹא
	תִּקְרָא	קָרְאָה	היא	
	נִקְרָא	קָרָאנוּ	אנחנו	**הווה**
קִרְאוּ	תִּקְרְאוּ	קְרָאתֶם	אתם	יחיד קוֹרֵא
קִרְאוּ	תִּקְרְאוּ	קְרָאתֶן	אתן	יחידה קוֹרֵאת
קִרְאוּ	יִקְרְאוּ	קָרְאוּ	הם/הן	רבים קוֹרְאִים
(קְרֶאנָה)	(תִּקְרֶאנָה)		(אתן/הן)	רבות קוֹרְאוֹת

ציווי	עתיד	עבר		בניין : פָּעַל
	אֶקְנֶה	קָנִיתִי	אני	גזרה : נחי ל"י (ל"ה)
קְנֵה	תִּקְנֶה	קָנִיתָ	אתה	שורש : ק-נ-י (ק-נ-ה)
קְנִי	תִּקְנִי	קָנִית	את	שם פועל : לִקְנוֹת
	יִקְנֶה	קָנָה	הוא	מקור : קָנֹה, קָנוֹת
	תִּקְנֶה	קָנְתָה	היא	
	נִקְנֶה	קָנִינוּ	אנחנו	**הווה**
קְנוּ	תִּקְנוּ	קְנִיתֶם	אתם	יחיד קוֹנֶה
קְנוּ	תִּקְנוּ	קְנִיתֶן	אתן	יחידה קוֹנָה
קְנוּ	יִקְנוּ	קָנוּ	הם/הן	רבים קוֹנִים
(קְנֶינָה)	(תִּקְנֶינָה)		(אתן/הן)	רבות קוֹנוֹת

בניין : נִפְעַל

ציווי	עתיד	עבר		בניין : נִפְעַל
	אֶבָּדֵק	נִבְדַּקְתִּי	אני	גזרה : שלמים
הִבָּדֵק	תִּבָּדֵק	נִבְדַּקְתָּ	אתה	שורש : ב-ד-ק
הִבָּדְקִי	תִּבָּדְקִי	נִבְדַּקְתְּ	את	שם פועל : לְהִבָּדֵק
	יִבָּדֵק	נִבְדַּק	הוא	מקור : נִבְדּוֹק, הִבָּדֵק
	תִּבָּדֵק	נִבְדְּקָה	היא	
	נִבָּדֵק	נִבְדַּקְנוּ	אנחנו	**הווה**
הִבָּדְקוּ	תִּבָּדְקוּ	נִבְדַּקְתֶּם	אתם	יחיד נִבְדָּק
הִבָּדְקוּ	תִּבָּדְקוּ	נִבְדַּקְתֶּן	אתן	יחידה נִבְדֶּקֶת
הִבָּדְקוּ	יִבָּדְקוּ	נִבְדְּקוּ	הם/הן	רבים נִבְדָּקִים
(הִבָּדַקְנָה)	(תִּבָּדַקְנָה)		(אתן/הן)	רבות נִבְדָּקוֹת

Table 1

בניין: נִפְעַל
שורש: ר-ד-מ
שם פועל: לְהֵרָדֵם

		עתיד	
נֵרָדֵם	אנחנו	אֵרָדֵם	אני
תֵּרָדְמוּ	אתם	תֵּרָדֵם	אתה
תֵּרָדְמוּ	אתן	תֵּרָדְמִי	את
יֵרָדְמוּ	הם/הן	יֵרָדֵם	הוא
(תֵּרָדַמְנָה)	(הן)	תֵּרָדֵם	היא

		ציווי	
את	הֵרָדְמִי	הֵרָדֵם	אתה
אתן	(הֵרָדַמְנָה)	הֵרָדְמוּ	אתם

Table 2

בניין: נִפְעַל
גזרה: שלמים, פ' גרונית א' ה' ע'
שורש: ה-ר-ג
שם פועל: לְהֵהָרֵג
מקור: נֶהֱרוֹג, הֵהָרֵג

ציווי	עתיד	עבר	
	אֵהָרֵג	נֶהֱרַגְתִּי	אני
הֵהָרֵג	תֵּהָרֵג	נֶהֱרַגְתָּ	אתה
הֵהָרְגִי	תֵּהָרְגִי	נֶהֱרַגְתְּ	את
	יֵהָרֵג	נֶהֱרַג	הוא
	תֵּהָרֵג	נֶהֶרְגָה	היא
	נֵהָרֵג	נֶהֱרַגְנוּ	אנחנו
הֵהָרְגוּ	תֵּהָרְגוּ	נֶהֱרַגְתֶּם	אתם
הֵהָרְגוּ	תֵּהָרְגוּ	נֶהֱרַגְתֶּן	אתן
יֵהָרְגוּ	יֵהָרְגוּ	נֶהֶרְגוּ	הם/הן
(הֵהָרַגְנָה)	(תֵּהָרַגְנָה)	(אתן/הן)	

	הווה	
נֶהֱרָג	יחיד
נֶהֱרֶגֶת	יחידה
נֶהֱרָגִים	רבים
נֶהֱרָגוֹת	רבות

Table 3

בניין: נִפְעַל (some verbs)
גזרה: שלמים, פ' גרונית ח'
שורש: ח-ק-ר
שם פועל: לְהֵחָקֵר
מקור: נֶחְקוֹר, הֵחָקֵר

ציווי	עתיד	עבר	
	אֵחָקֵר	נֶחְקַרְתִּי	אני
הֵחָקֵר	תֵּחָקֵר	נֶחְקַרְתָּ	אתה
הֵחָקְרִי	תֵּחָקְרִי	נֶחְקַרְתְּ	את
	יֵחָקֵר	נֶחְקַר	הוא
	תֵּחָקֵר	נֶחְקְרָה	היא
	נֵחָקֵר	נֶחְקַרְנוּ	אנחנו
הֵחָקְרוּ	תֵּחָקְרוּ	נֶחְקַרְתֶּם	אתם
הֵחָקְרוּ	תֵּחָקְרוּ	נֶחְקַרְתֶּן	אתן
יֵחָקְרוּ	יֵחָקְרוּ	נֶחְקְרוּ	הם/הן
(הֵחָקַרְנָה)	(תֵּחָקַרְנָה)	(אתן/הן)	

	הווה	
נֶחְקָר	יחיד
נֶחְקֶרֶת	יחידה
נֶחְקָרִים	רבים
נֶחְקָרוֹת	רבות

Table 1

הווה		עתיד		בניין : נִפְעַל, ע׳ גרונית
נִשְׁאָר	יחיד	תִּשָּׁאֲרִי	את	שורש : ש-א-ר
נִשְׁאֶרֶת	יחידה	תִּשָּׁאֲרוּ	אתם	שם פועל : לְהִשָּׁאֵר
		יִשָּׁאֲרוּ	הם/הן	

עבר		צֵיווי	
הִשָּׁאֲרִי	את	נִשְׁאֲרָה	היא
הִשָּׁאֲרוּ	אתם/ן	נִשְׁאֲרוּ	הם/הן

Table 2

הווה		עתיד		בניין : נִפְעַל, ל׳ גרונית
נִפְגָּע	יחיד	אֶפָּגַע	אני	שורש : פ-ג-ע
נִפְגַּעַת	יחידה	תִּפָּגַע	אתה	שם פועל : לְהִפָּגַע
		יִפָּגַע	הוא	
		תִּפָּגַע	היא	
		נִפָּגַע	אנחנו	

עבר		צֵיווי	
נִפְגַּעְתִּי	אני	הִפָּגַע	אתה
נִפְגַּע	הוא		

Table 3

בניין : נִפְעַל — גזרה : פ"י — שורש : י-ל-ד — שם פועל : לְהִוָּלֵד — מקור : נוֹלֹד, הִוָּלֵד

צֵיווי	עתיד	עבר	
	אֶוָּלֵד	נוֹלַדְתִּי	אני
הִוָּלֵד	תִּוָּלֵד	נוֹלַדְתָּ	אתה
הִוָּלְדִי	תִּוָּלְדִי	נוֹלַדְתְּ	את
	יִוָּלֵד	נוֹלַד	הוא
	תִּוָּלֵד	נוֹלְדָה	היא
	נִוָּלֵד	נוֹלַדְנוּ	אנחנו
הִוָּלְדוּ	תִּוָּלְדוּ	נוֹלַדְתֶּם	אתם
הִוָּלְדוּ	תִּוָּלְדוּ	נוֹלַדְתֶּן	אתן
יִוָּלְדוּ	יִוָּלְדוּ	נוֹלְדוּ	הם/ן
(הִוָּלַדְנָה)	(תִּוָּלַדְנָה)		(אתן/הן)

הווה

נוֹלָד		יחיד
נוֹלֶדֶת		יחידה
נוֹלָדִים		רבים
נוֹלָדוֹת		רבות

Table 4

בניין : נִפְעַל — גזרה : חסרי פ"נ — שורש : נ-צ-ל — שם פועל : לְהִנָּצֵל — מקור : נִצוֹל, הִנָּצֵל

צֵיווי	עתיד	עבר	
	אֶנָּצֵל	נִצַּלְתִּי	אני
הִנָּצֵל	תִּנָּצֵל	נִצַּלְתָּ	אתה
הִנָּצְלִי	תִּנָּצְלִי	נִצַּלְתְּ	את
	יִנָּצֵל	נִצַּל	הוא
	תִּנָּצֵל	נִצְּלָה	היא
	נִנָּצֵל	נִצַּלְנוּ	אנחנו
הִנָּצְלוּ	תִּנָּצְלוּ	נִצַּלְתֶּם	אתם
הִנָּצְלוּ	תִּנָּצְלוּ	נִצַּלְתֶּן	אתן
יִנָּצְלוּ	יִנָּצְלוּ	נִצְּלוּ	הם/ן
(הִנָּצַלְנָה)	(תִּנָּצַלְנָה)		(אתן/הן)

הווה

נִצָּל		יחיד
נִצֶּלֶת		יחידה
נִצָּלִים		רבים
נִצָּלוֹת		רבות

Table 1

ציווי	עתיד	עבר	
	אֶסוֹג	נְסוֹגוֹתִי	*אני*
הִסוֹג	תִּסוֹג	נְסוֹגוֹתָ	*אתה*
הִסוֹגִי	תִּסוֹגִי	נְסוֹגוֹת	*את*
	יִסוֹג	נָסוֹג	*הוא*
	תִּסוֹג	נָסוֹגָה	*היא*
	נִסוֹג	נְסוֹגוֹנוּ	*אנחנו*
הִסוֹגוּ	תִּסוֹגוּ	נְסוֹגוֹתֶם	*אתם*
הִסוֹגוּ	תִּסוֹגוּ	נְסוֹגוֹתֶן	*אתן*
יִסוֹגוּ	יִסוֹגוּ	נָסוֹגוּ	*הם/הן*
(הִסוֹגְנָה)	(תִּסוֹגְנָה)		*(אתן/הן)*

בניין : נִפְעַל
גזרה : ע"ו
שורש : ס-ו-ג
שם פועל : לְהִסוֹג
מקור : נָסוֹג, הִסוֹג

הווה		
נָסוֹג		*יחיד*
נְסוֹגָה		*יחידה*
נְסוֹגִים		*רבים*
נְסוֹגוֹת		*רבות*

Table 2

ציווי	עתיד	עבר	
	אֶמָּצֵא	נִמְצֵאתִי	*אני*
הִמָּצֵא	תִּמָּצֵא	נִמְצֵאתָ	*אתה*
הִמָּצְאִי	תִּמָּצְאִי	נִמְצֵאת	*את*
	אֶמָּצֵא	נִמְצָא	*הוא*
	תִּמָּצֵא	נִמְצְאָה	*היא*
	נִמָּצֵא	נִמְצֵאנוּ	*אנחנו*
הִמָּצְאוּ	תִּמָּצְאוּ	נִמְצֵאתֶם	*אתם*
הִמָּצְאוּ	תִּמָּצְאוּ	נִמְצֵאתֶן	*אתן*
	יִמָּצְאוּ	נִמְצְאוּ	*הם/הן*
(הִמָּצֶאנָה)	(תִּמָּצֶאנָה)		*(אתן/הן)*

בניין : נִפְעַל
גזרה : נחי ל"א
שורש : מ-צ-א
שם פועל : לְהִמָּצֵא
מקור : נִמְצוֹא, הִמָּצֵא

הווה		
נִמְצָא		*יחיד*
נִמְצֵאת		*יחידה*
נִמְצָאִים		*רבים*
נִמְצָאוֹת		*רבות*

Table 3

ציווי	עתיד	עבר	
	אֶבָּנֶה	נִבְנֵיתִי	*אני*
הִבָּנֶה	תִּבָּנֶה	נִבְנֵיתָ	*אתה*
הִבָּנִי	תִּבָּנִי	נִבְנֵית	*את*
	יִבָּנֶה	נִבְנָה	*הוא*
	תִּבָּנֶה	נִבְנְתָה	*היא*
	נִבָּנֶה	נִבְנֵינוּ	*אנחנו*
הִבָּנוּ	תִּבָּנוּ	נִבְנֵיתֶם	*אתם*
הִבָּנוּ	תִּבָּנוּ	נִבְנֵיתֶן	*אתן*
	יִבָּנוּ	נִבְנוּ	*הם/הן*
(הִבָּנֶינָה)	(תִּבָּנֶינָה)		*(אתן/הן)*

בניין : נִפְעַל
נחי ל"י (ל"ה)
שורש : ב-נ-י (ב-נ-ה)
שם פועל : לְהִבָּנוֹת
מקור : הִבָּנֶה, הִבָּנוֹת

הווה		
נִבְנֶה		*יחיד*
נִבְנֵית		*יחידה*
נִבְנִים		*רבים*
נִבְנוֹת		*רבות*

בניין: פִּעֵל

ציווי	עתיד	עבר		
				בניין: פִּעֵל
	אֲדַבֵּר	דִּבַּרְתִּי	אני	גזרה: שלמים
דַבֵּר	תְּדַבֵּר	דִּבַּרְתָּ	אתה	שורש: ד-ב-ר
דַבְּרִי	תְּדַבְּרִי	דִּבַּרְתְּ	את	שם פועל: לְדַבֵּר
	יְדַבֵּר	דִּבֵּר	הוא	מקור: דַבֵּר
	תְּדַבֵּר	דִּבְּרָה	היא	
	נְדַבֵּר	דִּבַּרְנוּ	אנחנו	**הווה**
דַבְּרוּ	תְּדַבְּרוּ	דִּבַּרְתֶּם	אתם	יחיד מְדַבֵּר
דַבְּרוּ	תְּדַבְּרוּ	דִּבַּרְתֶּן	אתן	יחידה מְדַבֶּרֶת
דַבְּרוּ	יְדַבְּרוּ	דִּבְּרוּ	הם/הן	רבים מְדַבְּרִים
(דַבֵּרְנָה)	(תְּדַבֵּרְנָה)		(אתן/הן)	רבות מְדַבְּרוֹת

ציווי	עתיד	עבר		
				בניין: פִּעֵל
	אֲבָרֵךְ	בֵּרַכְתִּי	אני	גזרה: שלמים
בָּרֵךְ	תְּבָרֵךְ	בֵּרַכְתָּ	אתה	שורש: ב-ר-כ
בָּרְכִי	תְּבָרְכִי	בֵּרַכְתְּ	את	שם פועל: לְבָרֵךְ
	יְבָרֵךְ	בֵּרֵךְ	הוא	מקור: בָּרֵךְ
	תְּבָרֵךְ	בֵּרְכָה	היא	
	נְבָרֵךְ	בֵּרַכְנוּ	אנחנו	**הווה**
בָּרְכוּ	תְּבָרְכוּ	בֵּרַכְתֶּם	אתם	יחיד מְבָרֵךְ
בָּרְכוּ	תְּבָרְכוּ	בֵּרַכְתֶּן	אתן	יחידה מְבָרֶכֶת
בָּרְכוּ	יְבָרְכוּ	בֵּרְכוּ	הם/הן	רבים מְבָרְכִים
(בָּרֵכְנָה)	(תְּבָרֵכְנָה)		(אתן/הן)	רבות מְבָרְכוֹת

הווה		עתיד		בניין: פִּעֵל גזרה: שלמים, ע' גרונית
מְנַהֲלִים	רבים	תְּנַהֲלִי	את	שורש: נ-ה-ל
מְנַהֲלוֹת	רבות	תְּנַהֲלוּ	אתם	שם פועל: לְנַהֵל
		יְנַהֲלוּ	הס/הן	

ציווי		עבר	
נַהֲלִי	את	נִהֲלָה	היא
נַהֲלוּ	אתם/ן	נִהֲלוּ	הס/הן

Table 1

בניין : פִּעֵל   גזרה : שלמים, ל׳ גרונית ח׳ ע׳
שורש : נ-צ-ח
שם פועל : לְנַצֵחַ

הווה		עתיד	
מְנַצֵחַ	*יחיד*	אֲנַצֵחַ	*אני*
מְנַצַחַת	*יחידה*	תְּנַצֵחַ	*אתה*
		יְנַצֵחַ	*הוא*
		תְּנַצֵחַ	*היא*
		נְנַצֵחַ	*אנחנו*

עבר		ציווי	
נִצַחְתִּי	*אני*	נַצֵחַ	*אתה*
נִצַח	*הוא*	נַצַח	

Table 2

בניין : פִּעֵל
גזרה : עו״י, כפולים (ע״ע)
שורש : ק-ו-מ (=ק-מ-מ)
מקור : קוֹמֵם

הווה	
מְקוֹמֵם	*יחיד*
מְקוֹמֶמֶת	*יחידה*
מְקוֹמְמִים	*רבים*
מְקוֹמְמוֹת	*רבות*

ציווי	עתיד	עבר	
	אֲקוֹמֵם	קוֹמַמְתִּי	*אני*
קוֹמֵם	תְּקוֹמֵם	קוֹמַמְתָּ	*אתה*
קוֹמְמִי	תְּקוֹמְמִי	קוֹמַמְתְּ	*את*
	יְקוֹמֵם	קוֹמֵם	*הוא*
	תְּקוֹמֵם	קוֹמְמָה	*היא*
	נְקוֹמֵם	קוֹמַמְנוּ	*אנחנו*
קוֹמְמוּ	תְּקוֹמְמוּ	קוֹמַמְתֶּם	*אתם*
קוֹמְמוּ	תְּקוֹמְמוּ	קוֹמַמְתֶּן	*אתן*
	יְקוֹמְמוּ	קוֹמְמוּ	*הם/הן*
(קוֹמֵמְנָה)	(תְּקוֹמֵמְנָה)		*(אתן/הן)*

Table 3

בניין : פִּעֵל
גזרה : נחי ל״א
שורש : מ-ל-א
שם פועל : לְמַלֵא
מקור : מַלֵא

הווה	
מְמַלֵא	*יחיד*
מְמַלֵאת	*יחידה*
מְמַלְאִים	*רבים*
מְמַלְאוֹת	*רבות*

ציווי	עתיד	עבר	
	אֲמַלֵא	מִלֵּאתִי	*אני*
מַלֵא	תְּמַלֵא	מִלֵּאתָ	*אתה*
מַלְאִי	תְּמַלְאִי	מִלֵּאת	*את*
	יְמַלֵא	מִלֵּא	*הוא*
	תְּמַלֵא	מִלְּאָה	*היא*
	נְמַלֵא	מִלֵּאנוּ	*אנחנו*
מַלְאוּ	תְּמַלְאוּ	מִלֵּאתֶם	*אתם*
מַלְאוּ	תְּמַלְאוּ	מִלֵּאתֶן	*אתן*
	יְמַלְאוּ	מִלְּאוּ	*הם/הן*
(מַלֶּאנָה)	(תְּמַלֶּאנָה)		*(אתן/הן)*

ציווי	עתיד	עבר		בניין : פִּעֵל
	אֲחַכֶּה	חִכִּיתִי	אני	גזרה : נחי ל"י (ל"ה)
חַכֵּה	תְּחַכֶּה	חִכִּיתָ	אתה	שורש : ח-כ-י (ח-כ-ה)
חַכִּי	תְּחַכִּי	חִכִּית	את	שם פועל : לְחַכּוֹת
	יְחַכֶּה	חִכָּה	הוא	מקור : חַכּוֹת
	תְּחַכֶּה	חִכְּתָה	היא	
	נְחַכֶּה	חִכִּינוּ	אנחנו	**הווה**
חַכּוּ	תְּחַכּוּ	חִכִּיתֶם	אתם	יחיד　מְחַכֶּה
חַכּוּ	תְּחַכּוּ	חִכִּיתֶן	אתן	יחידה　מְחַכָּה
	יְחַכּוּ	חִכּוּ	הם/ן	רבים　מְחַכִּים
(חַכֶּינָה)	(תְּחַכֶּינָה)		(אתן/הן)	רבות　מְחַכּוֹת

ציווי	עתיד	עבר		בניין : פִּעֵל
	אֲגַלְגֵּל	גִּלְגַּלְתִּי	אני	גזרה : מרובעים, שלמים
גַּלְגֵּל	תְּגַלְגֵּל	גִּלְגַּלְתָּ	אתה	שורש : ג-ל-ג-ל
גַּלְגְּלִי	תְּגַלְגְּלִי	גִּלְגַּלְתְּ	את	שם פועל : לְגַלְגֵּל
	יְגַלְגֵּל	גִּלְגֵּל	הוא	מקור : גַּלְגֵּל
	תְּגַלְגֵּל	גִּלְגְּלָה	היא	
	נְגַלְגֵּל	גִּלְגַּלְנוּ	אנחנו	**הווה**
גַּלְגְּלוּ	תְּגַלְגְּלוּ	גִּלְגַּלְתֶּם	אתם	יחיד　מְגַלְגֵּל
גַּלְגְּלוּ	תְּגַלְגְּלוּ	גִּלְגַּלְתֶּן	אתן	יחידה　מְגַלְגֶּלֶת
	יְגַלְגְּלוּ	גִּלְגְּלוּ	הם/ן	רבים　מְגַלְגְּלִים
(גַּלְגֵּלְנָה)	(תְּגַלְגֵּלְנָה)		(אתן/הן)	רבות　מְגַלְגְּלוֹת

בניין : פָּעַל

עתיד	עבר		בניין : פָּעַל
אֲבַטֵּל	בִּטַּלְתִּי	אני	גזרה : שלמים
תְּבַטֵּל	בִּטַּלְתָּ	אתה	
תְּבַטְּלִי	בִּטַּלְתְּ	את	שורש : ב-ט-ל
יְבַטֵּל	בִּטֵּל	הוא	
תְּבַטֵּל	בִּטְּלָה	היא	מקור : בִּטּוּל
נְבַטֵּל	בִּטַּלְנוּ	אנחנו	**הווה**
תְּבַטְּלוּ	בִּטַּלְתֶּם	אתם	יחיד　מְבַטֵּל
תְּבַטְּלוּ	בִּטַּלְתֶּן	אתן	יחידה　מְבַטֶּלֶת
יְבַטְּלוּ	בִּטְּלוּ	הם/ן	רבים　מְבַטְּלִים
(תְּבַטֵּלְנָה)		(אתן/הן)	רבות　מְבַטְּלוֹת

Table 1

	עתיד	עבר
בניין : פָּעַל		
גזרה : שלמים, ע׳ גרונית		
שורש : ת-א-מ		

	עתיד	עבר	
	אֶתְאַם	תֵּאַמְתִּי	אני
	תֵּתְאַם	תֵּאַמְתָּ	אתה
	תֵּתְאֲמִי	תֵּאַמְתְּ	את
	יְתְאַם	תֵּאַם	הוא
	תֵּתְאַם	תֵּאֲמָה	היא
	נְתְאַם	תֵּאַמְנוּ	אנחנו
	תֵּתְאֲמוּ	תֵּאַמְתֶּם	אתם
	תֵּתְאֲמוּ	תֵּאַמְתֶּן	אתן
	יְתְאֲמוּ	תֵּאֲמוּ	הם/ן
	(תֵּתְאַמְנָה)		(אתן/הן)

הווה		
מְתְאַם	יחיד
מְתְאֶמֶת	יחידה
מְתְאֲמִים	רבים
מְתְאֲמוֹת	רבות

Table 2

	עתיד	עבר
בניין : פָּעַל		
גזרה : עו״י, כפולים (ע״ע)		
שורש : ק-ו-מ (=ק-מ-מ)		

	עתיד	עבר	
	אֲקוֹמֵם	קוֹמַמְתִּי	אני
	תְּקוֹמֵם	קוֹמַמְתָּ	אתה
	תְּקוֹמְמִי	קוֹמַמְתְּ	את
	יְקוֹמֵם	קוֹמֵם	הוא
	תְּקוֹמֵם	קוֹמְמָה	היא
	נְקוֹמֵם	קוֹמַמְנוּ	אנחנו
	תְּקוֹמְמוּ	קוֹמַמְתֶּם	אתם
	תְּקוֹמְמוּ	קוֹמַמְתֶּן	אתן
	יְקוֹמְמוּ	קוֹמְמוּ	הם/ן
	(תְּקוֹמַמְנָה)		(אתן/הן)

הווה		
מְקוֹמֵם	יחיד
מְקוֹמֶמֶת	יחידה
מְקוֹמְמִים	רבים
מְקוֹמְמוֹת	רבות

Table 3

	עתיד	עבר
בניין : פָּעַל		
גזרה : נחי ל״א		
שורש : ד-כ-א		

	עתיד	עבר	
	אֲדַכֵּא	דִּכֵּאתִי	אני
	תְּדַכֵּא	דִּכֵּאתָ	אתה
	תְּדַכְּאִי	דִּכֵּאת	את
	יְדַכֵּא	דִּכֵּא	הוא
	תְּדַכֵּא	דִּכְּאָה	היא
	נְדַכֵּא	דִּכֵּאנוּ	אנחנו
	תְּדַכְּאוּ	דִּכֵּאתֶם	אתם
	תְּדַכְּאוּ	דִּכֵּאתֶן	אתן
	יְדַכְּאוּ	דִּכְּאוּ	הם/ן
	(תְּדַכֶּאנָה)		(אתן/הן)

הווה		
מְדַכֵּא	יחיד
מְדַכֵּאת	יחידה
מְדַכְּאִים	רבים
מְדַכְּאוֹת	רבות

עתיד	עבר		בניין : פִּעֵל
אֲזַכֶּה	זִכֵּיתִי	אני	גזרה : נחי ל״י (ל״ה)
תְּזַכֶּה	זִכֵּיתָ	אתה	שורש : ז-כ-י (ז-כ-ה)
תְּזַכִּי	זִכֵּית	את	
יְזַכֶּה	זִכָּה	הוא	
תְּזַכֶּה	זִכְּתָה	היא	
נְזַכֶּה	זִכֵּינוּ	אנחנו	**הווה**
תְּזַכּוּ	זִכֵּיתֶם	אתם	יחיד	מְזַכֶּה
תְּזַכּוּ	זִכֵּיתֶן	אתן	יחידה	מְזַכָּה
יְזַכּוּ	זִכּוּ	הם/ן	רבים	מְזַכִּים
(תְּזַכֶּינָה)	(אתן/הן)		רבות	מְזַכּוֹת

עתיד	עבר		בניין : פִּעֵל
אֲפַרְסֵם	פִּרְסַמְתִּי	אני	גזרה : שלמים, מרובעים
תְּפַרְסֵם	פִּרְסַמְתָּ	אתה	שורש : פ-ר-ס-מ
תְּפַרְסְמִי	פִּרְסַמְתְּ	את	
יְפַרְסֵם	פִּרְסֵם	הוא	
תְּפַרְסֵם	פִּרְסְמָה	היא	
נְפַרְסֵם	פִּרְסַמְנוּ	אנחנו	**הווה**
תְּפַרְסְמוּ	פִּרְסַמְתֶּם	אתם	יחיד	מְפַרְסֵם
תְּפַרְסְמוּ	פִּרְסַמְתֶּן	אתן	יחידה	מְפַרְסֶמֶת
יְפַרְסְמוּ	פִּרְסְמוּ	הם/ן	רבים	מְפַרְסְמִים
(תְּפַרְסֵמְנָה)	(אתן/הן)		רבות	מְפַרְסְמוֹת

בניין : הִתְפַּעֵל

ציווי	עתיד	עבר		בניין : הִתְפַּעֵל
	אֶתְלַבֵּש	הִתְלַבַּשְׁתִּי	אני	גזרה : שלמים
הִתְלַבֵּש	תִּתְלַבֵּש	הִתְלַבַּשְׁתָּ	אתה	שורש : ל-ב-ש
הִתְלַבְּשִׁי	תִּתְלַבְּשִׁי	הִתְלַבַּשְׁתְּ	את	שם פועל : לְהִתְלַבֵּש
	יִתְלַבֵּש	הִתְלַבֵּש	הוא	מקור : הִתְלַבֵּש
	תִּתְלַבֵּש	הִתְלַבְּשָׁה	היא	
	נִתְלַבֵּש	הִתְלַבַּשְׁנוּ	אנחנו	**הווה**
הִתְלַבְּשׁוּ	תִּתְלַבְּשׁוּ	הִתְלַבַּשְׁתֶּם	אתם	יחיד	מִתְלַבֵּש
הִתְלַבְּשׁוּ	תִּתְלַבְּשׁוּ	הִתְלַבַּשְׁתֶּן	אתן	יחידה	מִתְלַבֶּשֶׁת
הִתְלַבְּשׁוּ	יִתְלַבְּשׁוּ	הִתְלַבְּשׁוּ	הם/ן	רבים	מִתְלַבְּשִׁים
(הִתְלַבֵּשְׁנָה)	(תִּתְלַבֵּשְׁנָה)	(אתן/הן)		רבות	מִתְלַבְּשׁוֹת

ציווי	עתיד	עבר		בניין: הִתְפַּעֵל
	אֶסְתַּלֵּק	הִסְתַּלַּקְתִּי	אני	גזרה: שלמים, פ' = ס' שׂ' שׁ'
הִסְתַּלֵּק	תִּסְתַּלֵּק	הִסְתַּלַּקְתָּ	אתה	שורש: ס-ל-ק
הִסְתַּלְּקִי	תִּסְתַּלְּקִי	הִסְתַּלַּקְתְּ	את	שם פועל: לְהִסְתַּלֵּק
	יִסְתַּלֵּק	הִסְתַּלֵּק	הוא	מקור: הִסְתַּלֵּק
	תִּסְתַּלֵּק	הִסְתַּלְּקָה	היא	
	נִסְתַּלֵּק	הִסְתַּלַּקְנוּ	אנחנו	**הווה**
הִסְתַּלְּקוּ	תִּסְתַּלְּקוּ	הִסְתַּלַּקְתֶּם	אתם	יחיד מִסְתַּלֵּק
הִסְתַּלְּקוּ	תִּסְתַּלְּקוּ	הִסְתַּלַּקְתֶּן	אתן	יחידה מִסְתַּלֶּקֶת
	יִסְתַּלְּקוּ	הִסְתַּלְּקוּ	הם/הן	רבים מִסְתַּלְּקִים
(הִסְתַּלֵּקְנָה)	(תִּסְתַּלֵּקְנָה)		(אתן/הן)	רבות מִסְתַּלְּקוֹת

ציווי	עתיד	עבר		בניין: הִתְפַּעֵל
	אֶצְטַלֵּם	הִצְטַלַּמְתִּי	אני	גזרה: שלמים, פ' = צ
הִצְטַלֵּם	תִּצְטַלֵּם	הִצְטַלַּמְתָּ	אתה	שורש: צ-ל-מ
הִצְטַלְּמִי	תִּצְטַלְּמִי	הִצְטַלַּמְתְּ	את	שם פועל: לְהִצְטַלֵּם
	יִצְטַלֵּם	הִצְטַלֵּם	הוא	מקור: הִצְטַלֵּם
	תִּצְטַלֵּם	הִצְטַלְּמָה	היא	
	נִצְטַלֵּם	הִצְטַלַּמְנוּ	אנחנו	**הווה**
הִצְטַלְּמוּ	תִּצְטַלְּמוּ	הִצְטַלַּמְתֶּם	אתם	יחיד מִצְטַלֵּם
הִצְטַלְּמוּ	תִּצְטַלְּמוּ	הִצְטַלַּמְתֶּן	אתן	יחידה מִצְטַלֶּמֶת
	יִצְטַלְּמוּ	הִצְטַלְּמוּ	הם/הן	רבים מִצְטַלְּמִים
(הִצְטַלֵּמְנָה)	(תִּצְטַלֵּמְנָה)		(אתן/הן)	רבות מִצְטַלְּמוֹת

ציווי	עתיד	עבר		בניין: הִתְפַּעֵל
	אֶזְדַּקֵּק	הִזְדַּקַּקְתִּי	אני	גזרה: שלמים, פ' = ז
הִזְדַּקֵּק	תִּזְדַּקֵּק	הִזְדַּקַּקְתָּ	אתה	שורש: ז-ק-ק
הִזְדַּקְּקִי	תִּזְדַּקְּקִי	הִזְדַּקַּקְתְּ	את	שם פועל: לְהִזְדַּקֵּק
	יִזְדַּקֵּק	הִזְדַּקֵּק	הוא	מקור: הִזְדַּקֵּק
	תִּזְדַּקֵּק	הִזְדַּקְּקָה	היא	
	נִזְדַּקֵּק	הִזְדַּקַּקְנוּ	אנחנו	**הווה**
הִזְדַּקְּקוּ	תִּזְדַּקְּקוּ	הִזְדַּקַּקְתֶּם	אתם	יחיד מִזְדַּקֵּק
הִזְדַּקְּקוּ	תִּזְדַּקְּקוּ	הִזְדַּקַּקְתֶּן	אתן	יחידה מִזְדַּקֶּקֶת
	יִזְדַּקְּקוּ	הִזְדַּקְּקוּ	הם/הן	רבים מִזְדַּקְּקִים
(הִזְדַּקֵּקְנָה)	(תִּזְדַּקֵּקְנָה)		(אתן/הן)	רבות מִזְדַּקְּקוֹת

Table 1

בניין: הִתְפַּעֵל   גזרה: שלמים, ע׳ גרונית
שורש: נ-ה-ג
שם פועל: לְהִתְנַהֵג

עבר		ציווי	
הִיא	הִתְנַהֲגָה	אַת	הִתְנַהֲגִי
הֵם/הֵן	הִתְנַהֲגוּ	אַתֶּם/ן	הִתְנַהֲגוּ

	עתיד	הווה	
אַת	תִּתְנַהֲגִי	מִתְנַהֲגִים	רַבִּים
אַתֶּם	תִּתְנַהֲגוּ	מִתְנַהֲגוֹת	רַבּוֹת
הֵם/הֵן	יִתְנַהֲגוּ		

Table 2

בניין: הִתְפַּעֵל   גזרה: שלמים, ל׳ גרונית ח׳ ע׳
שורש: ק-ל-ח
שם פועל: לְהִתְקַלֵּחַ

עבר		ציווי	
אֲנִי	הִתְקַלַּחְתִּי	אַתָּה	הִתְקַלַּח
הוּא	הִתְקַלֵּחַ	אַתֶּן	(הִתְקַלַּחְנָה)

	עתיד	הווה	
אֲנִי	אֶתְקַלֵּחַ	מִתְקַלֵּחַ	יָחִיד
אַתָּה	תִּתְקַלֵּחַ	מִתְקַלַּחַת	יְחִידָה
הוּא	יִתְקַלֵּחַ		
הִיא	תִּתְקַלֵּחַ		
אֲנַחְנוּ	נִתְקַלֵּחַ		

Table 3

בניין: הִתְפַּעֵל
גזרה: ע״ו, כפולים (ע״ע)
שורש: ק-ו-מ (=ק-מ-מ)
שם פועל: לְהִתְקוֹמֵם
מקור: הִתְקוֹמֵם

	ציווי	עתיד	עבר
אֲנִי		אֶתְקוֹמֵם	הִתְקוֹמַמְתִּי
אַתָּה	הִתְקוֹמֵם	תִּתְקוֹמֵם	הִתְקוֹמַמְתָּ
אַת	הִתְקוֹמְמִי	תִּתְקוֹמְמִי	הִתְקוֹמַמְתְּ
הוּא		יִתְקוֹמֵם	הִתְקוֹמֵם
הִיא		תִּתְקוֹמֵם	הִתְקוֹמְמָה
אֲנַחְנוּ		נִתְקוֹמֵם	הִתְקוֹמַמְנוּ
אַתֶּם	הִתְקוֹמְמוּ	תִּתְקוֹמְמוּ	הִתְקוֹמַמְתֶּם
אַתֶּן	הִתְקוֹמְמוּ	תִּתְקוֹמֵמְןָ	הִתְקוֹמַמְתֶּן
הֵם/ן		יִתְקוֹמְמוּ	הִתְקוֹמְמוּ
(אַתֶּן/הֵן)	(הִתְקוֹמֵמְנָה)	(תִּתְקוֹמֵמְנָה)	

	הווה
יָחִיד	מִתְקוֹמֵם
יְחִידָה	מִתְקוֹמֶמֶת
רַבִּים	מִתְקוֹמְמִים
רַבּוֹת	מִתְקוֹמְמוֹת

Table 4

בניין: הִתְפַּעֵל
גזרה: נחי ל״א
שורש: פ-ל-א
שם פועל: לְהִתְפַּלֵּא
מקור: הִתְפַּלֵּא

	ציווי	עתיד	עבר
אֲנִי		אֶתְפַּלֵּא	הִתְפַּלֵּאתִי
אַתָּה	הִתְפַּלֵּא	תִּתְפַּלֵּא	הִתְפַּלֵּאתָ
אַת	הִתְפַּלְאִי	תִּתְפַּלְאִי	הִתְפַּלֵּאת
הוּא		יִתְפַּלֵּא	הִתְפַּלֵּא
הִיא		תִּתְפַּלֵּא	הִתְפַּלְאָה
אֲנַחְנוּ		נִתְפַּלֵּא	הִתְפַּלֵּאנוּ
אַתֶּם	הִתְפַּלְאוּ	תִּתְפַּלְאוּ	הִתְפַּלֵּאתֶם
אַתֶּן	הִתְפַּלְאוּ	תִּתְפַּלְאוּ	הִתְפַּלֵּאתֶן
הֵם/ן		יִתְפַּלְאוּ	הִתְפַּלְאוּ
(אַתֶּן/הֵן)	(הִתְפַּלֶּאנָה)	(תִּתְפַּלֶּאנָה)	

	הווה
יָחִיד	מִתְפַּלֵּא
יְחִידָה	מִתְפַּלֵּאת
רַבִּים	מִתְפַּלְאִים
רַבּוֹת	מִתְפַּלְאוֹת

ציווי	עתיד	עבר		בניין : הִתְפַּעֵל
	אֶתְגַּלֶּה	הִתְגַּלֵּיתִי	אני	גזרה : נחי ל״י (ל״ה)
הִתְגַּלֵּה	תִּתְגַּלֶּה	הִתְגַּלֵּיתָ	אתה	שורש : ג-ל-י (ג-ל-ה)
הִתְגַּלִּי	תִּתְגַּלִּי	הִתְגַּלֵּית	את	שם פועל : לְהִתְגַּלּוֹת
	יִתְגַּלֶּה	הִתְגַּלָּה	הוא	מקור : הִתְגַּלֶּה, הִתְגַּלּוֹת
	תִּתְגַּלֶּה	הִתְגַּלְּתָה	היא	
	נִתְגַּלֶּה	הִתְגַּלֵּינוּ	אנחנו	**הווה**
הִתְגַּלּוּ	תִּתְגַּלּוּ	הִתְגַּלֵּיתֶם	אתם	מִתְגַּלֶּה	יחיד
הִתְגַּלּוּ	תִּתְגַּלּוּ	הִתְגַּלֵּיתֶן	אתן	מִתְגַּלָּה	יחידה
	יִתְגַּלּוּ	הִתְגַּלּוּ	הס/ן	מִתְגַּלִּים	רבים
(הִתְגַּלֶּינָה)	(תִּתְגַּלֶּינָה)		(אתן/הן)	מִתְגַּלּוֹת	רבות

ציווי	עתיד	עבר		בניין : הִתְפַּעֵל
	אֶתְקַלְקֵל	הִתְקַלְקַלְתִּי	אני	גזרה : שלמים, מרובעים
הִתְקַלְקֵל	תִּתְקַלְקֵל	הִתְקַלְקַלְתָּ	אתה	שורש : ק-ל-ק-ל
הִתְקַלְקְלִי	תִּתְקַלְקְלִי	הִתְקַלְקַלְתְּ	את	שם פועל : לְהִתְקַלְקֵל
	יִתְקַלְקֵל	הִתְקַלְקֵל	הוא	מקור : הִתְקַלְקֵל
	תִּתְקַלְקֵל	הִתְקַלְקְלָה	היא	
	נִתְקַלְקֵל	הִתְקַלְקַלְנוּ	אנחנו	**הווה**
הִתְקַלְקְלוּ	תִּתְקַלְקְלוּ	הִתְקַלְקַלְתֶּם	אתם	מִתְקַלְקֵל	יחיד
הִתְקַלְקְלוּ	תִּתְקַלְקְלוּ	הִתְקַלְקַלְתֶּן	אתן	מִתְקַלְקֶלֶת	יחידה
	יִתְקַלְקְלוּ	הִתְקַלְקְלוּ	הס/ן	מִתְקַלְקְלִים	רבים
(הִתְקַלְקֵלְנָה)	(תִּתְקַלְקֵלְנָה)		(אתן/הן)	מִתְקַלְקְלוֹת	רבות

בניין : הִפְעִיל

ציווי	עתיד	עבר		בניין : הִפְעִיל
	אַכְנִיס	הִכְנַסְתִּי	אני	גזרה : שלמים
הַכְנֵס	תַּכְנִיס	הִכְנַסְתָּ	אתה	שורש : כ-נ-ס
הַכְנִיסִי	תַּכְנִיסִי	הִכְנַסְתְּ	את	שם פועל : לְהַכְנִיס
	יַכְנִיס	הִכְנִיס	הוא	מקור : הַכְנֵס, הַכְנִיס
	תַּכְנִיס	הִכְנִיסָה	היא	
	נַכְנִיס	הִכְנַסְנוּ	אנחנו	**הווה**
הַכְנִיסוּ	תַּכְנִיסוּ	הִכְנַסְתֶּם	אתם	מַכְנִיס	יחיד
הַכְנִיסוּ	תַּכְנִיסוּ	הִכְנַסְתֶּן	אתן	מַכְנִיסָה	יחידה
	יַכְנִיסוּ	הִכְנִיסוּ	הס/ן	מַכְנִיסִים	רבים
(הַכְנֵסְנָה)	(תַּכְנֵסְנָה)		(אתן/הן)	מַכְנִיסוֹת	רבות

Table 1

בניין: הפעיל			
גזרה: שלמים, פי גרונית א׳ ה׳ ח׳ ע׳			
שורש: ע-ס-ק			
שם פועל: להעסיק			
מקור: העסק, העסיק			

ציווי	עתיד	עבר	
	אעסיק	הֶעֱסַקְתִּי	אני
הַעֲסֵק	תַּעֲסִיק	הֶעֱסַקְתָּ	אתה
הַעֲסִיקִי	תַּעֲסִיקִי	הֶעֱסַקְתְּ	את
	יַעֲסִיק	הֶעֱסִיק	הוא
	תַּעֲסִיק	הֶעֱסִיקָה	היא
	נַעֲסִיק	הֶעֱסַקְנוּ	אנחנו
הַעֲסִיקוּ	תַּעֲסִיקוּ	הֶעֱסַקְתֶּם	אתם
הַעֲסִיקוּ	תַּעֲסִיקוּ	הֶעֱסַקְתֶּן	אתן
הַעֲסִיקוּ	יַעֲסִיקוּ	הֶעֱסִיקוּ	הם/ן
(הַעֲסֵקְנָה)	(תַּעֲסֵקְנָה)		(אתן/הן)

הווה		
מַעֲסִיק	יחיד
מַעֲסִיקָה	יחידה
מַעֲסִיקִים	רבים
מַעֲסִיקוֹת	רבות

Table 2

בניין: הפעיל   גזרה: שלמים, פי גרונית
שורש: ח-ל-ט
שם פועל: להחליט

		עבר	
הֶחְלַטְנוּ	אנחנו	הֶחְלַטְתִּי	אני
הֶחְלַטְתֶּם	אתם	הֶחְלַטְתָּ	אתה
הֶחְלַטְתֶּן	אתן	הֶחְלַטְתְּ	את
הֶחְלִיטוּ	הם/ן	הֶחְלִיט	הוא
		הֶחְלִיטָה	היא

ציווי		הווה	
הַחְלֵט	אתה	מַחְלִיט	הוא
הַחְלִיטוּ	אתם/ן	מַחְלִיטָה	היא

Table 3

בניין: הפעיל גזרה: שלמים, ל׳ גרונית
שורש: ב-ט-ח
שם פועל: להבטיח

הווה		עתיד	
מַבְטִיחַ	יחיד	אַבְטִיחַ	אני
מַבְטִיחָה	יחידה	תַּבְטִיחַ	אתה
		יַבְטִיחַ	הוא
		תַּבְטִיחַ	היא
		נַבְטִיחַ	אנחנו

ציווי		עבר	
הַבְטַח	אתה	הִבְטַחְתִּי	אני
(הַבְטַחְנָה)	אתן	הִבְטִיחַ	הוא

Table 4

בניין: הפעיל			
גזרה: נחי פ״י			
שורש: י-ר-ד			
שם פועל: להוריד			
מקור: הוֹרֵד, הוֹרִיד			

ציווי	עתיד	עבר	
	אוֹרִיד	הוֹרַדְתִּי	אני
הוֹרֵד	תּוֹרִיד	הוֹרַדְתָּ	אתה
הוֹרִידִי	תּוֹרִידִי	הוֹרַדְתְּ	את
	יוֹרִיד	הוֹרִיד	הוא
	תּוֹרִידָה	הוֹרִידָה	היא
	נוֹרִיד	הוֹרַדְנוּ	אנחנו
הוֹרִידוּ	תּוֹרִידוּ	הוֹרַדְתֶּם	אתם
הוֹרִידוּ	תּוֹרִידוּ	הוֹרַדְתֶּן	אתן
הוֹרִידוּ	יוֹרִידוּ	הוֹרִידוּ	הם/ן
(הוֹרֵדְנָה)	(תּוֹרֵדְנָה)		(אתן/הן)

הווה		
מוֹרִיד	יחיד
מוֹרִידָה	יחידה
מוֹרִידִים	רבים
מוֹרִידוֹת	רבות

בניין : הִפְעִיל
גזרה : חסרי פ״נ, פיי״צ
שורש : נ-פ-ל
שם פועל : לְהַפִּיל
מקור : הַפֵּל, הִפִּיל

ציווי	עתיד	עבר	
	אַפִּיל	הִפַּלְתִּי	אני
הַפֵּל	תַּפִּיל	הִפַּלְתָּ	אתה
הַפִּילִי	תַּפִּילִי	הִפַּלְתְּ	את
	יַפִּיל	הִפִּיל	הוא
	תַּפִּיל	הִפִּילָה	היא
	נַפִּיל	הִפַּלְנוּ	אנחנו
הַפִּילוּ	תַּפִּילוּ	הִפַּלְתֶּם	אתם
הַפִּילוּ	תַּפִּילוּ	הִפַּלְתֶּן	אתן
	יַפִּילוּ	הִפִּילוּ	הם/הן
(הַפֵּלְנָה)	(תַּפֵּלְנָה)		(אתן/הן)

הווה

מַפִּיל		יחיד
מַפִּילָה		יחידה
מַפִּילִים		רבים
מַפִּילוֹת		רבות

בניין : הִפְעִיל
גזרה : עו״י
שורש : ק-ו-מ
שם פועל : לְהָקִים
מקור : הָקֵם, הָקִים

ציווי	עתיד	עבר	
	אָקִים	הֲקַמְתִּי	אני
הָקֵם	תָּקִים	הֲקַמְתָּ	אתה
הָקִימִי	תָּקִימִי	הֲקַמְתְּ	את
	יָקִים	הֵקִים	הוא
	תָּקִים	הֵקִימָה	היא
	נָקִים	הֲקַמְנוּ	אנחנו
הָקִימוּ	תָּקִימוּ	הֲקַמְתֶּם	אתם
הָקִימוּ	תָּקִימוּ	הֲקַמְתֶּן	אתן
	יָקִימוּ	הֵקִימוּ	הם/הן
(הָקֵמְנָה)	(תָּקֵמְנָה)		(אתן/הן)

הווה

מֵקִים		יחיד
מְקִימָה		יחידה
מְקִימִים		רבים
מְקִימוֹת		רבות

בניין : הִפְעִיל
גזרה : כפולים (ע״ע)
שורש : ק-ל-ל
שם פועל : לְהָקֵל
מקור : הָקֵל

ציווי	עתיד	עבר	
	אָקֵל	הֵקַלְתִּי	אני
הָקֵל	תָּקֵל	הֵקַלְתָּ	אתה
הָקֵלִי	תָּקֵלִי	הֵקַלְתְּ	את
	יָקֵל	הֵקֵל	הוא
	תָּקֵל	הֵקֵלָה	היא
	נָקֵל	הֵקַלְנוּ	אנחנו
הָקֵלוּ	תָּקֵלוּ	הֵקַלְתֶּם	אתם
הָקֵלוּ	תָּקֵלוּ	הֵקַלְתֶּן	אתן
	יָקֵלוּ	הֵקֵלוּ	הם/הן
(הָקֵלְנָה)	(תָּקֵלְנָה)		(אתן/הן)

הווה

מֵקֵל		יחיד
מְקֵלָה		יחידה
מְקֵלִים		רבים
מְקֵלוֹת		רבות

בניין: הִפְעִיל

ציווי	עתיד	עבר		
	אַמְצִיא	הִמְצֵאתִי	אני	בניין: הִפְעִיל
הַמְצֵא	תַּמְצִיא	הִמְצֵאתָ	אתה	גזרה: נחי ל"א
הַמְצִיאִי	תַּמְצִיאִי	הִמְצֵאת	את	שורש: מ-צ-א
	יַמְצִיא	הִמְצִיא	הוא	שם פועל: לְהַמְצִיא
	תַּמְצִיא	הִמְצִיאָה	היא	מקור: הַמְצֵא, הַמְצִיא
	נַמְצִיא	הִמְצֵאנוּ	אנחנו	**הווה**
הַמְצִיאוּ	תַּמְצִיאוּ	הִמְצֵאתֶם	אתם	מַמְצִיא — יחיד
הַמְצִיאוּ	תַּמְצִיאוּ	הִמְצֵאתֶן	אתן	מַמְצִיאָה — יחידה
	יַמְצִיאוּ	הִמְצִיאוּ	הם/הן	מַמְצִיאִים — רבים
(הַמְצֶאנָה)	(תַּמְצֶאנָה)		(אתן/הן)	מַמְצִיאוֹת — רבות

ציווי	עתיד	עבר		
	אַרְשֶׁה	הִרְשֵׁיתִי	אני	בניין: הִפְעִיל
הַרְשֵׁה	תַּרְשֶׁה	הִרְשֵׁיתָ	אתה	גזרה: נחי ל"י (ל"ה)
הַרְשִׁי	תַּרְשִׁי	הִרְשֵׁית	את	שורש: ר-ש-ה
	יַרְשֶׁה	הִרְשָׁה	הוא	שם פועל: לְהַרְשׁוֹת
	תַּרְשֶׁה	הִרְשְׁתָה	היא	מקור: הַרְשֵׁה, הַרְשׁוֹת
	נַרְשֶׁה	הִרְשֵׁינוּ	אנחנו	**הווה**
הַרְשׁוּ	תַּרְשׁוּ	הִרְשֵׁיתֶם	אתם	מַרְשֶׁה — יחיד
הַרְשׁוּ	תַּרְשׁוּ	הִרְשֵׁיתֶן	אתן	מַרְשָׁה — יחידה
	יַרְשׁוּ	הִרְשׁוּ	הם/הן	מַרְשִׁים — רבים
(הַרְשֶׁינָה)	(תַּרְשֶׁינָה)		(אתן/הן)	מַרְשׁוֹת — רבות

בניין: הֻפְעַל

עתיד	עבר		
אֻגְבַּל	הֻגְבַּלְתִּי	אני	בניין: הֻפְעַל
תֻּגְבַּל	הֻגְבַּלְתָּ	אתה	גזרה: שלמים
תֻּגְבְּלִי	הֻגְבַּלְתְּ	את	שורש: ג-ב-ל
יֻגְבַּל	הֻגְבַּל	הוא	
תֻּגְבַּל	הֻגְבְּלָה	היא	מקור: הֻגְבַּל
נֻגְבַּל	הֻגְבַּלְנוּ	אנחנו	**הווה**
תֻּגְבְּלוּ	הֻגְבַּלְתֶּם	אתם	מֻגְבָּל — יחיד
תֻּגְבְּלוּ	הֻגְבַּלְתֶּן	אתן	מֻגְבֶּלֶת — יחידה
יֻגְבְּלוּ	הֻגְבְּלוּ	הם/הן	מֻגְבָּלִים — רבים
(תֻּגְבַּלְנָה)		(אתן/הן)	מֻגְבָּלוֹת — רבות

עתיד	עבר		בניין : הֻפְעַל
אֶעֱבַר	הָעֱבַרְתִּי	*אני*	גזרה : שלמים, פ׳ גרונית
תֻּעֱבַר	הָעֱבַרְתָּ	*אתה*	
תֻּעֲבְרִי	הָעֱבַרְתְּ	*את*	שורש : ע-ב-ר
יֻעֲבַר	הָעֱבַר	*הוא*	
תֻּעֲבַר	הָעֶבְרָה	*היא*	מקור : הָעֱבֵר
נֻעֲבַר	הָעֱבַרְנוּ	*אנחנו*	
			הווה
תֻּעֲבְרוּ	הָעֱבַרְתֶּם	*אתם*	מֻעֲבָר	*יחיד*
תֻּעֲבְרוּ	הָעֱבַרְתֶּן	*אתן*	מֻעֲבֶרֶת	*יחידה*
יֻעֲבְרוּ	הָעָבְרוּ	*הם/הן*	מֻעֲבָרִים	*רבים*
(תֻּעֲבַרְנָה)			מֻעֲבָרוֹת	*רבות*

	הווה		עתיד		בניין : פֻּעַל גזרה : שלמים, ע׳ גרונית
מֻזְהָרִים	*רבים*		תֻּזְהֲרִי	*את*	שורש : ז-ה-ר
מֻזְהָרוֹת	*רבות*		תֻּזְהֲרוּ	*אתם*	מקור : הֻזְהֵר
			יֻזְהֲרוּ	*הם/הן*	עבר
					הֻזְהֲרָה	*היא*
					הֻזְהֲרוּ	*הם/הן*

עתיד	עבר		בניין : הֻפְעַל
אֻפַּל	הֻפַּלְתִּי	*אני*	גזרה : חסרי פ״נ, פי״צ
תֻּפַּל	הֻפַּלְתָּ	*אתה*	
תֻּפְּלִי	הֻפַּלְתְּ	*את*	שורש : נ-פ-ל
יֻפַּל	הֻפַּל	*הוא*	
תֻּפַּל	הֻפְּלָה	*היא*	מקור : הֻפֵּל
נֻפַּל	הֻפַּלְנוּ	*אנחנו*	
			הווה
תֻּפְּלוּ	הֻפַּלְתֶּם	*אתם*	מֻפָּל	*יחיד*
תֻּפְּלוּ	הֻפַּלְתֶּן	*אתן*	מֻפֶּלֶת	*יחידה*
יֻפְּלוּ	הֻפְּלוּ	*הם/הן*	מֻפָּלִים	*רבים*
(תֻּפַּלְנָה)			מֻפָּלוֹת	*רבות*

עתיד	עבר		בניין : הֻפְעַל
אוּקַם	הוּקַמְתִּי	אני	גזרה : נחי פ"י, ע"י
תּוּקַם	הוּקַמְתָּ	אתה	שורש : ק-ו-מ
תּוּקְמִי	הוּקַמְתְּ	את	
יוּקַם	הוּקַם	הוא	מקור : הוּקַם
תּוּקַם	הוּקְמָה	היא	

			הווה
נוּקַם	הוּקַמְנוּ	אנחנו	
תּוּקְמוּ	הוּקַמְתֶּם	אתם	מוּקַם	יחיד
תּוּקְמוּ	הוּקַמְתֶּן	אתן	מוּקֶמֶת	יחידה
יוּקְמוּ	הוּקְמוּ	הם/ן	מוּקָמִים	רבים
(תּוּקַמְנָה)		(אתן/הן)	מוּקָמוֹת	רבות

עתיד	עבר		בניין : הֻפְעַל
אוּחַל	הוּחַלְתִּי	אני	גזרה : כפולים (ע"ע)
תּוּחַל	הוּחַלְתָּ	אתה	שורש : ח-ל-ל
תּוּחֲלִי	הוּחַלְתְּ	את	
יוּחַל	הוּחַל	הוא	מקור : הוּחַל
תּוּחַל	הוּחֲלָה	היא	

			הווה
נוּחַל	הוּחַלְנוּ	אנחנו	
תּוּחֲלוּ	הוּחַלְתֶּם	אתם	מוּחָל	יחיד
תּוּחֲלוּ	הוּחַלְתֶּן	אתן	מוּחֲלָה	יחידה
יוּחֲלוּ	הוּחֲלוּ	הם/ן	מוּחָלִים	רבים
(תּוּחַלְנָה)		(אתן/הן)	מוּחָלוֹת	רבות

עתיד	עבר		בניין : הֻפְעַל
אֻקְפָּא	הֻקְפֵּאתִי	אני	גזרה : נחי ל"א
תֻּקְפָּא	הֻקְפֵּאתָ	אתה	שורש : ק-פ-א
תֻּקְפְּאִי	הֻקְפֵּאת	את	
יֻקְפָּא	הֻקְפָּא	הוא	מקור : הֻקְפָּא
תֻּקְפָּא	הֻקְפְּאָה	היא	

			הווה
נֻקְפָּא	הֻקְפֵּאנוּ	אנחנו	
תֻּקְפְּאוּ	הֻקְפֵּאתֶם	אתם	מֻקְפָּא	יחיד
תֻּקְפְּאוּ	הֻקְפֵּאתֶן	אתן	מֻקְפֵּאת	יחידה
יֻקְפְּאוּ	הֻקְפְּאוּ	הם/ן	מֻקְפָּאִים	רבים
(תֻּקְפֶּאנָה)		(אתן/הן)	מֻקְפָּאוֹת	רבות

עתיד	עבר		בניין : הֻפְעַל
אֶפָּנֶה	הֻפְנֵיתִי	אני	גזרה : נחי ל״י (ל״ה)
תֻּפְנֶה	הֻפְנֵיתָ	אתה	שורש : פ-נ-י (פ-נ-ה)
תֻּפְנִי	הֻפְנֵית	את	
יֻפְנֶה	הֻפְנָה	הוא	מקור : הֻפְנֵה
תֻּפְנֶה	הֻפְנְתָה	היא	
נֻפְנֶה	הֻפְנֵינוּ	אנחנו	**הווה**
תֻּפְנוּ	הֻפְנֵיתֶם	אתם	*יחיד* מֻפְנֶה
תֻּפְנוּ	הֻפְנֵיתֶן	אתן	*יחידה* מֻפְנֵית
יֻפְנוּ	הֻפְנוּ	הם/ן	*רבים* מֻפְנִים
(תֻּפְנֶינָה)		(אתן/הן)	*רבות* מֻפְנוֹת

Summary Tables of Irregularities in Verbs

Abbreviations for root consonants: C_1=פה״פ, C_2=עה״פ, C_3=לה״פ

Group 1: Irregularities within the שלמים.

A. שלמים עם פ', כ', ב'
i. ב', כ', פ' realized as *b/k/p.*
1. When they are the first segment in the word:

בָּדַק, פּוֹחֵד, כְּתֹב	עבר, הווה, ציווי	פָּעַל
בִּקֵּר, פִּקֵּד, כִּבֵּס	עבר, ציווי	פִּעֵל
בֻּטַּל, פֻּתַּח, כֻּבַּס	עבר	פֻּעַל

2. When they follow a zero vowel in the middle of the verb form:

יִשְׁבֹּר, יִשְׁפֹּךְ, יִשְׁכַּב	עתיד	פָּעַל
הִתְבַּקֵּשׁ, מִתְפַּלֵּא, יִתְכַּנֵּס	entire conjugation	הִתְפַּעֵל
הִסְבִּיר, יַשְׁכִּיר, לְהַסְפִּיק	entire conjugation	הִפְעִיל
הֻסְבַּר, מֻשְׁפָּע, יֻשְׁכַּר	entire conjugation	הֻפְעַל

3. When the pattern of the verb demands it:

יִבָּדֵק, הִפָּרֵד, לְהִכָּנֵס	פה״פ- עתיד, ציווי, שם פועל	נפעל
דִּבֵּר, מְסַפֵּר, יְסַכֵּן	עה״פ- entire conjugation	פִּעֵל
שִׁבְּחוּ, מְשֻׁפָּר, תְּסֻכְּמוּ	עה״פ- entire conjugation	פֻּעַל
הִתְבַּקֵּשׁ, מִתְפַּלֵּא, יִתְכַּנֵּס	עה״פ - entire conjugation	התפעל

ii. ב', כ', פ' realized as *v/kh/f.*

1. When they follow a vowel:

סָבַל, סוֹפֵר, שִׂכְרִי	עתיד, הווה, ציווי	פָּעַל
מְבַקֵּשׁ, יְפַחֵד, מְכַבֵּס	הווה, עתיד	פִּעֵל
מְבַקֵּשׁ, יְפַתַּח, מְכֵנֵן	הווה, עתיד	פִּעֵל
הִבְחִין, מַפְסִיק, יַכְתִּיב	entire conjugation	הפעיל
הֻבְרַח, מֻפְעָל, יֻכְנַס	entire conjugation	הֻפְעַל

2. When they follow a zero vowel derived from an underlying one (e.g., אָסְפוּ below), and/or when they are the last consonant in the root:

עָזַב, אָסְפוּ, יִדְרֹךְ, עֻזְבִי, לֶאֱסֹף	entire conjugation	פָּעַל
נֶעֶזְבָה, נֶאֱסָף, יִדָּרְכוּ, לְהֵעָזֵב	entire conjugation	נפעל
עִצֵּב, מְקַלֵּף, תְּשַׁדְּכִי, מְאַלְפוֹת, לִשְׁכֵּךְ	entire conjugation	פִּעֵל
עֻצַּב, מְקֻלָּף, יְשֻׁכְכוּ, יֵשְׁבוּ	entire conjugation	פֻּעַל
הִתְיַצֵּב, מִתְהַלְּכִים, יִתְרַךְ, תִּשְׁתַּלְּבִי	entire conjugation	התפעל
הֶעֱלִיב, מַדְלִיף, יַדְרִיךְ	entire conjugation	הפעיל
הֻרְכַּב, הֻרְכְּבָה, מֻדְלָף, יֻדְרְכוּ	entire conjugation	הֻפְעַל

B. שלמים עם גרוניות - with 'guttural' root consonants.
Insertion of a 'helping' vowel (where a zero vowel is hard to pronounce).

אֲמַרְתֶּם, הֲלַכְתֶּם, חֲשַׁבְתֶּם, עֲבַדְתֶּם	פה"פ	עבר	פָּעַל
שׁוֹאֲלִים, נוֹהֲגוֹת, בּוֹחֲרִים, בּוֹעֲרוֹת	עה"פ	הווה	
אֱסֹף, אֶסְפְּנָה	פה"פ א'	ציווי	
הֲרֹג, הַרְגְנָה, חֲזוֹר, חֲזֹרְנָה, עֲזֹר, עֲזֹרְנָה	פה"פ ה' ח' ע'		
שַׁאֲלִי, נַהֲגוּ, גַּעֲרִי	עה"פ		
תִּשָּׁאֲרִי, יִבָּהֲלוּ, תִּשָּׁחֲקוּ, יִפָּעֲרוּ	עה"פ	עתיד	נפעל
הִשָּׁאֲרִי, הִבָּהֲלוּ		ציווי	
תֵּאָמַה, נֵהֲלָה, שֵׂחֲקוּ, שֵׂעֲרָה	עה"פ	עבר	פִּעֵל
מְתַאֲמִים, מְנַהֲלוֹת, מְשַׂחֲקִים, מְשַׂעֲרוֹת		הווה	
תְּתַאֲמִי, תְּנַהֲלוּ, יְשַׂחֲקוּ, יְשַׂעֲרוּ		עתיד	
נַהֲלִי, שַׂחֲקוּ		ציווי	
תֹּאֲמוּ, נֹהֲלָה, נֻחֲמוּ, נֹעֲרָה	עה"פ	עבר	פֻּעַל
יִתְאָמוּ, תְּנֹהֲלִי, תְּנֻחֲמוּ, יְנֹעֲרוּ		עתיד	
הִתְפָּאֲרָה, הִתְנַהֲגָה, תִּתְנַהֲגוּ, הִתְפַּעֲלָה	עה"פ	עבר	התפעל
מִתְפָּאֲרִים, מִתְנַהֲגוֹת, מִתְנַחֲלִים, מִתְפַּעֲלוֹת		הווה	

Similar insertion of a vowel and 'echo' in the prefix (optional for ח').

בניין	זמן	פה"פ	דוגמאות
פָּעַל	עתיד	פה"פ א' (ח')	תֶּאֱסֹף, תַּאַסְפִי, תֶּחֱזַק, תֶּחֶזְקִי
		פה'פ ה' (ח') ע'	יַהֲרֹג, תַּהַרְגִי, יַחֲזֹר/יַחְזֹר , תַּעֲבֹד , תַּעַבְדוּ
		פה"פ ח'	תַּחְבּוֹשׁ, תַּחְבְּשִׁי
נפעל	עבר	פה"פ א' ה' י' ע'	נֶאֱלַץ, נֶהֱרַס, נֶחֱרַב/נֶחְרַב, נֶעֶלְמוּ
		פה"פ ח'	נֶחְקַר, נֶחְקְרָה
	הווה	פה"פ א' ה' י' ע'	נֶאֱלָץ, נֶהֱרֶסֶת, נֶחֱרֶבֶת/נֶחְרֶבֶת, נֶעֱלָמִים
		פה"פ ח'	נֶחְקָר, נֶחְקֶרֶת
הפעיל	עבר	פה"פ	הֶאֱמַנְתְּ, הֶחֱרִיב/הֶחְרִיב, הֶעֱסַקְתִּי
		פה"פ ח'	הֶחְלִיט, הֶחְכִּים
	הווה	פה"פ	מַאֲמִין, מַחֲרִיבָה/מַחְרִיבָה, מַעֲסִיקִים
		פה"פ ח'	מַחְלִיט, מַחְכִּימִים
	עתיד	פה"פ	יַאֲמִינוּ, יַחֲרִיב/יַחְרִיב, תַּעֲסִיק
		פה"פ ח'	יַחְלִיט, יַחְכִּים
	ציווי	פה"פ	הַאֲמֵן, הַחֲרֵב/הַחְרֵב, הַעֲסִיקוּ
		פה"פ ח'	הַחְלֵט
הֻפְעַל	עבר	פה"פ	הָאֱשַׁם, הָחֳרַם/הָחְרַם, הָעֳסְקָה
		פה"פ ח'	הָחְלַט
	הווה	פה"פ	מָאֳשָׁמִים, מָחֳרֶמֶת/מֶחְרֶמֶת, מָעֳסָקוֹת
		פה"פ ח'	מֻחְלָט
	עתיד	פה"פ	יָאֳשַׁם, תָּחֳרְמִי/תֶּחְרְמִי, יָעֳסְקוּ

Furtive *patah* insertion.

בניין		דוגמאות
פָּעַל	הווה	תָּמֵהַּ, שׁוֹלֵחַ, יוֹדֵעַ
פָּעֵל	entire conjugation	נִצַּח/נֻצַּח, מְנַצֵּחַ, יְנַצַּח/יְנֻצַּח,
הִתְפַּעֵל	entire conjugation	הִתְקַלַּח/הִתְקַלֵּחַ, לְהִתְקַלֵּחַ
הפעיל	entire conjugation	הִבְטִיחַ, מַבְטִיחַ, יַבְטִיחַ

Avoidance of vowel deletion in the environment of gutturals

(alternatively, may also be regarded as insertion of a 'helping' vowel where a zero vowel is hard to pronounce – see above)

בניין		דוגמאות
נפעל	עבר	נִשְׁאֲלוּ
פָּעַל	עבר, עתיד	תֹּאֲרוּ, תִּנְהֲלוּ, יִשְׁעֲרוּ
הֻפְעַל	עבר, עתיד	הֻשְׁאֲלָה, יֻשְׁאֲלוּ

Stem vowel in future and imperative of *pa`al* (when C2, C3 is guttural).

בניין		דוגמאות
פָּעַל	עתיד	תִּשְׁאַל, תִּנְהַג
	ציווי	שְׁלַח, קְרָא

The feminine singular in the present tense (when C3 is guttural).

נִשְׁלַחַת, נִשְׁמַעַת	נפעל	שׁוֹלַחַת, שׁוֹמַעַת	פָּעַל
מְנַצַּחַת, מְשַׁגַּעַת	פִּעֵל	מְנַצַּחַת, מְשַׁגַּעַת	פִּעֵל
מִצְטַלַּחַת, מֵפְרַעַת	הֻפְעַל	מִתְפַּתַּחַת, מִשְׁתַּגַּעַת	התפעל

'Compensatory lengthening' before gutturals.

תֹּאַר, בֹּרַר	פֻּעַל	תֵּאֵר, בֵּרֵר	פִּעֵל	יֵהָרֵג, יֵחָשֵׁב	נפעל

Group 2: חסרים - one of the root consonants is absent

1. חסרי פ"י – י' is omitted: תֵּשֵׁב, תֵּלֵךְ, תֵּרֵד, תֵּצֵא :פָּעַל

2. חסרי פ"נ – נ' is fully assimilated.

יִפֹּל, סַע	עתיד, ציווי	פָּעַל
נִצַּל, נִצְּלוּ	עבר, הווה	נפעל
הִפִּיל, מַפִּיל, יַפִּיל, הַפֵּל, לְהַפִּיל	entire conjugation	הפעיל
הֻפַּל, מֻפָּל, יֻפַּל	entire conjugation	הֻפְעַל

3. נ' and ת' assimilated to a stem beginning with the same letter

לַנּוּ, נִשְׁעַנּוּ, סִמַּנּוּ, שְׁכַּנּוּ, הִזְדַּקַּנּוּ, הִזְמַנּוּ, הֵכַנּוּ	נ + נ-
שַׁבְּתִּי, אַמַּתִּי, צֹוַתִּי, הִתְעַשַּׁתִּי, הִפְחַתִּי, הִשְׁחַתִּי	ת + ת-
הִדַּרְדֵּר	ת + ד-

4. ע"ע – two identical root consonants sometimes merge .ג.נ.נ

גּוֹנַנְתִּי, גּוֹנֵן, גּוֹנְנוּ, מְגֹונֵן, מְגֹונְנוֹת, יְגֹונֵן, יְגֹונְנוּ, גֹּונְנִי, לְגֹונֵן	no merger	פָּעַל
הִתְגּוֹנַנְתִּי, הִתְגּוֹנֵן, מִתְגּוֹנֵן, מִתְגּוֹנְנוֹת, יִתְגּוֹנֵן, הִתְגּוֹנְנִי, לְהִתְגּוֹנֵן	no merger	התפעל
הֵגַנְתִּי, הֵגֵן, הֵגֵנָּה, מֵגֵן, מְגִנָּה, מְגִנּוֹת, יָגֵן, יָגֵנּוּ, הָגֵן, הָגֵנּוּ, לְהָגֵן		הפעיל
הוּגַנְתִּי, הוּגַן, הוּגְנָה, מוּגָן, מוּגָנִים, תּוּגַן		הֻפְעַל

Group 3: נחים - a root consonant is weakened or silent

1. נחי פ"א – stem-initial א' muted: תֹּאכַל, תֹּאהַב, תֹּאמַר -פָּעַל
2. נחי ל"א – syllable-final א' muted

קָרָא, קָרָאתִי, קוֹרֵא, קוֹרֵאת, יִקְרָא, קְרָא, לִקְרֹוא	פָּעַל
נִקְרָא, נִקְרֵאתִי, נִקְרֵאת, יִקָּרֵא, הִקָּרֵא, לְהִקָּרֵא	נפעל
מִלֵּא, מִלֵּאתִי, מִלֵּאת, מְמַלֵּא, מְמַלֵּאת, יְמַלֵּא, מַלֵּא, לְמַלֵּא	פִּעֵל
מֻלָּא, מֻלֵּאתִי, מֻלֵּאת, מְמֻלָּא, מְמֻלֵּאת, יְמֻלָּא	פֻּעַל
הִתְמַלֵּאתִי, הִתְמַלֵּא, מִתְמַלֵּא, מִתְמַלֵּאת, יִתְמַלֵּא, לְהִתְמַלֵּא	התפעל
הִמְצִיא, הִמְצֵאתִי, הִמְצֵאת, מַמְצִיא, יַמְצִיא, הַמְצֵא, לְהַמְצִיא	הפעיל
הֻמְצָא, הֻמְצֵאתִי, הֻמְצֵאת, מֻמְצָא, מֻמְצֵאת, יֻמְצָא	הֻפְעַל

3. נחי פ"י – stem-initial י weakened to a vowel.

פָּעַל	עתיד	תִּישַׁן, יִשְׁנוּ, תִּירַשׁ, יִירְשׁוּ
נפעל	עבר, הווה	נוֹלַדְתִּי, נוֹלַד
הפעיל	entire conjugation	הוֹשִׁיב, מוֹשִׁיב, תּוֹשִׁיב
הֻפְעַל	entire conjugation	הוּשַׁב, מוּשָׁב, תּוּשַׁב

4. נחי ל"י – stem-final י muted

פָּעַל	קָנִיתִי, קָנָה, קָנְתָה, קוֹנֶה, קוֹנִים, תִּקְנֶה, תִּקְנִי, קְנֵה, לִקְנוֹת
נפעל	נִקְנֵיתִי, נִקְנְתָה, נִקְנֶה, נִקְנֵית, תִּקָּנֶה, תִּקָּנוּ, הִקָּנֵה, לְהִקָּנוֹת
פִּעֵל	בִּלִּיתִי, בִּלָּה, בִּלְּתָה, מְבַלֶּה, מְבַלֶּה, תְּבַלֶּה, בַּלֵּה, בַּלִּי, לְבַלּוֹת
פֻּעַל	גֻּלֵּיתִי, גֻּלָּה, גֻּלְּתָה, גֻּלּוּ, מְגֻלֶּה, מְגֻלָּה, מְגֻלִּים, תְּגֻלֶּה, תְּגֻלּוּ
התפעל	הִתְגַּלֵּיתִי, הִתְגַּלְּתָה, מִתְגַּלֶּה, מִתְגַּלָּה, יִתְגַּלֶּה, יִתְגַּלּוּ, הִתְגַּלֵּה, לְהִתְגַּלּוֹת
הפעיל	הִפְלֵיתִי, הִפְלְתָה, הִפְלוּ, מַפְלֶה, מַפְלָה, יַפְלֶה, תַּפְלוּ, הַפְלֵה, לְהַפְלוֹת
הֻפְעַל	הֻפְלֵיתִי, הֻפְלָה, הֻפְלְתָה, הֻפְלוּ, מֻפְלֶה, מֻפְלָה, מֻפְלִים, יֻפְלֶה, תֻּפְלוּ

5. נחי ע"ו/ע"י – medial ו and י are deleted or muted.

פָּעַל	קַמְתִּי, קָם, קַם, קָמָה, קָמִים, יָקוּם, תָּקוּמוּ, קוּם, קוּמִי, לָקוּם
נפעל	נְסוּגוֹתִי, נָסוֹג, נָסוֹגָה, נְסוֹגָה, יִסּוֹג, תִּסּוֹגִי, הִסּוֹג, הִסּוֹגִי, לְהִסּוֹג
פִּעֵל	קוֹמַמְתִּי, קוֹמֵם, קוֹמְמָה, מְקוֹמֵם, יְקוֹמֵם, יְקוֹמְמוּ, קוֹמְמִי, לְקוֹמֵם
התפעל	הִתְקוֹמַמְתִּי, הִתְקוֹמְמָה, מִתְקוֹמֵם, יִתְקוֹמֵם, יִתְקוֹמְמוּ, לְהִתְקוֹמֵם
הפעיל	הֵקַמְתִּי, הֵקִים, הֵקִימוּ, מֵקִים, מְקִימוֹת, תָּקִים, תָּקִימוּ, הָקֵם, לְהָקִים
הֻפְעַל	הוּקַמְתִּי, הוּקַם, הוּקְמָה, הוּקָם, מוּקָם, יוּקַם, יוּקְמוּ

Appendix 2: noun tables

The nouns in this table are **representative** of many of the patterns of Hebrew nouns. They provide one illustration of each of the patterns represented. They are presented in their singular and plural forms, in their independent and dependent forms, and with pronoun suffixes of the first person singular and second person masculine plural.

There are two sets of pronoun suffixes: one set is attached to singular nouns, and the other set is attached to plural nouns.

Pronoun suffixes attached to singular nouns

Plural ending			Singular ending		
3rd	2nd	1st	3rd	2nd	1st
‑ָם	‑ְכֶם	‑ֵנוּ	‑וֹ	‑ְךָ	‑ִי
‑ָן	‑ְכֶן		‑ָהּ	‑ֵךְ	

Pronoun suffixes attached to plural nouns

Plural ending			Singular ending		
3rd	2nd	1st	3rd	2nd	1st
‑ֵיהֶם	‑ֵיכֶם	‑ֵינוּ	‑ָיו	‑ֶיךָ	‑ַי
‑ֵיהֶן	‑ֵיכֶן		‑ֶיהָ	‑ַיִךְ	

Below are full paradigms of the various forms of nouns and nouns with their pronoun suffixes. The asterisked forms represent the four 'default' forms of the construct state: the sing. masc. and fem. pl. forms are unchanged; the fem. sing. ‑ָה becomes ‑ַת, and the pl. masc. ‑ִים becomes ‑ֵי. In some of the tables following the paradigms, the construct form may not be represented if it is realized in the default form.

Masculine Paradigm

uncle					דּוֹד (ז)	יחיד
דּוֹדָהּ	דּוֹדוֹ	דּוֹדְךָ	דּוֹדְךָ	דּוֹדִי	דּוֹד‑*	
דּוֹדָן	דּוֹדָם	דּוֹדְכֶן	דּוֹדְכֶם	דּוֹדֵנוּ		
					דּוֹדִים	רבים
דּוֹדֶיהָ	דּוֹדָיו	דּוֹדַיִךְ	דּוֹדֶיךָ	דּוֹדַי	דּוֹדֵי‑*	
דּוֹדֵיהֶן	דּוֹדֵיהֶם	דּוֹדֵיכֶן	דּוֹדֵיכֶם	דּוֹדֵינוּ		

Feminine Paradigm

aunt						דּוֹדָה (נ)	יְחִידָה
דּוֹדָתָהּ	דּוֹדָתוֹ	דּוֹדָתֵךְ	דּוֹדָתְךָ	דּוֹדָתִי	*דּוֹדַת-		
דּוֹדָתָן	דּוֹדָתָם	דּוֹדַתְכֶן	דּוֹדַתְכֶם	דּוֹדָתֵנוּ			
						דּוֹדוֹת	רַבּוֹת
דּוֹדוֹתֶיהָ	דּוֹדוֹתָיו	דּוֹדוֹתַיִךְ	דּוֹדוֹתֶיךָ	דּוֹדוֹתַי	*דּוֹדוֹת-		
דּוֹדוֹתֵיהֶן	דּוֹדוֹתֵיהֶם	דּוֹדוֹתֵיכֶן	דּוֹדוֹתֵיכֶם	דּוֹדוֹתֵינוּ			

A. Noun patterns not subject to vowel reduction

Vowel reduction occurs when stress shifts to an added suffix, or to the second noun in a construct phrase. In general, it does not apply in the following cases:

(i)   Vowels other than *kamats* or *tsere* are not reduced.

(ii)   Reduction of a *kamats* tends to occur only two syllables away from the syllable with the main stressed syllable.

(iii)   Deletion does not occur if a three-consonant cluster would have resulted (a consonant with a *dagesh ḥazak* counts as two). This also explains why a *pataḥ*, which usually occurs in a syllable closed by a consonant or by a *dagesh ḥazak*, is not affected, while a *kamats* is).

Some illustrations:

1. No reduction in vowels other than *kamats* or *tsere*:

Gloss	רבים			יחיד		
sound	קוֹלוֹתֵיכֶם	קוֹלוֹתַי	קוֹלוֹת	קוֹלְכֶם	קוֹלִי	קוֹל
song	שִׁירֵיכֶם	שִׁירַי	שִׁירִים	שִׁירְכֶם	שִׁירִי	שִׁיר
stamp	בּוּלֵיכֶם	בּוּלַי	בּוּלִים	בּוּלְכֶם	בּוּלִי	בּוּל

2. No reduction of *kamats* immediately before the stress, but it does occur two syllables before the stress (יְדֵיכֶם etc.):

Gloss	רבים			יחיד		
fish	דְּגֵיכֶם	דָּגַי	דָּגִים	דָּגְכֶם	דָּגִי	דָּג
hand	יְדֵיכֶם	יָדַי	יָדַיִם	יֶדְכֶם	יָדִי	יָד

3. No reduction if a three-consonant cluster would have resulted:

Gloss	רבים			יחיד		
fight	קְרָבוֹתֵיכֶם	קְרָבוֹתַי	קְרָבוֹת	קְרָבְכֶם	קְרָבִי	קְרָב
student	תַּלְמִידֵיכֶם	תַּלְמִידַי	תַּלְמִידִים	תַּלְמִידְכֶם	תַּלְמִידִי	תַּלְמִיד
candy	מַמְתַּקֵּיכֶם	מַמְתַּקַּי	מַמְתַּקִּים	מַמְתַּקְכֶם	מַמְתַּקִּי	מַמְתָּק
bride	כַּלּוֹתֵיכֶם	כַּלּוֹתַי	כַּלּוֹת	כַּלַּתְכֶם	כַּלָּתִי	כַּלָּה
reason	סִבּוֹתֵיכֶם	סִבּוֹתַי	סִבּוֹת	סִבַּתְכֶם	סִבָּתִי	סִבָּה

4. Relative immunity to reduction of *kamats* and *tsere* in nouns ending in ־וּת or ־ית, even in open syllables (note that their plural forms replace ־וּת with ־יּוֹת and ־ית with ־יוֹת, respectively):

Gloss	רבות			יחידה		
testimony	עֵדֻיּוֹתֵיכֶם	עֵדְוִיֹתַי	עֵדֻיּוֹת	עֵדֻתְכֶם	עֵדֻתִי	עֵדוּת
exile	גָּלֻיּוֹתֵיכֶם	גָּלֻיּוֹתַי	גָּלֻיּוֹת	גָּלוּתְכֶם	גָּלוּתִי	גָּלוּת
angle	זָוִיֹּתֵיכֶם	זָוִיֹּתַי	זָוִיֹּת	זָוִיַּתְכֶם	זָוִיָתִי	זָוִית

B. Noun patterns undergoing changes other than vowel reduction

1. A *patah* sometimes reverts to an underlying *i* when a suffix is appended:

Gloss	רבות			יחידה		
loaf	פִּתֵּיכֶם	פִּתַּי	פִּתִּים	פִּתְּכֶם	פִּתִּי	פַּת

2. When the noun is derived from a root with identical second and third consonants (e.g., שֵׁן < ש.נ.נ), the original *i* from which the *tsere* developed resurfaces:

Gloss	רבות			יחידה		
tooth	שִׁנֵּיכֶם	שִׁנַּי	שִׁנַּיִם	שִׁנְּכֶם	שִׁנִּי	שֵׁן

3. There is a similar relationship between *o* and *u* in forms derived from a root with identical second and third consonants, and a few other items:

Gloss	רבים			יחיד		
drum	תֻּפֵּיכֶם	תֻּפַּי	תֻּפִּים	תֻּפְּכֶם	תֻּפִּי	תֹּף
ankle	קַרְסֻלֵּיכֶם	קַרְסֻלַּי	קַרְסֻלַּיִם	קַרְסֻלְּכֶם	קַרְסֻלִּי	קַרְסֹל

C. Noun patterns that generally undergo vowel reduction

Generally, only *kamats* and *tsere* are subject to reduction, which occurs when the stress shifts forward (with the addition of suffixes, or with the formation of the construct state). Some illustrations:

1. A *kamats* in the plural of monosyllabic words that do not have that vowel in the singular. The forms with a hyphen are the dependent forms of the noun.

day	רבים			יחיד		
day	יְמֵיכֶם	יָמַי	־יְמֵי	יָמִים	יוֹמְכֶם	יוֹמִי	יוֹם

2. A basic *kamats* in some inflected forms of monosyllabic words (cf. Section A.2 above)

fish	רבים			יחיד		
fish	דְּגֵיכֶם	דָּגַי	־דְּגֵי	דָּגִים	דַּגְכֶם	דָּגִי	דָּג

3. A *kamats* in word-initial position in bi-syllabic nouns:

clerk	פְּקִידְכֶם	פְּקִידִי	פְּקִיד-	פָּקִיד	יחיד
	פְּקִידֵיכֶם	פְּקִידַי	פְּקִידֵי-	פְּקִידִים	רבים

but no reduction of a *patah* vowel

hammer	פַּטִּישְׁכֶם	פַּטִּישִׁי	פַּטִּישׁ -	פַּטִּישׁ	יחיד
	פַּטִּישֵׁיכֶם	פַּטִּישַׁי	פַּטִּישֵׁי-	פַּטִּישִׁים	רבים

thing,	דְּבַרְכֶם	דְּבָרִי	דְּבַר-	דָּבָר	יחיד
word	דִּבְרֵיכֶם	דְּבָרַי	דִּבְרֵי-	דְּבָרִים	רבים

but no reduction of a *patah* vowel

carpenter	נַגָּרְכֶם	נַגָּרִי	נַגָּר-	נַגָּר	יחיד
	נַגָּרֵיכֶם	נַגָּרַי	נַגָּרֵי-	נַגָּרִים	רבים

year	שְׁנַתְכֶם	שְׁנָתִי	שְׁנַת-	שָׁנָה	יחידה
	שְׁנוֹתֵיכֶם	שְׁנוֹתַי	שְׁנוֹת-	שָׁנִים	רבות

but no reduction of a *patah* vowel

map	מַפַּתְכֶם	מַפָּתִי	מַפַּת-	מַפָּה	יחידה
	מַפּוֹתֵיכֶם	מַפּוֹתַי	מַפּוֹת-	מַפּוֹת	רבות

field	שְׂדְכֶם	שָׂדִי	שְׂדֵה-	שָׂדֶה	יחיד
	שְׂדוֹתֵיכֶם	שְׂדוֹתַי	שְׂדוֹת-	שָׂדוֹת	רבים

but no reduction of a *patah* vowel

staff, rod	מַטְּכֶם	מַטִּי	מַטֵּה-	מַטֶּה	יחיד
	מַטּוֹתֵיכֶם	מַטּוֹתַי	מַטּוֹת-	מַטּוֹת	רבים

4. A *kamats* in word-medial position:

memory	זִכְרוֹנְכֶם	זִכְרוֹנִי	זִכְרוֹן-	זִכָּרוֹן	יחיד
	זִכְרוֹנוֹתֵיכֶם	זִכְרוֹנוֹתַי	זִכְרוֹנוֹת-	זִכְרוֹנוֹת	רבים

but *hataf patah* vowel replaces zero *shva* when a guttural is involved:

interview	רַאֲיוֹנְכֶם	רַאֲיוֹנִי	רַאֲיוֹן-	רֵאָיוֹן	יחיד
	רַאֲיוֹנוֹתֵיכֶם	רַאֲיוֹנוֹתַי	רַאֲיוֹנוֹת-	רַאֲיוֹנוֹת	רבים

gift	מַתְּנַתְכֶם	מַתְּנָתִי	מַתְּנַת-	מַתָּנָה	יחידה
	מַתְּנוֹתֵיכֶם	מַתְּנוֹתַי	מַתְּנוֹת-	מַתָּנוֹת	רבות

but no reduction when a *dagesh hazak* closes the syllable:

request	בַּקָּשַׁתְכֶם	בַּקָּשָׁתִי	בַּקָּשַׁת-	בַּקָּשָׁה	יחידה
	בַּקָּשׁוֹתֵיכֶם	בַּקָּשׁוֹתַי	בַּקָּשׁוֹת-	בַּקָּשׁוֹת	רבות

5. A *kamats* in word-final position:

institution	מוֹסַדְכֶם	מוֹסָדִי	מוֹסַד-	מוֹסָד	יחיד
	מוֹסְדוֹתֵיכֶם	מוֹסְדוֹתַי	מוֹסְדוֹת-	מוֹסָדוֹת	רבים
sentence/	מִשְׁפַּטְכֶם	מִשְׁפָּטִי	מִשְׁפַּט-	מִשְׁפָּט	יחיד
trial	מִשְׁפְּטֵיכֶם	מִשְׁפָּטַי	מִשְׁפְּטֵי-	מִשְׁפָּטִים	רבים

6. If the consonant **preceding** a deletable *kamats* is ר׳ ,נ׳ ,מ׳ ,ל׳ ,י׳, or the **following** consonant is a guttural, the *kamats* is not deleted. Instead, it is reduced to *e* (the vowel sign is still a *shva*):

food	מְזוֹנְכֶם	מְזוֹנִי	מְזוֹן-	מָזוֹן	יחיד
	מְזוֹנוֹתֵיכֶם	מְזוֹנוֹתַי	מְזוֹנוֹת-	מְזוֹנוֹת	רבים
river	נְהַרְכֶם	נְהָרִי	נְהַר-	נָהָר	יחיד
	נַהֲרוֹתֵיכֶם	נַהֲרוֹתַי	נַהֲרוֹת-	נְהָרוֹת	רבים
hour	שְׁעַתְכֶם	שְׁעָתִי	שְׁעַת-	שָׁעָה	יחידה
	שְׁעוֹתֵיכֶם	שְׁעוֹתַי	שְׁעוֹת-	שָׁעוֹת	רבות

7. A *tsere* in monosyllabic words:

name	שְׁמְכֶם	שְׁמִי	שֶׁם-	שֵׁם	יחיד
	שְׁמוֹתֵיכֶם	שְׁמוֹתַי	שְׁמוֹת-	שֵׁמוֹת	רבים

8. A *tsere* in bi-syllabic words or longer; some cases involve both a *kamats* and a *tsere*:

elder	זְקַנְכֶם	זְקֵנִי	זְקַן-	זָקֵן	יחיד
	זִקְנֵיכֶם	זְקֵנַי	זִקְנֵי-	זְקֵנִים	רבים
fence	גְּדֵרְכֶם	גְּדֵרִי	גֶּדֶר-	גָּדֵר	יחיד
	גְּדֵרוֹתֵיכֶם	גְּדֵרוֹתַי	גְּדֵרוֹת-	גְּדֵרוֹת	רבים
yard	חֲצֵרְכֶם	חֲצֵרִי	חֲצַר-	חָצֵר	יחיד
	חַצְרוֹתֵיכֶם	חַצְרוֹתַי	חַצְרוֹת-	חֲצֵרוֹת	רבים
hair	שְׂעַרְכֶם	שְׂעָרִי	שְׂעַר-	שֵׂעָר	יחיד
	שַׂעֲרוֹתֵיכֶם	שַׂעֲרוֹתַי	שַׂעֲרוֹת-	שְׂעָרוֹת	רבים
brick	לְבֵנַתְכֶם	לְבֵנְתִי	לְבְנַת-	לְבֵנָה	יחידה
	לְבֵנֵיכֶם	לְבֵנַי	לְבְנֵי-	לְבֵנִים	רבות

9. A *tsere* is also reduced **immediately before** the stressed vowel, mostly in nouns that are identical to active participles of verbs.

assistant	עוֹזֶרְכֶם	עוֹזְרִי	עוֹזֵר-	עוֹזֵר	יחיד
	עוֹזְרֵיכֶם	עוֹזְרַי	עוֹזְרֵי-	עוֹזְרִים	רבים

ḥataf pataḥ replaces *shva* when the medial consonant is a guttural

worker	פּוֹעֲלְכֶם	פּוֹעֲלִי	פּוֹעֵל-	פּוֹעֵל	יחיד
	פּוֹעֲלֵיכֶם	פּוֹעֲלַי	פּוֹעֲלֵי-	פּוֹעֲלִים	רבים

caretaker	מְטַפֶּלְכֶם	מְטַפְּלִי	מְטַפֵּל-	מְטַפֵּל	יחיד
	מְטַפְּלֵיכֶם	מְטַפְּלַי	מְטַפְּלֵי-	מְטַפְּלִים	רבים

ḥataf pataḥ replaces *shva* when the medial consonant is a guttural

manager	מְנַהֶלְכֶם	מְנַהֲלִי	מְנַהֵל-	מְנַהֵל	יחיד
	מְנַהֲלֵיכֶם	מְנַהֲלַי	מְנַהֲלֵי-	מְנַהֲלִים	רבים

volunteer	מִתְנַדֶּבְכֶם	מִתְנַדְּבִי	מִתְנַדֵּב-	מִתְנַדֵּב	יחיד
	מִתְנַדְּבֵיכֶם	מִתְנַדְּבַי	מִתְנַדְּבֵי-	מִתְנַדְּבִים	רבים

ḥataf pataḥ replaces *shva* when medial letter is א׳, ע׳, ח׳, ה׳

settler	מִתְנַחֶלְכֶם	מִתְנַחֲלִי	מִתְנַחֵל -	מִתְנַחֵל	יחיד
	מִתְנַחֲלֵיכֶם	מִתְנַחֲלִי	מִתְנַחֲלֵי-	מִתְנַחֲלִים	רבים

10. Similarly, a *tsere* is reduced in pre-stress position when the second consonant has a *dagesh ḥazak*:

stick	מַקֶּלְכֶם	מַקְּלִי	מַקֵּל-	מַקֵּל	יחיד
	מַקְּלוֹתֵיכֶם	מַקְּלוֹתַי	מַקְּלוֹת-	מַקְּלוֹת	רבים

11. When a final ה׳ originated from a root with final consonant ה׳ from historical י׳, that ה׳ is elided when a suffix is appended.

Gloss		רבים				יחיד		
teacher	מוֹרֵיכֶם	מוֹרַי	מוֹרִים	מוֹרְכֶם	מוֹרִי	מוֹרֵה-	מוֹרֶה
patient	חוֹלֵיכֶם	חוֹלַי	חוֹלִים	חוֹלְכֶם	חוֹלִי	חוֹלֵה-	חוֹלֶה
occurrence	מִקְרֵיכֶם	מִקְרַי	מִקְרִים	מִקְרְכֶם	מִקְרִי	מִקְרֵה-	מִקְרֶה
structure	מִבְנֵיכֶם	מִבְנַי	מִבְנִים	מִבְנְכֶם	מִבְנִי	מִבְנֵה-	מִבְנֶה

D. *Segolate* nouns

(i). Masculine *Segolates*:

1. When the base is פֶּעֶל-

king	מַלְכְּכֶם	מַלְכִּי	מֶלֶךְ-	מֶלֶךְ	יחיד
	מַלְכֵיכֶם	מַלְכַי	מַלְכֵי-	מְלָכִים	רבים

When consonant 1 is a guttural

slave	עַבְדְּכֶם	עַבְדִּי	עֶבֶד-	עֶבֶד	יחיד
	עַבְדֵּיכֶם	עַבְדַּי	עַבְדֵּי-	עֲבָדִים	רבים

When consonant 2 is a guttural

gate	שַׁעַרְכֶם	שַׁעֲרֵי	שַׁעַר-	שַׁעַר	יחיד
	שַׁעֲרֵיכֶם	שַׁעֲרֵי	שַׁעֲרֵי-	שְׁעָרִים	רבים

When consonant 3 is a guttural

rock	סַלְעֲכֶם	סַלְעִי	סֶלַע-	סֶלַע	יחיד
	סַלְעֵיכֶם	סְלָעַי	סַלְעֵי-	סְלָעִים	רבים

2. When the base is -פֶּעֶל

clothing	בִּגְדְּכֶם	בִּגְדִּי	בֶּגֶד-	בֶּגֶד	יחיד
	בִּגְדֵיכֶם	בְּגָדַי	בִּגְדֵי-	בְּגָדִים	רבים

When the base is -פֶּעֶל and the independent form is פֵּעֶל

book	סִפְרְכֶם	סִפְרִי	סֵפֶר-	סֵפֶר	יחיד
	סִפְרֵיכֶם	סְפָרַי	סִפְרֵי-	סְפָרִים	רבים

When the last consonant is a guttural

quarter	רִבְעֲכֶם	רִבְעִי	רֶבַע-	רֶבַע	יחיד
	רִבְעֵיכֶם	רְבָעַי	רִבְעֵי-	רְבָעִים	רבים

3. When the base is -פֹּעֶל (*kamats katan=o*) and the independent form is פֹּעֶל

month	חָדְשְׁכֶם	חָדְשִׁי	חֹדֶשׁ-	חֹדֶשׁ	יחיד
	חָדְשֵׁיכֶם	חֳדָשַׁי	חָדְשֵׁי-	חֳדָשִׁים	רבים

With a guttural as second root consonant

width	רָחְבְּכֶם	רָחְבִּי	רֹחַב-	רֹחַב	יחיד
	רָחֳבֵיכֶם	רְחָבַי	רָחֳבֵי-	רְחָבִים	רבים

With a guttural as third root consonant

manner	אָרְחֲכֶם	אָרְחִי	אֹרַח-	אֹרַח	יחיד
	אָרְחוֹתֵיכֶם	אָרְחוֹתַי	אָרְחוֹת-	אֲרָחוֹת	רבים

ii. Feminine *segolates*:

1. When the pattern is פַּעְלָה

young girl	יַלְדַּתְכֶם	יַלְדָּתִי	יַלְדַּת-	יַלְדָּה	יחידה
	יַלְדוֹתֵיכֶם	יַלְדוֹתַי	יַלְדוֹת-	יְלָדוֹת	רבות

When the first consonant is a guttural

maiden	עַלְמַתְכֶם	עַלְמָתִי	עַלְמַת-	עַלְמָה	יחידה
	עַלְמוֹתֵיכֶם	עַלְמוֹתַי	עַלְמוֹת-	עֲלָמוֹת	רבות

When the second consonant is a guttural

girl	נַעֲרַתְכֶם	נַעֲרָתִי	נַעֲרַת-	נַעֲרָה	יחידה
	נַעֲרוֹתֵיכֶם	נַעֲרוֹתַי	נַעֲרוֹת-	נְעָרוֹת	רבות

2. When the pattern is פְּעָלָה

dress	שִׂמְלַתְכֶם	שִׂמְלָתִי	שִׂמְלַת-	שִׂמְלָה	יחידה
	שִׂמְלוֹתֵיכֶם	שִׂמְלוֹתַי	שִׂמְלוֹת-	שְׂמָלוֹת	רבות

With a guttural as a first consonant

position	עֶמְדַּתְכֶם	עֶמְדָּתִי	עֶמְדַּת-	עֶמְדָּה	יחידה
	עֶמְדוֹתֵיכֶם	עֶמְדוֹתַי	עֶמְדוֹת-	עֲמָדוֹת	רבות

3. When the pattern is פָּעְלָה (*kamats katan=o*)

wisdom	חָכְמַתְכֶם	חָכְמָתִי	חָכְמַת-	חָכְמָה	יחידה
	חָכְמוֹתֵיכֶם	חָכְמוֹתַי	חָכְמוֹת-	חָכְמוֹת	רבות

4. When the pattern is פְּעֶלֶת

lady	גְּבִרְתְּכֶם	גְּבִרְתִּי	גְּבֶרֶת -	גְּבֶרֶת	יחידה
	גְּבִירוֹתֵיכֶם	גְּבִירוֹתַי	גְּבִירוֹת-	גְּבָרוֹת	רבות

5. When the pattern is פַּעֶלֶת

(tree)top	צַמַּרְתְּכֶם	צַמַּרְתִּי	צַמֶּרֶת-	צַמֶּרֶת	יחידה
	צַמְּרוֹתֵיכֶם	צַמְּרוֹתַי	צַמָּרוֹת -	צַמָּרוֹת	רבות

6. When the pattern is פּוֹעֶלֶת

assistant/ maid	עוֹזַרְתְּכֶם	עוֹזַרְתִּי	עוֹזֶרֶת-	עוֹזֶרֶת	יחידה
	עוֹזְרוֹתֵיכֶם	עוֹזְרוֹתַי	עוֹזְרוֹת-	עוֹזְרוֹת	רבות

With a guttural as the second root consonant

worker	פּוֹעַלְתְּכֶם	פּוֹעַלְתִּי	פּוֹעֶלֶת-	פּוֹעֶלֶת	יחידה
	פּוֹעֲלוֹתֵיכֶם	פּוֹעֲלוֹתַי	פּוֹעֲלוֹת-	פּוֹעֲלוֹת	רבות

With a guttural as the third root consonant

passenger	נוֹסַעְתְּכֶם	נוֹסַעְתִּי	נוֹסַעַת-	נוֹסַעַת	יחידה
	נוֹסְעוֹתֵיכֶם	נוֹסְעוֹתַי	נוֹסְעוֹת-	נוֹסְעוֹת	רבות

7. When the pattern is מְפַעֶלֶת

visitor/ comptroller	מְבַקַּרְתְּכֶם	מְבַקַּרְתִּי	מְבַקֶּרֶת-	מְבַקֶּרֶת	יחידה
	מְבַקְּרוֹתֵיכֶם	מְבַקְּרוֹתַי	מְבַקְּרוֹת-	מְבַקְּרוֹת	רבות

With a guttural as the second consonant

worker	מְנַהַלְתְּכֶם	מְנַהַלְתִּי	מְנַהֶלֶת-	מְנַהֶלֶת	יחידה
	מְנַהֲלוֹתֵיכֶם	מְנַהֲלוֹתַי	מְנַהֲלוֹת-	מְנַהֲלוֹת	רבות

With a guttural as the third consonant

surgeon	מְנַתַּחְתְּכֶם	מְנַתַּחְתִּי	מְנַתַּחַת-	מְנַתַּחַת	יחידה
	מְנַתְּחוֹתֵיכֶם	מְנַתְּחוֹתַי	מְנַתְּחוֹת-	מְנַתְּחוֹת	רבות

8. When the pattern is מִתְפַּעֶלֶת

| volunteer | מִתְנַדְּבַתְכֶם | מִתְנַדַּבְתִּי | -מִתְנַדֶּבֶת | מִתְנַדֶּבֶת | יחידה |
| | מִתְנַדְּבוֹתֵיכֶם | מִתְנַדְּבוֹתַי | -מִתְנַדְּבוֹת | מִתְנַדְּבוֹת | רבות |

9. When the pattern is פְּעֶלֶת (note: *kamats katan=o*)

| address | כְּתָבְתְּכֶם | כְּתָבְתִּי | -כְּתֹבֶת | כְּתֹבֶת | יחידה |
| | כְּתוֹבוֹתֵיכֶם | כְּתוֹבוֹתַי | -כְּתוֹבוֹת | כְּתוֹבוֹת | רבות |

10. When the pattern is תִּיעֶלֶת (note: *kamats katan=o*)

| baby girl | תִּינָקְתְּכֶם | תִּינַקְתִּי | -תִּינֹקֶת | תִּינֹקֶת | יחידה |
| | תִּינוֹקוֹתֵיכֶם | תִּינוֹקוֹתַי | -תִּינוֹקוֹת | תִּינוֹקוֹת | רבות |

11. When the pattern is פְּעֶפֶעֶת (note: *kamats katan=o*)

| skull | גֻּלְגָּלְתְּכֶם | גֻּלְגָּלְתִּי | -גֻּלְגֹּלֶת | גֻּלְגֹּלֶת | יחידה |
| | גֻּלְגָּלוֹתֵיכֶם | גֻּלְגָּלוֹתַי | -גֻּלְגָּלוֹת | גֻּלְגָּלוֹת | רבות |

12. When the pattern is מִפְעֶלֶת (note: *kamats katan=o*)

| weight | מִשְׁקָלְתְּכֶם | מִשְׁקָלְתִּי | -מִשְׁקֹלֶת | מִשְׁקֹלֶת | יחידה |
| | מִשְׁקוֹלוֹתֵיכֶם | מִשְׁקוֹלוֹתַי | -מִשְׁקוֹלוֹת | מִשְׁקוֹלוֹת | רבות |

13. When the pattern is מַפְעֶלֶת

| salary | מַשְׂכֶּרְתְּכֶם | מַשְׂכֶּרְתִּי | -מַשְׂכֹּרֶת | מַשְׂכֹּרֶת | יחידה |
| | מַשְׂכּוֹרוֹתֵיכֶם | מַשְׂכּוֹרוֹתַי | -מַשְׂכּוֹרוֹת | מַשְׂכּוֹרוֹת | רבות |

14. When the pattern is פְּעֶלֶת (note: *kamats katan=o*)

| criticism | בִּקָּרְתְּכֶם | בִּקָּרְתִּי | -בִּקֹּרֶת | בִּקֹּרֶת | יחידה |
| | בִּקּוֹרוֹתֵיכֶם | בִּקּוֹרוֹתַי | -בִּקּוֹרוֹת | בִּקּוֹרוֹת | רבות |

iii. *Segolates* derived from ע״י/ע״י roots or other bi-consonantal bases:

| hue, | גּוֹנְכֶם | גּוֹנִי | -גּוֹן | גָּוֶן | יחיד |
| color | גּוֹנֵיכֶם | גּוֹנַי | -גּוֹנֵי | גְּוָנִים | רבים |

| house/ | בֵּיתְכֶם | בֵּיתִי | -בֵּית | בַּיִת | יחיד |
| home | בָּתֵּיכֶם | בָּתַּי | -בָּתֵּי | בָּתִּים | רבים |

| tool | כֶּלְיְכֶם | כֶּלְיִי | -כְּלִי | כְּלִי | יחיד |
| instrument | כְּלֵיכֶם | כֵּלַי | -כְּלֵי | כֵּלִים | רבים |

Appendix 3: particle tables

The paradigms for the particles below follow either the singular or the plural pattern for (possessive) pronoun suffixes (see pp. 168-170, pp. 233-235).

1. Following the Paradigm for Singular (Possessive) Pronoun Suffixes

בֵּין	בִּגְלַל	בְּ-	אֵת	אֶת=עִם	אֵצֶל
between	*because of*	*in/at*	*direct object*	*with*	*at someone's*
בֵּינִי	בִּגְלָלִי	בִּי	אוֹתִי	אִתִּי	אֶצְלִי
בֵּינְךָ	בִּגְלָלְךָ	בְּךָ	אוֹתְךָ	אִתְּךָ	אֶצְלְךָ
בֵּינֵךְ	בִּגְלָלֵךְ	בָּךְ	אוֹתָךְ	אִתָּךְ	אֶצְלֵךְ
בֵּינוֹ	בִּגְלָלוֹ	בּוֹ	אוֹתוֹ	אִתּוֹ	אֶצְלוֹ
בֵּינָהּ	בִּגְלָלָהּ	בָּהּ	אוֹתָהּ	אִתָּהּ	אֶצְלָהּ
בֵּינֵינוּ	בִּגְלָלֵנוּ	בָּנוּ	אוֹתָנוּ	אִתָּנוּ	אֶצְלֵנוּ
בֵּינֵיכֶם/	בִּגְלַלְכֶם/	בָּכֶם/	אֶתְכֶם/	אִתְּכֶם/	אֶצְלְכֶם/
בֵּינֵיהֶם/	בִּגְלָלָם/	בָּהֶם/, בָּם/	אוֹתָם/	אִתָּם/	אֶצְלָם/

לְבַד	לְ-	כֹּל	כְּמוֹת	כְּמוֹ	בִּשְׁבִיל
by self	*to/for*	*all of*	*like/as*	*like*	*for*
לְבַדִּי	לִי	כֻּלִּי	כְּמוֹתִי	כָּמוֹנִי	בִּשְׁבִילִי
לְבַדְּךָ	לְךָ	כֻּלְּךָ	כְּמוֹתְךָ	כָּמוֹךָ	בִּשְׁבִילְךָ
לְבַדֵּךְ	לָךְ	כֻּלֵּךְ	כְּמוֹתָךְ	כָּמוֹךְ	בִּשְׁבִילֵךְ
לְבַדּוֹ	לוֹ	כֻּלּוֹ	כְּמוֹתוֹ	כָּמוֹהוּ	בִּשְׁבִילוֹ
לְבַדָּהּ	לָהּ	כֻּלָּהּ	כְּמוֹתָהּ	כָּמוֹהָ	בִּשְׁבִילָהּ
לְבַדֵּנוּ	לָנוּ	כֻּלָּנוּ	כְּמוֹתֵנוּ	כָּמוֹנוּ	בִּשְׁבִילֵנוּ
לְבַדְכֶם/	לָכֶם/	כֻּלְּכֶם/	כְּמוֹתְכֶם/	כְּמוֹכֶם/	בִּשְׁבִילְכֶם/
לְבַדָּם/	לָהֶם/	כֻּלָּם/	כְּמוֹתָם/	כְּמוֹהֶם/	בִּשְׁבִילָם/

מִן	מוּל	לִקְרַאת	לְעֻמַּת	לְמַעַן
from	*facing*	*toward*	*versus*	*for the sake of*
מִמֶּנִּי	מוּלִי	לִקְרָאתִי	לְעֻמָּתִי	לְמַעֲנִי
מִמְּךָ	מוּלְךָ	לִקְרָאתְךָ	לְעֻמָּתְךָ	לְמַעַנְךָ
מִמֵּךְ	מוּלֵךְ	לִקְרָאתֵךְ	לְעֻמָּתֵךְ	לְמַעֲנֵךְ
מִמֶּנּוּ	מוּלוֹ	לִקְרָאתוֹ	לְעֻמָּתוֹ	לְמַעֲנוֹ
מִמֶּנָּה	מוּלָהּ	לִקְרָאתָהּ	לְעֻמָּתָהּ	לְמַעֲנָהּ
מִמֶּנּוּ/מֵאִתָּנוּ*	מוּלֵנוּ	לִקְרָאתֵנוּ	לְעֻמָּתֵנוּ	לְמַעֲנֵנוּ
מִכֶּם\	מוּלְכֶם\	לִקְרַאתְכֶם\	לְעֻמַּתְכֶם\	לְמַעַנְכֶם\
מֵהֶם\	מוּלָם\	לִקְרַאתָם\	לְעֻמָּתָם\	לְמַעֲנָם\

* מֵאִתָּנוּ is colloquial.

שֶׁל	עִם	עַל-יַד	עֲבוּר	סָבִיב	נֶגֶד
of	*with*	*next to*	*for*	*around*	*opposite*
שֶׁלִּי	עִמִּי	עַל-יָדִי	עֲבוּרִי	סְבִיבִי	נֶגְדִּי
שֶׁלְּךָ	עִמְּךָ	עַל-יָדְךָ	עֲבוּרְךָ	סְבִיבְךָ	נֶגְדְּךָ
שֶׁלָּךְ	עִמָּךְ	עַל-יָדָךְ	עֲבוּרֵךְ	סְבִיבֵךְ	נֶגְדֵּךְ
שֶׁלּוֹ	עִמּוֹ	עַל-יָדוֹ	עֲבוּרוֹ	סְבִיבוֹ	נֶגְדּוֹ
שֶׁלָּהּ	עִמָּהּ	עַל-יָדָהּ	עֲבוּרָהּ	סְבִיבָהּ	נֶגְדָּהּ
שֶׁלָּנוּ	עִמָּנוּ	עַל-יָדֵנוּ	עֲבוּרֵנוּ	סְבִיבֵנוּ	נֶגְדֵּנוּ
שֶׁלָּכֶם\	עִמָּכֶם\	עַל-יָדְכֶם\	עֲבוּרְכֶם\	סְבִיבְכֶם\	נֶגְדְּכֶם\
שֶׁלָּהֶם\	עִמָּהֶם\, עִמָּם\	עַל-יָדָם\	עֲבוּרָם\	סְבִיבָם\	נֶגְדָּם\

- Note that in the case of בֵּין 'between', the singular forms follow the singular possessive pronoun paradigm, בֵּינִי etc., whereas the plural ones follow the plural possessive pronoun paradigm, בֵּינֵינוּ etc.
- Note the variant forms of עמם/עמהם.
- Existential particles, such as 'exists' יֵשׁ, 'does not exist' אֵין and 'still exists' עוֹד also take singular type suffixes:

אֵינָם\	אֵינְכֶם\	אֵינֶנּוּ	אֵינֶנָּה/אֵינָהּ	אֵינוֹ/אֵינֶנּוּ	אֵינֵךְ	אֵינְךָ	אֵינֶנִּי/אֵינִי
יֶשְׁנָם\			יֶשְׁנָהּ	יֶשְׁנוֹ			*יֶשְׁנִי
עוֹדָם\	עוֹדְכֶם\	עוֹדֵנוּ	עוֹדָהּ/עוֹדֶנָּה	עוֹדוֹ/עוֹדֶנּוּ	עוֹדֵךְ	עוֹדְךָ	עוֹדֶנִּי

*The suffixed forms of יש are used only in the first and third persons.

2. Following the Paradigm for Plural (Possessive) Pronoun Suffixes

עַל *on/about*	אוֹדוֹת *about*	בִּלְעֲדֵי *without*	אֶל *to/toward*	אַחֲרֵי *after*
עָלַי	אוֹדוֹתַי	בִּלְעֲדִי	אֵלַי	אַחֲרַי
עָלֶיךָ	אוֹדוֹתֶיךָ	בִּלְעֲדֶיךָ	אֵלֶיךָ	אַחֲרֶיךָ
עָלַיִךְ	אוֹדוֹתַיִךְ	בִּלְעֲדַיִךְ	אֵלַיִךְ	אַחֲרַיִךְ
עָלָיו	אוֹדוֹתָיו	בִּלְעֲדָיו	אֵלָיו	אַחֲרָיו
עָלֶיהָ	אוֹדוֹתֶיהָ	בִּלְעֲדֶיהָ	אֵלֶיהָ	אַחֲרֶיהָ
עָלֵינוּ	אוֹדוֹתֵינוּ	בִּלְעֲדֵינוּ	אֵלֵינוּ	אַחֲרֵינוּ
עֲלֵיכֶם/ן	אוֹדוֹתֵיכֶם/ן	בִּלְעֲדֵיכֶם/ן	אֲלֵיכֶם/ן	אַחֲרֵיכֶם/ן
עֲלֵיהֶם/ן	אוֹדוֹתֵיהֶם/ן	בִּלְעֲדֵיהֶם/ן	אֲלֵיהֶם/ן	אַחֲרֵיהֶם/ן

מֵאֲחוֹרֵי *behind*	לִפְנֵי *in front*	עַל-יְדֵי *by*	מֵעַל *above*	תַּחַת *below*
מֵאֲחוֹרַי	לְפָנַי	עַל-יָדַי	מֵעָלַי	תַּחְתַּי
מֵאֲחוֹרֶיךָ	לְפָנֶיךָ	עַל-יָדֶיךָ	מֵעָלֶיךָ	תַּחְתֶּיךָ
מֵאֲחוֹרַיִךְ	לְפָנַיִךְ	עַל-יָדַיִךְ	מֵעָלַיִךְ	תַּחְתַּיִךְ
מֵאֲחוֹרָיו	לְפָנָיו	עַל-יָדָיו	מֵעָלָיו	תַּחְתָּיו
מֵאֲחוֹרֶיהָ	לְפָנֶיהָ	עַל-יָדֶיהָ	מֵעָלֶיהָ	תַּחְתֶּיהָ
מֵאֲחוֹרֵינוּ	לְפָנֵינוּ	עַל-יָדֵינוּ	מֵעָלֵינוּ	תַּחְתֵּינוּ
מֵאֲחוֹרֵיכֶם/ן	לִפְנֵיכֶם/ן	עַל-יְדֵיכֶם/ן	מֵעֲלֵיכֶם/ן	תַּחְתֵּיכֶם/ן
מֵאֲחוֹרֵיהֶם/ן	לִפְנֵיהֶם/ן	עַל-יְדֵיהֶם/ן	מֵעֲלֵיהֶם/ן	תַּחְתֵּיהֶם/ן, תַּחְתָּם/ן

Note

The particle לפני means 'before (ahead of me)' and consists of the preposition ל- and the dependent noun form of פנים. It has two variations, where the prepositional prefixes are altered to give it another meaning: prefix בפני 'in front of me (facing me)' and מפני 'from me, because of me'. These two particles are conjugated in the same manner as לפני in the above table. The same is true for the particle מאחורי, which means 'behind'. It has an alternate לאחורי where the preposition מ- is replaced by ל-, changing the direction. Instead of positional 'behind', לאחורי means 'to/toward the back'. It is conjugated in the same manner as מאחורי.

Appendix 4: Punctuation rules

Most punctuation marks are used in a manner similar to their use in English. The rules listed below follow those set by the Hebrew Language Academy (in abbreviated and simplified form).

1. Period   נקודה

A period is used at the end of a sentence that makes a statement. There is no space between the last letter and the period.

הלימודים התחילו מיד אחרי החגים.

A period is also used at the end of an indirect question.

ההורים רצו לדעת אם תהיה שביתת מורים.

2. Comma   פסיק

The comma indicates a pause in the sentence, and this is why it is often placed in the sentence where a change in structure has occurred. It is the most commonly used punctuation mark and has several functions.

1. With a list of items (coordinated)

A comma separates the coordinated parts when there is no conjunction.

משה שמיר, יגאל מוסנזון, נתן שחם ואהרון מגד היו מבין הסופרים הראשונים של המדינה.

2. Parenthetical expressions   ביטויים מוסגרים

A qualified expression is separated from the main sentence by commas, one that comes before it and one that concludes it.

We can say, without any reservation, that the proposal is a daring one.	<div dir="rtl">אנחנו יכולים לומר, ללא כל הסתייגות, שההצעה היא הצעה נועזת.</div>

In very short parenthetical expressions it is possible to omit the comma.

My Dad for instance always thinks about the future.	<div dir="rtl">אבא שלי למשל תמיד חושב על העתיד.</div>

3. Apposition   תמורה

Commas separate items in apposition:

Dr. Michael Schwartz, the leader
of the Reform movement, will
make a speech in the session.

ד״ר מיכאל שוורץ, מנהיג התנועה
הרפורמית, ינאם בישיבה.

However, when apposition is very short, it can come without commas:

The philosopher Mendelssohn was
the grandfather of the composer
Mendelssohn.

מנדלסון הפילוסוף היה סבו של
מנדלסון המלחין.

4. Topic and comment   משפטי ייחוד

In topicalized sentences it is possible, but not obligatory, to separate the
topic from the comment by a comma:

The next elections, there will be
serious struggles there among the
parties.

הבחירות הבאות, יהיו שם מאבקים
רציניים בין המפלגות.

It is not common to insert commas into shorter expressions or fixed
conventional expressions:

Such a mother, there is only one.

אמא כזאת יש רק אחת.

5. Clauses of coordinate sentence   בין איברים של משפטי איחוי

In a coordinate sentence, a comma separates the individual sentences.

The rains will stop, the winds will
gradually lessen, and the
temperatures will be higher.

הגשמים ייפסקו, הרוחות ייחלשו
בהדרגה, והטמפרטורות יהיו גבוהות
יותר.

If the two sentences are short, there is no need for a comma.

Rain fell and the wind was blowing.

ירד גשם והרוח נשבה.

6. The coordinator אלא

In a sentence where the conjunction אלא separates and contrasts the
two parts, a comma is often inserted before the conjunction.

He did not want go to the movies, but
rather to the theater.

הוא לא רצה ללכת לקולנוע,
אלא לתיאטרון.

However, when it is used for emphasis, in an expression such as
אין...אלא 'nothing ...but', no comma is inserted.

There is nothing here but trivial things.

אין כאן אלא דברים בטלים.

7. After a subordinate clause

A comma is inserted after a subordinate clause, provided that it is long.

After all the guests arrived and sat themselves in the seats reserved for them, the show began.	אחרי שכל האורחים הגיעו והתיישבו במקומות שהוקצו להם, התחילה ההצגה.

8. Separating non-restrictive relative clauses

A non-restrictive relative clause is usually separated from the main sentence by commas. (A restrictive relative clause does **not** have a comma).

<u>Non-restrictive clause</u>

Those rumors, that the tabloids published, were not true.	השמועות הללו, שהתפרסמו בעיתונות הצהובה, לא היו נכונות.

<u>Restrictive clause</u>

I don't trust rumors that are spread by tabloids.	אני לא מאמין בשמועות שמתפרסמות בעיתונות הצהובה (צהובונים).

3. Dash   קו מפריד (–)

A dash is a line that separates parts of a sentence. It replaces a comma, serving as a 'super-comma', especially when a comma is perceived to be not quite strong enough. It is a line that has a space before and after the part that is being separated from the rest of the sentence. It is used more frequently in Hebrew than in English. Sometimes two hyphens are used instead of a dash.

1. It can be used after a topic, before a part of the sentence that includes a special comment, especially if several items are listed in it that themselves are separated by commas:

All of their children – Danny, Ro`ie, Yossi and Dina – all of them have good careers.	כל הילדים שלהם – דני, רועי, יוסי ודינה – כולם הצליחו בעבודה.

All of his manuscripts and the many letters sent to him – were all lost.	כל כתבי היד שלו והמכתבים הרבים שנשלחו אליו – כולם הלכו לאיבוד.

2. When ellipsis has occurred in the sentence:

One man wants learning, and the other – goods.	פלוני רוצה תורה, ואלמוני – סחורה.

3. Before words or phrases detailing an explanation that preceded them.

The train is very fast – about 100 miles per hour.	הרכבת מאוד מהירה – כמאה מייל לשעה.

4. It sometimes separates a subject and a predicate in a verbless sentence that has no copula, especially in newspaper headlines.

The party's candidate for mayor – inexperienced in politics.	מועמד המפלגה לראשות העירייה – חסר ניסיון בפוליטיקה.

5. A parenthetical expression can be separated from the main sentence by dashes instead of commas, before and at the end of the sequence.

Many years ago – I was then a young and strong lad – I studied during the day and worked at night.	לפני הרבה שנים – אז הייתי בחור צעיר וחזק – למדתי ביום ועבדתי בלילה.

6. To separate lengthy apposition phrases from the main part of the sentence.

All the holy things – the Land of Israel, Jerusalem, Temple Mount, the Tablets – they have no holiness of themselves and only became sanctified by the doing of good deeds.	כל הקדושות – ארץ ישראל, ירושלים, הר הבית, המקדש, הלוחות – אין בהן קדושה בעצמן ולא נתקדשו אלא במעשה המצוות.

4. Parentheses   סוגריים ( )

The following rules govern material within parentheses:

1. When a period or comma comes at the end of a parenthetical segment, it is placed outside of the parentheses.

Slang changes very rapidly (especially in Israeli Hebrew).	הסלנג משתנה במהירות עצומה (במיוחד בעברית ישראלית).

2. When a complete sentence is followed by a loosely related one that is bounded by parentheses, a period follows the last segment in each.

Driver: I am a driver. It is my responsibility to deliver the passengers safely. (A dreadful shout is heard from outside.)	נהג : אני נהג, התפקיד שלי להביא את הנוסעים בשלום. (נשמעת זעקה איומה מבחוץ.)

3. When a question mark, an exclamation mark or three dots is part of the sentence in parentheses, it stays within the parentheses. A period still follows (outside of the parentheses).

And you know what else? It is not just that the principal did not react to what I told him; he even refused to listen (who ever heard such a thing?).	ואת יודעת מה?! זה לא רק שהמנהל לא הגיב למה שאמרתי לו ; הוא אפילו סרב להקשיב (איפה נשמע דבר כזה?!).

5. Hyphen   מקף (-)

It is important to distinguish between מקף 'hyphen', which is inserted to <u>join</u> items, and the קו מפריד 'dash' inserted to <u>separate</u> items.

1. A hyphen can be used to join two nouns that are closely bound, sometimes constituting a fixed expression and considered to be a single semantic unit.

attorney	עורך-דין	landlord	בעל-בית
human being	בן-אדם	school	בית-ספר
courtroom	בית-משפט	backpack	תרמיל-גב

2. Hyphens can be used to join nouns or adjectives into compound structures.

French-Canadian	צרפתי-קנדי	Ashkenazi-Jew	יהודי-אשכנזי
ethno-religious	אתני-דתי	socio-economic	חברתי-כלכלי

3. They can be used (not obligatory) in noun phrases where the noun repeats itself to create an adverbial phrase, which in English can be translated in the following way:

one by one	איש-איש	step by step	שלבים-שלבים
one by one	אחד-אחד	day by day on a daily basis	יום-יום

4. They can be used with prefix words.

unambiguous	חד-משמעי	international	בין-לאומי
no confidence	אי-אמון	bi-lingual	דו-לשוני

6. Quotation marks מירכאות

Quotation marks are used to set off material that represents quoted or spoken language. A colon usually marks the beginning of quoted speech (although in newspaper articles a comma can introduce a direct quote), and quotation marks are present in the beginning and at the end of the quoted speech.

There are two ways of inserting a punctuation mark at the end of the quoted sentence:

One way, following the American system of punctuation, puts the punctuation marks of the quoted speech within the quotation marks.

אורן : ״הלו רות, אני לא בא הערב.״

רות : ״אבל אתה אמרת שתבוא.״

Another way, following the European system of punctuation and used in most media publications, is to put the quotation mark before the final punctuation mark of the sentence (the following is from *Maariv*).

בלשכת ראש הממשלה הביעו זעם : ״אם יש ביקורת, היא צריכה להיאמר ישירות לראש הממשלה״.

When the quote precedes the rest of the sentence, a comma follows the quotation mark.

״מסכן אבא״, אמרה לי בצאתנו משער החצר.

However if the quote has a question mark, an exclamation mark or three dots at the end of the quote, the appropriate punctuation mark will be present inside the quotation mark, and there will be no comma separating the two.

״למה אפשר לצפות?״ שאל.

Quotation marks can also set off the titles of things that do not normally stand by themselves: short stories, movies, poems, and articles.

The interactive show, 'Medea X', was staged in Akko.

המופע האינראטקטיווי, ״מדיאה אקס״, הוצג בתיאטרון עכו.

Quotation marks are also used to set off the titles of institutions:

She is a physician in the 'Ha`emek' hospital in Afula.

היא רופאה בבית החולים ״העמק״ בעפולה.

Quotation marks can also be put around concepts that the writer wants to highlight:

Are there real possibilities for choice?	האם קיימות אפשרויות אמיתיות
Will 'Sacrifice' always follow 'Love'?	של בחירה? האם ״הקרבה״
These are the question that the	תמיד תבוא אחרי ״אהבה ״? אלו
audience is being asked.	השאלות שנשאל הצופה.

Note
In English single quotation marks are used in the above cases, rather than double quotations marks, which are used in Hebrew.

7. Exclamation mark   סימן קריאה (!)
An exclamation mark is used at the end of an emphatic declaration, interjection, or command.

Do it, now!   עשו את זה, עכשיו!

An exclamation mark may be used to close questions that are meant to convey extreme emotion, as in:

In God's name, what are you doing!   אלוהים אדירים, מה אתם עושים!

8. Question mark   סימן שאלה (?)
The question mark is used at the end of a direction question.

What do you plan on doing?   מה אתם מתכוננים לעשות?

A tag question is a device used to turn a statement into a question. It nearly always consists of a pronoun, a helping verb, and sometimes the word *not*. A question mark is used at the end of such a sentence.

You are coming tomorrow, right?   אתם באים מחר, נכון?

9. Semicolon   נקודה פסיק (;)
The rules for the use of a semicolon are not always clear. It is used to separate large lists or long clauses, without ending the sentence.

1. A semicolon can help out sort a very large list:

There were many participants in the	היו הרבה משתתפים בכינוס :
conference: representatives from the	נציגים מהגליל ; מורים מבאר-
Galilee; teachers from Beer Sheva; social	שבע ; עובדים סוציאלים
workers from Haifa; and journalists from	מחיפה ; ועיתונאים מכל
all parts of the country.	קצוות הארץ.

2. A semicolon is used to separate closely related independent clauses:

And you know what else? It is not just
that the principal did not react to what I
told him; he even refused to listen.

ואת יודעת מה? זה לא רק
שהמנהל לא הגיב למה שאמרתי
לו ; הוא אפילו סרב להקשיב .

The semicolon allows the writer to imply a relationship between ideas without actually stating that relationship.

10. Colon נקודתיים (:)

A colon is used before a list or an explanation that is preceded by a clause that can stand by itself.

The following people were elected to
the committee:

לוועדה נבחרו האנשים הבאים :

the mayor	ראש העיר
the deputy mayor	סגן ראש העיר
representatives of the firemen	נציגי ארגון הכבאים

A colon is used to separate an independent clause from a quotation that the clause introduces:

Ofir continued speaking: "The nurse
understood all of a sudden how much
laughter actually helps health."

אופיר המשיך וסיפר : "האחות
הבינה פתאום עד כמה הצחוק
באמת עוזר לבריאותי".

11. Inverted commas/apostrophe גרש (') וגרשיים (")

The single inverted comma, or apostrophe, is used in abbreviation of words. It is inserted after the last letter of the abbreviated word.

no. (number)	מס' (=מספר)	etc. (etcetera)	וגו' (=וגומר)
Mr. (mister)	הא' (= האדון)	pg. (page)	עמ' (= עמוד)

The double inverted commas are used in the following:

1. In acronyms:

Bible	תנ"ך	silverware	סכו"ם
	תורה, נביאים, כתובים		סכין, כף ומזלג

2. In spelling out names of letters of the alphabet:

Double inverted commas are inserted between the last two letters of the name.

אל"ף, בי"ת, וי"ו, כ"ף, צד"י, תי"ו

Appendix 5: *plene* writing   כתיב מלא

Plene writing rules (according to the Hebrew Language Academy, simplified and abbreviated)

1. Any vowel represented by an אם קריאה *mater lectionis* י ,ו ,ה׳ ,א׳ in
   nikud ḥaser maintains its אם קריאה :ראש, שנה, יבוא, תקום, כתיבה

2. Any *u* vowel is represented by וּ, or by ו if the symbol וּ is not
   available: שולחן, תמונה, שום, סודר

3. The vowel *o* is generally represented by וֹ, or by ו if the symbol וֹ is
   not available. It is always inserted when the *o* is a *ḥolam ḥaser* in
   ktiv ḥaser: בוקר, כוח, יכתוב, למצוא

   When it is a *kamats katan* or *ḥataf kamats* in *ktiv ḥaser*, no ו is
   inserted if the *kamats katan* or *ḥataf kamats* is found in all
   realizations of the word (the assumption being that it is easy to
   reconstruct this way): אמנם, חכמה, תכנית ; צהריים, למחרת, אנייה

   When the *kamats katan* or *ḥataf kamats* alternates with *ḥolam ḥaser*
   in some of its realizations, ו is inserted: שורשי (שורש), חומרי (חומר),
   ציפורים, ציפורניים, חודשים

4. The vowel *i* is represented by י in an open syllable, or in words
   whose base has an open syllable: דיבר, סיבה, זיכרון, ביקורת, מגילה,
   תיזהר, נטייה, שנייה ; דיברו, לימדה, פיקחים, כיסאות

   It is not inserted in:
   * a closed syllable that is closed in all realizations (again, the
     assumption being that it is easy to reconstruct this way): הסביר,
     התלבש, שמלה, מכתב, דמיון, ארגון
   * some words whose base is not *i*: לבי, עזים
   * *hif'il* forms where an initial נ was assimilated: הפיל, הפלתי
   * before יו or יו: דיון, קיום, נטיות, טריות
   * after the prefix -מ: משם, מחוץ
   * in frequent (and thus easy to recognize) function words: אם, עם, מן

5. Generally, the vowel *e* is represented by י when it comes from a *tsere*, and provided that the following conditions are met:
   * the *tsere* replaces a basic *i* before a guttural: בירך, תיאכל, תיעשה,
     גירושים, שירות, חירש, חירשים, תיאבון
   * when the *tsere* is maintained in all realizations of the word: תיבה,
     לידה, קיבה

   The vowel *e* from *segol* is represented by י only in one pattern,
   heCeC: הישג, היתר

6. The consonant *v* from ו is represented by just one ו at the beginning
   of the word and at its end: ועד, ועידה, ותיק; קו, צו, עכשיו

   In the middle of the word it is represented by וו, even after a prefix
   word: הוועד, בוודאי, שווה, תקווה

   No more than two ו symbols can come in sequence: מקוות, מצוות,
   כוון

7. The consonant *y* from י is represented by just one י at the beginning
   of the word, regardless of whether or not it is preceded by a prefix
   word: ילד, יפה, ישב; הילד, כיום

   In the middle of the word and at its end it is represented by יי,
   provided that it is not adjacent to an קריאה אם :בניין, עניין, הייתה,
   התיישבות, רגליים; צייר, עליי, בניי
   But: קיום, איום, חיה, היה, יהיה, מצוין, מסוים, שינוי, גוי, ודאי

8. *Ktiv male* rules do not apply to native proper nouns: משה, אפרים, בעז,
   הלל, נח, ירושלים, כנרת, יקנעם, זכרון יעקב, יד מרדכי

   In foreign words, any *u*, *o* or *i* is represented with קריאה אם :מונסון,
   אופטיקה, היסטוריה, מיליון

Index of grammatical topics